DELHI AND AWADH
DURING 1857

DELHI AND AWADH DURING 1857

STUDIES

IMAGES AND DOCUMENTS

Editor

Saiyid Zaheer Husain Jafri

GYAN

Published, 2019

Published by

Gyan Publishing House
5, Ansari Road
Daryaganj, New Delhi-110002
Phone: 011-47034999, 9811692060
www.gyanbooks.com
E-mail: books@gyanbooks.com

Printed at: G. Print Process, Delhi.

Cataloging in Publication Data—DK
Courtesy: D.K. Agencies (P) Ltd. <docinfo@dkagencies.com>

Delhi and Awadh During 1857: studies, images and documents.
pages cm
ISBN 9788121214131

1. Delhi (India)—History—19th century. 2. India—History—Sepoy Rebellion, 1857-1858.

DS486.D3D45 2017 DDC 954.560317 23

Dedicated
To the memory of

LATE PROFESSOR IQBAL HUSAIN SAHEB
(20th July, 1935-22nd Feb, 2017)

Centre of Advanced Study, Department of History
Aligarh Muslim University

Contents

Review Article

Preface

The Mughal imperial capital, Delhi, and the Nawabi principality of Awadh were major centers of the uprising of 1857. Initially, the sepoys, military commander and the leaders of the uprising from the other centers looked towards the Mughal Emperor Bahadur Shah Zafar as the legitimate leader for the cause of the rebels. They rallied around him and the Red Fort, taking them to be the symbols of sovereignty. Reluctantly and with different motives, the leadership was provided by the Mughal royal household: they came up to the expectations of the sepoys. At Lucknow, the erstwhile capital of Nawabi regime, things were different: the reluctance of ex-King's immediate household and his other queens brought Begum Hazrat Mahal and her infant son Birjis Qadr as the principal leaders of the rebellion. In addition to them, the religious divines like Maulavi Syed Sarfaraz Ali, Maulavi Ahmadullah Shah and Maulavi Liyaqat Ali, the *ta'alluqadars* namely Rana Beni Madhav Singh of Baiswara, Raja Devi Baksh Singh of Gonda, Muhammad Husain, the *Nazim* of Gorakhpur and others could muster the huge following due to their charismatic appeals, caste associations and anti-Colonial sentiments of landholders, artisans and peasantry as a result of highly devastating impact of the annexation and Summary settlement. In Bundelkhand, Rani Lakshmi Bai, Nana Saheb and Tatya Tope held the field against the Company, while in Rohilkhand stiff opposition to the British presence was offered by Khan Bahadur Khan, the scion of Rohilla chief Hafiz Rahmat Khan. There is plenty of primary material available on the subject: both in English official records as well as in indigenous literature produced by the rebel leaders and their sympathizers. Competent and detailed studies on almost every region have come up in the past decades; some of them have ignored/or tenaciously used the indigenous discourse. Hence, their conclusions match with the official British interpretation of the uprising. Worst, crucial evidences have been totally ignored in some of these studies. The files of *Delhi Urdu Akhbar* and *Tilism-e Lucknow* have yet to find any mention in the mainstream historiography, except for few sporadic references from the secondary works.

I

A large number of printed proclamations, appeals and pamphlets were issued by rebel leaders in the various centers of uprising. These documents were seized by Company's troops and officers and were not destroyed, most of them passed into the private and public collections. An analysis of this documentation yields enough data for an understanding of the motives of the rebels, the power of mobilizing the rebels and the classes and the strata sought to be mobilized. Such data also helps us to examine the questions as to how far the appeal remained within the traditional framework and how far the sepoy's background as members of the Bengal army, the most modern army in the east of Suez, and the influence of the new medium- the 'printed word' facilitated rebel's mobilization. It is just possible that the ideas which germinated under the influence of the British rule might have played a greater role in the course of the events than has been recognized so far in modern historical writings. The questions like the conflicts between the sepoys on one hand and more traditional elements on the other, the kind of 'polity' or the 'polities' that the leaders of the rebellion envisioned can also be examined in the light of such data.

Some of the studies on the revolt are quite interesting but unfortunately they are missing from the large literature on the subject. In all modesty, there is no claim for any major intervention on the subject from our side, but we do claim that some of the studies included in this volume provide important complimentary information, which in itself is a major corrective to much of the current literature. There is little justification for ignoring the data from extremely important weekly newspaper *Tilism-e Lucknow* published from Lucknow, (file of 42 weekly issues, July 1856-8th May 1857 are available), or not using the data from the only versified biography of the famous rebel leader Maulvi

Ahmadullah Shah (composed as early as 1862) in the larger historiography. Though unfortunate, but it is a fact that most of the people who have written on the subject are linguistically handicapped to use the indigenous sources.

Similarly, there had been few scholars in India who were able to use the well researched monographs written in Urdu by the scholars in India as well as in Pakistan. The scholars writing in Urdu on the other hand, have made every effort to make use of the works in English. Therefore, the works of Intizam Ullah Shahabi, Ghulam Rasul Mehr, Abrar Husain Farooqi, Ayyub Qadri, Ateeq Ahmad Siddiqi and a host of other Urdu writers whose works were easily available in all the major libraries and were most accessible, were simply ignored by the modern authors. Surprisingly, the large corpus left by Khwaja Hasan Nizami (d.1953) on the memory, history and the documents on the uprising (in twelve thick volumes) were never thought to be worthy enough as the historical source. The end result of such lopsided studies was quite unfortunate. It led to a 'vertical divide' between the perceptions of the 'English reading public' and the 'Urdu reading public' about their understanding of the events, causes of the failures and their 'respective heroes'.

Surprisingly, the mainstream historiography 'with all its arrogance' did not bother to correct such a growing divide and never thought of utilizing the indigenous discourse in their writings to 'balance the picture'. This attitude is well reflected in the recent historiography where the writers of the modern standard works such as Rudrangshu Mukherjee, Rajat Kanta Ray and Gautam Bhadra seem to be unaware of the writings about Maulavi Ahmadullah Shah and most of them have depended on an article by late Professor Iqbal Husain, where he had used the information of extremely important newspaper from Lucknow i.e. *Tilism-e Lucknow*. The 150th anniversary of the uprising was celebrated with much fanfare in the academic circles in 2007. The period saw experts of writing on the subject. But it was almost surprising that no mention was ever made to the seminal work on the city of Delhi by S.A.A. Rizvi. This monograph titled as *Swatantra Dilli* was an official publication of the Government of UP and was published in 1957 itself. Another such seminal work by Ateeq Ahmad Siddiqui titled as *1857: Akhbarat wa Dastawezat,* containing the facsimiles of the rare records from the Mutiny Papers, contemporary Urdu Akhbars and other indigenous material was simply ignored even in the authoritative Urdu works. This type of ignorance is really unfortunate.

The endeavor here is to utilize such indigenous discourse on the life and activities of the important rebel leaders like Maulavi Ahmadullah Shah and to see how the modern historiography has treated him and how his biography has been reconstructed by reading (and by not reading) the crucial documents and how this has affected the approach of the many modern notice(s) of Maulavi Ahmadullah Shah. This exercise is not only limited to highlighting the value of the indigenous discourse but also seeks to show that how the ultimate interpretation of the events has been distorted by not cross-checking the 'victor's narrative' with that of the 'vanquished' which is mainly in Urdu. In the recent debates it has been pointed out that since Ahmadullah Shah had very strong 'Sufic' antecedents being a *Qadri Pir,* his sympathies could not have been with the *Wahabis*. Hence, his movement is sought to be seen independent of the movement of *Wahabis*. But it is very difficult at that stage to separate the 'Sufic' antecedents of a person from that of the orthodoxy. In fact all the *Wahabi* leaders and their followers have enrolled themselves in one or more than one Sufi orders. Their campaign was never against *Tassawuf* per se, they were only trying to purify *Tassawuf* from what they considered as the corrupt practices. Such an argument has little strength and Ahmadullah Shah's antecedents as Sufi *Pir* does not make him different from those subscribing to the *Wahabi* ideas.

However, on the basis of the study of the indigenous discourse along with the reports in the contemporary newspapers and the dispatches of the British officers, a picture of Maulavi Ahmadullah Shah emerges which is quite at variance with the projections of the modern scholars. Most of the studies on Maulavi Ahmadullah Shah heavily rely on the report of the British Officers who crushed the uprising in the province of Awadh and Rohilkhand. No doubt they speak in respectful terms of his personal qualities, and organizing capacity yet they don't offer a complete picture of the person and his movement. Little attempt had been made to utilize his versified biography[1] in Urdu and to have a substantive idea of his career during these years. Similarly, the reports in the contemporary newspapers and the short notices in the lesser known works of the contemporaries have also escaped the notice of the historians.[2]

The other important proclamation issued from Lucknow by the group closely associated with Maulavi Ahmadullah Shah, has been translated by the British officers as 'a Cry of *Jehad* in Oudh' (*Futteh Islam/Fateh-i Islam)* and has been used as an evidence of the religious bigotry and 'holy nature of the war' waged against the Christians. It was used to highlight the crucial role played by the *Wahabis* or *jehadis* during the course of rebellion.[3] In the Subaltern historiography, this

---

1. Fath Muhammad Taib, *Tawarikh-i Ahmadi*, Lucknow, Tegh Bahadur Press, 1925. The author of this *masnavi* (composed in A.H. 1280/A.D. 1863) was a landed aristocrat of Lucknow and had become a disciple of Ahmadullah Shah in 1856. On the instructions of Mehrab Shah Qadri of Gwalior, the spiritual guide of author's *pir*, he had composed this *masnavi*. The work is divided into 40 sub-sections, and the main discussion on the activities of Ahmadullah Shah is confined to sections 11 to 35, but the verses are numbered in continuation. For the purpose of precise reference, the numbers of the verses has been cited. This edition has been reprinted with copious notes and a useful introduction by Abrar Husain Farooqi, as *Mirat-i Ahmadi*, Hardoi, 1973.

   Although in English works Ahmadullah is invariably referred to as Maulavi or Maulavi of Fyzabad, to be in taune with Taib the epithet 'Shah' has been retained in this article.

2. By way of exception, Syed Moinul Haq, *The Great Revolution of 1857*, Pakistan Historical Society, Karachi, 1968, had made full use of Taib's account but unfortunately he had no access to the weekly Newspapers in Indian Archives and Libraries. Similar is the case with a number of important Urdu works for example Intizamulla Shahabi, *East India Company our Baghi Ulema*, Delhi (no date), Ghulam Rasool Mehr, *Atharah Sau Sattawan ke Mujahid*, Lahore, 1957, Mufti Intizamullah Shahabi, *Ghadr ke Chand Ulema*, Delhi, (n.d.). Abrar Husain Farooqi, *Masir-i Dilawari*, Lucknow, 1965, utilizes all the evidences about Maulavi Ahmadullah Shah with a number of photo plates of the rare documents. See also Muhammad Ayub Qadri, *Jang-i Azadi 1857 Waqiat aur Shakhsiyat* (in Urdu), Karachi, 1976, pp. 525-540 for a fairly comprehensive account of Shah's activities.

3. After the events of 1857 it was a widely held belief among the British that it was mainly due to the Muslim conspiracy against the British rule that such a catastrophe has happened. The suspicion increased further when it

document has been singled out as a representative document showing extreme hatred for the British and using 'the most insulting language to describe the British especially. Queen Victoria'; it has also been chided for 'its abusive condemnation of the whole chain of British authority from the Crown to the common soldiers'. However, it is significant here to compare the British who describe the 'rebels and their leaders as scoundrels, *badmash, shuhda'*, and the *mujahideens* as a 'debased class of the people and the fanatics' and also employ the most abusive language which they never did for the Irish rebels or the Australian convicts or during the American War of Independence.

Apart from the purportedly 'fire and sword' nature of the document for which it has been rather harshly criticized by all the modern writings, there is enough which can be culled from it to examine the vision of the people participating in the 'Battle unto death' and as to what they felt about the ongoing struggle and the strategies they had worked out under the extreme circumstances and yet they were conscious about the death of the English Women and children as something which was totally unacceptable under the tenets of any religion. Besides, making

---

was found in 1863 that the *Wahabis* were still active in the Northwest Frontier as they were now confronting directly the British after the collapse of the Sikh kingdom they were regularly in receipt of the money and the recruits from areas as far as Bengal and Bihar. This followed a series of 'Wahabi trials' during1863-72. In the context of this witch hunt W W Hunter wrote his famous *Our Indian Musalmans,* London, 1871. His main assumption was that the notion of *jehad* had the historical continuity from the time of Shah Waliullah (d.1762) and his son Shah Abdul Aziz (d. 1824) to Syed Ahmed of Balakot fame (died in action 1831). This becomes the most important interpretation in the 20th Century Nationalist Discourse when Maulana Azad reaffirmed the theory of *jehad* in the above continuum. This interpretation got full-fledged support by Maulana Ghulam Rasul Mehr, who served as the secretary to Maulana Azad as well to develop this interpretation in his monumental Urdu biography of Syed Ahmed Rae Bareilley after the partition. This understanding remains the most dominant trend in the modern writings especially. Urdu historiography. See Marc Gaborieau, 'The "Forgotten obligation": A Reinterpretation of Sayyid Ahmed Barelwi's *Jihad* in the North-West Frontier. 1826-1831, in *The Resources of History: Tradition, Narration and Nation in South Asia,* Ed. Jackie Assayag, Paris-Pondicherry, 1999, pp. 297-8.

a strong plea for Hindu-Muslim unity it underlines the importance of firearms and canons which were now available to the sepoys and its decisive impact in the final outcome of the Battle!

Risala Fateh Islam was issued sometime between 5th-17th July 1857 (the date has been worked out by Prof. S A A Rizvi on the basis of the internal evidence of the text) after the Battle of Chinhat on 30th June 1857. In the preamble of the document, the atrocities committed by the British have been highlighted in great details and thus, the people, Muslims as well as Hindus have been asked to unite and to wage a 'Holy War' against the 'inhuman and ungodly Christians'. It also talks about the British attempts to 'deprive the troops of their religion by applying impure substances to the cartridges and pressing those troops to use them' which ultimately had resulted to their destruction. There is a warning to the people that in case the British succeed in reestablishing their 'authority great misfortune will fall on all the Hindus, Muslims, the people, the Sepoys, the kings and the *Wazirs*. Hence, the call is to unite, fight and annihilate them without delay'. Interestingly enough, the deadly impact of the fire-power of the artillery has been exalted to the highest limits as the Proclamation says that since they possess the guns which 'formerly the people of Hindustan needed badly' are now in possession of the kings of Delhi and Lucknow. Hence, it becomes very clear that in the perception of the rebels it was this deadly weapon which had tilted the balance in favour of the English earlier was now at the command of the rebels to be deployed and used as effectively and as quickly as possible. Probably, this refers to the sepoys joining in large number the army of the rebels with artillery pieces and large guns which boosted their morals.

II

It was a matter of honor for me to have organized the two annual sessions of Indian History Congress almost in succession (i.e. 68th & 70th annual sessions of Indian History Congress in Dec 2007 and May 2010) during the period when I was heading the Department of History, University of Delhi (July 2007-June 2010). The souvenirs we have brought on the occasion were focused on the city of Delhi itself. The focus of the first brochure, prepared during the 68th session was *Delhi though the Ages,* giving a glimpse of and also compiling original extracts from the documentary material on ancient, medieval and modern pasts of the city of Delhi. The souvenir for the 70th session of the congress was focused on *Delhi during 1857: Studies, Images and Documents*. Both these publications were in a way complimentary to each other. The focus of our study was to highlight the proclamations and other evidences from the 'rebel's world' along with the 'victors narratives', mutiny papers the other data related to the 'suppression' of the uprising. The two diametrically opposed narratives sometimes complimented each other in the matter of details of the events but there was a vast difference in the perceptions, future vision and the methods of mobilization. Thus, we sought to fill the vital gaps in some of the studies and also to present somehow a 'complete' historiography by highlighting the missing (yet interesting) details of the period between the uprising and its suppression.

The souvenir was well received in the academic circles. Later on, it was decided to extend the scope of the publication by adding more studies on Delhi, the major centre of the uprising and also to include the city of Lucknow (the capital of erstwhile Nawabi kingdom of Awadh). Hence, the material available on the city of Lucknow like the famous rebuttal Begum Hazrat Mahal has issued (under the name of Prince Birjis Qadar) in reply to Queen Victoria's much talked about proclamation are integrated. We decided to supplement this material with a fresh study of the conditions of Lucknow just prior to the outbreak of the rebellion. The period between annexation of the kingdom of Awadh (Feb., 1856) and the uprising of 1857 was the time of extreme complexity with communitarian relations between Hindus and Muslims and the sectarian divide between Shia and Sunni within the Muslim community were at lowest ebb. Yet, during the course of uprising exemplary unity was displayed by the people of Awadh for a cause. This, being an aspect that offers a silver-line and pin-point the deep rooted pluralistic ethos of the region, where the personal enmities and deep rooted prejudices were given up; thus the colonial establishment was effectively challenged.

It is well known that the charter act of 1813 and 1833 have allowed various Evangelical missions to carry on the religious propaganda of Christianity in the blatantly pushy manner, something noticed by Sir Syed Ahmad Khan in his *Causes for the Uprising of 1857*. The

Christian-Muslims debates were organized in the principal towns of Upper Gangetic Valley. This has created major fissures within the Indo-Islamic elite. The polemical and intellectual debate was taken up by a section of the Muslim scholars as a challenge. Some of these debates [*munazra]* had a huge impact into the making of the 'rebel psychic'. This aspect needs further investigation.

The 'middle class' citizenry came up mainly from the erstwhile landed elite which was effectively marginalized by the administrative measures of the EIC: the resumption of the revenue grants, the sale and auction of the proprietary rights of the *zamindars*, high rates of taxation, the destruction of the handicraft and the artisanal products has led to the impoverishment of almost all the section of society. The process of marginalization of the Indo-Islamic elite at the city of Delhi and the principal towns of Awadh will provide a perspective for the anguish which became the hall mark of the urban citizenry during the period of uprising.

The retribution and vengeance with extreme brutality awaited the rebels as well as the physical symbols of authority. It is important to interrogate how blatantly the British officials were treating the royal stores and personal property of Nawab Wajid Ali Shah, the illegally deposed King of Awadh, as their own. Thus, the contemporary newspaper from Lucknow graphically describes the loot of Nawab's library and his personal zoo. It was the naked display of power by the English to humiliate the erstwhile elite and the middle class. Worst, was the fate of the physical landscape of Delhi and Lucknow after the suppression of Uprising. Historical, religious, antiquarian buildings were raised to the ground in addition to the huge private properties which were not even counted. True, the Jama Masjid of Delhi was not converted into a Church or blown up, as it was planned. It was released and restored for the prayers after much bargaining, in a gradual manner. Numerous conditions and administrative restrictions were put up. Thus, the citizenry of Delhi were told how to behave!

The EIC was supported by numerous chieftains, Rajas and other collaborators. Each of them were duly compensated according to their worth. The official papers and gazetteers compiled after the uprising has a section on these 'loyal collaborators'. Thus, a new class of people was created, who became the 'die-hard' supporters of the Raj. Rewards, by way of cash and land grants were made available to the chiefs, commanders and other notables. The ordinary soldier already had their pound of flesh during the suppression of uprising and after the 'peace' was restored. The army from Nepal 'helped' British EIC to subjugate the area from Gorakhpur to Lucknow. From there they were asked to return back to Kathmandu. While going back, the Nepali army had thousands of bullock carts full of booty and this was more than enough for them! These aspects are also important to understand the event and its aftermath in a better way. Some studies included in the volume were invited from the young scholars working on the related areas: hopefully, new insights will emerge with these researches.

It is a matter of honor for me to reproduce the two notable pieces by Professor Irfan Habib in this volume. I am thankful to my teachers Prof. Shireen Moosvi and late Prof. Iqbal Husain, whose numerous chapters are included in this volume. I am equally grateful to my friends Prof. S.N.R.Rizvi, Prof Amar Farooqui and Ms. Rana Safavi who has kindly permitted me to reproduce their researches in the volume. I am placing on record my thanks to Dr. Madhu Prasad and Dr. Zakir Husain for allowing me to reproduce their articles in the souvenir for the 70th session of Indian History Congress, which are now included here. My students have always been a source of strength for me. I acknowledge Drs. Farha Khan, Nida Arshi, Shaheen Islamuddin, Sana Aziz, Heena Ansari, Ms. Sadia Aziz, Ms. Yusra Farooqui Mr. Mohammad Wasim and Ms. Suman Yadav for their contributions in the volume. At the final stage of preparation of the manuscript, I received immense help from Ms. Heena Ansari.

Once again, I take the opportunity to express my gratitude to my wife, Mrs. Tayyaba Jafri and to my kids Saiyid Naseer Jafri (Tariq), Haleema Sadia Jafri and Saiyid Ashraf Jafri (Abbas) for being considerate: graciously allowing me to work in the Department up to the late hours.

1st July 2019

Saiyid Zaheer Husain Jafri
Department of History
University of Delhi

Previous Publication Details

Chapter I, 'Remembering 1857', *Delhi during 1857: Studies, Images and Documents*, Souvenir 70th Session of Indian History Congress, Department of History, Delhi University, 2010.

Chapter II, 'The Sepoys and Middle Class Citizenry into the Making of Rebellion', Keynote Address for the Conference held at Kurukshetra University, titled as *1857 Revisited,* 16-18th January 2008.

Chapter III, 'Rebel Journalism *Dehli Urdu Akhbar*, May-September 1857' *Delhi during 1857: Studies, Images and Documents*, Souvenir 70th Session of Indian History Congress, Department of History, Delhi University, 2010.

Chapter IV, 'Lucknow between the Annexation and the Mutiny', *Religion and Ideology of the Rebels of 1857*, Iqbal Husain, Primus, 2013, pp. 24-37.

Chapter V, 'Voices of the Vanquished: The 'Indigenous Discourse' in the 'Rebel's World' of 1857', *Delhi during 1857: Studies, Images and Documents*, Souvenir 70th Session of Indian History Congress, Department of History, Delhi University, 2010.

Chapter VI, 'The Rebel Administration of Delhi, 1857', *Religion and Ideology of the Rebels of 1857*, Iqbal Husain, Primus, 2013, pp. 91-101.

Chapter VII, 'Religious Debates and the Making of 1857 in North India', extracted from *Christian Muslim Encounter and Debates in Northern India, 1579-1857,* Ph. D Dissertation, Department of History, University of Delhi, 2014.

Chapter VIII, "Royals', Property and Prize Agents: Fate of the Mughal Capital in the aftermath of 1857', extracted from *'The Indo-Muslim Aristocracy under the 'Siege': Colonial Expansion and the Muslim 'Elite' in Delhi, c.1800-1860,* Ph. D Dissertation, Department of History, University of Delhi, 2015.

Chapter IX, 'Delhi, Meos and the Great Uprising: A Study of Anti-British Resistance during 1857', *Delhi during 1857: Studies, Images and Documents*, Souvenir 70th Session of Indian History Congress, Department of History, University of Delhi, 2010, pp. 52-67.

Chapter X, 'Communitarian Relations, Colonial Remodeling, and the British in Pre-Mutiny Awadh', extracted from *The Indigenous Discourse of Great Uprising of 1857: A Study of Delhi Urdu Akhbar* (Delhi) and *Tilism-e Lucknow* (Lucknow), M.Phil Dissertation, Department of History, University of Delhi, 2015.

Chapter XI, 'Fazl-e Haq Khairabadi: A Scholarly Rebel of 1857', *Religion and Ideology of the Rebels of 1857*, Iqbal Husain, Primus, 2013, pp. 178-188.

Chapter XII, 'Indigenous Discourse and Modern Historiography of 1857: The Case Study of Maulavi Ahmadullah Shah', *Rethinking 1857*, (ed.) Sabyasachi Bhattacharya, Orient Blackswan, 2018, pp. 237-260.

Chapter XIII, 'Bakht Khan: A Leading Sepoy General of 1857', *Religion and Ideology of the Rebels of 1857*, Iqbal Husain, Primus, 2013, pp. 91-101.

Chapter XIV, 'Maulavi Liyaqat Ali', *Religion and Ideology of the Rebels of 1857,* Iqbal Husain, Primus, 2013, pp. 91-101.

Chapter XV', Wlliam Hodson and the Abduction of Bahadur Shah Zafar', extracted from Amar Farooqui, *Zafar and the Raj: Anglo-Mughal Delhi C.1800-1850,* Primus, 2013.

Chapter XVI, 'Fishing in the Troubled Waters: The Revolt of 1857 and Jung Bahadur Rana, the Prime Minister of Nepal', *The Great Uprising of 1857: Commentaries, Studies and Documents*/edited by Syed Najmul Raza Rizvi and Saiyid Zaheer Husain Jafri, Delhi, Anamika, 2009, pp. 94-107.

Chapter XVII, ' The Battle for Delhi: Myths and the Construction of the Raj', *Delhi during 1857: Studies, Images and Documents*, Souvenir 70th Session of Indian History Congress, Department of History, University of Delhi, 2010, pp. 40-51.

Chapter XVIII, 'The Concept of Booty, Revolt of 1857 and Delhi as a 'Prize'', extracted from *Delhi in 1857: Shifting landscapes and Memories,* Ph.D Dissertation, Department of History, University of Delhi, 2018.

Chapter XIX, '*Masjid-e Jahan Numa* at Shahjahanabad during and after the Uprising of 1857', for its earlier version, see, *Polish Journal of Aesthetics*, Vol. 47, No.4 Jagiellonian University, Krakow, 2017, pp. 13-29.

Chapter XX, 'Literature, History and Memory: A study of the Selected Writings of Khwaja Hasan Nizami on the Great Uprising of 1857. Presented in a panel on 'Literature and Reality', sponsored by Aligarh Historians Society, at the 73rd session of Indian History Congress, University of Bombay, Mumbai, 29th December 2012.

Chapter XXI, for an initial argument see, *'Dehli ki Jankani'*, Delhi in 1857: Shifting landscapes and Memories, *Pluralities of Past Upper Gangetic Valley through the Millenium*, ed. S.Z.H.Jafri & N.R.Farooqui, UP History Congress Proceeding, 2012, pp. 267-278.

'Some Stories from *Begamat* ke *Aansoo*', an excerpt from *City of My Heart: Accounts of Love, Loss and Betrayal in Nineteenth - Century Delhi*, Ms. Rana Safvi, Hachette India, 2018.

Chapter XXII, for an initial argument see her review of this book in *Studies in People's History*, Vol. 5, No.1, June 2018, Sage, Delhi, pp. 114-115.

Contributors

IRFAN HABIB, Professor Emeritus, Centre for Advanced Study in History, Aligarh Muslim University.

SHIREEN MOOSVI, Professor [retd.], Centre for Advanced Study in History, Aligarh Muslim University.

IQBAL HUSAIN, Professor [late], Centre for Advanced Study in History, Aligarh Muslim University.

AMAR FAROOQUI, Professor, Department of History, University of Delhi.

SAIYID ZAHEER HUSAIN JAFRI, Professor, Department of History, University of Delhi.

SYED NAJMUL RAZA RIZVI, Professor [retd.], Department of Medieval and Modern History, DDU University of Gorakhpur.

MADHU PRASAD, Associate Professor [retd.], Zakir Husain College, University of Delhi.

ZAKIR HUSAIN, Assistant Director [retd.], National Archives of India, New Delhi.

RANA SAFVI, Historian, Author, Blogger and Journalist.

FARHA KHAN, Assistant Professor, Maharaja Agrasen College, University of Delhi.

NIDA ARSHI, Assistant Professor, Shaheed Bhagat Singh College, University of Delhi.

SHAHEEN ISLAMUDDIN, Assistant Professor, Bhagini Nivedita College, University of Delhi.

SANA AZIZ, Assistant Professor, Centre for Advanced Study in History, Aligarh Muslim University.

HEENA ANSARI, Ph.D. Department of History and Culture, Jamia Millia Islamia, New Delhi.

SADIA AZIZ, Ph.D Scholar, Department of History, DU.

YUSRA FAROOQUI, Ph.D. Scholar, Department of History, DU.

MOHAMMAD WASIM, Ph.D. Scholar, Department of History, DU.

PERSPECTIVES OF THE UPRISING OF 1857

Chapter - 1

Remembering 1857

— ***Professor Irfan Habib***

The year 2007 marked the 150th Anniversary of the Revolt of 1857. It is difficult in free India to recall the times under the British, when no free and open discussion of the events of 1857 was possible. It was, then, only after independence that people became more and more familiar about the rebellion itself. Documents not known to scholars before 1947 have now been published, especially rebels' proclamations, and other documents, newspaper accounts of the Mutiny, etc.

Largest Uprising

We did not, indeed, have merely an armed revolution-the only armed revolution on that scale that we have ever known in India. But it was more than that: it was the largest anti-colonial uprising anywhere in the world in the nineteenth century. If one looks at the whole of the nineteenth century, among anti-colonial revolutions all over the world, one will find successful anti-colonial revolutions in Latin America, but even there none remotely on this scale. There were armed revolutionaries under the great Bolivar, but they never exceeded more than a few thousands of armed men at any time.

Here in India, on the other hand, there were over 1,25,000 Bengal Army sepoys going into armed revolt. According to official figures, the Bengal Army consisted of over 1,35,000 'native' sepoys. Of these only some 7,000 remained loyal. According to a report laid before

British Parliament in 1858, no less than 1,35,000 men thus went into rebellion. We are here referring to what was the most modern army in Asia at that time, and the largest army within the British Empire overseas. In terms of the percentage of people inhabiting the rebellious territory involved, it consisted of about 30 per cent of the population of the territory of the present Union of India. Thus, if we look at the scale from any angle whatsoever, then 1857 was not only a major event in Indian history, it was a major event in modern world history.

Revolutions often break out in situations frequently created by the ruling classes themselves. The revolt of the Bengal Army, seemingly the favoured child of the British regime (as Marx had noted) was brought about in part by a new phase in British colonial expansion, the *Imperialism of Free Trade,* which put this entire army under unprecedented pressure.

Role of the Bengal Army

The Bengal Army was the 'sword arm' of British Imperialism in India and outside of it. Marx was completely skeptical about the peace pretensions of the Free Traders, who dominated British politics from the early 1830s onwards, a fact not known even to Lenin, for these articles of Marx had not yet been traced and published. His scepticism proved to be fully justified when historians like John Gallagher and Ronald Robinson, in England, began to analyse the phenomenon of 'the imperialism of free trade'. They underlined the empirically observed fact that after the British Parliamentary Reforms of 1832, when British industrial classes virtually came into power, a new powerful wave of British colonial expansion began. It was in the process of this expansion that the Bengal Army sepoys were continuously made canon-fodder, to fight and die in battlefields from Crimea to China.

The first campaign the Bengal Army was thrown in, was the gruesome First Afghan War, in 1839-42; then it fought in the Gwalior War of 1843, a half-forgotten war causing great losses on both sides; this was followed by the war to conquer Sind in 1844; then came the Punjab Wars, with huge losses for the Bengal Army in 1845-6 and in 1848-9. In 1852, the Army was sent to Burma for the Second Burma War, during which, amidst dreadful pestilence, it conquered southern Burma for the British. In 1840-2, it had to fight in China in the infamous Opium War, and then again during 1856-60. In 1854, a contingent was sent off to Crimea, to fight against Russia. It had thus been continuously fighting from 1839 to 1857. Even in 1856-7, a war was going on with Persia, with Indian troops fighting there. No other army in the world was so continuously involved in wars in contemporary times. It is an ordinary perception of professional generals that armies need rest; for eighteen years, such rest remained unknown to the Bengal Army.

John William Kaye, who was more honest than other British military historians of the day, notes that it was common for British officials, while reprimanding the sepoys of the Bengal Army, for any fault, to say that they would be 'sent to Burma, or to China where the men would die.' It was not that the *sepoys* were excessively religious; it was just that they were human beings. Why was the British Army, the home army, not sent on all those expeditions? The only exception was the war in Crimea, the single war, and that seemingly bled Britain white.

Bengal Army: Not Communal

The frustration that the sepoys felt as soldiers were given expression to in ways that were determined by the very kind of army that the British had built. For reasons of convenience, the British recruited soldiers for the Bengal Army from an area where people spoke and understood the same language, namely, Hindustani. Therefore, the recruits came basically from an area comprising the present territories of Uttar Pradesh, western Bihar and Haryana. A very large recruiting ground in Uttar Pradesh, consisted of the two present Divisions of Faizabad and Lucknow, which constituted before 1856, the kingdom of Oudh. Some 40,000 of Bengal Army men came from Oudh alone. Another aspect about this army was that it was recruited largely on a caste basis. The Brahmans constituted a very large part of the infantry. They were often literate, and were seen to be more prone to accept the discipline needed for modern warfare, than the usual 'martial' elements in traditional Indian armies. Rules were framed in 1850 to include the stipulation that upper caste men alone would be recruited to the Bengal Army. At the same time in order to encourage cohesive action at command, divisions on religious lines were not introduced in the Bengal Army. Imperialism had not discovered till then that it could everywhere use religious divisions between Hindus and Muslims. For this lapse they were censured by a loyal official and future educationist, Syed Ahmed Khan, when he wrote his book, *Asbab-e Bagawat-e Hind* (Causes of the Indian Rebellion), in which he argued that it was a mistake for the British Government to put both Hindu and Muslim sepoys in the same regiments and companies, for when they shed their blood together, they became closer than brothers to each other, and could no longer be used against each other. Soldiers of this modern army, which had very little to do with the Indian ruling classes of older days, and which was perhaps the most numerous modern element in Indian society of that time, had thus evolved two important features. It was very highly caste sensitive, and yet it was not communal.

Fundamental Causes

That is why the greased cartridges were particularly difficult for the sepoys to accept. Caste was important for them. That kind of status was perhaps the only thing left to them: they could not become officers, or get promotions. At best, one out of twenty, or it could be thirty, could become a *jamadar*. Then from such *jamadars*, one out of thirty, perhaps, could become a *subedar*; from those, just a few could become a Subedar Major; and that was the end in the promotion ladder. They had hardly any dignity as men left to them in the army. They were paid, but constantly humiliated by their officers as people of an inferior race. Only the pride of caste had been left to them and the British government was now taking even that away with its greased cartridges containing tallow from cow and pig fat. It is true, many good reasons could be given in favour of the use of greased cartridges. The difference between biting the cartridge or breaking it by fingers, could be one between life and death in battle.

When Bahadur Shah was put on trial, the British prosecutor said that the mutineers who had objected to the greased cartridges when issued by their British officers, were using and biting the very same cartridge when they were firing them against the British. The claim was, however, that was done by them at their own free will, not under coercion. Their rejection of the greased cartridges stemmed from all the cumulative humiliations, especially the racial and religious humiliations they had been constantly subjected to, such as having to march off on a Sunday to hear some White missionary glorifying his faith at the cost of theirs, or suffering personal insults at the hands of European officers.

But there were more fundamental causes behind the Bengal Army's mutiny than the 'accident' of the greased cartridges. It was, however, no 'accident' that the area the bulk of its sepoys came from, had been turned into the highest taxed area of the country. The peasantry as well as the 'village *zamindars*' here had been made subject to an ever rising burden of tax under the Mahalwari system since 1822. Bengal proper was under the Permanent Settlement, with land tax permanently fixed; the Rayatwari of the Madras Presidency was also a permanent settlement, made mainly with peasants; Bombay had settlements of thirty years. In Mahalwari, not only were the settlements made for twenty years only, but the revenue-rates could be changed at any time. There was also collective responsibility for payment: even if one peasant or landholder paid his tax, but his neighbour had not, then his own land would also stand forfeited to the government. In Aligarh district, Eric Stokes tell us, between 1839 and 1858, half of the land changed hands; in Muzaffarnagar, a quarter, between 1841 and 1861. The tax-free (*mafi*) lands had also been resumed wholesale after 1833. The Brahmans and also '*shaikhs*', from amongst Muslims, who were particularly recruited in the Bengal Army, often held *mafi* lands, which were ordinarily given to pundits and Muslim scholars under the pre-British regimes. Both as peasants and as *mafi*-holders, the classes that the sepoys came from, were increasingly adversely affected, and this, of course, led to discontent spreading among the sepoys as well.

Whatever sources of the discontent might have been, the fact that practically the entire Bengal army revolted, step by step, but with increasing tempo, remains a dramatic phenomenon. Over 1,25,000 revolting out of 1,35,000 is itself, as we have mentioned earlier, an incredible development however one looks at it. It began in West Bengal, in Dumdum first, in January 1857; then, Mangal Pandey, enacted the first bold act of defiance, in March at Barrackpore. The flames spread to Lucknow early in May; and on 9 and 10 May full scale mutiny erupted at Meerut. The Meerut Sepoys occupied Delhi on 11 May. This proved to be the decisive general signal for the whole army to revolt.

Popular Response

Till now, despite much speculation, there has been no solid evidence that behind this sudden upsurge there was any long premeditated plan or a recognisable leadership, beyond a strong sense of brotherhood among the sepoys. The brotherhood that had long been developed through shedding blood together in their masters' wars alone can explain how the mass of sepoys decided to follow the call of solidarity with the first rebels. Hindu and Muslim sepoys of the Bengal Army thought that they had a common identity. Hence, when one set of sepoys revolted, the others could not hold back. When we deprecate the term 'Mutiny' given to the Revolt of 1857, we should not at the same time underestimate the vital role of the rebelling soldiers in the uprising. They remained throughout its course the backbone of the Revolt. The proper estimation of the *sepoys'*

role in the rebellion is found in even the conventional narrative of Vincent Smith in his *Oxford History of India* (1916). One finds him speaking of how these 1,20,000 men, went to their deaths, on the battlefield, or on the gallows, or in the Tarai defiles; anyone hardly escaping, with few ever surrendering. The Bengal Army Sepoys certainly deserve every tribute we can offer them, and the memory of their staunchness in resistance and suffering would hopefully live forever in the heart of the Indian people.

It is also true that the rebel soldiers immediately found a response in the civil population. The areas, where the Sepoys were recruited from, were immediately convulsed by a widespread sense of sympathy for the rebels; and in turn other classes also revolted.

A very well documented article by Talmiz Khaldun in a volume on 1857 edited by P.C. Joshi argues that the Revolt turned into 'a peasant war against indigenous landlordism and foreign imperialism', and was thus primarily an anti -feudal movement, and only secondarily an anti colonial uprising. One would agree with P.C. Joshi that this is an unjustified dilution of the anti-colonial character of 1857 and very unrealistic in its excluding the landlord classes from the ranks of the rebels. It is naturally also not in consonance with Marx's assessment of the rebellion of 1857, as we have seen. To him, it was 'a revolution', 'a national revolt', in which the peasants, as well as a section of the *zamindars* and *talukdars* were also involved. All the classes in India were adversely affected by imperialism at that time, and the contradiction between Imperialism and the Indian people was at that particular juncture concentrated in those areas, where the Bengal Army Sepoys mostly came from. The land tax was intensely heavy there; and the land rights of the *zamindars* were being rendered increasingly vulnerable to forfeiture. The annexation of Oudh had taken place in 1856; and the *talukdars*, who were the great landed magnates of Oudh were threatened with the imposition of the same Mahalwari system that had ruined landed classes in the rest of the province. So there was a situation, in which both the peasants and the landed classes had to bear oppression from the same source.

As would happen in any agrarian revolution, the conditions on the ground undoubtedly varied. Mark Thornhill claimed in a report (15 November 1858) that the upper landed castes, who had suffered most in the Mahalwari system in Uttar Pradesh, remained loyal to the British, whereas the peasants, 'who have derived the most benefit from our rule(!) were the most hostile to its continuance'. This is an obviously one-sided version, foreshadowing the subsequent British policy of winning over the landlords and repressing the peasantry. In any case, in Oudh the Governor-General Canning himself thought that the *talukdars* were the leaders of the rebellion and, therefore, issued his famous proclamation of 1857, in which he declared that the entire land of Oudh under the *talukdars*' possession was now forfeited to the British Government. It was stated repeatedly on the floor of the British Parliament that both the *talukdars* and the peasants of Oudh had joined hands in the rebellion against the British Government.

Moreover, apart from the rural roots of the rebellion that Marx has underlined, urban elements were also involved in it. British rule had meant considerable growth of urban unemployment. Lucknow might not have had a population of one million at the time of annexation (1856), as estimated by some British observers, but it certainly had a population of above 600,000, at that time, to judge from a police-house-survey made just before the Mutiny. It was therefore, a large city, possibly even larger at the time than Kolkata. After the annexation it thronged with people deprived of their livelihood, because the court was gone. The artisans, especially weavers, were the hardest hit because of imports of British products. This was notably because while, on the one hand, there was an influx of cheap factory-made cloth and other products from Britain, there was simultaneously the loss of their traditional markets for town artisans, as the princely courts and their dependents were destroyed. As L.E.S. Rees, an English eyewitness of the events at Lucknow in 1857 admitted:

> 'That the Lucknow people should rise against us was a very probable event...We had done very little to deserve their love and much to merit their detestation.'

What was true of Lucknow was true, in varying measure, of most towns of the affected region. Therefore, the revolt of 1857 was more than an agrarian war: people of cities also joined the rebellion: Delhi, Lucknow, Bareilly, Kanpur, Jhansi and other towns became determined centres of resistance.

Appeal to the Masses

We must remember that the British regime by the processes of tribute extraction and deindustrialisation, it had unleashed, had caused extreme impoverishment among millions of Indians. Tribute was the cause behind heavy taxation; and it had to be remitted constantly to meet what would later be known as the 'Home Charges', and for transfers of private wealth to Europe. The degree of colonial exploitation was so extreme that many classes, which perhaps did not understand what their misery was due to, still took to the path of revolt. They sensed that in the overthrow of the British, lay the only source of relief; and so, whether in villages or in towns, they joined the Revolt.

The documents that became known to us in the 1950s are important in this regard, as they bring out some of these sentiments of the rebels. For example, the Mughal Prince Firoz Shah's proclamation of 25th August 1857 lists many of the popular grievances of the time and seeks by certain specific promises to attract many sections of the population to the rebel banner. It begins with an appeal to the *zamindars* : the British were levying heavy taxes on them, and the *Badshahi* Government would only take half the produce in tax; those landowners who aided it with money and men will be made tax-exempt; those who gave money only would need to pay only a fourth of the produce in tax. Moreover, their dignity as against 'common Ryots' would be protected. The merchants would be aided with funds and 'will have the benefit of the Government steam vessels and steam-carriages for the conveyance of their merchandise gratis'-this has the appearance of a particularly 'modern' project. Salaries of public servants and soldiers would be raised. Artisans were promised employment, their present plight being described thus:

> 'The Europeans by the introduction of English articles into India, have thrown the weavers, the cotton dressers, the carpenters, the blacksmiths and the shoemakers, etc., out of employ...so that every description of native artisan has been reduced to beggary.' Finally, 'pundits, fakirs and learned men', both Hindu and Muslim, would be given lands, provided they declare in favour of the rebels.

It will be seen that practically every class of society is appealed to-except the peasants. Clearly, even among the more intelligent and determined rebel leaders, as Firoz Shah turned out to be, the full potential of peasant unrest and its value for the success of the Rebellion was still not understood.

Yet, even the most traditional of rebel leaders were conscious of the need for making an appeal to the masses. This is particularly to be seen in their use of the printing press to publish their proclamations. The Oudh Court, in the name of Birjis Qadr, issued a printed 'General Notice (*Ishtiharnama*) to the *Zamindars* and General Inhabitants of this Country', which was a bilingual document in Hindustani in Urdu characters (on the right) and Nagari (on the left). The language was deliberately kept simple, and the document shows that the days of Hindi Urdu controversy had not yet dawned. S. Athar Abbas Rizvi has published a facsimile of this 'Notice' as well as a printed *ishtihar* of Nana Sahib, printed at Kanpur in July 1857, in similarly idiomatic but simple Urdu. Throughout the period of rebel control of Delhi (May-September 1857) weekly Urdu newspapers continued to be printed and issued in the city.

Religious Differences Recede

The last-mentioned proclamation of Nana Sahib is also important in another respect. It has long been the custom of certain historians to treat Nana Sahib and Lakshmi Bai of Jhansi as representing the chiefly 'Hindu' centres of the Rebellion, while Delhi and Bareilly were regarded as particularly 'Muslim' centres, with an assumption of an underlying sense of hostility between them. One can see how this assumption is at work in Smith's account of the Revolt in his *Oxford History of India.* How wrong such a conception could be, is shown by the fact that not only is Nana Sahib's *ishtihar* published in Urdu, and bears a *Hijri* date, but its main theme is that the Sultan of Turkey had intervened on behalf of the Indians, so that when the British ships had brought the European troops to Egypt on their way to India, the Sultan issued a *farman* to the Pasha of Egypt to slaughter the English, and he had done so. This was nothing but fantasy, of course. Yet the expectation of support from the Sultan is good evidence that Nana Sahib's world-view was not clouded by religious prejudices. As for the Rani of Jhansi, some of her most determined fighters were Muslim gunners and Pathan guards. On the supposedly 'Muslim ' side, the way the standard of *jihad* was removed from the Jama Masjid in May 1857 at Delhi, lest it be apprehended as being directed against the Hindus, and all cow and buffalo-slaughter was banned at the Muslim *Iduz Zuha* festival in July, showed the rebels' determination to prevent all religious disputation-a realm in which Percival Spear *(Twilight of the Mughals)* in his detailed account of the rebel regime in Delhi, credits them with the 'most striking success'. At Bareilly, Bahadur Khan, the principal rebel leader, printed an appeal to Hindu chiefs to join the struggle against the British, detailing the attacks on Hindu customs and taboos by the British and offering, on behalf of Muslims, to utterly abjure cow-slaughter and the eating of beef!

In his important book, *Felt Community,* Rajat Kanta Ray has very comprehensively dealt with the attitude of mind of the various sections of the rebels. He particularly underlines the fact that in the rebellion of 1857, in the minds of most of the participants, even when they were not *sepoys,* but civilians, the sense of religious differences receded to a surprising degree. Hindu contingents would elect Muslims as their representatives; Muslim contingents would accept a Hindu Subedar Major as their head. Among the Muslims who voluntarily joined the Rebellion, under the impulse of joining a righteous war, or *jihad* and so were called *mujahids* or *jihadis* ('fanatics' in official British translation and often wrongly identified with Wahabis), there was the same acceptance of the need for Hindus and Muslims coming together to fight for a common cause: the target was the British alone.

In the *Risala Fath-i Islam* (Tract on the Victory of Islam) composed under the supposed aegis of the famous rebel leader-and-theologian Ahmadullah Shah, the appeal is repeatedly made to both Hindus and Muslims to fight unitedly to defend their respective faiths against their English oppressors. In a contemporary eyewitness description of a mass rebel ceremony at Bareilly that Rajat Ray extracts from a Bengali source, we are told of Bahadur Khan moving through Bareilly with two banners, one the banner of Islam, the green banner, and another large banner, the holy *dhvaj.* A similar ceremony had been undertaken by Nana Sahib at Kanpur.

The final aspect, and one that is often ignored in the discussions about the rebellion, is the racial question. W.W. Hunter, in the preface to his book *Indian Musalmans* (1871), admitted that 'the chronic peril, which environs the British power in India, is the gap between the Rulers and the Ruled'. It was a barrier, set by not just power and wealth, but also and most visibly, by race. Though India was always familiar with social hierarchies, and the rebel leaders themselves often wanted to restore and strengthen the traditional social hierarchy, this kind of racial difference, based on colour, was unknown to them. (Later on, there would be railway carriages for the Europeans' exclusive use, separate from those for Indians. Those who, like our Prime Minister, praise the Indian Civil Service as the great contribution of the British to India, forget that as late as 1916, out of every twenty ICS officers only one was an Indian). The first common perception once the English were overthrown in any locality was obviously that now the relationship stood reversed, infusing a sense of elation in the consciousness of the Indians that Rajat Ray does well to emphasise.

Reasons for Failure

There were many reasons that could be advanced for the failure of India's great Rebellion. As we have noted, there had been no organised conspiracy behind this. Plots and plans began only once the initial sepoy mutinies had occurred. There is no proof of detailed plans of the kind that the BJP put in its NCERT textbooks, attributing these to Nana Sahib, and bemoaning a 'premature' outbreak spoiling a well-prepared design. Marx's statement that one could not expect the Indian revolt to be a kind of modern European revolution introduces for us an important element of caution. There was neither a large bourgeoisie as yet, nor a working class in India. There were no political parties. The French Revolution would have not developed the way it did, if the Jacobins had not established through their Jacobin clubs a true political party. Such organisations gave direction, thrust, and boldness to the French Revolution. Mao Zedong in his characterisation of the long series of Chinese peasant revolutions notes especially as the cause of their failure that there were then no political parties to guide the revolts. One of the great Marxist thinkers, Antonio Gramsci, in his essay, 'The Modern Prince' has, indeed, said that the political party is the basic unit of modern polity. And, for the working class, of course, its own party is a crucial instrument of action. There was not yet any working class or even a modern, educated middle class in the zone of the rebellion. In the absence of these classes, and any organisation answering to the form of a political party, the rebel leaders could conceive only of a polity of the old type, envisioning basically a restoration of pre-British system of local regimes bound together with vague loyalties to a central monarchy. They could not think of a modern Indian national state, though they did definitely think of India as a country to which they owed loyalty.

It is relevant here to refer to the spirited reply that the rebels gave to Queen Victoria's proclamation of November 1858 in the name of Birjis Qadr. They said that the promises the Queen was holding forth to Indians were totally deceptive; the British had never fulfilled their promises. The British had destroyed Indian states, one after another, and the rebels gave a list which included practically every important state in India demolished by Britain, from that of Tipu Sultan in Mysore, to that of Duleep Singh in the Punjab. The rebels were thus concerned with what had happened to the whole of 'Hindustan'. The proclamation told the sepoys, and all rebels, not to believe the British, who would ultimately kill them. Queen Victoria's promises meant nothing: the Indians were destined under her to be only the hewers of wood and drawers of water, and not masters of their own house. The reply is totally defiant and uncompromising, even when as in November 1858, everything seemed lost. One's heart is warmed by the fact that the rebels still spoke of India and remained steadfast in what they believed to be her cause.

Such firmness of sentiment did not, however, change the situation on the ground, which was that even the Bengal Army sepoys never attained unity of command; they in their different units co-operated with or even joined the service of different traditional authorities. They had no single high command, because among the sepoys, none had any experience of being officers; they were only soldiers, though their leaders might now be called generals or colonels. It is true that they did not only follow English military titles, they also almost everywhere tended to form 'councils', to manage their affairs. In Delhi, they formed the famous Council of Administration, which in every way was modelled after British practises. But these organs of power were no substitute for a unified command of the whole rebel movement, which was not only a political but a military necessity. One of the great advantages of the British was that they could devise strategies and plan troop movements according to need. The sepoys could decide only on tactics, and could not concentrate their military strength at vital points. Despite their large numbers, they could yet be overthrown in detail.

The result was that the rebels were actually placed between two enemy pincer movements, one from the east, and the other from the north-west; and ultimately so trapped, they were destroyed. They were not, however, destroyed easily. The defence of Delhi lasted for more than four months, with Bakht Khan as its leading commander. Lucknow lasted for almost ten months, repulsing the first invasion by General Campbell himself. The Gwalior contingent defeated the British troops and occupied Kanpur, inflicting on General Windham one of the few defeats in an open engagement, ever suffered by the British in India. The bitter defence of Jhansi under its brave Rani remained memorable.

And forever an epic was the campaign over a surprisingly large area by that old and able chieftain, Kunwar Singh of Jagdishpur. Tatiya Tope valiantly continued his battle against the British for almost two years and was hanged on 18 April 1859. The rebels hardly ever went down without fighting, or without resisting.

One needs to remember here the recurring descriptions of the rebels, who were tortured and hanged. They went to their deaths unbowed, and hardly anyone craved pardon. There was often the same stoical and defiant streak, which was to be seen later in the Singapore Mutiny of 1915. And not only among sepoys, but also among ordinary men. Let us read J.W. Kaye, author of *The Sepoy War,* on the conduct of Peer Ali, a simple bookseller of Patna:

> Brought before the Commissioner and other English gentlemen, 'heavily fettered, his soiled garments stained deeply with blood from a wound in his side', he was asked whether he had any information to give that might induce the government to spare his life. With dignified composure, such as our people (i.e. the English) did not always maintain under exciting circumstances, he confronted his questioners....He denounced the oppression of the English... Peer Ali was [then] taken out to execution...He was hanged, his house was razed to the ground and his property was confiscated.

British Atrocities

It had repeatedly been said that many English women had been dishonoured; this was said on the floor of British Parliament again and again. Marx disbelieved such inflammatory rumours with remarkable prescience, as may be seen an article of his in *New York Tribune,* 15 April 1858. After the rebellion was suppressed, despite the English assiduously trying to find evidence against the Rebels for molesting English women nothing by way of evidence could be found. Yet the cry that 'the natives have dishonoured our women', was a very important piece of hate propaganda spread in England against the mutineers and used to justify all barbarities perpetrated.

Even before they could have possibly known of the Kanpur massacre that took place later, the English had begun committing atrocities on Indian men, women and children. Here is what J.W. Kaye, says about the haunting dilemma that British atrocities posed for him.

> An Englishman is almost suffocated with indignation when he reads that Mrs Chambers or Miss Jennings was hacked to death by a dusky ruffian. But in native histories, or history being wanting in native legends and traditions, it may be recorded against our people, that mothers, wives and children with less familiar names, fell miserable victims to the first swoop of English vengeance, and these stories may have as deep a pathos as any that rend our own hearts.

Such atrocities undertaken by the English from the beginning of the Mutiny enflamed the rebels and hardened their hearts. The English gave no quarter to their opponents: as Engels recalled in 1870 they violated all laws of war in killing the prisoners of war; and they did so by ever imaginable, fiendish means, like hanging after binding their victims in contorted forms or-a special favourite-blowing the captives from mouths of their guns.

Right from the beginning, with Col. James Neill's expedition in early June 1857 horrible bouts of atrocities were committed by the British as they regained each village or town from the rebels. There was a frenzied general massacre of civilians at Delhi upon its fall in

September 1857, devastating and depeopling the whole city-an account of which may be read in William Dalrymple's *Last Mughal.* Every subsequent success of the British was similarly marked by a general massacre and plunder of civil populations. William Russell of the *London Times* was a witness to the British loot of Lucknow in March 1858. A Maharashtrian pilgrim caught in the rebellion similarly described the slaughter of civilians, including women and children, wrought by the British at Jhansi and neighbouring places. The repression continued even after the end of the rebellion. There were pursuits, trials and executions. Confiscations of lands and properties followed. Not only individual rebels but whole families, whose members were suspected of having been involved in any way in the Mutiny were deprived of their lands. The confiscated lands were given to British families and to such 'natives' as could claim to have rendered service against their own compatriots.

The defeat of the Rebellion of 1857 seemed at the time total, and as a consequence, the repressive and exploitative nature of British rule now appeared in a still more naked form. And yet even in its defeat, the Revolt weakened the capacity of British imperialism to continue with its policy of territorial aggrandisement, since it could no longer rely on Indian troops for external adventures. Before 1857, there were over 2,00,000 Indian sepoys in the three Presidency Armies. This number had been reduced to 1,21,000 by 1862-3, while the number of European soldiers in India was increased from 38,000 to 76,000-so that there was now one European soldier to watch over every two Indian sepoys! Moreover Indians were excluded from the artillery branch. Since a European soldier's pay was several times that of an Indian, the burden of military expenditure fell ever more heavily on the Indian tax-payers' shoulders. Yet the army was far less effective. Thus, the grand designs of British imperialism which had been based on the use of Indian troops as cannon fodder, could no longer be pursued with the same elan. To this extent 1857 helped to shield other Asian nations from British onslaughts for a long time.

Bahadur Shah, the last Mughal king, is not one of the heroic figures of the Revolt of 1857. But he was a poet, and as he was being tried, deprived of pen and paper, he scrawled with charcoal on the walls of his cell, verses of sorrow and sadness at the tragic end of the Great Rebellion. The bulk of the verses I translate below belong to a poem that was already being sung by 'the minstrels of India', according to a report of the Political Agent of Bhopal, dated 14 June 1862.

The way the wind has changed so suddenly and totally,
my heart now knows no quiet.

How can I recount that tale of cruelty, for my breast is shattered by sorrow?

How have the people of India been destroyed!
What cruelties have been perpetrated on them!

Whomever the victorious masters saw, they said,

'He is fit enough for the gallows.'

No one buried the dead under the earth, no one gave them a shroud,

They could never attain their native place, nor is there any sign anywhere of their graves.

'Friends, I am that slaughtered man, at whose corpse,

a whole world will continue to look with grief and envy.

O Zafar, so long as the country of India endures,

the star of the glory of this flower will ever shine.'

میں وہ کشتہ کہ میری لاش پر اے دوستوں
اک زمانہ دیدۂ حسرت سے تکنے جائے گا
اے ظفر قائم رہے گی جب تلک اقلیم ہند
اختر اقبال اس گل کا چمکاتا جائے گا

The last lines contained a proud boast on behalf of the rebel dead. It is for the people of India to show over a hundred and fifty years later how much they care for the memory of those who died so bravely for her.

Chapter - 2

The Sepoys and Middle Class Citizenry into the Making of Rebellion

—Professor Irfan Habib

The Bengal Army was very different from the traditional Indian armies. It comprised three major branches: 1. Infantry called 'Telingas' in colloquial speech, presumably because the original sepoys had been initially recruited from the Madras Presidency; 2. Cavalry, Popularly called 'Turk Sawar', presumably because Turks were supposed to be skilled horsemen; and 3. Artillery (less than 5000 men), commonly known by the Persian word *Topkhana.* The Infantry formed the largest branch with 112,000 men. In its total strength the Bengal Army comprised some 139,807 'natives' or 'Hindustanies' watched over by some 26,089 European officers and men (Goras), on the eve of the rebellion. British recruitment policies were guided by various needs and prejudices. They had come to think that the Bengal Army needed to be linguistically cohesive, and so recruited it from areas where Hindustani was either spoken or at least widely understood. This restricted its area of enlistment to the present Uttar Pradesh and western Bihar and Haryana. About 40,000 men came from the territory of Awadh (the present Lucknow and Faizabad divisions) alone/ the second consideration was to recruit mainly Brahmans into the infantry branch. The Brahmans were considered to be disciplined and often literate and so best suited to serve in infantry, Rajputs too were recruited into the infantry, but apparently as second list. Pathan and other Muslims were preferred for the cavalry (19000 men). Educated sepoys (like the later rebel commander Bakht Khan) were recruited to the artillery, which however had less than 5000 sepoys in it. Such compositions led to the supposition that inducing lower-caste men would reduce the army's cohesiveness. Thus, by the regulations of 1855 all recruitment from the lower caste was prohibited. On the other hand, in order to preserve cohesiveness Hindu and Muslim soldiers were put in the same military units. The result of this, noted Syed Ahmad Khan in his near contemporary work on the causes of the Indian Rebellion (*Asbab-e Baghawat-e Hindustan)*, was that Hindu and Muslim sepoys came to regard each other as closed than blood brothers, since the life of each in battle depended on the other.

I

The composition of the Bengal Army was accordingly such that the sepoys felt proud of their caste status, while at the same time close ties grew between both Hindus and Muslim sepoys. It thus came about that in the case of the greased cartridges, the Brahman sepoys in or near Calcutta were in the first instance greatly influenced by the propaganda of the *Dharma Sabha,* the organ of Bengali Brahman conservatism; and then, the Muslim sepoys were affected, not so much because of the suspect pig-fat, but because they could not stand aside when their Hindu brethren were so much concerned. *'Deen'*, for once, became a unifying and not a divisive slogan for both Hindus and Muslim sepoys.

But there was much else in the sepoy mind than a concern for either *'deen'* or injustice over allowances. The spoys formed one very large group of Indians who had both in war and peace lived so close to British personnel and institutions. Ever since 1839 the Bengal Army sepoy had continuously fought in Afghanistan (1839-42), in China (1840-42, 1856-60), with Sindhia's troops (1843), in Sind (1844), in Punjab (1845-46 and 1848-49), in Burma (1852) and in Crimea (1854). He had in the process not only been worn down but learnt much about the principles of modern military organization.

Such military organization consisted, in the first place, of a system of transmission of command through a hierarchy of military ranks. The sepoys in revolt aspired to build such a command system by giving their leaders the same military ranks from General down to Captain. The word officer was Urdu-ised into 'afsar'. All military units retained their previous identities, and the plural 'platoons' referring generally to infantry. The word 'command' became 'kaman'. This usage can be seen in the numerous rebel documents at Delhi preserved in the National Archives.

The rebel sepoys were also admirers of the British methods of consultation and of their committees and councils. The constitution (*dasturul amal)* of the Court of Administration in Rebel Delhi by the sepoys, whose original text in cursive hand is preserved in the National Archives, is well-known. It is established not by an order of the Mughal king, but by a decision of the sepoys taken in July 1857. It begins:

> "Let there be established a 'Court', whose name shall be 'Court-e Administration' [the –e representing Persian possessive or *izafat,* meaning 'of'], that is an assembly for the military and civil affairs."

It was to consist of ten members, six of whom were to be elected (*muntakhib),* two from each branch, '*paltan*' (infantry), '*risala*' (cavalry) and '*topkhana*' (artillery). The chairman of the court was given the English name of 'President'. Decisions were to be by vote, the president to have casting vote. Five members were to form a quorum.

The numerous documents in the National Archives leave us in no doubt that the Court actually functioned on a day-to-day basis with many matters being referred to it by the king himself.

The sepoys set up a similar court or council at Lucknow as well, so that there is no doubt that this was a mode of government and command they spontaneously counterposed to the traditional method of government: of the princely court.

If the sepoy was impressed with British methods of organization, he was also influenced, through his own experience, of successful resistance abroad to British aggression. The National Archives contain a paper written by a half-literate sepoy who had presumably seen service in Afghanistan: 'we have proposed', it says, 'that just as Kabul was a country which rose against the English. So should Hindustan similarly rise, only then these English (*Nasara*) would be killed, otherwise there is no way of killing them...Every Hindu and Muslim should avoid falling victim to their deceit and unite in order to expel the English quickly from *Hindostan.* Otherwise as we will have all to repent. Nothing will be of any avail."

Here, then, is a simple sepoy's understanding that if the country is to be freed of the English, the Hindu and Muslims will have to unite. From a simple fight for defense of '*Deen*' and '*Dharma*' there is thus emerges a perception here, however vague, of a Freed India.

In many ways Bakht Khan the "republican" sepoy commander at Delhi, distills this perception of unity in the artless orders that he issued and that are preserved for us in the National Archives of India.

On 30th July 1857 he issued an order to the Kotwal (police head) of Delhi that he should by beat of drum announce that no one would be allowed to engage in cow slaughter during the "*Id-ul-azha*" festival. Such persons should be forthwith arrested. "It is heard," he syas, "that certain *Mujahids* (muslim volunteer- soldiers) have this object their in mind. Go and tell *Maulavi* saheb to convince the *mujahids,* not to do so this year. If quarrel breaks out, this will not be good; only the enemy will become stronger. And those *mujahids*, who having gone into the Jami Masjid, which is a sacred place of God, are spoiling it by their dirtiness, should also be told that such mischief coming from religious people is not proper. They desist, otherwise it is not good to invite trouble."

Subsequently, he went to the extent of demanding that all cows kept by Muslims be impounded so that they may not be able to slaughter cows. It is surprising that such a man should be described as a "*Wahabi*" by some historians, with William Dalrymple as the latest one. In fact, in to fight at Kashmiri Gate in the last stand on 10 September is telling in this respect.

> "to all officers of infantry, cavalry and artillery, the order is issued; that let every Hindu, bound to respect the cow, and every Muslim, undefiled by pig, deem it a matter of *deen* and *dharma*, and, if you have regard for your dignity and life, then do in one body, prepare the infantry, cavalry and artillery, and march to Kashmiri Gate…"

II

The next class to be considered is that of the intelligentsia, Delhi, unlike Lucknow, was in a peculiar position in that the Mughal royal presence here was merely in the form as a fort-State, with the British controlling the city since as early as AD 1803. The result was that within Delhi, there was no great presence of *zamindars* and landed magnates, to dominate its cultural scene. Lucknow, which the old Awadh state, annexed only in 1856, was not only much larger than Delhi, but was far more dependent on the *talluqdars* and *zamindars* who had been the dominant classes within the old regime. When the rebellion broke out in 1857, the rebel sepoys in Delhi, surrounded by English forces, had to depend far more on the Delhi citizenry for support; and among these citizens, the educated classes occupied an important position.

When in 1847, Syed Ahmed Khan issued the first edition of his *Asar-us-Sanadid,* 'The Monuments of Kings', he appended to his account of the monuments of Delhi, an account also of contemporary notables. In this supplement, he gave an enthusiastically sympathetic account of Shah Isma'il, the "*Wahabi*" martyr, who had been killed at Balakot in a battle with Ranjit Singh's troops in AD 1831. He recalled his sermons at Delhi calling for *jihad* or holy war. And added:

> "every year the *mujahids* leave their different native places to go to those territories [where Maulvi Shah Isma'il had been killed] and the spiritual merit of this noble act reaches his [Ism'il's] soul constantly."

The *Wahabis* were then fighting against the Sikhs, and so their activities were of little concern to the English .The situations changed only some time after the British occupation of Peshawar after the first Punjab war, 1844-45, and then Syed Ahmed Khan prudently dropped the supplement altogether from the subsequent edition of his book.

We are here, however, concerned with whether the picture he draws of the response to Shah Ismail's religious speeches was an accurate representation of the intellectual state of Delhi at the time. Such religiosity at best represents a part of Delhi's intellectual sphere, but not the whole or the main part of it. There were other influences at play, especially strengthened by the printing press. Recalling his youth before the revolt, Zaheer Dehalvi mentions how he was able to obtain volumes of collections of the great Persian poets– songs of the world, of love, which were much irreligious – that come off the printing presses of Lucknow.

The printing press also brought a whiff of air from the Bengal Renaissance. This was seen in the arrival of the weekly newspaper. The pre-eminent Delhi weekly was the *Delhi Urdu Akhbar,* edited by Maulvi Muhammad Baqir, father of the great historian, Muhammad Husain Azad. It began to be issued from 1836 and appeared regularly until the fall of rebel Delhi in September 1857. Issues of this paper just one year, from 26th January 1840 to 12th December 1840 have been reprinted by Khwaja Ahmad Farooqui, (Delhi, 1972).

An examination of the extant issues of this weekly shows that the *Delhi Urdu Akhbar* was able to include reports translated into Urdu news and comments from the English Delhi Gazette, a paper for the English communities in upper India. It also extracted news from Urdu paper printed elsewhere, notably in Calcutta. It often quoted the Bengali paper *Samachar Darpan*, through the Calcutta Urdu paper *Jam-i Jahan Numa*. One issue even carried news of "a reception with dance- performance and fire-works" given by Dwarkanath Tagore at Calcutta.

What is of much interest is the critical attitude towards British imperialism that the *Delhi Urdu Akhbar* shared with part of the Calcutta "native" press. In its issues of 1840, admired the defiance exhibited by Muhammad Ali Pasha of Egypt against the British (p. 78 of the Farooqui vol.); it proclaimed the wide unpopularity of Shah Shuja in Afghanistan, the British puppet at Kabul (pp. 103-4 and passm); and it criticized Britain's opium trade with China and her preparations to go to war with that country over the issue. On the other hand, it welcomed modern learning and science. It commended the graduates of the Delhi College (p. 192) and hailed advances in modern medicine (p. 230).

How did such a paper react to the entry of the sepoys in Delhi? It is our good fortune that we have in the National Archives the file of this weekly for the year 1857, until its demise on the British storming of

Delhi and the execution of its editor at English hands. Before the revolt it maintains the same attitude of criticism towards the British as it had in 1840. Giving a report about English success in Iran, translated from the Delhi Gazette, it says in its issue of 8th March 1857 that such news "would gladden the European and their well-wishers and disturb the equanimity of all others". Otherwise its reports on the greased cartridges are surprisingly neutral. Remarkably, it shows no indignation at the English insistence that they be used by the sepoys. Indeed, it shows little concern with religious matters. Its issue of 10th May (just a day before the sepoys broke into Delhi) bears no trace of any knowledge of things to come.

When the sepoys from Meerut broke into Delhi, the paper maintained an attitude of wonder and neutrality. For the sepoys it employs the usual colloquial terms, "*telinga*", "*turk sawar*" , "*poorbi*". The editor gave a clinically impartial but detailed account of what happened at Delhi on 11th May and afterwards . On 24th May it published a poem by the editor's son expressing astonishment at how the poor had overthrown the mighty English, but only comparing the event to what had happened in the past to great and powerful empires.

But then the attitude changes from astonishment to admiration and from neutrality to total support of the rebels. The sepoys are no longer '*Telingas*', "*Poorbeas*", etc. They are the "*Sipha-I Hindostan*" or "*Fauj-i- Hindostan*"—India's army; or "*Fauj-i-Zafar*", the victorious army; and, then, above all, "*Hamari Fauj*" – Our army By 2nd August its major hero is Bakht Khan, the Rebel Army Commander. In a Persian poem after recording perfunctorily courteous praise of Bahadur Shah, it tells of the changes Bakht Khan's presence had brought about, and says.

> "Let the army of the Commander be victorious; Let all the English be put in Hell"

What is of interest is how this spokesman of the pre-1857 "Delhi Renaissance" justifies the overthrow of the English. It produces an argument which Indian economic nationalism was so much to develop later: the thesis of Colonial Tribute. In its issue of 21 June 1857, under the heading "Let us seize this opportunity". Its editor wrote:

> "In the times of the English, all the high offices, which were so numerous and each of which produced hundreds of rupees per

month were distributed among men of the same (white) colour..., they hardly spent anything here, being most careful, tight-fisted and narrow-minded. All the thousands and lakhs of rupees they saved, they took to their own country. Thus nothing of what they obtained was spread out in this country, and we got no benefit out of it, when on the other Indians obtained employment, from a few people out of hundreds, the hundreds too benefited".

Now the paper hoped that as the Indians would supplant the English, "our fellow countrymen and men of competence" would be in great demand. "So you should bear with fortitude the difficulties of the early days of the new regime (*amaldari*)."

For the success of the regime it was important for Hindus and Muslims to unite. On 14th June it urged both: Muslims and Hindus to look into their scriptures. They would find that nothing is mortal. In appealing to the Hindus, it used words like "*dharma*", "*gyan*", "*prakash*", and "*Adipurush*". But Dalrymple is wrong in stating that the appeal is addressed to Hindus only, who were supposedly weakening. Quite the contrary, it is addressed to both Muslims and Hindus in that order. It ends with a quotation (slightly altered from the original) from the Urdu poet Mir;

> "This is the beginning of love; why are you afraid?
> Look! what will happen, by and by"

On 19th July it made the hemistich of Saadi, Hafiz of Shiraz the foundation for another such appeal. Hafiz had said: "All human beings are parts of one another" This, says the paper, applies to Hindus and Muslims for they believe in one God, unlike the English who believe in Trinity. Muhammad Baqir then adds: "So O! brothers, O! fellow countrymen, especially O men of the army! It is obligatory for all of you, Hindus and Muslims, to unite with one heart, regarding each other as parts of the same body, and destroy this race [of the English)."

On 5th July and 12th July the editor severely condemned a *Wahabi*-inspired poster (which had been put up at the Jami Masjid) which had claimed that the English being Christians were *People of the Book* to Muslims and so are no enemy. While the Hindus being Infidels (*kafirs*) were the real enemy of Muslims. The *Urdu Akhbar* denounced the poster as the work of English agents and printed its editorial as a pamphlet, priced 4 annas. It concluded: 'There is no doubt that at this time and in these circumstance, for every Hindu and Muslim, cooperation and endeavour in this cause conforms to the needs of *jihad* (holy war) and *deen* (religion). To this paper, then, those undertaking "*jihad*" embraced both Hindus and Muslims.

Such were the ideas and sentiments of the major rebel newspaper at Delhi. It is seldom that the paper refers it, a conspiracy of the English to Christianize India, religion, as we see above, is rather sought to be made the cementing bond between Indians. *Nor, it will be seen as the restoration of the Mughal Empire as the object.* It is the independence of the country ("Hindostan" is to frequently invoked) that the paper seeks- a state of independence, it is true where "fellow countrymen and men of competence" -not aristocrats, by the way-would be needed to govern its several parts.

I would class Firoz Shah's proclamation of 25th August as representative of the same intellectual environment which produced the *Delhi Urdu Akhbar*. Although a distant member of Delhi's royal family, Firoz Shah was a scholar rather than prince. He could not reach Delhi in time to join the rebels there, but his proclamation (extant now only in an official English translation) was obviously designed to furnish a programme of concessions to various classes, in order to win them over to the side of the Delhi rebels ("the *Badshahi* Government') The proclamation offered to the *zamindars* a land-tax not exceeding half of the produced and promised to protect their dignity in relations with the common *rayats*. Merchants were to receive subsidies, and were promised free or cheap transport by rail and steamboat for their goods (a refreshing piece of salute to modern technology!) The pay of government servant would be raised. Import of foreign manufactures would be prohibited to protect the livelihood of local artisans.

Finally, grants of land would be made to both mullahs and pundits—provided they loyally supported the new regime!

One may regret that peasants are totally excluded from the ambit of Firoz Shah's programme, and that so much regard has been paid to the dignity of the *zamindars*. But for the rest the programme seems unexceptionable and astonishingly modem in its reasoned composition.

In the late second and third week of September 1857, the British stormed Delhi, and lane by lane the Sepoys and their supporters fought, until the later retreated over the Yamuna in full order to continue the fight another day. The ordinary citizen now became subject to a wholesale massacre and spoliation by the victors. The special targets is of the executioners were the educated classes of Delhi, whom the English rightly suspected of widespread sympathy with the rebels. This infamous act of genocide put a forcible end to the literary and scholarly resurgence that has been called the Delhi Renaissance. But if there had a Renaissance its most memorable chapter was surely penned by the likes of the rebel journalist Muhammad Baqar or the princely rebel Firoz Shah.

No one can improve on the elegy for the rebel dead that the ex-king, of a Delhi poet who himself saw it all, has left for us:

> "Friends, I am that murdered one on whose corpse a world will
> gaze long on with grief and envy.
> O Zafar, so long the country of India endures,
> The star of the glory of that flower will ever remain bright."

The Indigenous Voices from Rebels' World

Chapter - 3

Rebel Journalism, *Dehli Urdu Akhbar*, May-September 1857

—Professor Shireen Moosvi

At the height of the Rebellion, in June 1857, the Governor-General Lord Canning is reported to have said that the 'native press', on the pretext of publishing news, was very cleverly and craftily spreading seditious sentiments among the Indian people.[1] This reminds us that the rebels were able to use the printed word to serve their cause. The four months that Delhi re-mained in the hands of the rebels (May-September 1857) saw the city served by three weekly newspapers, of which perhaps the major one, to judge by its detailed reporting and commentaries, was the *Dehli Urdu Akhbar*. Sixteen issues of this paper from 1857 are preserved in the National Archives of India, New Delhi.[2] Of these three, viz., 8th March, 12th April and 10th May, are pre-Mutiny. The remaining thirteen issues belong to the period,

Facsimile of the news printed by Dehli Urdu Akhbar about the rebellion in Kol (Aligarh), Bulandshahar and Saharanpur.

17th May to 13th September 1857. Unfortunately, five issues, namely of 7th and 28th June, 26th July, 30th August and 6th September, are missing and copies of them have not yet been traced anywhere else. Atiq Ahmad Siddiqi rendered yeoman service to research on 1857 when in 1966 he published a volume containing transcriptions of the texts of all the Urdu newspapers of Delhi, during the Mutiny available in the National Archives of India: the *Siraj-ul-Akhbar* (Persian) of 11th May, thirteen issues aforementioned of the *Dehli Urdu Akhbar* (of which seven appeared under the changed name *Akhbar-al-Zafar),* and six of the *Sadiq-ul-Akhbar.* Facsimile of the rebuttal issued by *Dehli Urdu Akhbar* to a communal notice put up by the British.

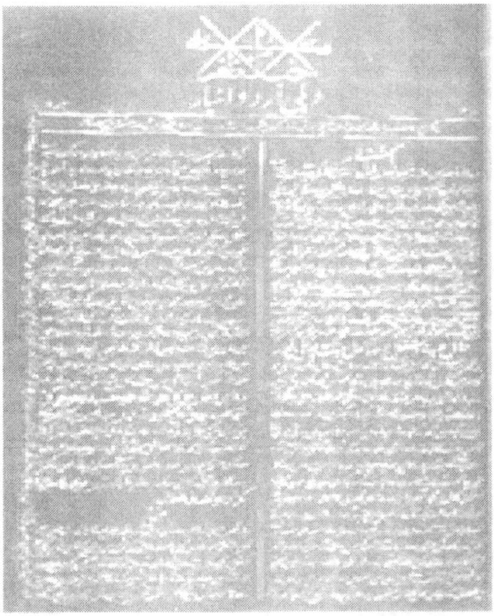

Facsimile *of* the rebuttal issued by *Dehli Urdu Akhbar to* a communal *notice put up by the British.*

The *Urdu Akhbar* has received much attention from scholars of the history of Urdu journalism who have explored matters relating to its dates of issue, ownership, editors, publishers and printers. It has also been used as an important source for the period of the rebel regime in Delhi in *Swatantra Delhi* (Varanasi, 1957) by Athar Abbas Rizvi, well known as the editor of *History of Freedom Struggle in Uttar Pradesh,* 5 Vols., Lucknow, 1957-60, the largest collection of documents on the revolt so far published. It is, therefore, rather strange that William Dalrymple should have made the following statement:

> No less exciting was it to discover that Delhi's two principal Urdu newspapers, the wonderfully opinionated Dihl! Urdu Akbhar [sic] and the more staid and restrained Court Circular, the *Siraj ul-*

Akbhar [sic], had continued publication without missing an issue throughout the Uprising, and that the National Archives contained almost complete sets of both. Again only fragmentary translations of these have previously been available.[3]

It is unbelievable that the imperial weekly newspaper *Siraj-ul-Akhbar,* noted for its chaste Persian, can be declared to be one of the 'two Principal Urdu newspapers'. Nor is it true that almost all the issues of these weekly newspapers for 10 May-20 September 1857 are available in National Archives of India, as we have seen. It is also strange that Nadir Ali Khan's important book in Urdu should appear in Dalrymple's 'Bibliography' only in the garb of its English translation.

The *Dehli Urdu Akhbar,* began to be issued from 1837. By 1857, it come to be owned and edited by Maulvi Muhammad Baqar, a well respected Shi'ite scholar and a member of the Delhi elite, with access to the Court and the Urdu literati. Particularly friendly relations existed between him and the famous Urdu poet, Zauq. According to the print-line on all the surviving issues of 1857 it was 'printed and published' by Sayyid Abdullah, the manager of the *Dehli Urdu Akhbar* Press. The press was located at Baqar's own house in Guzar Aitiqad Khan, near Panja Sharif. It appears from a glance at the three pre-Mutiny issues that the *Urdu Akhbar* followed the practise of other contemporary Urdu newspapers (like *Tilism* of Lucknow), in providing news drawn from government gazettes, other newspapers both English and Urdu, with unpaid free-lancers supplying reports or information from other places by letters sent to the editor. Its coverage was not confined to India and, contrary to Dalrymple's statement that it only remained concerned with ' local political and religious matters'[4] its columns regularly gave news of Europe *(Firangistan)* and England *(Englistan)*, keeping its readers informed on such matters as changes in the British cabinet or an attempt on the life of the King of France. However, from the issue of 17th May, with Delhi having been cut off from the rest of the country by the English, and the postal system destroyed, the paper naturally enough could only report events happening in and around Delhi, or such places outside about which the editor was able to learn from people coming from other parts of the country. This was, of course, not by choice. The issue of 17th May reports under the account of the Cantonment that the Englishmen looking after the postal system had been killed. Again on

24th May the editor laments that no arrangements for *dak* (postal system) have yet been made (by the rebel regime), so that information from outside was hard to get.

Eyewitness Account

The issue of 17th May is exceptionally important because it contains the editor's eyewitness (as well as hearsay) account in great detail of the events at Delhi on 11th May and the subsequent days. The report is preceded by Quranic extracts and Persian and Urdu passages on how God can make totally unforeseen events happen. The initial reaction to the Mutiny in the first two issues of 17th and 24th May is, indeed, that of gleeful surprise on so sudden a turn of events, leading to the fall of the mighty English. There is no sympathy or compassion shown for the English, even for their women and children who were now killed. A degree of unabashed pleasure is perceptible in the report on the killing of Nixon, the head of the 'Chancellery' and Taylor, the Principal of the Delhi College.[5] The terms used are almost invariably *Angrez* for the English and *Tilanga* for the rebel sepoy. There is a grudging approval of the *Tilangis* when they killed the English,[6] but disapproval of their trigger-happy conduct when they killed a Khatri horseman or injured a vegetable vendor in Chandni Chauk.[7] The paper complains of the helplessness of the City Kotwal in maintaining law and order in the presence of the army of 'the *Tilangis*' that has descended upon Delhi. Reflective of this attitude is the poem that was composed by Muhammad Baqar's son, Muhammad Husain Azad (who unlike his father survived the rebellion to join British service and become the first historian of Urdu literature). This was printed on the first page of the issue of 24th May, with the editor's special commendation, under the title 'Chronogram for this Instructive Revolution'. Recalling how great rulers and conquerors like Soloman and Alexander, cruel tyrants like Hajjaj, Chengiz, Halaku and Nadir, great epic heroes and sages, have all disappeared, the poem glories the fact that, similarly, the English too, once so knowledgeable, so mighty, so cruel, have had their day. 'Nothing came of their knowledge, skill, wisdom and character: The *Tilangs* of Purab (present eastern UP) have done to death all of them here.' Still the wonder is: 'How every trace of the Christian rulers, despite their wisdom and foresight, has all of a sudden disappeared from amongst the people (*khalq*).'

However, from 14th June both the vocabulary and attitude change. Now the *sipah-i diler* ('the brave army') the *Tilingan-i nar sher* (the lion-like *Tilangis)* are being enjoined, if Muslims, to take the name of God and the Prophet, and, if Hindus, to pray to Parmeshar and Narain. The sepoys are to follow the examples of Bhim and Arjun, of Rustam, Chengiz, and Halaku, along with Timur and Nadir Shah, and defeat the English. Thus, the simple sense of wonder is replaced by a great sense of sympathy with the sepoys, and there is the greatest anxiety to encourage them, in the name of Both Hindu and Muslim traditions, in their battle against the English.

The terminology continues to change in accordance with the new spirit as the days pass. The rebel army becomes the *sipah-i Hindostan* (the army of India) and there are appeals now to 'fellow countrymen' *(ahl-i watan),* 'dear compatriots' *(aziz ham-watan),* with specific exhortations for a united rallying of Hindus and Muslims. The English being Christians and so believing in the Trinity of God are now held to be polytheists and infidels *(kafir),* while the Hindus being believers in 'Adi Purush' share the basic belief in One God with Muslims and so are close to them.[8] Both Hindus and Muslims are therefore called upon to fight and destroy the Christian English.

The next issue of 21th June recalls various grievances against the English: under them there was utter lack of any respectable or gainful employment for Indians. The English rulers were not only of a different religion but also of a different race speaking a different language. They cornered all the high offices and wealth and did not spend it in our country, but took it away to their own country thus depriving 'our Hindustan' of its own wealth. It goes on to criticise the lethargy and lack of industry on the part of the Indian upper classes, their practice of looking down upon business and artisanal professions and their reluctance to move from their native places in search of better opportunities.

The issue of 5th July is of special importance. It reproduces as the first item a copy of the *ishtihar* (public notice) that was pasted on the Jama Masjid, allegedly by agents of the English, to 'threaten and mislead the citizenry and the army'. The notice called upon Muslims to wage a 'holy war against Hindus', for the Christians were the natural allies of Muslims as 'People of the Book' according to the *Shariat.* It asserted that the use of pig-tallow in the greased cartridges was a totally false rumour. The *Urdu Akhbar* declares this notice to be a conspiracy, the handiwork of enemies of both *Dharm* and *Iman* (the faith of Hindus and Muslims). The paper provides a point-by-point rebuttal of the pamphlet, saying sarcastically.that the English should not try to deceive anyone by invoking the *Shariat*. In its later issues too the paper strongly espouses the perception that all Indians are one, while the English are absolute aliens.

Dalrymple's Misleading Remarks

Here it is necessary to correct certain very misleading remarks made by Dalrymple about the reason behind the appeals for unity and resistance printed in the *Dehli Urdu Akhbar*. He tells us that 'Maulvi Muhammad Baqir included in his columns a call for the Hindus of the city not to lose heart-which of course implied that they were beginning to do just that'. He, then, goes on to give a passage in translation from a 'remarkable letter aimed at his Hindu readers' published in the *Akhbar's* issue of 14th June. The fact is that the appeal was addressed to both Muslims and Hindus, and Dalrymple's translation of the passage is deliberately doctored by omitting all references to Muslims. Without bothering about small inaccuracies, I reproduce below his translation, inserting what he has omitted:

> O my countrymen, Looking at the strategy and devious cleverness of the English...and their overflowing treasuries you may feel disheartened and doubt that such a people could ever be overcome. But those who are my Muslim brothers by faith, let them consider-if they are anxious and concerned out of worldly considerations-to look at their [not 'your'] religious books, such as the Qur'an, the Tafsir and Hadis, and those who belong to the Hindu dharm [not 'my Hindu brothers'], let them [not 'you'], by the light of their gyan (wisdom) and dharm (faith), illumine their hearts [not 'look into your Holy books'] and first see that except the Adipurush, the primaeval Deity, nothing is permanent.[9]

It can thus be seen from the reproduction of what the paper actually wrote that there is no sanction for the inference drawn by Dalrymple about the Hindus alone being addressed and so there being any implication of their being less committed to the revolt than the Muslims.

An ordinary reader would find even in the last issue of the paper (13th *Muharram* = 13th September) the same spirit of defiance, and not the depressed resignation which Dalrymple reads into it.[10] The issue actually exists in two separate prints. Of one only the front page exists. In both the prints news is carried that everywhere from Benares to Muzaffarnagar the rebellion is being met with success. The readers are urged not to be demoralised from 'the long period' *(tulkashi)* of the struggle, a phrase used in both prints.

Dalrymple also quotes an English report (date not mentioned) purporting to be a translation of a letter from Muhammad Baqar to the effect that he had been persuading Bahadur Shah Zafar to make peace with the British, which Hakim Ahsanullah Khan was preventing. In this letter he is also reported as mentioning that there was much outrage among Muslims at the killing of five butchers by Hindu sepoys.[11] Whether such a letter was actually sent by Baqar or not cannot be established; but the English, at least, did not treat him as their informer: he was seized and hanged, while Hakim Ahsanullah flourished.[12] The rebels knew well enough that the latter was in league with the English. In the issue of 18th *Zilhij*/9th August, just after the *Id-al-Azha* when the cow-slaughter issue came up, there is a report at the bottom of page 3 that Hakim Ahsanullah Khan had been proved to be an agent of the English and so arrested by 'the Victorious [Rebel] Army'[13]

In the *Dehli Urdu Akhbar* there is not the slightest mention of the cow-slaughter episode, which in some accounts of the rebel regime in Delhi is given much importance. The omission of any reference to this incident in the *Dehli Akhbar* in either its issue of 11th *Zilhij* 19th August immediately after the *Id-al-Azha* (18th August), or in that of 18th *Zilhij*, suggests that the editor did not regard the issue as very serious. It is, however, worth quoting how its contemporary, the *Sadiqul Akhbar* commented on the matter in its issue of 12th *Zilhij* 13th *Sawan*, under the heading 'Thanks' (*Shukriya*):

> A thousand thanks to Almighty God that the auspicious day of the *Id-i Qurban* passed off peacefully despite the machinations of the mischievous opponents of religion, the irreligious English, and no dispute arose between Hindus and Muslims on account of cow-slaughter. Both communities remained united, like milk and sugar.

The paper attributed the success in maintaining unity to the efforts of Bahadur Shah and his 'Prime Minister' Hakim Ahsanullah Khan. Apparently, the editor was not yet aware of the Hakim's links with the English.

It is clear that the *Dehli Akhbar* mirrors the feelings of much of the Delhi populace, especially its educated section-its elite-and it is singular how from the early feelings of estrangement towards the sepoys, they become in its pages, much before the fall of Delhi, the object of admiration, and then begin to be viewed as the valiant defenders and protectors of the city. All this tells us much not only about what Rajat K. Ray calls 'the Mentality of the Mutiny', but about how the very process of resistance transformed that mentality and created a patriotic surge that prevailed over everything else.

Notes

1. M. Donough, *History of Law and Sedition,* New York, 1952, p. 183.
2. The extant issues available at National Archives of India (NAI) are of following dates: 8th March, 12th April, 10th, 17th, 24th and 31th May, 14th and 21th June, 5th, 12th and 19th July, 2nd, 9th, 16th and 23th August and 13th September. Four of these, beginning from 12th July, appeared under the changed name *Akhbaruz Zafar* written on top in ornamented hand with *Delhi Urdu Akhbar* inscribed below it, the last three issues, from 16th August onward, no more carry the previous name and only bear the title *Akhbaruz* Zafar.
3. William Dalrymple, *The Last Mughal: the Fall of a Dynasty.* Delhi, 1857, p. 14.
4. *Ibid.,* p. 86.
5. *Dehli Urdu Akhbar,* 17th May 1857.
6. *Ibid.,* 23rd May 1857, (Account of the City).
7. *Ibid.*
8. *Ibid.,* 14th June 1857.
9. William Dalrymple. The *Last Mughal,* pp. 268-269.
10. *Ibid.,* p. 346.
11. *Ibid.,* pp. 301-302.
12. *Ibid.,* pp. 375-376.
13. The report was true. The Hakim was, *however,* released at the intervention of Bahadur Shah.

Chapter - 4

Lucknow between the Annexation and the Mutiny

—Professor Iqbal Husain

This essay aims at introducing *Tilism,*[1] a less widely known Urdu weekly newspaper edited and published by Muhammad Yaqub[2] from Firangi Mahal, Lucknow during the short period elapsing between the annexation of Awadh and the Mutiny. The annexation was proclaimed on 11th February 1856, whereas the first issue came out on 25th July 1856. Only one copy of *Tilism* is available in the National Archives of India, New Delhi. A few copies are reportedly preserved in the libraries of Osmania University, Hyderabad and the *Urdu Research Institute* of the *Anjuman-i Islam,* Bombay.[3] The Department of History, Aligarh Muslim University has acquired 41 issues of *Tilism,* beginning from number 1, dated 25th July 1856 till number 42, dated 8th May 1857 (number 37th is missing) through the courtesy of Mufti Muhammad Raza Ansari[4] Sahib of Firangi Mahal. It seems that with the outbreak of the Mutiny in May 1857, the *Tilism* had to cease its publication, though the editor survived the Mutiny to issue yet another journal.[5]

The *Tilism* covered news of varied nature, such as local events, cases of theft, dacoity and murder. It also published government notices and news of appointments, transfers and removal of the Company's officials. There also appear prescriptions or advice of varied kinds to deal with particular maladies or epidemics, such as cholera. Finally, the paper gave considerable space to news from other parts of the country and foreign countries. Since the telegraph was then costly and the mails slow, the English[6] and the Urdu[7] newspapers (see Appendix A) depended largely on news borrowed from newspapers at other centres or on private correspondence. The *Tilism* similarly gathered news from the Urdu, Persian and English newspapers.[8] An interesting aspect of the news coverage by *Tilism* is that it gave prominence to the information relating to the deposed king of Awadh, Wajid Ali Shah and members of his family. The *Tilism* also published government notices which throw light on the effects of the annexation on the people, the status of *zamindars* and *taluqdars,* the role of the *mustajirs* (revenue-farmers), the civil and military organisations, etc. It also refers to the growing discontent caused by unemployment, and it records an increase in thefts, robberies and murders in Lucknow. From the pages of the *Tilism,* one learns that the Company authorities conducted a ward-wise census of houses with complete information of caste, religion and economic condition of the dwellers of each house. This information is given in six issues of *Tilism,* covering 272 mohallas (wards) out of an estimated total of 800 mohallas.[9] The census indicates how the mohallas were divided on the basis of caste, class and occupation.[10]

The *Tilism* is written throughout in versified Urdu, a style popularized and developed by Rajab Ali Saroor[11] who enjoyed considerable influence at that time.[12] Though, *Tilism* was published during a period of political-uncertainty, the editor is quite fearless and candid. He praised the Company officers for their suppression of disorder and crime, but he also criticized them for their unfair treatment meted out to their new subjects.[13]

It seems that the *Tilism* became one of the popular news weeklies in north and central India. Its subscribers were found in Delhi, Lahore, Banares, Alwar, and Gwalior among other places, as appears from the names of subscribers it printed in each issue. Apart from the common people,[14] the subscribers belonged to aristocratic families of the Nawabs of Awadh like the sons of Muhammad Ali Shah, the Maharajas of Banares and Alwar, and the Nawab of Rampur. A number of British officers (see Appendix B) including Sir John Lawrence, the Agent and Chief Commissioner of Punjab, was also one of the subscribers.

The *Tilism* appears so far, to have escaped the notice of the scholars working on the Awadh history. Since it contains much valuable information of the period, it is only possible here to select some reports published in it, which shed light on the situation at Lucknow in the fateful year preceding the Mutiny.

Occupation of Palaces

After the annexation of Awadh, the immediate task before the East India Company was to disarm the retainers of the 'Nawabs', or family members of the deposed King. The Chief Commissioner of Lucknow, issued an order No. 374, dated 10th June 1856 allowing only eleven[15] prominent members of the family of Wajid Ali Shah including the Wazir Ali Naqi Khan to keep arms.[16] Still the disarmament was not complete as a large quantity of arms was stored in various palaces. On orders from the Chief Commissioner, Carnegi[17] made a futile bid to secure information from Sahib-i-Ali, Mirza Ali, Mirza Khush Bakht.[18] Having failed in persuading the prince to disclose the arms stored there, Carnegi resorted to coercive methods and compelled the *darogha* of the palace to declare the arms![19] The authorities also made a determined bid to occupy the royal palaces. They refused to accept any excuse put forward by the palace servants and forced a hurried vacation by the *Harem* of the deposed king overnight.[20] The ladies thus ejected took shelter in different mohallas where Wajid Ali Shah and his predecessors had built houses.[21] Having obtained control over the palaces, the Company's officers recovered the arms and transferred them to safe places.[22] A large quantity of conventional arms such as daggers, swords, spears including some of historical value[23] as well as obsolete firearms were auctioned in public causing great resentment among the public.[24] Despite the recovery of arms from several palaces the Chief Commissioner suspected the existence of secret arm dumps. When every attempt proved ineffective in getting clues *from* high ranking Awadh servants like *Miftah-ud-Daulah*, *Iqbal-ud Daulah* and *Sihat-ud Daulah* their freedom of movement was restricted and they were forced to produce cash security of Rs. 10,000.[25] With the seizure of arms, the Company 'officers also carried on a systematic plunder of the royal palaces and removed all the valuables they could lay their hands on'.[26]

Demobilization of the Awadh Army

The annexation was followed by wholesale dismissal of the Awadh troops. Scores of old servants[27] and troopers were removed on one pretext or the other.[28] The *Tilism* gives interesting information about the technique adopted by the British officers in demobilisation of the Awadh troops in its issue dated 25th July 1856. It reported:

> After the annexation, the Awadh army was retrenched and most of the troopers received their salary. The Company's government ordered the recruitment of three battalions. Captain Dohli, Captain Hardinge and Captain Gall were appointed to lead each battalion. Thereafter, the deposed king's soldiers were granted option to join service under the Company's government. Specially the *Turk Sawars* and *Khud Aspas* were repeatedly asked to give their assent. Two hundred of them agreed to serve the Company and the rest refused. Now Hardinge is removing one hundred and fifty of them. Learning this news they were upset and approached the *Sahib Bahadur* (Hardinge) and wanted to know their offences for removal, saying that they were neither idle nor thieves nor cowards. The *Sahib* kept quiet and gave no reply. When the news was conveyed to the Chief Commissioner, he instituted a committee to enquire into the case. The enquiry committee also held them innocent but they were not taken back into service due to the enmity of Hardinge. Now the papers have been forwarded to the Chief Commissioner for consideration. Let us see what orders come forth.[29]

In the next issue, the *Tilism* continues to report of the case:

> On 29th July 1856 Captain Gall lined up 250 horsemen of the royal Awadh cavalry, whom he had appointed after great persuasion. He then said that the Company intended to maintain mares instead of horses and asked them to deposit rupees one hundred and fifty within one month so that the company could supply them (with mares). He also said that those who did not pay the money would be removed from service. All of them expressed their inability to pay such an amount and said that there was no one who would buy their horses; the government was their master, it depended on its sense of justice whether to keep them or dismiss them.[30]

Finally the *Tilism* reported in its issue dated 22th August 1856:

> By the end of July 1856, sixty-seven horsemen were removed for not having deposited Rs. 150 the cost of a mare. The rest are also

> likely to suffer the same fate. It is said that in the Amausi cantonment orders have been given to the *Akhtari* and *Nadiri* battalions that those who desired to quit service could do so by the end of this month failing which resignations of none would be accepted.[31]

With this policy of the Company unemployment increased and led to cases of theft and murder.[32]

Economic Effects of Annexation

The increase in the prices of essential goods added to popular misery.[33] Their impoverishment became so great that they could not file appeals in the court of law for the restoration of their rights.[34] The annexation also greatly affected the demand of indigenous goods, particularly cloth manufactured at Mubarakpur (District Azamgarh, UP). The *Tilism* reports:

> The English (*Sahib*) Magistrate was informed that the weavers of Mubarakpur are emigrating in large numbers. He asked the *thanadar* of Muhammadabad to report the number of the emigrants and the causes of their desertion. The *thanadar* reported that the weavers are suffering from hunger and they have no means of subsistence. One thousand weavers have already emigrated with their families to Mecca (!), since there are no buyers of cloth in Lucknow and they are not in a position to meet their expenses. Their trade declined; hence they migrated.[35]

People's Reaction Over the Annexation

The attitude of the Company authorities towards the members of the family of the deposed King, unemployment and high prices of foodgrains led to a feeling of general resentment among the local population. This found reflection in conspirational anti-British activities. The *Tilism* records three such secret attempts:

1. Qadir Ali Shah, posing as a saint, managed to raise a force of 12,000 men secretly. He had fixed 11th September 1856 (tenth day of Muharram) for an uprising against the Company's rule at Lucknow. But the conspiracy was foiled by the alertness of the authorities. *Muhsin-ud-Daulah* was suspected of

involvement in the conspiracy and his house was put under surveillance. He was called upon-to explain his position. Later on he was acquitted of this charge for want of proof.[36]

2. In November 1856, Maulvi Ahmadullah[37] the famous figure in the Mutiny, arrived in Lucknow and stayed at Ghasiyari Mandi as a saint. Soon he- became popular and a centre of attraction. People in large numbers paid frequent visits. He gave the call of a holy war against the Company's government. The Company authorities, therefore, began to stop visitors from seeing him and posted troops. It seems that due to such rigorous restrain, Ahmadullah Shah went away to Faizabad. He stayed in a *sarai* where he continued to preach *jihad* against the Company's rule. The local police administration took notice of it and the Kotwal pressed him in vain to give up the *jihad* campaign. This led to deployment of two companies around the *sarai*. The forces made an unsuccessful attempt to disarm the Shah and his men. Consequently, a battle ensued in which some of the supporters of Shah Ahmadullah were killed and he was himself arrested after being wounded seriously.[38]
3. In December 1856, another person claiming to be a saint settled near the *Tare Wali Kothi*. He also became a centre of attraction. He claimed that his mission was to restore the King to the throne. The authorities having failed to dissuade the people, expelled the saint from the city. An order was issued to all the *thanadars* to see that no crowd gathered around the saints in the city. The order authorized the *thanadars* to banish everyone who did not obey these orders.[39]

Taluqdars and the *Zamindars*

It is interesting to note from the pages of *Tilism* that the *taluqdars* in the kingdom of Awadh had adopted a peculiar technique for obtaining the land rights from the *zamindars*. Exercising their superior powers, the *taluqdars* entered into a league with the *Amils* to increase the *jama* (revenue) imposed on the *zamindars*. When the *zamindars* failed to pay the amount, the *taluqdars* stood as their surety, paying up the government demand. Within two or three years the *zamindars* were compelled either to sell the land to the *taluqdars* for meeting the outstanding dues or the *zamindars* gave their lands in farm *(ijara)* to the *taluqdars*.[40] Thus, the *taluqdars* appropriated the rights of the *zamindars* and held the *zamindaris* under their control by the use of armed men.[41] This in turn led to a general discontent among the *zamindars* and a perpetual conflict between the *zamindars* and the *taluqdars*. Since the *taluqdars* were the creation of the Awadh rulers and their loyalties were to their King, the Company sought now to win over the confidence of the *zamindars* by issuing a series of orders with a view to restoring the old *zamindars* to their lands.[42]

The *Mustajirs* and the Custom Duties

The Company's government in principle was opposed to the *ijara* system.[43] but it transpires that it continued to farm out the markets for some time even after annexation. It, however, specified the commodities on which the custom duties were to be levied. The *Tilism* refers to the following commodities on which the custom duties could be levied:

1.	Grains of every quality	@[44] Rs. 1 per cart load
2.	*Paan* (betel)	@ Rs. 15 per cart load
3.	Whire silk cloth	@ Rs. 5 (on value of Rs. 100)
4.	Fruirs	@ Rs. 3 (on value of Rs. 100)
5.	Spices	@ Rs. 3 (on value of Rs. 100)
6.	*Kandla tarkashi* (gold and silver wires)	@ Rs. 3 (on value of Rs. 100)
7.	Horses, camels, oxes and cows	@ Rs. 5 (on value of Rs. 100)
8.	Wood of all varieties except for cooking	@ Rs. 10 (on value of Rs. 100)

The cloth manufactured in the city and the vegetables were exempted from custom duties.[45]

It seems that the first farming of the markets under the Company's rule took place on 25th July 1856.[46] It is interesting to note that even the high Awadh officials took interest in taking the markets on *ijara*. When the markets were auctioned, the agent of Ali Naqi Khan the ex-wazir was the highest bidder offering Rs. 1,65,000. However, the *mustajir* was assigned to Sharf-ud-Daulah the next day for a lesser amount of Rs. 1,41,000 considering his past experiences and services.[47] Such a high bid for securing the markets on *ijara* does not necessarily indicate the quantum of trade in the commodities which were really taxable. The *musrajirs* expected to levy a number of unauthorised cesses. The Company realising the position, issued a notice to the people directing them not to pay a single pie to the *mustajirs* on the commodities exempted from custom duties.[48] The *mustajirs* were also instructed to desist from charging extra cesses. But ignoring the instructions, Sharf-ud-Daulah levied Rs. 5 on coarse cloth. The traders appealed to Simson,[49] the Deputy Commissioner of Lucknow, who upheld the Company's orders.[50] We are, however, not in a position to ascertain the extent to which the Company government's orders were followed by the *mustajirs*. From the pages of the *Tilism* it transpires that one of the causes of price rise in the city was the prevailing corruption among the officials such as the *daroghas* and *thanadars* who gave a free hand to the traders for hoarding.[51] The *mustajirs* also took advantage of the situation and earned money unscrupulously.[52]

Social and Religious Life

From the first day of *Muharram*, the *Imambaras* in Lucknow used to be illuminated during the Nawabi days. Sweets and cereals used to be served to the destitute.[53] People thronged the courtyards of the *Imambaras* in multitudes to celebrate the *Muharram*. Recital of *nauhas* (elegies); and preparations of new *tazias*[54] and *zarih*[55] were a common feature.[56] But the departure of King Wajid Ali Shah from Lucknow, the economic difficulties and the direct rule by the East India Company, all worked adversely to affect the social and religious life of Lucknow. The *Imambaras* remained unlighted till the 6th day of *Muharram*, causing great gloom and sorrow among the people of Lucknow. In utter helplessness, they prayed for the return of their king and bewailed the prevailing state of affairs.[57]

Mutiny in Lucknow

It has been suggested that the mutiny started in Lucknow after the proclamation of 20th May 1857.[58] As a matter of fact the *Tilism* shows that there was resentment among the sepoys encamped at Mandiyaon[59] and Amausi[60] much before the popular outbreak in May 1857. A serious agitation was launched against an English doctor on a minor issue and the people set his bungalow on fire.[61] Subsequently, towards the end of April 1857, the cantonment of Mandiyaon was also set on fire by some unknown persons.[62] The British brought the guns in position and fortified their residences.[63] In the meantime the sepoys stationed at Amausi defied Captain Meagan's orders and refused to use the new cartridges. A detailed report gives the names of Sarnam Singh (*subedar*), Shiv Deo Singh (*jamadar*), Bhawani Singh, Mughal Beg (*naiks*), Gulzar Khan, etc., as the leaders of this movement.[64] They sent a message to fellow sepoys in the cantonment of Mandiyaon to join hands with them. However, the messenger was captured; and he disclosed the whole scheme. Having learnt of the failure of their plan, the sepoys at Amausi seized the magazine. On 4th May 1857, the Chief Commissioner sent the Seventh Company and thus the insurrection was suppressed.[65] However, the mutineers were not really suppressed; and the failure of the 43rd issue of the *Tilism,* proclaimed silently the momentous seizure of Lucknow by the rebels.

Notes

1. Ahsan Marahri had mentioned, -*Tilism* in his work but he does not give the name of the editor nor the place of its publication. *Tarikh-i Nasr-e Urdu,* Aligarh, 1930, pp. 405-6.
2. His full name was Maulvi Muhammad Yaqub Ansari. He belonged to the family of the *ulema* of Firangi Mahal. He died in 1903. Preface, *Fasana-i Ibrat,* Lucknow, 1957, p. 7; Muhammad Raza Ansari, *Ajkal* (Urdu), June 1951.
3. I am thankful to Dr Asghar Abbas of the Department of Urdu for this information.
4. He is one of the most known scholar from Firangi Mahal of the modern time. After serving as a Lecturer in the Department of Theology (Sunni), Aligarh Muslim University, Aligarh, Mufti Sahib is now engaged in writing the History of the *Ulema-i Firangi Mahal* after taking retirement from the University. Unfortunately he could not complete his work due to illness followed by his death.
5. *Karnamah* came out on 31th July 1865 and survived till the death of the editor in 1903. Garcin De Tassy also quotes *Karnamah* in one of his lectures, *Khutbat, Anjuman-i Taraqqi-i Urdu,* Aurangabad, 1935, p. 521; *Ajkal, 1951.*

6. In 1851, *the Friend of India* gathered news from a number of newspapers like *Hurkaru, Englishman, Bombay Times,* etc. See O' Malley, *Modern India and the West,* London, 19 41, p. 204.
7. The list of such papers is pretty long containing more than 25 Urdu and Persian newspapers. See Appendix 'A' where the papers alongwith their places of publication are listed.
8. *The Evening Mail,* London; *The Telegraph,* Bombay; *The Morning Chronicle,* Calcutta; *the Friend of India,* Bombay; *The Chronicle,* Lahore; *Bombay Times, The Muffissilite,* Agra; *Bombay Gezette,* etc.
9. *Proceedings of Indian History Congress,* 1970, p. 169.
10. *Tilism,* nos. 35, 36, 38, 39, 40 and 4 1; 20th, 27th March, 10th, 17th and 24th April and 1st May 1857.
11. He was an admirer of the editor of *Tilism* and gave him the right of publication of several of his works. Preface, *Fasana-i Ajaib,* p. 7.
12. A modern writer's contention that Saroor's style was confined to Lucknow and around (Rais Ahmad Jafri, *Wajid Ali Shah Aur Unka'Ahd,* p. 198) does not hold good in view of the fact that a number of newspapers published outside Lucknow like the *Chashma-i Faiz, Koh-i Noor, Doorbin, Noor-i Maghrabi, Umdat-ul Akhbar,* etc., also imitated the style of Saroor.
13. An English gentleman carelessly rode a horse and was involved in an accident with a *dakvan* (mail-carrier) causing serious injuries to the latter. The fault of the gentleman was ignored and the poor *dakvan* was arrested. *Tilism* reporting the whole case concludes with the saying, *Hakim hare to munh men mare* (If the ruler loses (a game), he slaps you on the face). At another place reporting the growing lawlessness in the city under the Company's rule, *Tilism* wrote, *Shahar men hukumat-sahiban-i angrez hai, char taraf berez berez hai* (Under the rule of Englishmen in the city, there is a cry 'save, save' from every corner). *Tilism,* no. 26, 16th January 1857.
14. Some subscribers who are otherwise known to us were: Shaikh Qutbuddin Saudagar (Delhi), Shah Makhan Lal, Babu Har Prasad, Diwan Kalika Prasad, Rai Krishna Sahai, Munshi Ram Bhajan Lal, Ram Prasad, Munshi Fazle Rasool, Mir Munshi of the Agent of Rajputana, Muhammad Hikmatullah, Chaudhari Ahmad Yar, Mirza Azad Beg, Mirza Azam Ali Beg, Chaudhari Ranjit Singh, Asmatullah Khan and others., For details, *Tilism,* Nos. 3, 4, 8, 11, 12, 14, 25, 26, 31, 33 and 40.
15. *Tilism,* no. 4, 15th August 1856; *Qaisar-ul Tawarikh,* vol. II, pp. 7-9.
16. *Tilism,* no. 4, 15th August 1856.
17. He was appointed City Magistrate of Lucknow upon Annexation. During the Mutiny he rendered valuable services to the Company and was raised to the rank of Major, *Qaisar-ul Tawarikh,* vol. II, p. 141; S.A.A. Rizvi, *Freedom Struggle in UP* Vol. II, pp. 11, 13, 52, 54, 228.

18. Sixth son of Wajid Ali Shah born of *Akhtar Mahal. Qaisar-ul Tawarikh,* vol. II, p. 8; Najmul Ghani places him at number 8. *Tarikh -i Awadh,* vol. V, Lucknow, p. 113.
19. *Tilism,* no. 5, 22th August 1856.
20. *Tilism,* no. 7, 5th September 1856, gives a detailed list of houses where 14 prominenr ladies took shelter.
21. *Ibid.*
22. *Tilism,* no. 7, 5th September 1856, Kamaluddin Haider only mentions the transfer of valuables. *Qaisar-ul Tawarikh,* vol. II, p. 166.
23. A dagger of Hafiz Rahmat Khan and sword of Mahabat Jang were also auctioned. *Tilism,* no. 10, 26th September 1856.
24. *Tilism,* nos. 9, 10, 19; 19 and 26th September, and 28th November 1856.
25. *Tilism,* no. 8, 12th September 1856; *Qaisar-ul Tawarikh,* vol. II, p. 166.
26. (i) Captain Flecher Hayes removed all the books preserved in the royal library to the bungalow of Captain Martin, Deputy Commissioner 1. *Tilism,* no. 5, 22 August 1856.

    (ii) Murray, incharge of the British artillery in Lucknow, secretly sold the stock of lead stored in the Mangal Sen Kothi to a *baniya* of Kanpur. *Tilism,* no. 16, 7th November 1856. For more such cases see *Tilism,* nos. 7 and 19, 5th September and 28th November 1856.
27. Kamaluddin Haider estimates that there were 87,000 men including 14,000 retainers designated *Shagird Pesha: Qaisar-ul Tawarikh,* vol. II, p . 170.
28. *Tilism,* nos. 1, 2, 4 and 5; 1th and 15th August 1856.
29. *Tilism,* no. 1, 25th July 1856.
30. *Tilism,* no. 2, 1th August 1856.
31. *Tilism,* no. 5, 22th August 1856.
32. *Tilism,* nos. 3, 22, 23, 26 and 33; 8th August, & 26th December 1856, 16th January, 6th March 1857; *the Rajas and Taluqadars of Oudh,* p. 16.
33. *Tilism,* nos. 3, 4, 22, 23, 26 and 33, 8 and 15th August, 19th and 26th December 1856 and 16th January, 6th March 1857.
34. *Tilism,* no. 5, 22th August 1856.
35. *Tilism,* no. 6, 29th August 1856.
36. *Tilism,* nos. 9 and 10; 19th and 26th September 1856; *Qaisarr-ul Tawarikh,* vol. II, p. 193.
37. He was a grandson of Nawab *Umdat-ul Mulk Amir-ul Hind Walajah Bahadur* of Carnatic. He received religious, administrative and military training at an early age. From the very beginning he had a mystic bent of mind. He went to Hyderabad at the age of 16 and from there he travelled to a number of countries including Arabia and England After the annexation, he came to Lucknow and from there to Faizabad. where he was imprisoned on the

charge of creating religious disturbance. For his later career, M. Abrar Husain Faruqi, *Ma'asiri Dilawari,* Hardoi, 1966, pp. 8-43,181-92; S.Z.H. Jafri, 'Indigenous Discourse and Modern Historiography of 1857: The Case Study of Maulvi Ahmadallah Shah', in *Rethinking* 1857, ed. Sabyasachi Bhattacharya, New Delhi, 2007, pp. 237-60; *Freedom Struggle in UP,* vol. II, pp. 13, 18, 54, 81, 102, 104, 141, 142-4, 147, 419. Also see *Qaisar-ul-Tawarikh,* vol. II, pp. 203-4. Conspicuously the *District Gazetteer,* Lucknow is silent. *Tilism,* nos. 18, 19, 28 and 33; 27th November, 12th December 1856; 30th January and 6th March 1857.

38. *Tilism,* nos. 18, 21, 28 and 33; 21th November, 12th December 1856; 30th January and 6th March 1857; *Qaisar-ul Tawarikh,* vol. II, p. 203.
39. *Tilism,* nos. 20 and 21, 5 and 12th December 1856.
40. *Tilism,* nos. 3, 4 and 5; 8th, 15th and 22nd August 1856; Lalji, *Mirat-ul Auza,* Aligarh Ms., ff. 9a-11 a.
41. *Mirat-ul Auza,* ff. 9a-11a.
42. *Tilism,* nos. 3,4 and 5; 8th, 15th and 22th August 1856.
43. G.D. Bhatnagar, *Awadh under Wajid Ali Shah,* Varanasi, 1968, p. 171.
44. @ denotes at the rate of.
45. *Tilism,* no. 1, 25th July 1856.
46. *Ibid.*
47. *Tilism,* no. 2, 1st August 1856.
48. *Tilism,* no. 3, 7th August 1856.
49. He was appointed as Deputy Commissioner of Lucknow under Young when Awadh was annexed. During the mutiny he was the incharge of British Artillery in Lucknow. *Qaisar-ul Tawarikh,* vol. II, p. 64; *Freedom Struggle in UP* vol. II, p.64.
50. *Tilism,* no. 3, 7th August 1856.
51. *Tilism,* nos. 22, 23; 19th and 26th December 1856.
52. *Tilism,* no. 33, 6th March 1857.
53. *Tilism,* nos. 2, 6 and 8; 1st, 19th August and 14th September 1856.
54. A model of the Tomb of Imam Husain.
55. A model of the grave.
56. *Tilism,* nos. 2, 6 and 8; 1st, 29th August and 14th September 1856.
57. *Tilism,* no. 6, 29th August 1856.
58. *Freedom Struggle in UP* vol. II, pp. 5-7. 'The first outward manifestation of discontent took place on 18th April, when a clod of earth was thrown at the Chief Commissioner while driving.' *The District Gazetteer,* Lucknow, p. 156.
59. Mandiyaon or Mariaon is a small town lying at a distance of 4 miles north of Lucknow. *the District Gazetteer,* Lucknow, p. 254.

60. A village 7 miles-south-west of Lucknow. *The DIstrict Gazetteer,* Lucknow, p. 168.
61. *Tilism,* no. 41, 1st May 1857.
62. *Ibid.*
63. *Ibid.*
64. *Tilism,* no. 42, 8th May 1857.
65. *Ibid.*

Appendix - A

Newspapers with their Places of Publications

S.No.	*Name of the newspaper*	*Place of publication*
1.	*Koh-i Noor*	Lahore
2.	*Sadiq-ul Akhbar*	Delhi
3.	*Jam-i Jahan Numa*	Meerut
4.	*Riyaz-i Noor*	Multan
5.	*Matla-ul Akhbar*	Agra
6.	*Noor-i Maghrabi*	Delhi
7.	*Punjabi*	Lahore
8.	*Subh-e Sadiq*	Madras
9.	*Kashf-ul Akhbar*	Bombay
10.	*Noor-e Mashriqi*	Delhi
11.	*Shua-us Shams*	Siyalkot
12.	*Chashma-i Faiz*	Siyalkot
13.	*Mufid-i Khalaiq*	Agra
14.	*Amir-ul Akhbar*	Madras
15.	*Umdat-ul Akhbar*	Bareilly
16.	*Aftab-i Hind*	Banares
17.	*Sultan-ul Akhbar*	Lucknow
18.	*Safir-e Agra*	Agra
19.	*Murtaza'ee*	Peshawar
20.	*Mathura Akhbar*	Mathura
21.	*Qiran-us Sa'adain*	Delhi
22.	*Doorbin*	Calcutta
23.	*Jam-e Jamshed*	Meerut
24.	*Muhtashim*	—
25.	*Gulshan-i Nau Bahar*	Calcutta
26.	*Dayar-i Magharib*	—
27.	*Nayrang-i Zamana*	—

Appendix - B

British Officers with their Designations

1. Captain Weston *Sahib Bahadur.*[1]
2. Brigadier W Ramsay *Sahib Bahadur*, Gwalior.
3. John Lawrence Sahib Bahadur, Chief Commissioner and Agent, Punjab.
4. Captain R. Sahib *dam daulat-ho.*[2]
5. Alexendar Orr *Sahib Bahadur,*[3] *Thanadar, dam daulat-bo.*
6. Captain William Hearsay *Sahib Bahadur.*[4]
7. Joseph Johannes *Sahib dam daulat-ho.*[5]
8. Dr Patridge *Sahib.*[6]
9. Captain Halnegi *Sahib dam daulat-ho.*
10. Hauckins *Sahib Bahadur dam daulat-ho.*
11. George Cooper, Secretary to Chief Commissioner, Lucknow.

Notes

1. He was the superintendent of Frontier Police. *Qaisar-ul Tawarikh,* vol. II, pp. 140-1; *Awadh Under Wajid Ali Shah,* pp. 59-60.
2. He was the Deputy Commissioner, Class I, under the Commissioner of Khairabad and Muhammadi. *Qaisar-ul Tawarikh,* vol. II, pp. 140-l.
3. He was appointed Deputy Commissioner, Faizabad after the annexation. He was killed by the mutineers in the Mutiny. *Qaisar-ul Tawarikh,* vol. II, p. 142; *Freedom Struggle in UP* vol. II, p. 109.
4. Assistant Superintendent Awadh Frontier Police, *Awadh under Wajid Ali Shah,* p. 188.
5. An employee in the Residency, *Freedom Struggle in UP,* vol. II, pp. 77, 191, 199.
6. Nos. 8 to 10 require identification. Here the names as found in the *Tilism* have been recorded.

Chapter - 5

'Voices' of the 'Vanquished' The 'Indigenous Discourse' in 'the Rebels World' of 1857

— *Prof. S. Zaheer Husain Jafri*

One comes across numerous printed proclamations, appeals and pamphlets issued by the rebel leaders in the various centres of the uprising making a plea for the ouster of the foreign rulers from the Indian subcontinent. These pamphlets, apart from making a very strong case for Hindu -Muslim unity also sought to revive the notion of Mughal sovereignty and invoked the concept of *Khalq Khuda ki, Mulk Badshah ka* and *Hukum* of various local leaders who were issuing these pamphlets.'[1] These proclamations were widely circulated. This fact runs quite contrary to the popular perception that the rebels and their leaders had spread their 'fanatical', 'religio-centric' appeal against the British through word of mouth, by circulation of 'lotus-symbols' and by distribution of *chapatis* (small pieces of home-baked bread) among the sepoys'[2] and the masses as symbolic images for an 'endangered' religion which was under threat because of the activities of the Christian missionaries that enjoyed official patronage.

Documents of this nature were seized by East India Company's troops and officers but were not destroyed. Most of these papers passed into the private and public collections. An analysis of such documentation yields enough data to draw on for an understanding of the motives and the power of mobilising the rebels and the people. Such data also helps us examine questions regarding the sepoy's background as a member of the modern army and the influence of the new medium-the 'printed word' which introduced modern elements. It is possible that the modern ideas that germinated were under the influence of the British rule and might have played a greater role in the course of the events than has been recognised so far in modern historical writings. Issues like the conflicts between the sepoys on the one hand, and more traditional elements on the other, the kind of 'polity' or the 'polities' that the leaders of the rebellion envisioned can also be examined in the light of such data.

The attempt is to evaluate the information from the rebels' own writings, for the uprising, their attempts to have a framework to fill the vacuum after the British administration was uprooted in Delhi, the question of religion, their perception of the threat of the conversion of people to Christianity, the manner in which the organisation of the rebellion took place, the internal dissensions and the contradictions among the rebels, the degree of the clashes between the sepoys and the more traditional elements and finally their reading of the failures of the movement. This information is not used in isolation, it has been supplemented with the 'Victor's Narrative'. This essay tries to study the aspirations of the rebel leaders as well. Although, the nature of these documents is very different yet, there is a striking similarity in many respects: they talk about the layers and the groups within the rebels with contradictory and even antagonistic aspirations, they unequivocally condemn the killing of the innocent English women and children (strangely enough the much-talked about Queen Victoria's Proclamation maintains an absolute silence as it had never condemned the 'White Terror' against the sepoys or against the helpless citizens in the aftermath of 1857).

I

To establish a semblance of order and to check lawlessness in Delhi important efforts were made by Bahadur Shah and the princess of royal blood. Certain appointments were made within civil and police jurisdiction. However, since the situation was not very clear as to what role the military commanders coming from various garrison towns were supposed to play, a necessity was felt and a *Dastur ul Amal* was promulgated with the specific purpose of looking into such affairs under the given circumstances. The preamble of this document is worth quoting in full 'Whereas to avoid disorder *(Mauqufi-i Bad Intezami)* in the sections of administration of the military and civil departments, it is absolutely necessary to form a constitution *(Dastur ul Amal),* whereas to work out the constitution it is necessary first to appoint a Court'[3] the following regulations are laid down.... '

The preamble and the first two clauses of *Dastur ul Amal* in the original is reproduced in this essay. The first clause states, 'A court should be established and named administration court *(Jalsa-e Intezam Fauji wa Mulki),* i.e. a court to administer military and civil affairs.' The second clause states, 'This association *(Jalsa)* should appoint 10 members among whom 6 are to be appointed from military and 4 from civil. From among the military side 2 members are to be from infantry *(Paltan-i Piyadgan);* two from cavalry *(Risala-hae-Sawaran);* and two from artillery *(Sarishta Topkhana).*'[4]

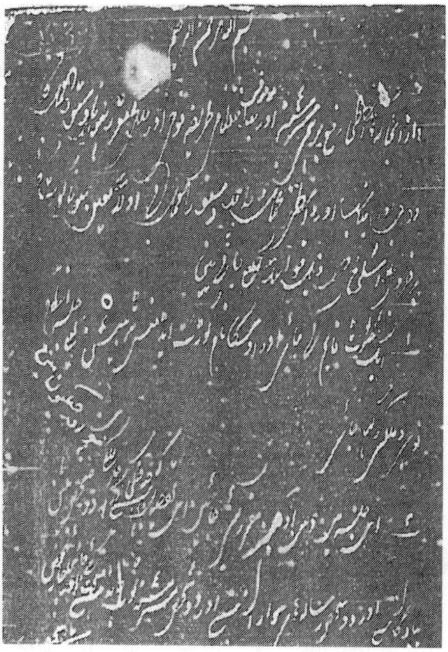

It is a remarkably coherent document which ought to have been drafted by a person(s) well acquainted with the working of the Company's administration. The English vocabulary has been freely employed. It talks about the *Sadr-i Jalsa* and *Naib Sadr-i Jalsa.* Secrecy of deliberations were to be maintained; there was a provision for election after any vacancy; 'His Majesty' was to be communicated about the decisions of the court, the meeting of the court was never to be attended by any outsider except Mirza Mughal-the Chief Commander (the *Sahib-e Alam)* and 'His Majesty'. It has been commended by no less a person than Sir John Lawrence, who has praised it for the 'remarkable manner in which Bahadur Shah was trying to conduct the affairs'. In fact Lawrence says that Bahadur Shah did make an effort for 'preserving the order in the city and to restrain the excesses of the soldiery.'[5]

The draft Constitution had twelve provisions, mainly relating to the 'affairs of the Court'. The actual power was vested in the hands of the military officers while His Majesty *(Huzur Zill-e Subhani;* and Mirza Mughal's *(Sahib-i Alam Bahadur),* presence in the meeting of the court appears to be more ceremonial, as every decision had to be taken by a majority vote without any veto power vested in either Bahadur Shah or any of the princess. As was argued, the sepoys of the Bengal Army were the only group who had been exposed to the techniques and the art of warfare and were the members of the most advanced fighting forces of the subcontinent. Their familiarity with British institutions was used in organising the skeleton of the framework of the rebellion, when they joined the uprising in an overwhelming majority.'[6] The importance of such a document need hardly be emphasised. It is here that we find certain initial attempts being made by those involved in the uprising to evolve a system which could take care of the colossal task which would follow the uprooting of the British system from the city of Delhi and its neighbourhood.

II

Another important proclamation was issued from Lucknow, the capital of the erstwhile kingdom of Awadh, by the group closely associated with the famous Maulavi Ahmadullah Shah, the hero of the Battle of Chinhat, who defeated the British forces. This pamphlet has been translated by the British officers as 'a Cry of *Jehad* in Oudh' *(Futteh Islam/Fateh-i Islam)* and has been used as evidence of the religious bigotry and holy nature of the war waged against the Christians. An attempt has been made to highlight the crucial role played by the *Wahabis* or *jihadis* during the course of the rebellion.'[7] Within Subaltern historiography, this document has been singled out as a representative document depicting extreme hatred for the British and using 'the most insulting language to describe the British especially Queen Victoria'. It has also been chided for 'its abusive condemnation of the whole chain of British authority from the Crown to the common soldiers'. Apart from the 'fire and sword' nature of the document for which it has been rather harshly criticised by modern writings, there is enough material which can be culled from it to examine the vision of the people participating in the 'Battle unto Death' and as to what they felt about the ongoing struggle and the strategies they had worked out under the extreme circumstances. Yet, they were conscious about the death of the English women and children as something unacceptable under the tenets of any religion. Besides making a strong plea for Hindu-Muslim unity, it emphasises the importance of firearms and canonns which were now available to the sepoys and its decisive impact in the final outcome of the battle.

Risala Fateh Islam was issued some time between 5-17 July 1857 (the date has been worked out by S.A.A. Rizvi on the basis of the internal evidence of the text) after the Battle of Chinhat on 30 June 1857. Maulavi Ahmadullah Shah had emerged as the most powerful military commander at Lucknow and his group was contemplating appointing him as an *amir* (leader) who could control indiscipline and restore law and order.'[8]

In the preamble to the document, the atrocities committed by the British have been highlighted in great detail, and, thus, the people, Muslims as well as Hindus have been asked to unite and wage a 'Holy War' against the 'inhuman and ungodly Christians'. It also discusses British attempts to 'deprive the troops of their religion by applying impure substances to the cartridges and pressing those troops to use them'. The preamble also holds a warning to the people that if the British were to succeed in re-establishing their 'authority great misfortune will fall on all the Hindus, Muslims, the people, the Sepoys, the kings and the Wazirs. Hence, the call is to unite, fight and annihilate them without delay.' It also becomes clear that in the perception of the rebels it was deadly weapons like guns which tilted the balance in favour of the English but which the rebels could now handle effectively. This might refer to the sepoys joining the army of the rebels in large numbers, carrying with them artillery pieces and large guns.

In fact, the fear of loss of religion and the forcible imposition of the Christian creed are the twin themes which continue to recur in most of the proclamations and within indigenous discourse. Such an apprehension should not be considered only as rhetoric propagated during the course of the rebellion or an exaggerated account of the activities of the British officials and policy-makers. This impression was so popular that even after the suppression of the Mutiny and restoration of British authority, a loyalist like Sir Syed Ahmad Khan in his *Asbab-e Bagawat-e Hind* (1858) has spoken in detail about the 'the apprehension of interference of government with the religious customs of the Indians'. In the opinion of Sir Syed the people generally believed that 'the government intended to force the Christian religion and foreign customs upon Hindus and Muslims alike'. It was firmly believed by everyone that slowly but surely the government was developing its plan. Even well-intentioned people thought that indirect steps were being taken, such as

> doing away with the study of Arabic and Sanskrit and reducing the people to ignorance and poverty…this way people would be deprived of a knowledge of the principles of their own faith and their attention turn to books containing principles of the Christian creed...the government would then work on their cupidity and poverty of its subjects and on condition of abjuring their faith, offer them employment in its own service. Similarly, after every drought and famine, the orphanages were opened where the orphans were 'reared in the principles of Christian faith throughout the North Western Frontier Provinces as per the scheme of the governrnent.'[9]

There are issues of academic importance which have been highlighted in the most argumentative and yet reasoned manner. One of these is about the origin of the notion of the leadership of the Quraysh, which was adopted as a cardinal principle of Sunni Muslim theories of governance. However, the leadership of the community did not always stay confined to the Quraysh tribe irrespective of the prevailing theory. This notion, it appears cropped up during this hour of crisis as well. Therefore, it has been asserted that since:

> the infidels have become paramount in power and a Qurayshi is not found…any Muslim chief endowed even with a few of the qualities of the leader and observing the tenets of Muslim law (*Shari'at*) can as a matter of necessity be selected as the chief. This leader will be called *Imam-i Akbar* and great benefits will be derived in the cause of your faith.

Since the important point of the struggle during 1857 was Hindu-Muslim unity, hence it is also argued that:

> such *rajas* who are dependant on the Muslim kings infinitely better than that, under the infidel Victoria and the English, are the enemies of our faith.

A special appeal was made to the Hindus to join the chief with a view to defend their religion as the Hindus and the Muslims were viewed as brethrens, and they should butcher the English.'[10]

The pamphlet, apart from suggesting practical measures to the people, to the women and even to the old and infirm during the actual fight with the English, also included an *Ishitihar* (public appeal) which was supposed to be circulated among the Hindus and the Muslims of Hindustan. Such an appeal was to be popularised among the sepoys and the common man by the 'maulavis and pundits'. They were supposed to explain in every village and city the 'misfortune which the success of the English will entail on the people and the advantages and spiritual benefit which will occur on their extirpation'. An extract from the preamble of this *Ishitihar* is reproduced here:

اشتہار

The original document runs into 12 closely printed pages which have been in the private collection of Saiyid Hamid Ali Sahib of Gorakhpur. I was able to obtain a copy of it, courtesy my teacher Professor Iqbal Husain saheb of Aligarh Muslim University. The extract is from the last paragraph of p.11. It is difficult to speculate about the source of this printing, and at the same time, it will be much more difficult to find out how these printing facilities were available to the rebels. Yet, one can be sure that the rebels were using modern printing mediums to spread their ideas and that they had their sympathisers among those who owned such facilities.

Apart from these technical aspects one also needs to study the evolution of the language. For instance, instead of Queen Victoria it says *'Malka Biktoria'* and instead of using percentage it uses the 'sense of proportion' which might be more understandable to the audience of the pamphlet.

It repeats the fear more forcefully that Queen Victoria (here she is spoken of in the most abusive manner: 'the ill-fated, dead bitch *(badbakht kutiya murdar)*'[11] has in fact approved the proposal of the British officials from India to kill 15 per cent of the learned men from among the Muslims and Hindus and also to kill 500,000 Hindu and Muslim sepoys and *raiyat* so that in a short while the people of India could become Christians. It can be argued that such an appeal might have been made to sensationalise and galvanise the people into action.'[12]

The main thrust of this document appears to be the issue of religion being in danger, and for this reason Hindus and Muslims have been asked to unite; while the usage of guns and artillery was reiterated to ensure their victory and the *Ghazis* under the leadership of an *imam* would definitely play a major role in the ensuing battle with the English. It is a document written in haste (before the fall of Delhi, Kanpur and Lucknow) when the threat from the English to reconquer the places of resistance was perceived to be most emminent. It does not discuss the grievances of the different sections of the Indian people against the British, the injustices done to the Indian rulers and princes by the East India Company (themes which were raised in the proclamations of Prince Firoz Shah, commonly known as the Azamgarh Proclamation or the one issued by Begum Hazrat Mahal). It simply tries to capture popular sentiment by positing the war as a people's fight against the British, where among other themes the most important concern appears to be a call for unity.

III

The third document under study is of a slightly different nature: it is a reminiscence of Maulana Fazl-e Haq Khairabadi (d.1862), an ideologue and important member of the Revolutionary Council in Delhi during 1857. He was an eyewitness as well as a participant in the many military events at Lucknow, Bareilley and Shahjahanpur. He was arrested, put to trial and finally transported to serve a life-term at the Andaman Islands *(Saza-e Habs-e Dawam ba Ubur Dariya-e Shor).* Here, fortunately for us, he has penned his reading of the events during 1857-9, the causes of the failure and has also hinted at the atrocities committed by the British during and after the events. The account is in chaste Arabic prose, written in the most figurative style, and, hence, is often difficult to understand. The manuscript of this work: *Risala as Saurat at Hindiya* was written secretly and smuggled out of the Andamans by a fellow detainee Maulavi Inayat Ahmad of Kakori, who was freed before the completion of his term as he had helped the jailor in translating a unique Arabic text. The manuscript was carefully preserved by the family and could not see the light of the day till 1947'[13] It is strange that such a unique text has remained most unnoticed in modern historiography-a text which provides an insight into the rebel's point of view. The *ecriture* of the last page of the Rampur Manuscript is reproduced from Mahdi Husain's *Bahadur Shah II.*

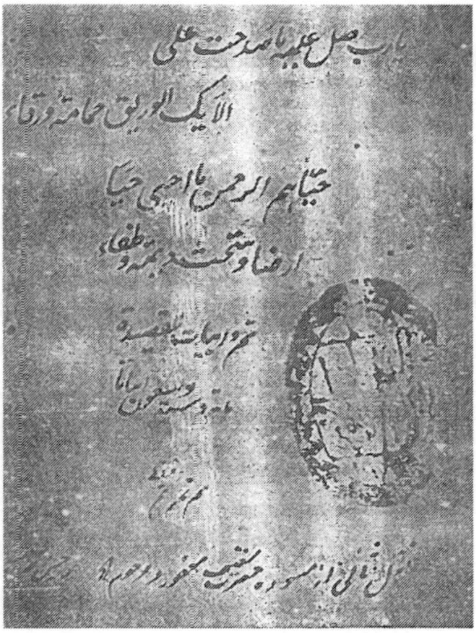

The text talks about the incidents related to the life of the author. His description of his sufferings is revelatory-perhaps the only document of its kind. The account was written at a time when he was trying hard for his release. Apart from describing in detail his dejection, isolation and the sufferings, he makes an important point that since he is a scholar of religion and law and has firm faith in Islam, and because of his staunch and zealous defence of his faith, he has been made to suffer. In this way the tyrant aimed at removing the traces of learning, destroying the banner of knowledge from the pages of history.'[14] This finds a strange collaboration with the earlier pamphlet where it was specifically stated that the British have decided to kill 15 out of every 100' (note the absence of the use of percentage) of the 'maulavis and pundits' so that they can Christianise the entire Indian subcontinent. He says that all this suffering was due to that 'painful event *(Waqi'a Faz'a)* which has rendered the cities and towns desolate such a calamity, it was this event which turned the nobles into beggars and the kings into prisoners and slaves'. Then he goes on to recount the reasons behind the occurrence of the rebellion.

He begins his story with the grudge that the British harboured, and who after the capture of the major part of the territories, had decided to Christianise the country, which was in consonance with their political belief that differences between various religious communities would disrupt the continuance of their domination in government. With this aim in mind they have not only established schools in villages and towns (to teach the books of their religion and faith) but have also wiped out the existence of the centres of knowledge and *madrasas* which were established in the earlier days. For this purpose they also attempted to control the prices of foodgrains and essential commodities. The sepoys became their first targets as it was considered that getting the sepoys to change their religion meant that the civil population would not dare disobey the command of the English officials. Here he points out that this, however, was their greatest mistake as the Hindu soldiers who were in overwhelming majority made a common cause with the Muslim sepoys who were in a minority to safeguard their religion and faith. Thus, both these people *(Fariqayn)* began to murder, loot and kill their officers. But here the author becomes conscious and talks about the excesses they have committed and the cruelties they have perpetuated on the women and children.'[15]

Regarding the organisation of the Rebellion in Delhi, he does not make any complementary references to the Emperor Bahadur Shah and repeats the allegation made against him that he is under the influence of his wife Zeenat Mahal and *Wazir Hakim* Ahsanullah Khan who was secretly in league with the British and was a friend of the Christians as was the case with other members of the royal family. About the king he specifically says that 'he could not decide anything openly or in secret and had no power of doing harm or good to anyone' and in that background he says that in such a sorry state of affairs when arose 'a party of strong and brave Muslims for *jihad* and fighting after having asked for a *fatwa* from the pious *ulema'*. He talks about *these jihadis* in a very laudatory manner and while speaking about the defence of Delhi he specifically says that these were the only people who exhibited courage and fought the Christians, met and attacked them'[16] When every defence has failed and every section had almost given up hope and had abandoned the fight, these strong and brave *mujahids* 'offered severe resistance and put up a strong fight against them. They kept their feet firm even in hard encounters and met everybody who tried to advance forward many of them tasted the honey of martyrdom and attained high ranks of good fortune they passed the nights in hunger, but rushed to fight at dawn and waged war against the enemy.

He is bitter when he speaks about the Company's forces which included among their ranks 'the white faced soldiers and their mercenaries who were drawn from the base and mean Hindus and those Muslims...who have sold their religion for a very low price'. They were supported by the thousands of residents of the city while the entire Hindu population turned out to support them. The money-changers, servants of the king, princes and Hindus continued to devise schemes to destroy the *jihadis* and to restrict their supplies. As a result of this blockade, these *jihadis* 'passed their days and nights in hunger. thirst. excessive heat and anxiety. Since the perplexity was extremely great and they fled in helpless manner' now it was easy for the 'Christians to take possession of the city, its gates, its walls, houses and mansions'. In other words. with the *jihadis* gone. the fortunes of the city also declined.

He has given a graphic description of the destruction of the city. the slaughter of its population, the digging of the houses of the nobles and the villas of the princess in search of hidden treasures. He has also given details of the arrest of Emperor Bahadur Shah at Humayun's tomb along with his sons and grandsons.

After the fall of Delhi the author moved with his family members to Awadh where Birjis Qader, under the guardianship of his mother Hazrat Mahal was still holding ground. He did not have a good opinion of their administration in Lucknow, for he says that 'they did not have the ability to understand the intricacies of the administration nor were they capable of issuing orders and leading the army…most of them were supporters and allies of the Christians'. He has praised Maulavi Ahmadullah Shah for his leadership qualities and the ability to withstand the onslaught of the company's forces. It appears that he was with Maulavi Ahmadullah Shah when the latter was treacherously killed by the Raja of Pawayan. in district Shahjahapur, at Rohilkhand. He has spoken at length about the treachery of the raja and the manner in which the rebels' cause suffered as a result of his death.

In the last pages of the text the author appears more concerned about his sufferings and complains bitterly that despite their victories. the British have made good on the promises made in the Queen Victoria Proclamation. Thinking himself immune from being booked for any crime as he was not involved in the killing of the Englishmen. he came out of hiding. Instead, he was captured. prosecuted and sentenced to life imprisonment at the newly developed penal settlement at Andarnan, where he remained a convict till he died in AD 1862.

The 'narrative of the vanquished ' ought to be an important source to understand the aspirations of the rebels, their *raison d'etre* for the rebellion and the vision they had for the future. The documents examined give only a few aspects of the rebels' point of view. There appears to be a striking similarity in these documents insofar as the causes of the rebellion are concerned: a threat to religion. There was a danger (real or perceived) of Hinduism and Islam being wiped out and Christianity to be promulgated thoroughout the subcontinent under official patronage. A crucial role has been ascribed to the sepoys of the Bengal Army who incidentally happened to be the members of the most advanced and progressive army of the East and who had been in action for 18 years in the various countries of Asia.'[17] It is possible to suppose that it was the sepoys who had the most advanced training in handling firearms and heavy artillery-a factor that made tremendous contribution during the initial stages of the rebellion. On the other hand, we notice a few laudatory references to the ideological commitment of the fighters who were described as *jihadis.* They appear as the most disciplined, organised and dependable fighting force at Delhi and Lucknow, with leaders like General Bakht Khan and Maulavi Ahmadullah Shah.

While the Proclamation lays much emphasis on achieving Hindu-Muslim unity-something achieved during the early stages of rebellion-the British were later successful in creating a disunity and destroying the communal harmony.'[18] Fazl-e Haq highlights this aspect when he recounts events at Andaman.

The importance of analysing the text produced by the rebel leaders during the course of the rebellion and thereafter, is a venture worth undertaking as it is through the analysis of such data that one can comprehend the mind and the aspirations of the *prime movers* of the rebellion. It gives us a glimpse into the causes and the failure of the movement as understood by the leaders immediately after its suppression by the British. One also gets to understand 'the vision' of the ideologues once the British were expirated. These narratives gain further importance because they were penned in a language fully understood and comprehended by the masses and the local elites; hence their idioms and phraseology could be seen to be closer to the then popular psyche. It is through such literature that the 'voices of the vanquished' can be recovered rather than looking for their voices and aspirations in the 'victor's narrative' which predominantly presents a 'loaded account'.

Notes

1. A large number of the pamphlets were issued by the rebel leaders at the centres of the uprising and were found scattered at various district Collectorates when the British finally captured those centres of resistance. Now most have been compiled and edited by Professor Iqbal Husain as, *Proclamations of the Rebels of* 1857 (forthcoming). However, the draft

containing translations (and retranslations) of 43 documents and two appendices were circulated at the ICHR 'Seminar on 1857', organised at India International Centre on 9-10 December 2006. It is quite interesting to note that Rani Lakshmibai of Jhansi or Nana Sahib also sought legitimacy from the Mughal sovereign Bahadur Shah II rather than appealing to the notion of Hindu *Padpadshahi* or seeking legitimacy from the Mararatha chiefs of Satara Raj or Peshwa.

2. The rebellion reached its highest intensity in rural Awadh. It has been estimated that in 1845 'the three-fourth of Bengal's Native Infantry came from Oudh'. It has been suggested that 50,000 men from Oudh were serving with the army of the East India Company. As a member of the sepoys' army, these soldiers enjoyed various privileges. They were entitled to have their grievances within the Kingdom of Oudh redressed through the intercession of the British Resident. To the great detriment of the king's authority, the sepoys always got what they wanted through the British Resident. Infact a keen observer (Henry Lawrence) in 1845 wrote that the 'Oudh Government is molested and degraded by the sepoys claims...by the Resident's interference litigation is promoted, hopes are excited...resulting into the agrarian instability...' The annexation of Awadh in February 1856 left the sepoys no more a pampered lot. It appears that they were highly dissatisfied with the new arrangements and hence displayed extreme resentment on this count as well. I have examined some of these issues in details in: 'Bengal Army Sepoys and Agrarian instability in the kingdom of Awadh: AD 1801-56', *PIHC,* 65th Session, Bareilley, 2004, pp. 642-5.

3. Bahadur Shah II in a letter to his son Mirza Mughal, dated 8 July 1857 specifically tells that 'when the officers of the regiment deliberate and decide on the means to be adopted for raising funds to meet the daily necessary and emergent expenses such a meeting of this kind in the language of the soldiery is called a "Court". ct. Mahdi Husain, *Bahadur Shah II and the War* of 1857 *in Delhi with its Unforgettable Scenes,* Delhi, 1958, p. 187. Besides S.N. Sen's *Eighteen Fifty Seven,* this document has been given in full with a facsimile of the original and its translation with a commentary in Mehdi Husain, op. cit., pp. 182-9; see also Ateeq Siddiqui, *Atharah Sau Satavan:Akhbar aur Dastavezein* (in Urdu), Delhi, 1966, pp. 279-91. Apart from the facsimile of the original, he has given the deciphered text as well.

4. Generally it is assumed that such an arrangement was made after the arrival of General Bakht Khan with his Bareilley contingent, i.e. after 2 July 1857. Spear, p. 206. However, Mahdi Husain has argued that it was done before his arrival, as the document freely employs English vocabulary and displays a familiarity with the working of the then British institutions, in which Maulana Fazl-e Haq Khairabadi was instrumental. Mahdi Husain, op. cit., p. 190; see also Ateeq Siddiqui, op. cit., pp. 279-91. Simultaneously, Dr Wazir Khan, the London-returned renowned physician who was a

'Muslim Hero' in the then ongoing Christian-Muslim disputes of the earlier decades, was also present at Delhi and was a member of the inner council of Bahadur Shah II. Khan could also have been one of the persons who drafted the document, along with Khairabadi. For a short biography of Wazir Khan see, Ghulam Rasul Mehr, 1857 *ke Mujahid,* (in Urdu), Lahore, 4th rpt, 1982, pp. 238-49. (For the specific reference of his being a part of the king's council, see p. 246). For the reaction of the British officials and the Christian missionaries against Wazir Khan and other well-placed Muslims see, Avril A. Powell, *Muslims and Missionaries in Pre-Mutiny India,* Curzon Press, London, 1993. See especially pp. 275-81.

5. Mahdi Husain, ibid., p. 194.
6. As per the testimony of the British government, out of 1,39,000 soldiers of the Bengal Army, only about 7,000 remained loyal to the British by March 1858. Irfan Habib, 'The Coming of 1857', in *Red the Earth, That Year, That Year,* Sahmat, New Delhi, 2007, pp. 3-21.
7. After the events of 1857 it was a widely-held belief among the British officers and civilians that it was mainly due to the 'Muslim Conspiracy' against the British rule that such a catastrophe had occurred. The suspicion increased when it was found in 1863 that the Wahabis who were still active in the North-west Frontier and were now directly confronting the British after the collapse of the Sikh kingdom, were regularly in receipt of money and recruits from areas as far as Bengal and Bihar. This followed a series of 'Wahabi trials' during 1863-72. In the context of this witchhunt, WW. Hunter wrote his famous *Our Indian Musalmans,* London, 1871. His main assumption was that the notion of *jihad* had a historical continuity from the time of Shah Waliullah (d.1762) and his son Shah Abdul Aziz (d.1824) to Syed Ahmed of Balakot fame (died in action 1831). This becomes the most important interpretation in the twentieth century nationalist discourse when Maulana Azad reaffirmed the theory of *jihad* in the above continuum. This interpretation received full-fledged support by Maulana Ghulam Rasul Mehr, who served as the secretary to Maulana Azad. This understanding remains the most dominant trend in modern writings, especially Urdu historiography. See Marc Gaborieau, 'The "Forgotten obligation": A Reinterpretation of Sayyid Ahmed Barelwi's *Jihad* in the North-West Frontier, 1826-1831', in *The Resources* of *History: Tradition, Narration and Nation in South Asia,* ed., Jackie Assayag, Paris-Pondicherry, 1999, pp. 297-8.
8. Contrary to the expectations of Ahmadullah Shah, the army leaders and the notables of the Awadh kingdom decided in favour of Prince Birjis Qadar, the minor son of Wajid Ali Shah, the former king of Awadh who was on a forced exile at Kolkata. Maulavi Ahmadullah Shah reacted to this very sharply. His major objection against the choice of Birjis Qadar seems to be that *jihad* could be conducted only under the leadership of an *imam* or *amir*. Therefore, it was necessary that the creed of the *imam* should be the

same as that of the *Mujahideens.* Moreover, *jihad* was not obligatory for the *Shi'as;* therefore, it was argued by his group that by choosing Birjis Qadar as the leader of the resistance, the most important ingredient of *jihad* was definitely missing. Hence, in such a situation, the fight against the British would not be a 'war of religion' but it would simply be a 'fight in self-defence'. Therefore, the religious sanction behind the resistance would be diluted.

The differences between Birjis Qadar and Shah are referred to in the versified biography of the latter composed by his disciple Maulana Fateh Muhammad Taib. See especially couplet numbers 1261-88 where some of the arguments given in the pamphlet *Fateh Islam* are reflected. See, Abrar Husain Faruqi, ed., *Tawarikh Ahmadi* of Taib as *Mirat-i Ahmadi,* with notes and a lengthy introduction, Hardoi, 1973. See pp. 239-42.

9. Sir Syed Ahmad Khan has spoken about some of these apprehensions in greater detail and about the manner in which British officials handled the matter in an extremely insensitive way. Some of these aspects are discussed here. He elaborates on the following points in a somewhat detailed manner. While the religious discussions and open debates by the Christian missionaries had the tacit approval of the government. The military and civil officers were in the habit of inviting their subordinates and servants 'to listen to the preaching of the missionaries thus, in the course of time, no man felt sure that his creed would last even his own time. The missionaries were printing and circulating tracts containing religious discussions. In some districts the missionaries were provided complete police protection. With such a protective cover the missionaries 'employed violent and unmeasured language...while attacking the followers and the holy places of other creeds, annoying and insulting...those who listen to them'. Similarly, genuine doubts about village schools, female education and colleges were also expressed.. These institutions were thought of as the places through which the 'government wished to wipe out the religions which it found in Hindustan'. See, Syed Ahmad Khan, *The Causes of the Indian Revolt,* ed., Francis Robinson, Karachi, Oxford University Press, 2000 (rpt of 1873 edition). See between pp. 16-22.

10. The fact that Hindu and Muslim sepoys fought together like brothers led loyalists like Sir Syed Ahmed Khan to suggest after the uprising that 'government should not have put the two antagonistic races into the same regiment as the constant intercourse between the two had done its work and the two races in regiment had almost become one'. *Ibid.,* p. 50.

11. This most 'insulting language to describe the British Queen Victoria', has injured the sensitivity of the subaltern scholars, while they seem to be equally unhappy with such an 'abusive condemnation of the whole chain of British colonial authority from Queen to the common administrators'. See Rudrangshu Mukherjee, *Awadh in Revolt,* Delhi, 1984, p. 148; Gautam

Bhadra, 'Four Rebels of 1857', in *Subaltern Studies,* Vol. IV, p. 271. The lack of any sensitivity among these 'subalterns' about the manner in which the British wrote about and butchered the sepoys and the civilians alike and the way they describe the rebel leaders in the most offensive manner is really unfortunate.

12. Thus, one is amused to see Sir Syed Ahmed stating his 'firm belief that the Muslims never dreamed of forming a combination in order to carry a religious war against the Christians'. He also adds that 'it was the ignorant and disaffected men who raised the cry of *jihad* and raising the *haidari* war cry'. *Ibid.,* p. 10.

13. It is generally believed that a fellow prisoner of the Khairabadi Penal settlement at Andaman, viz., Mufti Enayat Ahmad Kakorvi at the behest of his British jailor there had translated the difficult Arabic text of *Taqwim al Buldan* and provided the copious notes for him. Apparently, he was able to complete the task with the help of Khairabadi. The English jailor was pleased with him and had recommended his release in AH 1277/ AD 1862. While returning from Andaman, Mufti Enayat Ahmad Kakorvi took the notes of Khairabadi to hand them over to the latter's son, Maulana Abdul Haq Khairabadi. It was the son who edited the whole text and gave it its present shape. A number of copies were made and given to very close friends and students of Khairabadi. As per the testimony of Maulana Abul Kalam Azad, a copy of the same was sent to his father, Maulana Khairuddin by the editor at Mecca. That is how the manuscript of this volume has survived with the selected few who were in no position to make it public prior to 1947.

    The Arabic text with its Urdu translation was published by Mohammad Shahid Khan Sharwani (who has based his edition on the copy which was with Maulana Muinuudin Ajmeri [d. AH 1359]) with copious notes and a useful introduction as *Baghi Hindustan,* Bijnor, 1947. Since then it has run into several revisions and editions.

    Saiyid Muinul Haq has translated it into English with the help of (Maulana) Zikriya Mail as, 'The Story of the War of Independence 1857-58', in *Journal of Pakistan Historical Society,* Vol. V, Pt. I, January 1957, Karachi, pp. 23-57. For the recent attempts to reconstruct his biography and assess his role during the rebellion see, Iqbal Husain, 'Fazl-e Haq of Khairabad; A Scholarly Rebel of 1857', *PIHC,* 48th Session, Goa University, Bambolim, Panajim, 1987, Delhi, pp. 355-65; see also, Jamal Malik, 'Letters, Prison Sketches and autobiographical literature: The case of Fadl-e Haqq (sic!) Khairabadi in the Andaman Penal Colony', *IESHR,* Vol. XLIII, Pt. I, January-March 2006, Delhi, pp. 77-100. It is interesting to note that Malik has used Saiyid Muinul Haq's translation of *Risala* as *Saurat al Hindiya* throughout with a few com ments either on the manuscripts or about the history of the document as it has been traced by Shahid Khan Sharwani.

In 1961, Naadim Sitapuri raised doubts about the authenticity of the text penned by Khairabadi. Sitapuri's comments are mainly regarding the way in which Shahid Sharwani has traced the history of the manuscript rather than on the manuscript itself. According to him, Sharwani has worked out the history of the manuscript in a rather dramatic manner, which raises doubts about the veracity of the entire narration. See, *Ghalib Nam Awaram,* Lucknow, 1961.

While we know for certain that Kakorvi, the carrier of this manuscript has himself written two books while in the Andamans (and these books are still acknowledged as important contributions in their respective fields), in all probability there was no restriction on the writing and it appears that stationery was freely available to the prisoners. Hence, the very understanding that it was written by 'charcoal on pieces of paper and cloth' has little basis. Moreover, a bare reading of the text reveals stringent comments and harsh descriptions of the atrocities of the British and the character of the Britons—a fact which belies the suggestion that it was ever edited or toned down by his son to avoid the suspicions of the British government. For a detailed discussion on the academic contribution of the prisoners of 1857 in Andaman and Nicobar see an important chapter by Ayub Qadri, *Jung-e Azaadi* 1857: *Waqiat aur Shakhsiyat,* Pakistan Academy, Karachi, 1976. See especially pp. 429-61, while the discussion on Khairabadi and Naadim Sitapur is between pp. 437-48.

14. Khairabadi, besides being a representative of the 'Khairabad' school of logic had a chequered career involving teaching, polemics, debates, as well as serving the British at Delhi in various capacities prior to 1857. His stay in Delhi as the *Sarishtadar* at the English Residency coincided with the activities of Maulavi Shah Ismail (d.1831 at Balakot) whose controversial text *Taqwiat ul lman (The Strengthening* of *the Faith)* has created a fissure among the Sunni Muslims. By raising issues of *Shifa 'at* (intercession by the Prophet on behalf of the sinful members of his community with God on the Day of Judgement) and *Imkan un Nazir* (the possibility of the creation of another Prophet by God), Shah Ismail has advanced the Wahabi ideas of Abdul Wahab of Najd (d. 1799). These ideas were anathema for the Sunni Muslim followers of Hanafi *Fiqh.* Hence, these ideas were rebutted quite forcefully by scholars, among whom Khairabadi took a lead. His famous text on the issue was published in AH 1240/AD? entitled *Tahqiq al Fatwa fi Abtal* at *Taghwa* which was published within eight months of the publication of Shah Ismail's controversial track. Khairabadi also wrote couplets in Arabic where he severely criticized all the arguments of Shah Ismail by describing him as 'illiterate and a blind follower of Najdi's ideology' which led to 'dissensions within the community' and his movement for *jihad* against the Sikhs as a fight for 'amassing the war booty' and his followers as 'the people who were following the path of Satan'.

It is quite interesting to note that several leading contemporary poets like Momin (d. 1851/2), Zauq (d. 1854) and many others were sympathetic with Shah Ismail's movement and were highly critical of Khairabadi's criticism. Momin is well known for his *Jehadiya Masnawi* where being a disciple of Syed Ahmed he has espoused the cause of *jihad.* He had also openly criticised Khairabadi for opposing the same. He says, '*Gah junoo kehta hai Ishq ko; Gah kufr wa haram: jehl karne ko pade the mere naseh ne ulum*'. (On occasions you describe the *love]* as madness, and also as heresy and forbidden; O Preacher! have you acquired knowledge only to spread ignorance?'. It has also been suggested that since Shah Ismail used to deliver sermons at the historic Jama Mosque of Delhi which was attended by thousands, it was stopped for about two months by the English Resident at the behest of Khairabadi. It has also been suggested that when Shah Ismail was prevented from delivering sermons at Jama Mosque, an influential Punjabi Muslim businessman Maulavi Husain Baksh constructed a mosque and a *madrasa* in the same locality where he invited Shah Ismail to continue with his sermons. This institution still remains an important centre of the *Ahl-e Hadis* ideology even in the modern times. (For details see, Khwaja Manzur Husain, *Tahrik-e Jadd oJehad Bataur-e Mauzu*'e *Sukhan* (Urdu), National Book Foundation, Lahore, 1978; pp. 632-69. It is clear that the *jihadi* ideology propounded by Shah Ismail had opponents as well as proponents-a fact reflected in the indigenous literature prior to and during 1857.

15. It is important to mention here that both the documents which represent the 'authentic voices of the vanquished' quite unequivocally condemn the excesses committed by the sepoys, expecially when they killed British women and children. Similarly Begum Hazrat Mahal in her Proclamation was also sympathetic for such victims and condemned such acts by the sepoys. Queen Victoria in her 'famous Proclamation', however, did not either condemn the excesses committed by the Company's soldiers or show any sympathy for those who were butchered and looted.

16. Sir Syed Ahmad Khan has spoken very harshly about those indulging in *jihad,* calling them 'vagabond and ill conditioned men'. They were 'wine drinkers and men who spent their time in debauchery and dissipation'. They were 'men floating without profession or occupation on the surface of the society', with the sole aim 'to plunder government treasury and to steal government property'. He also adds that 'some scoundrels prompted by greed and hoping to gain their end by deceiving fools and increasing their own numbers, gave the disturbances the title of religious war'. Such a project was definitely, 'worthy of the men (those who are involved), but there was no Crusade'. *Ibid.,* pp. 8-9. At the same time he recognises the fact that at the time of the outbreak of the Mutiny in the city of Delhi itself there was a group of *maulavis* who thought of the 'deposed king Bahadur Shah, "little better than a heretic", *(bid* 'ati' as opposed to the Wahabi puritans) and they

avoided offering prayers in those mosques which were under the *Tauliyat* (trusteeship) of Mughal King'. Long before the outbreak of the mutiny they issued a *fatwa* on the above lines. Ibid. He points towards the vertical divide within the Sunni Muslim community due to the efforts of the Wahabis.

17. Irfan Habib, *The Coming of* 1857, p. 3.
18. Since the Muslim festival of sacrifice (*Id ul Azha*) was to be celebrated during the months of the rebellion in Delhi, we find dozens of orders issued (in the Mutiny Papers at National Archives of India) by Bahadur Shah Zafar and Bakht Khan asking the people to desist from cow slaughter and also to the *kotwal* of Delhi to sieze the cattle from the houses of the people who might go ahead with the sacrifices. There are numerous evidences to suggest that such an order was taken quite seriously and the police officials enforced it in letter and spirit.

Chapter - 6

The Rebel Administration of Delhi

—Professor Iqbal Husain

The Revolt of 1857 in Delhi has been a subject of much interest among historians of modern India. Some of them have, rather incidentally discussed the rebels' effort at establishing a working administration of Delhi. Percival Spear has assigned a few pages in his *Twilight of the Mughals* to the travails of the rebels within Delhi. A detailed study of the administration of Delhi under the rebels, is, however, long overdue. This article attempts to discuss the type of administration the rebels set up in Delhi. While effort has been made to set out information in a chronological order, details of Court politics and intrigues by princess and other members of the royal family, have been avoided unless directly relevant to our theme. Delhi was occupied by the rebel sepoys on 11th May. The rebels foisted upon Bahadur Shah the responsibility of administering the country.[1] The need for firm administration, indeed, immediately asserted itself. Taking advantage of the sudden disappearance of the British rule from Delhi the bad characters unsavoury elements and plunderers began to loot the people in the guise of sepoys.[2] Five of them were apprehended and thrashed by the rebel sepoys and were sent to jails.[3] With no leadership to control them some of the sepoys also seem to have joined in the plunder of the jewellers, *baniyas* and even petty shopkeepers such as sweetmeat sellers.[4] Many of those who were the plundered people appealed to the king for protection.[5] The developments, however, were so rapid and unprecedented that it was beyond the abilities of Bahadur Shah, already bereft of power and resources, to control the declining law and order situation in the city. On 12th May the condition of the city worsened. Munshi Jiwan Lal tells us that the unwilling king seemed distracted by the cries and petitions. The servants of the Europeans, shopkeepers and rich people whose houses had been plundered, all appealed to him for redress.[6] Bahadur Shah was keen to restore order and summoned Mirza Ziauddin Ahmad Khan, Aminuddin Ahmad Khan and Hasan Ali Khan (uncle of the *nawab* of Jhajjar) to form an Executive Council to maintain law and order in the city. Hasan Ali Khan's direct refusal foiled the King's attempt at restoring order in the city.[7] As an alternative, Mirza Moinuddin Hasan Khan, on the recommendation of Hakim Ahsanullah Khan[8] was directed to restore order in the city and its suburbs[9] These measures were hardly enough to satisfy the terrified people, specially the shopkeepers, to resume their occupations. On being persuaded (or rather pressed) by the rebels, Bahadur Shah personally visited the city, making appeals and giving assurances to the shopkeepers for their safety and asked them to resume their business.[10] The king's personal appeals also did not restore the confidence of the shopkeepers who kept their shutters down.[11] On the other hand, disputes between the rebels from Meerut and Delhi over the distribution of plunder posed a new problem. The king on returning from going around the city found the agitated sepoys occupying the courtyard of the *Diwan-i Khas*[12] The rebels, unaware of the Court's etiquette, addressed the king in a manner, which was deemed disrespectful.[13] The behaviour of the rebels and their conduct in the city led Mirza Ghalib to explain that, 'they (rebels) laid into dust both the honour and mansions of those who were distinguished for wisdom and good name, while those who had neither power nor pelf shot into prominence.' Men of valour were scared of their own shadows, and mere troopers ruled over all and sundry.[14] On 13th May Mirza Moinuddin Hasan Khan was appointed kotwal of Delhi and head of the Commissariate in the city. However, this was a mere formality. Reports of rapine and plunder continued to come into the fort. On 14th May Bahadur Shah shut himself up and refused audience to all.[15] Delhi remained at the mercy of the individual rebels and plunderers in the guise of rebels.

Similar conditions prevailed even within the Fort, the King's abode. A regiment of the Native Infantry occupied the fort and placed its own guards without an officer to command them.[16] On 15th May another effort to raise a police force of 100 men for the 'safety' of the city failed to yield any result.[17] Yet Bahadur Shah with all his limitations, was trying to restore order and punish the offenders connected with the imperial service.[18] To strengthen the city administration, he appointed Qazi Muhammad Faizullah and Abdul Hakim as city kotwal and Naib Qazi for the administration of justice.[19] These attempts were still far short of the requirement to control plunder and some of the sepoys, who were openly disobeying the orders of the civil authorities.[20] Apart from attempting to strengthen the city administration, endeavours were also being made to raise troops. Accordingly, on 15th May orders were issued to recruit horsemen at a salary of ₹ 30 and infantry at ₹ 10 per mensern.[21] The fast declining law and order situation necessitated the formal involvement of the princes in undertaking military responsibilities to contain uncontrolled elements in the city. Bahardur Shah assigned various offices to them.[22] Mirza Muhammad Jawan Bakht was appointed *wazir* of the empire perhaps on paper, practically though he did not function, and Mirza Zahiruddin Bakht (Mirza Mughal) was appointed 'Commander-in-Chief' of the forces (infantry, cavalry and other branches of the army). Mirza Abul Hasan alias Abdullah, Mirza Sohrab, Mirza Muhammad Khizr Sultan, Mirza Kochak Sultan and Mirza Muhammad Abu Bakr were assigned different military positions.[23] The expectation, perhaps, was that their royal prestige would enable the princes to enforce authority over the rebels. But none of the princess had the ability to discharge the responsibility with competence. Moreover, soon intrigues and conspiracies among the rival factions of the princess further distracted the fledgling administration. The princes began to exert such authority as they obtained, by proceeding to violate all norms of regular administration. In the meantime, the sepoys captured the king's private office. They placed guards at the *Diwan-i Khas* and substituted the king's personal staff with their own.[24] Bahadur Shah was thus surrounded by the sepoys. It is not yet clear as to how the princess reacted to the new situation. Their silence, however, suggests their connivance behind the capture of king's office. Armed with new authority, the princes' greed for money encouraged their troopers to exact money from the leading city bankers. In one of the petitions, two *mahajans,* Jugal Kishore and Sheo Prasad, drawing the attention of the king urged upon him to prohibit all the princes particularly Mirza Mughal, Mirza Khizr Sultan, Mirza Abu Bakr and Mirza Abdullah from deputing *tilangas* or sepoys to their residences for realising money. They also requested the king to depute soldiers *(najibs)* for their protection.[25] Though the king ordered Mirza Mughal to comply with the request, its implementation.[26] however, seems doubtful.

On 16th May 1857 the king appointed Mufti Yusuf Ali Khan, *Mir 'Adl Bahadur*, Captain Dildar Ali Khan *Bahadur*, Saiyid Sharif Ali Khan *Faujdar* and Nazrul Khan *Bahadur* to assist in the administration.[27] But the law and order condition of the city remained far from satisfactory, annoying the king. Even the king's servants, such as Kashi Nalei, a *thanedar,* pressurised the shopkeepers to pay him bribes. On receiving complaints, he was ordered to be sent to prison.[28]

On 18th May, another attempt was made to placate the princess by defining their ranks. The princes, Mirza Mughal, Mirza Khizr Sultan, Mirza Abu Bakr and Mirza Abdullah were appointed to different commands over the rebels.[29]

On 21st May some of the city bankers raised a sum of rupees one lakh for payment to the sepoys.[30] Still, the plunder continued for they were supporting different princes. Even the king's servants were not spared. To make matter worse the princes remained indifferent despite continuous complaints. Bahadur Shah was shocked at this state of affairs.[31] The passive attitude of the princess whose responsibility was to maintain law and order in the city added to the miseries of the people. Faced with the continuous disorderliness of the sepoys, Bahadur Shah gave orders to Mirza Mughal to direct them not to move within the city.[32]

On 24th May, Bahadur Shah was informed of the plight of the English prisoners under the control of the sepoys. Expressing his helplessness over the prevailing conditions he asked Mirza Mughal, Mirza Abdullah and Khizr Sultan to ensure the release of the prisoners and to look after them properly[33] as their execution was contrary to the religious texts expounded by the Prophet.[34]

By this time a number of rebel soldiers had collected a considerable amount through loot and plunder during the rebellion in Delhi. Some left the city with their booty but were plundered on the way, and returned only to add to the problems.[35] Those who stayed in the city began to change their silver into gold coins for hoarding. This resulted in doubling the price of goldcoins in Delhi from ₹ 16 to ₹ 32. Many soldiers in their attempts to change their silver coins with gold were duped. Counterfeit gold coins gained wide circulation in the market and the government had to issue a proclamation asking the soldiers to desist from such purchases. The duped soldiers, much chagrined over the loss of money, now began to plunder innocent people to recoup themselves.[36] The princes only saved such rich persons as bribed them, and the general population was thrown to the mercy of the plunderers.[37] Bahadur Shah on his part, again expressed the desire to retire to the tomb of Khwaja Bakhtiyar Kaki at Mahrauli.[38]

In the prevailing state of confusion and disorder, Bahadur Shah issued a proclamation that a *batta* would be levied on the Company's coins *(Putti Shahi),* The residents of Delhi were also warned not to give shelter to the mischief mongers in their homes; and in case of any untoward incidents, the offenders were threatened with being blown through the guns.[39] On 25th May, coins in the name of Bahadur Shah were introduced under the care of Munshi Ayodhya Prasad and a mint was established at Kara Mashro.[40] By 31st May, the *Dehli Urdu Akhbar* reported that some order was restored in the city due to the exertion of the *kotwal*.[41]

In the meantime, Bakht Khan.[42] appeared on the scene. He was an artillery subedar of 40 years experience who had served in the first Afghan war. It appears that he had entered Delhi soon after the revolt and had become a regular visitor to the Court. Khan had established his position among the sepoys and also to some extent enjoyed the confidence of Bahadur Shah. He was honoured with the title of 'Bakht Baland Khan' on 26th May.[43] Yet the circumstances were such that Bakht Khan always suspected the king and the princess of dealing secretly with the English. He, therefore, persuaded the king to send the princes on expeditions so as to keep them away from the city.[44] (27th May)

Gradually, the sepoys mounted pressure for the payment of their salaries. On 28th May a sum of ₹ 1,75,000 arrived from Rohtak. Orders were issued to pay the salary of the sepoys, but Mahbub Ali Khan's attempt to pay ₹ 9 and ₹ 7 against the promised ₹ 30 and ₹ 10 to the cavalry and infantry caused violent protests from the troops. The situation was saved by the timely intervention of the king's servants. Later, the cavalry was persuaded to agree to a payment of ₹ 20 per month.[45]

While the affairs of the soldiers were to some extent settled, the civil servants working in different branches of administration had little relief. At the end of May there was no indication of disbursement of their salaries. The *Dehli Urdu Akhbar* heralding their views urged the government to arrange and expedite payment of their salaries. It also appealed to the government to keep the *tilangas* (sepoys) under control.[46] The Imperial treasury remained vacant and the government faced acute financial difficulties. On 1st June the two leading bankers, Girdhari Lal and Girwar Singh, were asked to advance a loan of ₹ 3 lakhs. They yielded to the demand for fear of their lives and property.[47] The amount was still far short of the needs. On 3rd June all the *mahajans* of the city were summoned to the Fort. The houses of those who avoided to respond the summons were surrounded by the troopers.[48] Under compulsion, the bankers paid ₹ 1 lakh and promised to advance another lakh of rupees within four days.[49] Salig Ram, Zorawar Singh, Raja Bhole Nath, Aramji Ramji Mal, Gaurwala, Munshi Sultan Singh and Mathura Das assured the king that a regular supply of money would be provided in future.[50]

Apart from the normal functioning of the administration, the city municipal administration also suffered on account of increasing filth and uncleanliness.[51] The worst affected *mohallas* were Kucha Rahman, Billimaran, Kucha Malik Attar, etc. The miseries of the people further increased when the water carriers stopped attending to their normal duties.[52] Grocers and grain merchants made matters worse by creating an artificial scarcity of foodgrains and other essential commodities. The prices of all essential goods escalated. The *Dehli Urdu Akhbar* laments the state of affairs quoting the rates of various commodities and complaints of adulteration in *ghee,* oil, and flour, etc.[53]

Bahadur Shah continued to receive such distressing news. At last, fed up with the total breakdown of administrative machinery, he summoned the princess and expressed his desire to proceed to Mecca for Haj and spend his remaining days there. The princes, apparently moved by the king's gesture assured him of their sincere involvement in bringing normalcy to the administration.[54] The situation, however, did not improve.

The fast-collapsing civil and military administration needed immediate reforms. The more responsible elements in the army, undoubtedly influenced by the British army organisation and institutions, formed a 'Court' to eliminate mismanagement and restore order. How far Bakht Khan was behind the formation of the Court, is not far to seek. The Court was to function on a written 12-point Programme. According to this programme, the Court was to consist of ten 'members' *(membran)*. Of them, two were to be elected from each of the three wings of the army, i.e. the infantry, cavalry and artillery. The Court was to have one 'President' *(Sadr-i Jalsa)* and a 'Vice-President' (spelt vais-president and also styled *naib-Sedr-i Jalsa),* who were to nominate two members (one by each of them). The English words used for these two officers of the Court are noteworthy. The President, enjoying the right of a casting vote (literally, two votes) had a clear edge over other members including the Vice-President. The members of the Court were to work selflessly for the welfare of the people and the Empire. It was to function under the care of the 'Commander-in-Chief', Mirza Mughal. (The English word 'Commander-in-Chief' is used). All decisions were subject to his assent. In case of disagreement on any matter, the decision of the king was to be considered final and binding upon all. The king had the right to attend the meetings of the Court. All decisions concerning civil and military affairs were to be taken by a majority of votes.[55] The Court thus clearly represented the influence of English constitutional ideas on the minds of the sepoys.

But it seems that to a large degree the Court also remained a paper organisation. It could hardly successfully exercise its powers to maintain law and order. Prince Mirza Mughal, being the President of the Court and Commander-in Chief, continued to interfere in its affairs and violate its orders. On 1th July, Jugal Kishore and Sheo Prasad, *mahajans,* petitioned the king for protection against the princess.[56] The king ordered Mirza Mughal to desist from such acts in future. The king's orders were, as usual, ignored.[57] Under these conditions Bahadur Shah greatly valued Bakht Khan's offer to enforce general discipline.[58] Bakht Khan held a long meeting with Mirza Mughal and secured for himself the appointment of 'Commander-in-Chief' (whereby he also became President of the Court). Mirza Mughal was elevated to the position of 'Adjutant General'.[59] A proclamation was issued directing all officers to obey the orders of Bakht Khan.[60] Realising that the princes would continue to interfere in administrative affairs, Bakht Khan secured the king's mandate to deal with them severely if they again indulged in plunder,[61] On the same date the king issued elaborate instructions to Bakht Khan directing him to take the following action. First, to destroy the position of the English; second, to remove the infantry and cavalry occupying the fort and the city forbidding them sternly from plunder and rapine; third, to find out an immediate solution for the disbursement of salaries of the old *(qadim)* and new *(jadid)* servants; fourth, to make suitable arrangements for revenue collection and setting up of *thanas* outside the city to check plunder; and fifth, to punish the sepoys and imposters moving in the garb of sepoys and plundering the houses of the gentry *(shurafa and najaba)*.[62] Bakht Khan made vigorous efforts to restore law and order. His task was a truly hard one. The rebellion had evoked great apprehensions among the former *jagirdars,* pensioners and *madad-i ma'ash* holders residing in and around Delhi. Most of them, therefore, secretly sympathised with the English, and some were also working as enemy's spies. Bakht Khan immediately issued an order allaying their fears and assuring them that their grants and daily allowances would be maintained after the rebels' victory. He also assured them that all their losses would be made good. He, however, warned them of deterrent punishment if caught spying or supplying provisions to the enemy.[63]

Bakht Khan also attempted to allay the fears of the shopkeepers by a proclamation, asking them to keep arms at their shops. Shopkeepers carrying no arms were asked to obtain them from the headquarters. Severe punishment, such as amputation was prescribed for sepoys caught thieving and plundering. The general public was advised to surrender their arms, failing which severe punishment was threatened. Bakht Khan also inspected the magazine and ordered the stores and materials to be arranged properly.[64] His initiatives greatly impressed

Bahadur Shah. On 3rd July Khan was given absolute authority to make arrangements for civil and revenue administration. To make the work easier, the princes were relieved of all military duties. The emergence of Bakht Khan to such prominence, however, made the princess jealous as they were in no mood to concede to his authority. A letter with the king's forged signature was sent to Bakht Khan, censuring him. However, the king' s denial of having written such letters (11th July) cleared misunderstandings between them.[65] Though Khan enjoyed absolute power in revenue affairs, a levy of eight *annas* per *maund* on sugar was imposed without his knowledge (12th July). He got the tax withdrawn on the grounds that it was bound to affect regular supplies to the city causing great distress to the people and soldiers." Similarly[66] he also got the salt tax abolished.[67] Steps such as these were clearly intended to secure the confidence of the people.[68] The administrative reforms, however, did not bring adequate income to the exchequer to meet the financial difficulties. Bahadur Shah remained under constant pressure from the sepoys to provide them salaries. Despite financial problems, he was unwilling to raise the income through 'irreligious' means (probably because he was committed to fighting a religious war). He, therefore, did not allow Ayodhya and Thakur to set up wine shops in Delhi (19th July).[69] On 23rd July he also rejected the proposal of Moti Ram to reimpose taxes on salt (₹ 1 per *maund),* edible oil (12 *annas* per *maund),* burning oil (4 *annas* per *maund)* and sugar (8 *annas* per *maund).*[70]

Meanwhile, the British expelled from Delhi after 11th May 1857 were striving hard to recapture power. Their agents became quite active in Delhi as the festival of *Baqar-Id* approached. Rumours among the Muslims gained wide circulation that the sepoys, a majority of whom consisted of Hindus, were objecting to Muslims calling for *azan* (prayers) from the roadside mosques, and that they would not allow the performance of their obligatory practise of slaughtering big animals. Such rumours led to communal tension, leading to a breach in the communal harmony within the city and its suburbs, resulting in the killing of four butchers. In an effort at maintaining communal harmony, proclamations prohibiting cow-slaughter were issued warning the offenders of severe punishments.[71] The proclamations were resented by a section of the Muslims. Considering it an act of interference on their religious freedom, they declared a holy war. However, they were persuaded by Bahadur Shah to withdraw their agitation through the efforts of Mufti Sadruddin (31th July 1857).[72]

The prevalence of disorder in Delhi adversely affected trade and commerce. In one of the petitions to Bahadur Shah, the Muslim traders of Delhi (Haider Baksh, Haji Moula Bakhsh and 15 others) represented that due to the rebellion, they had suffered heavy losses, their trade with places such as Kanpur, Benares, kolkata, Ambala and Lahore, etc., had already been ruined and they had become destitute. Over and above this, Mirza Mughal demanded ₹ 50,000 from them and on their expressing their inability to pay, he placed guards at their houses, blocking their movements. They were not allowed even to offer their Eid prayers.[73] On 28th August four rich persons of Delhi, Ramsee Mull (brother of Umed Singh, the *Mir Munshi* of Indore state), Sa'adat Ali, Agha Jan (former *Mir Munshi* of Rajputana), and Zorawar Chand, (*sahukar*) were being pressurised for money. A sum of ₹ one lakh was being demanded from each of them and to make the demand effective, their water and food supplies were stopped, pending compliance.[74] Ironically, Bakht Khan could not forge discipline and order in the army ranks owing to the underhand intrigues of the princes. Conflicts between 'General' Sidhari Singh (under the influence of Mirza Mughal) and Bakht Khan divided the army.[75] The rebel army in Delhi was further weakened due to conflicts between the Sikh soldiers and the sepoys-mostly from eastern U.P. and western Bihar-generally called Purabia.[76] By the end of August several attempts were made to reform the administration by transfers and adjustments of the powers of the princes and Bakht Khan. Theoretically, Bahadur Shah commanded supreme authority, but in practise, he held little power. Regular defiance of Bakht Khan's orders and the failure of attempted reforms kept Delhi in the grip of disorder. A petition sent by the members of the Court to Bahadur Shah reveals how the princess were exacting money from the *mahajans* and interfering in the affairs of the Court. The members of the Court urged upon Bahadur Shah to direct the princes not to violate the Court's orders in future.[77] Efforts made by Bahadur Shah, the Court and Bakht Khan to restore administration and introduce reforms were foiled by the princess' self-interest. Bakht Khan expended much of his time and energy in countering the princess' intrigues, who were totally oblivious to the grave danger to which the rebels were exposed. Though Bakht Khan theoretically enjoyed absolute power to deal with the princess, he probably hesitated to take any action against the princess fearing further disunity among the sepoys.[78] Bakht Khan might have provided a viable administration in Delhi during the period of the rebellion, had he been free from such apprehensions and constraints. Consequently it is not surprising that a number of citizens of Delhi, hard-pressed and fed up with the continuous disorder, turned into spies and well -wishers of the British, paving the way for the reconquest of Delhi by the British.

Notes

1. Cf. Malleson, G.B., *The Indian Mutiny of* 1857, rpt, Delhi, 1977, p. 84 (hereafter Malleson). Abdul Latif, 1857 *Ka Tarikhi Roznamacha,* (ed.) K.A. Nizami, Delhi, (n.d.), pp. 119-120 (hereafter *Roznamacha),* says that the British Resident asked Bahadur Shah to assume responsibility to restore order in the city.
2. Atiq Siddiqui, 1857 *ke Akhbar aur Dastavezen,* Delhi, 1966, p. 45; *Roznamacha,* p. 123; Moinuddin Hasan Khan, 'Narrative of Moinuddin', tr., Metcalfe, C.T., in *The Two Native Narratives of the Mutiny of Delhi,* rpt, Delhi, 1974, pp. 41-53 (hereafter Metcalfe).
3. 1857 *ke Akhbar aur Dastavezen,* p. 45.
4. *Roznamacha,* p. 123 ; Metcalfe, pp. 41-53.
5. *Roznamacha,* p. 123.
6. Jiwan Lal in Metcalfe, *The Two Native Narratives of the Mutiny of Delhi,* rpt, Delhi, 1974, p. 86 (hereafter Metcalfe).
7. Metcalfe, p. 85. Abdul Latif says that Miyan Nizamuddin, Khan Jahan Khan, Iradat Khan, Mufti Sadruddin Khan and Karam Ali Khan were also present at the meeting. See *Roznamacha,* p. 123.
8. A renowned physician of Delhi since the days of Akbar Shah II. Bahadur Shah raised his honours conferring several titles. The people of Delhi viewed him with suspicion. He gave evidence against Bahadur Shah. See Garret, *The Trial of Bahadur Shah,* 1932, pp. 256-82.
9. *Roznamacha,* p. 123.
10. *Dehli Urdu Akhbar,* 17th May 1857, refers to the appointment of Mufti Sadruddin as *Sadr-i 'ala,* Maulvi Abbas Ali and Karam Ali Khan as *Munsif* criminal and civil court.
11. Metcalfe, p. 86.
12. *Dehli Urdu Akhbar,* 17th May 1857.
13. Jiwan Lal says that the king was addressed, '*Are Buddha!* listen', 'I say, you old fellow', etc. See Metcalfe, pp. 86-87. The *Dehli Urdu Akhbar* in its

issue of 17th May 1857 reported that the Red Fort looked like a military cantonment.

14. *Dastanboo,* cited by Ashraf, K.M., in *Rebellion of* 1857, ed., P.C. Joshi, Delhi, 1957, p. 249.
15. Metcalfe, p. 89.
16. Metcalfe, pp. 55-6; *Dehli Urdu Akhbar,* 17th May 1857.
17. *Ibid.,* p. 91.
18. *Ibid.*
19. *Ibid.,* p. 92. Abdul Latif writes that Qazi Faizullah was appointed *Kotwal* on 17th May. *Roznamacha,* pp. 124-125.
20. Metcalfe, pp. 57-58. On 24th May 1857, the Delhi *Urdu Akhbar* published the news of the plight of the people of Delhi who continued to suffer at the hands of plunderers who moved freely in the guise of *tilangas.*
21. Delhi Proclamation, May 1857, cited in Ball, Charles, *The History of Indian Mutiny,* Vol. I, p. 495. Also *Freedom Struggle in* U.P., 1957, pp. 438-439. Jiwan Lal writes that the infantry was to be paid ₹ 5/- per month. See, Metcalfe, p. 92. It may be pointed out that before the revolt the salary of a sepoy serving the company was ₹ 7 and a cavalry man got between ₹ 21 and ₹ 30 *(Eighteen Fifty-Seven,* 1958, p. 22) at a later date the king, under the pressure of the rebels, issued a proclamation inviting the services of sepoys and cavalry in the Company's employment offering ₹ 30 and ₹ 50 per month. See Metcalfe, pp. 60-61.
22. Earlier (on 11th May) the king had directed Mirza Mughal, Mirza Abdullah and other princes to help restore order in the city. See *Siraj-ul Akhbar,* Delhi, dated 11-12th May 1857.
23. Press List of Mutiny Papers, National Archives, (hereafter NAI), No. I, Vol. 13, 16-22nd May 1857. Jiwan Lal gives two more names, viz., Mirza Bakhtawar Shah and Mirza Sidu Beg.See, Metcalfe, p. 58. Sen refers to Mirza Mughal only. *Eighteen Fifty Seven,* p. 74.
24. Metcalfe, p. 60.
25. Press List of the Mutiny Papers, NAI, New Delhi.
26. Abdul Latif tells us that the king, unhappy over the conduct of the princes asked them to work for the welfare of the people as ordained by God. See, *Roznamacha,* p. 124.
27. Metcalfe, p. 93.
28. Metcalfe, pp. 93, 94-5.
29. Metcalfe, p. 96. On 24th May 1857, the *Delhi Urdu Akhbar* published a detailed report of prevailing disorder in Delhi.
30. Metcalfe, p. 99.
31. *Roznamacha,* p. 126.

32. *Akhbar Deorhi Khas Darbar-i Mualla,* 22nd May 1857, Press List of Mutiny Papers, No.2, SN, 22, NAI, New Delhi.
33. *Roznamacha,* pp. 127-128.
34. *Dehli Urdu Akhbar,* 31st May 1857; Metcalfe, p. 100; Press List of Mutiny Papers, No. 2, SN, 22, NAI, New Delhi.
35. *Roznamacha,* pp. 127-128.
36. Metcalfe, p. 101.
37. *Dehli Urdu Akhbar,* 24th May 1857; Press List of Mutiny Papers, Call No. I, No. 21, NAI, New Delhi; *Roznamacha,* pp. 127-128, refers to the king' s conversation with the princes advising them to win the goodwill of the subjects by good work.
38. *Roznamacha,* p. 129; Metcalfe, p. 102; *Dehli Urdu Akhbar,* 24 May 1857.
39. *Dehli Urdu Akhbar,* 24th May 1857.
40. *Roznamacha,* p. 129. The coins so minted carried the couplet:
    Sikka zad dar Jahan bafazl-i llah
    Shah-i Hindustan Bahadur Shah.
41. *Dehli Urdu Akhbar,* 31st May 1857.
42. He belonged to Sultanpur (Awadh), U.P. Jiwan Lal refers to his conversation with Bahadur Shah where Bakht Khan traced his descent to the Awadh rulers. During the revolt, Bakht Khan joined the rebels abandoning his employment with the Company. His rapid rise caused envy with the princes. He distinguished himself during the seige of Delhi and fought with great determination. When the British forces surrounded the city and the fall of the city became imminent, he suggested that Bahadur Shah accompany him to continue the struggle from outside. After the fall of Delhi, he disappeared and could not be caught despite the best efforts of the British forces. See Metcalfe, pp. 146-147; Ghulam Rasul Mehr, 1857 *Ke Mujahid* (Urdu), pp. 104, 119; Intizamullah Shahabi, *East India Company aur Baghi Ulema,* pp. 72-6; *Eighteen Fifty Seven,* pp. 83-84.
43. *Roznamacha,* p. 129. Sen and Spear say that Bakht Khan appeared before the king on 2 July, *Eighteen Fifty Seven,* p. 83. *Twilight of the Mughals,* rpt, Delhi, 1969, p. 208 which is based on Jiwan Lal's account.
44. See Metcalfe, p. 130.
45. *Ibid.,* pp. 104-105.
46. *Dehli Urdu Akhbar,* 31st May 1857.
47. Metcalfe, p. 111.
48. Press List of the Mutiny Papers, No. 63, SN, 4, dated 3rd June 1857, NAI, New Delhi.
49. Metcalfe, p. 113; *Roznamacha,* pp. 133-134.
50. *Roznemeche,* p. 134.

51. Press List of the Mutiny Papers, No. 61, SN-43, NAI, New Delhi, Dehli *Urdu Akhbar,* 14th June 1857.
52. Dehli *Urdu Akhbar,* 14th June 1857.
53. *Ibid.*
54. *Ibid.*
55. Press list of Mutiny Papers, Bundle No. 539-40, No. 57, NAI, New Delhi. Sen suggests that the Court was formed in the second week of May. See *Eighteen Fifty Seven,* p. 75. Documentary evidence, however, suggests that the Court was established much later. See, Press list of Mutiny Papers, No. 57 (Misc.), No. 35, NAI, New Delhi. For a detailed discussion on Court's functions, see Talmiz Khaldun (pseudonym of Sourin Roy?) 'The Great Rebellion', in *Rebellion* 1857: *A Symposium,* ed., P.C. Joshi, Delhi, 1957, pp. 36-62. The author of this paper is, however, in disagreement with some of the conclusions drawn by Khaldun about the courts' functioning.
56. Press list of Mutiny Papers, No. 146, SN 16, NAI, New Delhi Also see, *Roznamacha,* pp. 142-143.
57. Jiwan Lal writes (2nd July) that the 'King said it was no use his giving orders, as they were not obeyed, and he had no one to enforce them...' Metcalfe, p. 134.
58. *Ibid.*
59. Metcalfe, pp. 134-135; *Dehli Urdu Akhbar,* 12th July 1857 reported that the king also granted a sum of ₹ 4,000 to Bakht Khan for sweetmeats *shirini).*
60. Metcalfe, p. 134. Spear says that the title of 'lord Governor General' *Sahib- i Alam Bahadur,* was also conferred on him. See, Spear, *Twilight* of *the Mughals,* p. 213.
61. *Ibid.,* pp. 134-135.
62. *Dehli Urdu Akhbar,* 12th July 1857. Jiwan Lal says that Bakht Khan informed the *Kotwal* of the city that 'if any plundering took place he would be hanged'. Metcalfe, p. 135.
63. *Dehli Urdu Akhbar,* 12 July 1857.
64. Metcalfe, p. 135. *Sadiq-ul Akhbar,* dated 6th July 1857 reported that the appointment of Bakht Khan greatly increased the confidence of the people. The shopkeepers began to open their shops and there was no scarcity of provisions due to regular supply from outside the city. The city administration also became active. The *Kotwal* and *thanedars* took regular rounds of the city.
65. Metcalfe, p. 144.
66. *Ibid.,* pp. 149, 152.
67. Metcalfe, p. 152. Zakaullah says that Bakht Khan also offered five *bighas* of land to the descendants of soldiers who laid down their lives in fighting against the British. See, *Tarikh-i Uruj-i Sultanat-i Englishia Hind* (Urdu),

Delhi, 1904, p. 682. Jiwan lal elsewhere says that Bakht Khan had obtained the king's assent that the wounded soldiers should receive a pension as well as a grant of land. See Metcalfe, p. 146.

68. Bakht Khan's popularity is reflected from the fact that, *Sadiqul Akhbar,* 27th July 1857, gives a historical *masnavi* praising Bakht Khan.

69. *Roznamacha,* pp. 149-150.

70. *Roznamacha,* p. 150. On 25th August Baldeo Singh's request to secure the *mahals* of Delhi on farm with promises of regular supplies and payment to the imperial servants was rejected, *Roznamacha,* p. 165.

71. The ban orders were vigorously enforced. See, the proclamations of Bahadur Shah and Bakht Khan reproduced in original in Rizvi, S.AA, *Swatantra Dilli* (Hindi), Appendices 1, 2, 3, 5, 6, 7 and 8. Sen is doubtful about the implementation of the prohibition order. See, *Eighteen Fifty Seven,* p. 93, no. 67. Also see *Roznamacha,* pp. 153-4, for details on the communal issue raised at the time.

72. Jiwan Lal says that on 19th May 1857 some of the local Muslims in Delhi attempted to raise the standard of holy war to the great annoyance of Bahadur Shah. See Metcalfe, p. 95; *Roznamacha,* pp. 153-154.

73. Press List of Mutiny Papers, (n.d.), No. 166/377, NAI, New Delhi.

74. *Ibid.,* No. 19, SN 5, 8th August 1857.

75. Press List of Mutiny Papers, No. 19, SN 5, 8th August 1857, NAI, New Delhi.

76. Jiwan Lal vide Metcalfe, p. 183.

77. Press List of Mutiny Papers, No. 57, SN 352, NAI, New Delhi.

78. Metcalfe, p. 179.

THE MAKING OF 1857

Chapter - 7

Religious Debates and the Making of 1857 in Northern India

— ***Dr. Farha Khan***
Maharaja Agarsen Collage
University of Delhi

The great uprising of 1857 is an event which has attracted the attention of historians, members of the civil society and administrative officials who hold diverse views ever since it has taken place. Different views have been expressed regarding causes and character of this revolt. Various aspects related to the uprising have remained unexplored. The literature on the theme is daunting and large. Historiography of 1857 dealt with aspects of displeased army, endangered peasants, revenue or trading crisis, or religious threat. However, historians in recent times have paid more attention towards aspects like gender, marginals and tribal communities or popular resistance to political actions related to the events of 1857.[1]

The present study evaluates an important perspective around missionaries' activities. It attempts to question the thinking regarding the role played by evangelical societies in influencing the colonial government. Every policy of the colonial government was seen in the light of the activities of the various chaplains and missionaries in the major towns of the upper Gangetic valley. Establishments of schools, hospitals, orphanages were seen as institutions meant for promoting the Christianity through the means of education, health and charities. There were some individual Christian preachers who were not supported directly by the evangelical societies but they had become evangelists on their own.[2] Some of their publications too were highly offensive, making derogatory remarks against the highly reverend personalities of the Islam, especially the Prophet.[3] Traditionally the Hindu and the Muslims conducted their religious discourses at their private residences, temples or mosques, but the Christian missionaries literally took the matter to the streets and denounced other religions in the most violent terms.[4] Such an atmosphere created some sort of 'fear-psychosis' in the minds of the people, especially the Muslims. They considered that they and their progeny would be denied from practicing their religion and they will be forced to become the Christians.

Prior to the Charter Act of 1813, every single pamphlet to be printed for circulation, was duly examined and edited by the Company officials at Calcutta.[5] Hence no offensive pamphlet and no aggressive treatise could be circulated. The colonial authorities were very much concerned about the 'sensitivities of the natives in matter of religion'. For the safeguard of their empire they never wanted to antagonize them, instead their purpose was 'territorial expansion and governance'. Besides what concern them more, was the social evils like *sati*, child marriage, widow remarriage and human infanticide.[6] It was mainly due to the pressure from the merchants of Manchester and Lancashire (who wanted to push their textiles to be sold in an international market) who made the colonial government to change this policy of non-interference for the argument that they were failing in their duties, 'if the word of the Jesus was not spread in the land which had come to their possessions.'[7] Therefore, the new Charter Act gave a freedom to the missionaries of all denomination to come and 'spread the Gospel among the pagans'. It was this major policy shift on the part of the colonial administers which had transformed the earlier agenda and it made the things difficult for the Indians.

Another important charter which made the things easy for the evangelical societies and the missionaries was the Charter Act of 1833 which favored missionary expansion by permitting settlement in the Company's territories without the formality of a residence license.[8] Thus, opened the gate for the arrival and settlement of numerous missions and missionaries. These missionaries were now gearing up for open debates of the *munazara*[9] under the full protection of the colonial administrators. On such occasion, full administrative protection was available to the Christian side of the debaters, whereas, the debaters of the Muslim side were left to look for the defense of their own. The cities having the maximum concentration of the Indo-Muslim elites were having open religious debates (*munazara*). Now the Christian priests were challenging the Muslim scholars (*ulama*) to come up on certain supposedly contentious issues with the condition that the losing party shall have to abandon its creed.[10]

Beginning from 1840's and attaining its climax in 1850's, Religious curiosity, precisely, first brought the Muslims of the cities of Agra and Delhi in touch with the Evangelicals. It was the city of Lucknow where the first Christian-Muslim debate of the colonial era took place in AD1833, at the Nawab of Awadh, Nasir ul-din Haidar's (1827-37) Court. This unresolved debate was in many respects reminiscent of the medieval era. The publication of the *Mizan Ul-Haqq*, (Balance of the Truth, Urdu 1843) of the German Priest-the Rev. C.G. Pfander (1803-65) of Basel Seminary played the role of a catalyst that suddenly transformed these encounters into a bitter controversy. In comparison to all the previous missionary publications, this tract seemed to be all more offensive to Islam. Pfander did not have to wait long and consequent to his preaching and publications, from 1842-47, a number of *ulama* from Delhi,[11] Agra and Lucknow, have responded. In the midst of some unknown *munazara* one major and famous Agra *Munazara* of 1854 took place between Padre Pfander and Maulana Rahmat Ullah Kairanawi (1818-91) who was mainly assisted by Dr Wazir Khan.[12] In the debate which continued for two days, along with the main disputants of both religious groups, some British government official, leading citizens of Agra, and prominent *ulama* of the city were also present. Result of this debate remained open ended since 'both sides claimed victory.'[13] But more than the question as who wins and loss it's made up the Muslims to stand against the onslaught of Christian Evangelism.

The tone and the language employed in such disputes was highly offensive and further vitiated the feeling especially among the Muslim masses that the government had set the addendum of itself to destroy the creed of the Prophet from the Indian subcontinent. These aspects have contributed much into the making of 1857. The issue of religion provided an impetus to rise against the colonial government. Therefore, we find that a number of proclamations, which were issued by the rebel leaders in the various centers of uprising, urging for the ouster of the Christian rule from the Indian subcontinent.[14]

This work is not altogether new. Much has been written on the role of religion in the making of 1857. The importance of this enterprise is to look at the participation of the *ulama*, who prior to the uprising were the active participants in the religious debates with the evangelical Christian missionaries. Later these anti-missionary *ulama* became *mujahidin* who turned from engaging with missionaries in a discussion to fight the British government. Thus, the scope of this paper is limited. It is an attempt to examine the role played by the Christian evangelical endeavors in rousing religious sentiments which consequently prompted the opposite side to give a call to save one's own religion. And also to look at as how the echo of all these Christian-Muslim encounters which were taking place for almost two decades, helped in the making of 1857.

Threat of Conversion in the Indigenous Discourses

The Risala-i Fateh-Islam

Many proclamations[15] in the massive collection of documents were gathered meticulously together by Sayyid Athar Abbas Rizvi and M.L. Bhargava on behalf of the Uttar Pradesh Government. Recently, Iqbal Husain has made another important collection of the proclamations of 1857. One of the major Proclamation which raised the issue of alleged conversion to the Christianity as a major reason for the uprising was the *Risala-i Fateh-Islam* (Victory of Islam).[16]

This pamphlet was translated by British officers as 'a cry for Jehad in Oudh' and was used as evidence against the accusation of religious bigotry practiced by the Muslims. In Subaltern historiography this has been singled out as a representative document that expressed the extreme hatred that Indians had towards the British. Apart from the purportedly 'fire and sword' nature of the pamphlet for which it has been rather harshly criticized by modern writers, there is enough material through which the vision of people participating in a battle unto death can be deciphered. It revealed that they were conscious of the death of English women and children, something that was totally unacceptable under the tenets of any religion. Besides making a strong plea for the Hindu-Muslim unity, it underlined aspects related to the final outcome of the battle.[17] In the preamble to the document, atrocities committed by the British were highlighted in great detail. It also included an *Ishtihar* (public appeal) which was supposed to be circulated among the Hindus and the Muslims of Hindustan.[18] Such appeal was supposed to be popularized among the sepoy and the common man by the maulavis and pundits. It can be stipulated that such an appeal might have been made to sensationalize and galvanize the people into action.

Thus, the fear of the loss of faith was the main theme which continued to recur in most of the proclamations and within the indigenous discourse. Such an apprehension should not be considered only as rhetoric propagated during the course of the rebellion or an exaggerated account of the activities of the British officials and policy-makers. This impression was so popular that even after the suppression of the Mutiny and restoration of the British authority, a loyalist like Sir Syed Ahmad Khan in his *Asbab-e Bagawat-e Hind* (The Causes of Indian Revolt, 1858) raised his voice against 'the apprehension of interference of government with the religious customs of the Indians'.

Official Discourses and the Making of 1857

Asbab-e Bagawat-e-Hind

The Uprising of 1857 had a considerable impact on the relationship between the Christian missionaries and the Muslim community in India. It would not be wrong to say that this relationship had considerable impact in the making of the uprising. Sir Sayed Ahmad Khan, in his analysis of the causes of the rebellion, saw the people's perception of the government's involvement in missionary activity as a 'chief among the secondary causes of the rebellion'. The primary cause being the non-involvement of the indigenous people in the Legislative Council of India.[19] The people misapprehended the actions of the government and were convinced that it intended to force the Christian religion and foreign customs on Muslims and Hindus alike. They felt that this was not being done openly, but by indirect steps such as the removal of the study of Arabic and Sanskrit, and by reducing the people to poverty. The material assistance and the Christian education given to orphans after the drought of 1837 were also seen in this light.[20]

In addition to the government who were interfering into the faith of its subjects, Sir Syed faulted also actions of the missionaries and their methods. He argued that they had introduced a new system of preaching rather than holding to the traditional method of limiting religious discussion to a mosque or private home. They had taken to preaching in public places and publicized and circulated controversial tracts. They did not confine themselves to explain their own doctrines and books, but 'attacked the followers and the holy places of other creeds, which was annoying, and insulting beyond expression the feelings of those who listened to them.'[21] In all this, the missionaries enjoyed the protection of the authorities. They also opened Christian schools which the people were encouraged to attend by officers in high governmental positions, one of which could likely have been William Muir. The schools were tolerated because the people believed that such education would lead to a position in the civil service, but were nonetheless seen as instrumental in the erosion of their faith.[22]

Few Other Official Evidences

A number of unpublished letters in the National Archives of India, Delhi talks about the fear of danger amongst the 'natives' regarding their respective religion. In 1858, E.C. Bayley, the Deputy Secretary to the Government, North West Provinces, mentioned that a number of petitions that he received in the month of December were from some unknown figures, as well as some native of respectability from the city of Allahabad.[23] These petitions provided a curious evidence of the belief, which had obtained currency among, certain portions of the population of the Hindustan that the British government intended to convert them to Christianity.[24]

John William Kaye in 1864 published the first of his planned six-volume history of the revolt. He was the first person who, unlike other historian of his time, found religion was a factor that was composed by the reforming zeal of the state and missionaries activities.[25] Just ten years before this publication these shared evangelical enthusiasm was the talk of the town, especially, in the regions of northern India, where in 1854 a war of words had been on a high scale between the Muslim and missionaries. How three years afterwards this 'war of words' transformed into a 'battlefield war', and how the *ulama,* who were renowned for their theological understandings and argumentative qualities, 'abandoned the pen for sword' is interested to be looked into.

The Role of *Munazarist* in the Uprising

Maulana Rahmat Ullah Kairanawi and Dr. Wazir Khan

The Upper Gangetic Valley, where a war of words had been waged for nearly two decades, was transformed in the summer of 1857 into the epicenter of an armed rising which focused on the cities like Delhi, Lucknow, Kanpur and Bareilly. The former two were the foci of *munazara* confrontation. The role played by the *ulama* in the events of 1857 is a complex one. All those who joined were not of one doctrinal viewpoint. On the other hand many well-known *ulama* of different sects kept out.[26] Attention will be limited here in assessing the role during the rising only of those Muslims, who had taken an active public role in response to Pfander. This is being in order to test that how far the confrontational interface between the spokesmen of two religions contributed in the making of 1857.

Three years after the Agra debate of 1854, when Rahmat Ullah was busy in the writings and compositions of some of his books[27], news spread from nearby Meerut about the upheaval that broke out in the regiments stationed there in May 1857. It reached the district of Muzaffarnagar, and a series of attacks on the British started from here as well. Between July and September 1857, Kairana, Shamali and Thana Bhawan, the major towns of Muzaffarnagar, in the wake of the sepoy rebel of the adjacent region, seized the chance to throw off the Company rule.[28] It is generally agreed that the local Muslims participated in the risings in these districts, and that although many Muslim and cultivating Gujjars were involved. However, the scene was dominating by *ulama*.[29] In this context it is important to consider what Muhammad Taqi Usmani noted that the uprising of 1857 did not arise due to any long-drawn Muslim conspiracy, as it was generally believed. For him, indeed, the crisis was hundred years old that started from the Battle of Plassey in 1757. Gradual sufferings from the colonial government added to it, which finally resulted into an open outburst.[30] Thus it was a culmination of a long-standing unrest amongst the every section of the society, where, the Indian *ulama* had dedicated themselves to secure the eventual freedom of Indian Muslims from British rule. Therefore, the stage in Muzaffarnagar was set up by prominent *alim* of the city. Prominent among them being, Haji Imdad Ullah, Mamluk Ali, Hafiz Zamin, Muhammad Qasim Nanautawi, Maulana Munir Sahab, and Mualana Rashid Ahmad Gangohi. Rahmat Ullah was also said to be of their number, and have acted as an intermediary between the *ulama* in Delhi whose responsibility was to issue a *fatwa* on appropriate action, and the Muzaffranagar *ulama*, who were awaiting instructions.[31]

Historical opinions, however, are diversified at several points about his role in perceiving the real condition for waging a *jihad* against the British. It seems that the confused situation in Delhi after the initial outbreak at Meerut gave room for doubt about the appropriate actions to be taken. Maulavi Zaka Ullah described events in the vicinity of Delhi in May 1857 and argued that, although, Rahmat Ullah did indeed came to Delhi to find out if conditions were ripe for *jihad*. He quickly left again when he realized that the city was in the hands of the royal princes and other 'unreliable elements'.[32] Muhammad Mian attempted to reconcile Zaka Ullah's version with his own description of the event. He said that since no clear picture of the nature of events could be obtained in Thana Bhawan (which became the center of organization of the *mujahidin* camps), Rahmat Ullah was sent to Delhi to investigate the situation.[33] When he reached Delhi at the end of May he adjudged the effete Mughal court to be an unworthy pivot for *jihad*, and returned to Thana Bhawan with this advice. This, according to Muhammad Mian, was the visit which Maulavi Zaka Ullah mistakenly made the basis for his opinion that Rahmat Ullah at no point of time gave his support to *jihad*.[34] But probably in his estimation to find out the support provided by Rahmat Ullah to the *fatwa* of *jihad* in 1857 waged form Delhi, Muhammad Mian made a wrong perception by saying that the Mualana signed the *fatwa* as well.

Through *Rooznamchah* Abdul Lateef and through papers of the numbers of the mutiny participants) which Maulana Imdad Sabiri got from the Nazim of *Madrasa-i-Saulatiya,* Maulavi Mohammed Salim

Sahab, it can be estimated that Rahmat Ullah enjoyed deep influence upon the intellectuals of Delhi and the princes of the Red Fort and maintained good rapports with them. Therefore, Maulana Rahmat Ullah, along with Bahadur Shah Zafar and other *mujahidin* took active part in chalking out plans and guidelines for the war of independence and he did participate in the compilation of the *fatwa* as well. But he was not projected to sign the *fatwa* of *Jihad*.[35]

To turn back to the events, while the conditions were not yet ripe in Delhi, (which developed with the arrival in Delhi of Bhakt Khan's forces) the *ulama* of Thana Bhawan began to streamline their organization in preparation for a more favorable turn of events. Meanwhile they attacked on the neighboring *tahsil* of Shamli and very successfully retook it from the British army.[36]

It is uncertain whether Rahmat Ullah participated in the fighting of Shamli or not, but leadership of events in nearby Kairana was attributed to him in some of the Urdu accounts of the rising.[37] His position as a prominent rebel leader can be estimated on the account given by Taqi Usmani.

For the British, his presence and moreover supervision was there. It was enough to put him under the charge for the attacks of Shamali. Consequently, he became a wanted rebel.[38] However, forewarned about the danger, he escaped to a neighboring village of Muslim *Gujjars*. From there he stationed from one place to another and finally he moved to Mecca, where he spent the rest of his life.[39] On 20the January 1862, after his *hijrat,* the Deputy Commissioner of Karnal district began a *faujdari* case against him and confiscated all his property and put up for auction.[40]

In contrast to Rahmat Ullah, Wazir Khan's active role in the uprising can be pieced together with much completeness. Although even in his case some gaps remained in the order of events and sources as well. It was difficult to find his presence between the Agra debate of 1854 to the outbreak of 1857 and the similar scarcity remained in order to find him in the British records. Thus his presentation as a rebel leader apart from the Volume V of the *Freedom Struggle in Uttar Pradesh* can be corroborated only from some Urdu accounts.[41]

Through the correspondences that were taking place between Wazir Khan and Padri Pfander in Agra till late 1854, it can be confirmed that by the end of the year he was residing in Agra.[42] Plausibly prior to the Mutiny, he seemed to be in Agra. Ghulam Rasul Mehr's reference of the visit of Ahmadullah Shah, (the suggested compiler of the *Risala-Fateh-i-Islam*) to Agra did transform this probability into an assertion. Mehr stated that at some unspecified date from 1854 to 1857, Maulavi Ahmadullah Shah arrived at Agra. He was welcomed by a group of *ulama* of the city and later some good connection was also established between them that have contributed in the subsequent moves towards the British. As Mufti Intizam Ullah Shahabi also wrote that it was the influence of the Shah Sahab's company that Dr. Wazir Khan developed hatred towards the English and love for freedom.[43]

The participation of Wazir Khan in the events of 1857 is manifested with his arrival in Delhi in the very year. He soon became a part of *Jang-e-council* (war council) there.[44] Not long before his arrival did he asked Emperor Bahadur Shah Zafar to raise an *alam-e-baghawat* against the British.[45] He accompanied Bakht Khan in various military actions from Delhi to Awadh. In Awadh for their cause for the country they were honored with a *khillat* (robe of honour) by the Begum Hazrat Mahal.[46]

After investigating various official attributions that we found of Wazir Khan, it can be argued that his efforts were not confined to any limits. While at one place he was reported as the commanding officer in the infantry regiments of Khan Bahadur Khan at Bareilly,[47] at another one he was mentioned as the coachman of revolutionary government at Farrukhabad.[48] Referring to a *jihad* proclamation at Bareilly by Prince Feroze Shah, a son of king Bahadur Shah, a contemporary newspaper gave credit for its compilation to Wazir Khan, wherein he was mentioned with his government profile, the sub-assistant surgeon of Agra.[49] The proclamation's denunciated, in strident manner, the wicked Christian infidels who were intending to cause the spread of Christianity by violence and who wanted to do away with the religion of Hindus and Mussulmans. Avril Powell, in her little but important discourse on Wazir Khan's role in 1857, stated that the Proclamation bore the mark of the doctor who only three years before had achieved much against missionary aims.[50] His involvement was indicated by another newspaper report that Wazir Khan was superintending the cannon foundry of the Maratha rebel leader, Nana Sahib at Bareilly.[51]

However, when the British regained control of the N.W.P., he was put under trial.[52] But akin to his partner in debate, he also escaped from British hands and migrated to Mecca. While Maulana Rahmat Ullah even after his *hijrat* to Mecca continued his work of revitalizing Islam from the evangelical threat of the entire world via the medium of his writings, Dr Wazir Khan activities after his long lasted encounter-first *ilmi* and than *jangi*- is difficult to ascertain. Our limited information suggest that Wazir Khan's after his migration spent the last days of his life in Turkey by again enrolling himself in his medical work.[53] Dr Wazir Khan's activities in 1857 constituted the strongest evidence so far available for associating those Muslims who had earlier engaged in *munazara* with the Christians, with a readiness and capacity to wage active *jihad* against the British government.

Conclusion

The extent of anger waged upon the Churches and contemporary Christian community of the Upper Gangetic Valley, made up of some Indian converts, British Residents, and missionaries during the rebellion was one more reason to claim that it was related to religious sensitivities. The contemporary account of a missionary at work in Banaras and Mirzapore, Rev. M. A. Sherring, called *The Indian Church during the Great Rebellion* gave a detailed representation of the wrath and antagonism that befell on the missions in India, mostly situated in the N.W.P. during the rebellion.[54] There is undeniably some evidence that during the uprising, in some places like in Delhi for instance, the famous converts of the Delhi College Master Ram Chandra and Dr. Chaman Lal were the main target in the rebel list. While Ram Chadra successfully escaped, Chaman Lal was murdered.[55] When the converts were hunted down, the Christian religious institutions like Churches and Chapels were desecrated.[56] Destructing religious institution and to end some one's life in retaliation was not the work to be appreciated. But the manner in which the British addressed the rebels was no less appreciable. Once the Mutiny was over the measures, the British government implied in retribution of the hardships, they reported to have bore in 1857, is really pathetic. In a notification of 29th August

1857, the Commissioner of Allahabad ordered the Esquire of Calcutta, where in lieu of the maltreatment that the Christian woman and children face during the outbreak, and asked to hang ten Awadh nobels on every women and child.[57] Furthermore, he pointed out that besides the evangelical missionaries 'it was the native Catechists and Preachers who had to suffer more during the great devastation.[58]

However, despite the hardships the missionary writings claimed, restorations of the missions began within a year of the uprising of 1857.[59] In this new beginning the British government once again lent a hand of support. These shared evangelical sympathies were used to be the object of popular ire. Even Sir Syed Ahmad khan, who had established his firm loyalty towards the British rule, was bound to critique the government policies adopted for the Hindustani in every walk of their life that aimed to destroy their respective religion. No wonder that it was in such circumstances that the literate class of the Muslim community, who earlier through their writings provided the spirit, which made the Muslims to come out of its own and to withstand the onslaught of a powerful group and not to be shaken from the missionaries, later took a long-headed leadership and dedicated themselves to secure the eventual freedom of Indian Muslims from British rule.

In view of such weighty evidences that we have perceived from the indigenous and official discourses it would not be in correct to opine that the missionaries had played an important role in creating the feeling of religious insecurity among the masses and contributed substantially to the anxiety that led to the uprising of 1857. However, it is also true that the event of 1857 was not merely an outcome of the Christian evangelization.[60] There were certain political and economic factors in 1857 which were sufficient in themselves to bring about a country-wide upheaval, but it was the socio-religious causes which played a decisive role in the events of that year. Even S. N. Sen has no hesitation in agreeing with L.E.R. Rees who described the uprising 'as war of fanatic religionists against Christians',[61] which was not correct. Since this event was organized against an alien rule by disparate group of people with their distinctive grievances, where the feeling of religion superseded all other grudges and came as one of the major cause of the revolt.

Notes

1. Sabyasachi Bhattacharya, *Rethinking 1857*, Orient Longman, Delhi, 2007. For a detailed and upgraded information on the historiography of the event of 1857 in connection to such diverse aspects see, Sabyasachi Bhattacharya, *Rethinking 1857*, Orient Longman, Delhi, 2007; Shireen Moosvi, *Facets of the Great Revolt 1857*, Tulika press, Delhi, 2008; Biswamoy Pati, *The 1857 Rebellion*, OUP, New Delhi, 2007.
2. William Carey was known to be a part of the Serampore Baptist Society. In 1793 he entered India as an Indigo planter and started his missionary work with an enthusiastic zeal years before the passage of the Charter Act of 1813. He translated the early Christian literature available, with the help of locals, in various native languages. Arthur Mayhew, *Christianity and Government of India*, Faber & Gwyer Ltd., London, 1929, pp. 61-72.
3. '*Address from the Missionaries to all persons professing the Mohummudan Religion*'. It was published by the Serampore Baptist Mission Press under the supervision of William Carey in 1807. Due to its highly offensive tone, which described the Prophet Muhammad as a tyrant and a lustful man, it was asked by the Governor General, Lord Minto, to restrict its circulation, Foreign, Secret, No. 1, 1 Sep 1807, NAI.
4. The aggressiveness of their task could be measured by the assertion that even a loyalist like Sir Syed Ahmad Khan was forced to describe this change in much critical tone.
5. Arthur Mayhew, pp. 61-72.
6. At the outset, the Protestants had been more eager to preach among the Hindus than to the Muslims. John Thomas Thomason, the first evangelical missionary to the Mughal capital of Delhi, arrived in 1818 and in 1850 (sic) till he died in his missionary labors, registered to have focused on Hindus only. James Hough, *The History of Christianity in India from the Commencement of the Christian Era*, R.B. Seeley and W. Burnside, London, 1860, p. 214. One reason for this preference was that the initial encounter with certain features of the Hindu religious and social life, such as the custom of *sati*, which was particularly disturbing to the evangelical temperament. So they perceived that the Hinduism seemed to require more immediate attention than Islam, which had been a part of European consciousness in variously indistinct forms, for many centuries past. D. Kopf opined in this context that for the Evangelicals Hindus deserved their primary attention as they were the chief occupants of the land, the Muslims, on the other hand were considered intruders who did not merit their special attention- it would be difficult to then comprehend the entire history of Christian mission to Muslims in India. D. Kopf, *British Orientalism and the Bengal Renaissance: The Dynamics of Indian Modernization, 1773-1835,* University of California Press, Berkley, 1969, p. 103.

7. Penelope Carson, *The East India Company and Religion 1698-1858*, The Boydell Press, Woodbridge, 2012, Introduction.
8. Arthur Mayhew, p. 108.
9. In the 19th century this term was commonly used for religious disputation or debate.
10. It was a pre-condition, in the colonial India, of having *munazara,* which stated that the losing party in the debate had to renounce its faith and to convert to the religion of the winning group.
11. The religious character of the British rule till very late had not brought the Delhi *ulama* into a close touch with Christian Evangelism. It was only in May 1852 with the efforts of Rev. M.J. Jennings, an evangelical Company Chaplain that impact of missionary activity was felt in Delhi. The Delhi College became the ground for every religious controversy in the city, when Master Ram Chandra and Dr. Chaman Lal of the Science and Mathematics department, in the year1852, as being ardent supporter of Western scientific learning were baptized. Thus, here dissemination of knowledge became a tool for conversion for the people like Taylor the then Principle of Delhi College, who was accused by Maulavi Abdul Haq for having engineered the conversion of these professors of the College, *Ibid.*
12. It was only because of the command of this Muslim Surgeon over the Christian Theology that the Muslim would be able to know those in depth changes under the tenets of Christian Religion to which they themselves were ignored.
13. Hence neither in the case of this famous debate nor in the history of any other discussion in the colonial India does this prerequisite condition seem to turn into the results that were agreed upon, Avril Powell, *Muslim and Missionaries in Pre-Mutiny India,* Curzon Press, London, 1993.
14. Apart from Sayyid Athar Abbas Rizvi and M. L. Bhargava ed., *Freedom Struggle in Uttar Pradesh* in V Vols., Publication Bureau, Information Department, Uttar Pradesh, 1958, (hereafter, *FSUP*), a number of rebel proclamations from different source material is compiled by Iqbal Husain ed., *Proclamations of the Rebels of 1857*, Indian Council of Historical Research, New Delhi, 2007, (hereafter, *Proclamations*).
15. In records the term Proclamation and Pamphlet had been used interchangeably.
16. It was composed under the supposed aegis of the famous rebel leader, Maulavi Ahmadullah Shah of Lucknow. The English translation of the Pamphlet is found in the *FSUP,* Vol. II, *Awadh: 1857-59*, pp. 150-62.
17. *FSUI,* Vol. II, *Awadh: 1857-59*, pp. 150-62.
18. This *Istihar* was first produced from the original document in Urdu by S.Z.H. Jafri, in 'Voices of the Vanquished: The Indigenous Discourse in the Rebels World of 1857', pp. 69-82, collected in the Souvenir (*Delhi in 1857: Studies,*

Images and Documents) of the 70th Session of the Indian History Congress, held at Delhi, 15-17 May 2010, Department of History, University of Delhi,.

19. Syed Ahmad Khan, *Asbab-e Bagawat-e Hind*, pp. 13-16, 24-33.
20. *Ibid,* pp. 16-17.
21. *Ibid,* pp. 18, 21.
22. *Ibid,* pp.19-20.
23. Foreign Political, No. 679, *Proceeding Volume,* Dec 1858, NAI.
24. *Ibid.*
25. Kaye passed away before the anticipated six volumes could be completed. He was only able to write three volumes in his lifetime. The work was entitled, *A History of Sepoy War in India*. The project was completed by G.B. Malleson. He rewrote the work and renamed it as *A History of the Indian Mutiny*.
26. The Memoir of Fazle Haq Khairabadi (d. 1862), who was residing in Delhi during 1857, offered some interesting insights into the divided attitudes of the Muslim residents towards both the British and the rebel forces. He noted that some of the Muslims, along with the money changers and other wealthy Hindus remained loyal to the British, and therefore took steps to 'make ineffective the power of the Mujahidin and uproot them and then scatter and disrupt them'. 'The Story of the War of Independence', *Journal of the Pakistan Historical Society,* No. 5 Issue I, 1957, p. 33.
27. Muhammad Taqi Usmani, *Bible Se Quran Tak,* Karachi, 1968, p. 196; This book was the Urdu translation of the most prominent work of Maulana Rahmat Ullah called the *Izhar-ul Haqq*, which was a detailed reply to Pfander's challenges.
28. Ghulam Rasul Mehr, *1857 Ke Mujahideen*, p. 242.
29. R. M. Edwards, Magistrate of the Muzaffarnagar district wrote to F. Williams, Commissioner, Meerut Division on the People's part, '*I received information to the effect that the People had, at the instigation of King's emissaries, agreed to waive private and family feuds and all their energies should be leveled against the government*'. For the protracted struggle at Muzzafarnagar and adjacent regions see, *FSUP,* Vol. V. pp. 127-46.
30. *Bible Se Quran tak*, p. 196.
31. *Bible se Quran tak*, p.197; Muhammad Salim, *Ek Mujahid Memar*, Mecca, 1952, p. 29.
32. Maulavi Zakah Ullah, *'Tarikh-i Uruj Ahad-i Sultanat-i Inglishiya-i Hind',* Vol. II, p. 675 cited in *Asar-i Rahmat*, p. 220.
33. Muhammad Mian, *Ulama-i Hind ka Shandar Mazi*, Delhi, 1957, p. 291.
34. *Ek Mujahid Memar*, p. 29.
35. *Asar-i Rahamt*, pp. 220-23. Imdad Sabri mentioned a list of 30-32 (sic) *ulama* who were said to have signed the *jihad fatwa*. His description was

based on the report published in a Delhi newspaper, *Sadiq ul-akhbar* of 19 July 1857. Rahmat Ullah's name appeared first in the list. Imdad Sabri asserted that it was not the Maulana Rahmat Ullah Kairanawi but some Maulana Rahmat Ullah of Delhi.

36. *Ulama-i Hind ka Shandar Mazi,* p. 299; *Ek Mujahid Memar*, p. 29.
37. Imdad Sabri, *Firangiyon Ka Jaal*, Delhi, 1979, p. 233.
38. *Bible se Quran tak*, p. 197.
39. *Firangiyo ka Jaal*, p. 234; *Ek Mujahid Memar*, p. 32.
40. It is to be noted here that the account of the confiscation of his property was taken from some primary (*Bible se Quran Tak,* p. 200) and secondary (*1857 ke Mujahidin,* p. 245 and *Asar-i Rahmat*, p. 251) Urdu sources. Nothing is corroborated from the British Mutiny Records, since his name did not appear in any single British official record.
41. His official presentation is noted in *FSUP,* Vol. V. The Urdu accounts mentioned a very small but valuable biography of Dr. Wazir Khan is Ghulam Rasu Mehr, *1857 ke Mujahidin*.
42. *Asar-i Rahmat*, pp. 174-83.
43. *Ghadr ke Chand Ulama*, Delhi, p. 81.
44. Ghulam Rasul Mehar, Lahore, 1957, *1857 ke Mujahidin,* p. 246.
45. *Ibid,* p. 231, Imdad sabri cited *Rooznamachah* Abdul Lateef, p. 75 to talk about his role in the mutiny.
46. *1857 ke Mujahidin,* p. 233.
47. *FSUP,* Vol. V, *Western Districts and Rohilkhand, 1857-59*, p. 294.
48. *Ibid,* p. 251.
49. 'The Bengal Harkaru and India Gazette, 10 May 1858', p. 440, cited in *Ibid,* p. 381.
50. *Muslim and Missionaries*, p. 278.
51. 'The Friend of India, 6 May 1858', p. 414, in *FSUP,* Vol. V, *Western Districts and Rohilkhand, 1857-59,* p. 437.
52. 'The Bengal and Indian Gazette, 30 June 1858', p. 616, cited in Ibid, pp. 953-54 reported a Wazeer Khan a coachman of the revolutionary government of Farrukhabad-Fattehgurh with the *Nazim* of the ex-Nawab is under trial.
53. *1857 ke Mujahidin*, p. 248. His position during the last years of his life was traced by Mehr as following, 'While he was serving as the doctor of the sultan of Turkey, the English government in India wrote to the Sultan that the person who was sheltering in Mecca was a runaway culprit. It asked him to hand over the Doctor to India. The Sultan of Turkey wrote to Sharif Abdullah, the Governor of Mecca, who in response wrote to the Sultan that there were ten thousand men (members) in his tribe and Dr. Wazir Khan could be handed over to any one only after all of them are killed. Consequent

to which the Sultan wrote to the Indian government that handing over (deportation of) a culprit under such circumstances was almost impossible. The Indian government was compelled to keep quiet. Dr. Wazir Khan lived in Mecca for fourteen years. He breathed his last over there in 1873'.

54. M. A. Sherring, *The Indian Church during the Great Rebellion*, James Nisbet and Co., London, 1859. (Hereafter, *Church during the Great Rebellion*).
55. 'Narrative of the Escape of the Christian convert Babu Ram Chandra, late Professor of Mathematics in the Government College Delhi, and Now Professor of Mathematics in the Thomason College, Roorke', cited in *Church during the Great Rebellion*, pp. 62-8.
56. From a series a letter written from January to March by the Bishop and Vicar Apostate of Hindustan, J. Persico to the Lt. General and Chief Commissioner of Oudh, Sir James Outram, it was evident that the prominent tone was to make compensation for the loss sustained by the missions at Agra and Lucknow. It included establishing chapels, priests' house to mission houses and compensating for the personal loss faced by the missionaries, Foreign Political, Nos. 132-34, 19 March 1858, NAI.
57. Foreign, Secret, No. 219, 25 Sep 1857, NAI.
58. One name is here worthy to be mentioned is of Dhakul Prasad. He and his entire family were killed during the disturbances in Farrukhabad district. *Sixteen Annual Report of the Board of Foreign Mission of the Presbyterian Church, in the United States of America,* Published for the Board, At the Mission House, 23 Centre Street, 1853, P. 69. M. A. Sherring named 21 people in the list of missionaries, chaplains and their families killed during the rebellion while the number of native's converts who worked as catechists and teachers was 9, *Church during the Great Rebellion,* pp. 17-21. *The Imperial Gazetteer of India* in the year 1851 record 222 foreign and Eurasian ordained agents/preachers in India and Burma, while the number of native ordained agents/preachers was 21. After looking into such drastic difference in the number of presence it could be simply understood that who suffered more crises, Clarendon Press, Vol. II, 1908, p. 263.
59. Holcomb mentioned these re-establishments. *Historical Sketches of the Farrukhabad Mission,* p. 124.
60. An emphasis on the evangelical ventures of the English government and English missionaries were made over and over again, since this was the most important factor of dealing the Christian-Muslim encounters during the period of 1857 in India. This was the last important time period of these encounters and debates under study.
61. Surendra Nath Sen, 'The Inevitability of the Mutiny', pp. 80-82 cited in Mujeeb Ashraf, *Muslim Attitudes towards British Rule*, p. 156.

Chapter - 8

'Royals', Property and Prize Agents: Fate of the Mughal Capital in the aftermath of 1857

— *Dr. Nida Arshi*
Shaheed Bhagat Singh College
University of Delhi

Somewhere the city had to pay the price for having such a glorious past and being so famous in the world. Delhi wasn't just a cultural and political epicentre of the Mughal Empire, it had also garnered a lot of attention due to its immense wealth. So much so that many plunderers had made it a target for systematic looting in the late 18th and early 19th century. The riches of its citizens have been described as[1]

> "...its merchants and storekeepers, trading with the inhabitants of the richly-cultivated Doab and with more distant countries, became rich and prosperous, accumulating vast treasures, while the people, with the instinct of a penurious race, converted their ready-money into jewels and gold and silver ornaments and safely stored them away in hidden receptacles within their houses".

Delhi had seen many plunderers in the past, plunderers who came with the intention to loot the riches of the city and left leaving the city in an utter despair. These loots were random and were not targeted towards any particular group. But the Aftermath of 1857 was different, the British did not come as the plunderers they came to rule over the city. Their plunder was systematic, strategic and was full of revenge towards few individuals and people of a certain faith. The maliciousness, hostility and rancour displayed by the British towards their formal allies and residents of the city were unprecedented.

The city of Delhi was captured, the revolt was suppressed, several thousand innocent people lost their lives, the city was evacuated, properties were confiscated and a lot of fines were imposed in the aftermath of the revolt of 1857. The process went on for years, during which people were forced to live outside the walled city with the bare minimum resources. Meanwhile, the city was also changed physically with the British plan of clearance and demolition of the various buildings, houses, monuments and gardens.

In this study, we are going to explore three aspects of the aftermath of the revolt of 1857. Firstly, we will examine the failure of the British strategy of finding an ally in the Mughal house and the small principalities in the environs of Delhi. The setback of the British was expressed through a series of punishments assigned to the chiefs of these principalities. Likewise the British hunted and suppressed the members of the Mughal clan to avoid any rallying of the revolters around these Mughal successors.

In the second part of this work, we will explore the various forms of plunder which took place in Delhi after the suppression of the revolt. This plunder was both organised and unorganised. We will look at the appointment of the Prize Agents in the city which provided the plunder a legality, and how the native allies were used by the British to know the secrets of the hidden treasures in the city.

The last section will look at how the urban space of the city was recrafted according to the needs of the British in order to make the governing of the city easier for them. This recrafting and the demolition was well planned and strategic. The archival files show how the demolition and compensation was utilized by the British to reward the groups which helped them during the revolt and targeted some communities through their discriminatory policies.

The Royal Family and families of the Delhi Agencies after 1857

The repercussions and humiliation faced by the Mughal Emperor in the aftermath of the revolt are well known and documented. The revolt was suppressed and the city was recaptured on 20th September 1857. Two days later the 'pensioner monarch' of the British was the 'prisoner' of the British. General Wilson arrested him with a promise that his life would be spared. But the famous trial was held not at any official building in Calcutta or elsewhere but in the erstwhile court of *Diwan e Khas*, which added to the humiliation. The 'halo' of the Mughal sovereignty was to be shipwrecked in the highest temple of its creators and in the sight of its hundreds and thousands of believers, admirers and sympathisers.[2]

Mirza Jawan Bukht, the seventeen years old son of Bahadur Shah and Zeenat Mahal, was considered to be a threat to the Government because he could emergeas a rallying point for the disaffected.[3] Therefore, the Chief Commissioner of Punjab ordered that they should be kept in strict confinement with his father and mother and not allowed to go out under any pretext. He further stated that 'after the criminal conduct of this family, no male member of it, who was present at Delhi at any time, during the war, should be allowed to go free.'[4]

But it was not just the Emperor, Queen and the prince who were subjected to the wrath of the British, the entire Mughal clan was hunted down in Delhi and in the nearby area. The people,who had at some point been connected with the Mughal *darbar* or the family were also arrested and questioned by the British authorities. Since the rebels made the Mughal Emperor their leader and gathered huge support from the indigenous population in his name, the British feared any such rebellion to take place in future, therefore, they thought of uprooting the entire Mughal clan to evade any such possibility. Although removing the entire royal family was a tedious task due to its large number, orders were given to the officials to prepare a list of the near relatives of the ex-king to decide upon the course of action.[5]Numerous trials took place in and out of the city leading to the members of the royal family being put in prison. The trial of Shahzada Mirza Yakoob, who was the son of Nanhee Begum, a daughter of the ex-king, was one of them. He was arrested at Gwalior and sent to Delhi to undergo his trial before the special Commission which, on the 16th June 1858, sentenced him to imprisonment in transportation beyond seas for life. He was sentenced this harsh punishment just on the ground of him being a grandson of the ex-king and being unable to account for himself during the mutiny. But officials failed to find any evidence against him in the course of the trial. On the contrary two witnesses Mirza Halee Buksh and Rae Gunga Ram, who were the supporters of the British Government, affirmed that the prisoner had left Delhi before the insurrection broke out. No specific crime was proved against him and he was arrested only in consequence of him being a member of the Royal family of Delhi.[6] Although no act of rebellion was proved against him and he was released from the confinement, he was required to reside at a distance from Delhi with a small maintenance amount as small as Rs. 5 from the government.[7] This was the story of more or less all the members of the family and relatives of the Mughal King. They were taken to prison and trials against them ran for years. Few of them were lucky to have witnesses whom the British government saw as its supporters and they were released to die in misery with the bare minimum allowance from the government, far away from their baronial lives and ancestral home.

The aftermath even shows that it wasn't just the Mughal clan but many other royal families, from Delhi or part of the Delhi Agency system, were also punished for supporting the cause of the rebels. They were punished more because from the very inception these small royal households were placed and nurtured by the British on the outskirts of Delhi to have a greater control over the city and to secure their position. These small principalities were perceived by the British as trustworthy allies who will side with them in the time of need. But the revolt had presented them with a different outcome.

Therefore, after the revolt, the Chief Commissioner of Punjab asked the Commissioner of Delhi to furnish a list of all the chief and leading men in the custody at Delhi. As a rule, all those against whom any specific crime connected with the present insurrection could be proved were supposed to be brought to the trial as soon as possible and if found guilty to be put to death.[8] The Central Report on the administration of the Punjab territories prepared after the rebellion of 1857 clearly states a picture of the complete failure of the motive with which the British government had created the system of Delhi Agency.[9] At the time of need, the principalities constituted the Delhi Agency showed their allegiance towards Mughal Emperor and supported the rebels during 1857. This support, shook the British because, for the government, they were the feudatory chiefs whom they had maintained in power and affluence since the beginning of the century and most of them had now turned against the British government. Abdul Rehman Khan, *Nawab* of Jhajjar, Nahar Singh, *Raja* of Bullubhgurh and Ahmed Ali Khan, *Nawab* of Farukhnagar had sided with the rebels. The conduct of the Bahadur Jung Khan, *Nawab* of Dadree had been almost equally bad. Aminuddin Ahmad Khan, nawab of Loharu had done nothing for them. Such had been the 'traitarous' behaviour of the chiefs around Delhi.

Apart from these royal families, the British had to struggle to keep their control over the other surrounding areas of Delhi as well. The Karnal district having been constantly traversed by the British troops had remained in their possession. In the Haryana district (including Hissar and Hansi) and the Sirsa district, the native troops chiefly composed of the Haryana light infantry had mutinied soon after the outbreak at Delhi, and all Europeans had been either slain or driven out as fugitives. Then the Gujjar and the Mohamedan sections of the population gave the British a tough time, while the Jats and Hindus generally remained faithful. In the same manner, the Rohtak district had been lost to the British. It was only with the support of contingents from Punjab, Patiala and Bikaner that the British were able to recover their control over Sirsa, Hisar and Rohtak.

After curbing the revolt the chiefs of Jhajjar, Ballubhgurh, Dadree, Farukhnagar were either taken or surrendered themselves; their forts, treasure and equipages were seized as the prize for the troops and their lands were also confiscated. A Military Commission was forthwith convened to try and sentence the principal political prisoners. The chiefs of Jhajjar, Bullubhgurh, Farukhnagar were convicted and hung at Delhi, their moveable property was declared prize, their territorial fiefs were recommended to be confiscated to the British government. Their families were either allowed to retain their own private property or else they were pensioned. The Dadree chief, on account of extenuating circumstances, was spared the ordeal of being tried for his life, but his territory was recommended to be confiscated, and he himself was compelled to reside under surveillance at Lahore. The Loharu chief was acquitted of active participation in the revolt. The Dadree territory was given to the faithful Rajah of Jind and a portion of the Jhajjar territory worth three lakhs per annum was granted to the Maharaja of Patiala and the Rajah of Nabha in reward for their services. As the ceded territory was situated far to the south on a remote and troublesome frontier it was thought prudent and convenient to place the above chiefs, who were the friendly Sikh powers among a turbulent Mohamedan population.

The punishments which these chiefs had to go through were not restricted to them individually. They were set as an example for the future and the measures which were taken up against them had wide consequences. For instance, after with the confiscation of the property of the *Nawab* of Farukhnagar, the Government denied to acknowledge the rights of the debtors of the *Nawab* as well. Since the estates and the stipend of the *Nawab* were forfeited due to his treason it was declared that his debtors had no legal claims over the Government. The agents were barred from giving any guarantee that the British government will pay the debts of the chiefs under any circumstances.[10] This was done to teach everyone a lesson that any act of treason would not be tolerated by the Government, therefore, the punishments were much harsher in nature.

However, the *Nawab* of Bahadurgarh escaped the death sentence; even though he was accused of the same serious charges which were put on the other chiefs. Some of these charges were[11]-

- That he had recognized the usurpation and rebellion of the ex-king as his sovereign and kept an agent at his court.
- That his *sawars* mutinied and joined a portion of that insurgent band who murdered the magistrate and other European at Hissar and plundered the government treasury at the place.
- The mutineers and insurgents drew supplies without let or hindrance from his territory.
- That despite his engagements and the conditions of his tenure he did nothing to show his loyalty to or to aid the British Government.

It is interesting to note that after such allegations the authorities defended him by arguing in his favor. The Chief Commissioner recommended that his life should be spared. The chief was considered to be an individual plunged in debt and difficulty and it was argued that he had left his state for years to be mismanaged by others. Commissioner stated that 'notwithstanding all his misconduct of omission and commission it is not improbable, that he may hardly have been willing at heart to side against us. He was utterly weak and helpless, without any means and resources and his people were beyond his control and the *Nawab* of Jhajjar appeared to have intrigued with his troops.' Unfortunately, such consideration was not granted to the other chiefs, neither were they considered while punishing the Mughal Emperor.[12]

As a result, Bahadur Jung Khan was not tried by the Military Commission, but his territory was confiscated, a moderate amount of allowance was assigned for his life and he was supposed to live his rest of the life under surveillance.

After the revolt of 1857 and its suppression out of the above, only three states could safeguard their existence- Dojana, Loharu and Pataudi. Since none of them took part(at least direct part) in the revolt, therefore, they continued to be on the list of allies of the British. According to the *Memoranda on the Native States*, Dujana ranked nineteenth in order to precedence amongst the Native States in the Punjab and the *Nawab* was entitled to be received by the Viceroy. Loharu ranked eighteenth in order of precedence and the chief enjoys a salute of 9 guns, granted as personal distinction and was entitled to be received by the Viceroy. Pataudi also entitled to be received by Viceroy and ranked seventeenth in the order.[13]

Prize Agents as a means of an Organized Plunder

An evacuated city, empty houses and no residents to safeguard them, presented a golden opportunity for loot and plunder. The plunder took place in various forms the indigenous soldiers who fought on the British side plundered the city in an unorganized manner and took anything which they could get hold of. On the other hand, the British took the path of organized plunder; the city of Delhi was announced as the 'Prize' for the war for the soldiers. Army looked at it as an opportunity as recompensation for the toils and privations they had undergone,[14] but they soon realized that the Government had other plans for the city.

The law of military was "that a city taken by assault belonged as the prize to the conquerors." The plunder of the city was inevitable, the officials were sure that it would take place and it was beyond their control to stop every soldier from such doing, On 7th September 1857 General Wilson gave their words that a fund would be created for a common use of the soldiers from the plundered money, to be distributed according to the prize rules.[15]

After the capture of the city, the army waited for months for the fulfillment of the promises made to them, but the wait kept on increasing and the anxiety among the army started to go beyond control.[16] The wait resulted in the order from the Governor General that "there was an objection to the troops receiving the Delhi prize-money and in lieu thereof granted as a recompense for their arduous labors and patient in the field the magnificent sum of six months *batta*."[17] This order roused a storm of indignation not only amongst the Delhi force but throughout the British army in India. A burst of resentment led the Governor General to roll back his orders and he ordered to give the prize money in addition to six months *batta* to all the engaged.

The systematic plunder began with the election of the Prize Agents by the army as per the norm of the military. The Prize Agents were of three categories first, the ones who would take care of the share for the Generals and field officers, the second for the Queen's service and the third for the Company's army. During the plunder of the city initially, the Prize Agents obtained articles of lesser value like dresses and household goods. But as they started to dig deep and thorough searches were carried out, they soon started to acquire precious items like jewelry and precious stones, diamonds, rubies, emeralds, pearls, bracelets and bangles of solid metal, heaps of coins were collected from the various houses. The government never openly disclosed the amount of total prize money collected from the city.[18]

In the aftermath of 1857, the 'natives' also played a crucial role in the plunder of the city as spies or to put it in a more refined manner as guides for the Prize Agents. With the knowledge of the language and the local surroundings, they proved to be of immense help for the British.

Their services were utilized to interview the people who were allowed to enter the city, like traders, masons and builders to get the information about the hidden treasures in the houses of the former rich of the city. It was due to these people that they were even aware of the fact that the Muslims used to keep their precious things hidden in the floor and the Hindus used to keep it in the walls of their houses.[19]

The Prize Agents not only plundered the houses and the shops of the rebels and other residents, but the accounts of the bankers and merchants were thoroughly searched and if any rebel property was found in their register, it were also claimed by the Government.A sum of Rs. 42,575.8.3, jointly in the name of the ex Queen Begum Zeenat Mahal and the deceased chief Eunuch Mahboob Ali Khan was found amongst the books of Lalla Ramjee Das Gonwalla. The orders were issued to transfer the amount in the Government's treasury. Although due to the upheaval there was a considerable stagnation in the trade and it wasn't possible for the firm to act immediately on these orders, also because the amount was large. Therefore, a time of a month or two was given to arrange the money.[20]

There always had been a contradiction at the various levels of the authorities in the British Government. The records have often voiced out such differences between the various officials, often the officials dealing directly with a set of problem or area had to voice a different opinion from the officials at the highest level of authorities. At times these differences arose not because of the difference in the policy, but often because of personal reasons and greed. Similar differences could be found during the aftermath of the revolt of 1857 when the city of Delhi became an open ground for loot and plunder with the people of Delhi facing intolerable atrocities and severe loss of property. In the exchange of letters, some British officials shared their concern regarding the unrestrained plunder by the Sikh soldiers of the British side.The British govt. officials itself did not leave any chances to benefit from the ongoing loot by using 'subtle' methods. The British officials urged the higher authorities to earn whatever possible from the situation.

After the suppression of the revolt of 1857 the officiating Magistrate of Panipat, J.H. Richards wrote to C.B. Saunders, the Commissioner of Delhi, questioning his orders that no distribution of the property of the rebel should take place without further orders from the Government. Richards was in favour of giving away the property of the traitors in the district as a reward to their captors. Saunders disapproved of his proposal, stating that capturing the traitors was the bounded duty of the officials, and encouragement to such practices would lead to corrupt practices on the part of government officials and the ongoing Sikh plunder would become even more difficult to control. So, the officials were prohibited to take any action regarding the property of the traitors until the orders from the Governor General were received.[21]

The orders from the Government were clear, the officials were asked to report any existence of forts, fortified villages, or fortified houses and buildings of any kind in their division. They were asked to note the ownership, the extent of the state of repair of each such edifice, with the remarks on the behavior of the owner or occupier of the same during the late disturbances, and whether the defensive works have been erected or repaired since their commencement. The Lieutenant Governor ordered that no building of any description, except those in the occupation of Government and possibly of personages of high rank, who remained faithful and whom the official considered exempting from the operations of the disarming order, should be allowed to retain the semblance of a fortification. But they were not allowed to give any orders without the prior consultation with the Governor General.[22]

Even after the repeated orders of the Government, the officials at local levels continued with the practices of hiding the plunder or selling off the confiscated property without the consultation of the Government for personal benefits. The Governor General ordered that the officers of the Government, of whatever rank or class, were absolutely prohibited from selling or being concerned in the sale of property of any amount or description to native princes and chiefs or to their relatives or ministers or to any native gentlemen of rank or opulence residing under the protection of the British government. The officials were warned that any disobedience of these orders would lead to the displeasure of the Government and would result in heavy penalties for the person. These were the general orders for the people serving in all the British Residencies.[23]

The above description clearly shows that the Government wanted to control the entire process of the plunder to make the best possible profit out of it. Therefore, the Prize Agents were appointed to assess the property moveable and immovable, the officials were prohibited to act independently and even the army was denied of their right to plunder the city which they had captured. The system had many loopholes and it was next to impossible for the Government to keep a check on every official. Nonetheless, the Government had made huge profits and the total Prize money was never disclosed in public, leading to criticism from various corners.

Clearance, Confiscation and Compensations

After the city was captured, it was evacuated and all the residents were drawn out of the walled city since it was a necessity to execute the plans of the British in the city. The Governor General ordered that the authorities should proceed to demolish all the fortifications in and around Delhi. The authorities decided to demolish all the permanent or temporary settlements around the fort, making a clear area of 400 yards around the Fort. The authorities had many plans to utilize this open space in front of the fort, like a plan to construct a new staying bungalow at this station. A plan was proposed to utilize the ground in front of the palace and in the rear of the Ellenborough tank which was proposed to be cleared away for the purpose of procuring a suitable site. The alarming sanitary conditions around the fort were also described as the reason for the clearance, and it was also motivated by military and strategic reasons. The British planned to mount the heavy guns on the Lahore and Delhi Gate of the Palace and a clear ground was to be given as a musketry range to the soldiers. Some had even stated beautification of the city as the reason for demolition as well.[24] The reasons might be many and the British might have wished to gain many motives out of it, but for the people of Delhi, the clearing and demolition became a symbol of humiliation and the hardship they had to face during the period of the British suppression.

The entire plan of demolition and clearance was made with a target in mind, the Muslims of the city.Since the entire community was accused of treason, therefore, none of the policies whether of demolition or compensation were made keeping their well being in mind. Most of the area under the clearance plan was occupied by the Muslims of the city. Initially, the plan of clearing the ground in front of the Fort covered the entire area of Dareeba, it also contained the shops of some of wealthiest merchants of the city. Since their support was crucial for the Government, financially and politically, the plan was revised and the new plan was made. The starting of the Dareeba street was decided on to be the boundary of the clearance plan to leave the entire street intact.[25] It was stated that "the demolition should stop short of Dareeba and that street, for the preservation of which a large part of the community, which had remained loyal to us and the even retention of the street in no way affects the security of the palace and its garrison. [26] Against the demolition of the Dareeba, the *punchs* of the city of Delhi wrote several petitions to the government. The Superintendent Commander of Delhi found the petition the most reasonable one. The petition said that the whole Hindu population was interested in the Dareeba, not just those who would be the direct sufferers from the proposed demolitions. Another petition stated that the actual value of the property at Dareeba was around a crore of rupees, however, the estimation made by the British was only 10 lakhs. [27]

The religious sentiments of the Hindus and the Christians were also kept in mind during the demolition. The officials were ordered not to injure or demolish any Hindu temple existing within the area of the proposed plan of the Governor General.[28] The Roman Catholic Church, situated in the garden of the Begum Samru was ordered to be left intact, the wall around the garden was ordered to be demolished.[29] However, the Akbarabadi mosque was demolished by the authorities as it was accused as the centre of the '*Jihadis'* activities.

Initially, for the establishment of the main guard of the British, a site was selected in Chandni Chowk, but the Commissioner refused the idea stating that it would be too close to the palace and that rest of the city would go unchecked if they both were maintained at such close proximity. The area also consisted of Hindu population and the Government did not want to demolish their houses and pay heavy compensations to them. Therefore three other sites were suggested for the purpose by the Commissioner of Delhi. These locations were of the predominantly Muslim population, like Jama Masjid, Fatehpuri

Masjid and the Bhojla Pahadi. The Executive Engineer was keen to convert the Jama Masjid into the gun house due to its location being situated on an elevated platform, but the late Lt. Governor had already intimated officially the intention of the Government to restore it to Muslims when it was no longer required as quarters for the Sikh regiment. The Fatehpuri mosque was claimed unsuitable for similar reasons, but Bhojla Pahadi was considered for the gun house since the location was apt to have a clear view of the city and it was located in the area densely inhabited by the Muslims and orders were given to estimate the ground for the further demolitions.[30]

The interests of Muslims of Delhi were neither given any importance, nor while giving compensation for the loss of their properties. In fact, destroying a Muslim area became very convenient for the British due to the orders that the disloyal owners were not entitled to compensation, and since the entire community was treated as a 'traitor' it became considerably less expensive for the British to acquire the erstwhile Muslim properties.[31]Here the term Muslim Community might not designate each and every single person belonging to the faith, since there were sections who remained loyal to the British and earned favors from them by their act of treason towards the people, but here the term designated to the majority of the Muslim who suffered due to their religious affiliations. It's just not a personal assessment the Archival records, in general, use term like 'traitors' for the Muslim population without making any distinction.

The process of clearance and compensation was also taken up in a systematic manner, eventually resulting in a lot of profit for the Government. All the houses within the circle to be cleared were valued by a native surveyor, and finally the Deputy Commissioner was appointed to settle appeals on the spot. A register was made of all the demolished houses and their value, and a ticket was given to each house owner. A sufficient number of confiscated houses in other parts of the city to cover the value of the demolished houses represented by tickets were to be put up to auction and tickets holders were to be allowed to pay in their tickets at par in payment wholly or in part for houses they might purchase at the auctions. These tickets used to contain the following information:[32]

<table>
<tr><td colspan="8">General Number</td></tr>
<tr><td colspan="8">Ticket of value of demolished house</td></tr>
<tr><td colspan="8">Situated ____________________________________</td></tr>
<tr><td colspan="8">Dated 14th July 1860</td></tr>
<tr><td rowspan="2">No.</td><td rowspan="2">No in Register</td><td rowspan="2">Name of House</td><td rowspan="2">Owners name in census Register</td><td rowspan="2">Name of Ticket Holder</td><td colspan="2">Value</td><td rowspan="2">Remarks</td></tr>
<tr><td>Material</td><td>Ground</td></tr>
</table>

But problems started to rise as the process of ticket distribution started. As the tickets were issued, they began to change hands by endorsement without stamps. They were, at first, sold at 75 percent discount. In July 1860, a meeting of some of the influential native gentlemen of Delhi, who were the ticket holders, were convened. The 48 person present, represented only a small minority of the ticket holders.

The estimated value of the houses demolished as represented by tickets was Rupees 6,10,399, in the meeting it was decided by the Deputy Commissioner that out of the entire confiscated property in Delhi, valued at about 15 lakhs, the ticket holders should select property valued at Rupees 6,92,585 (being rupees 82,186 in excess of the value of the houses destroyed).It was also decided that the government should sell this property through auction and that the ticket holders should bear the losses or share the profit on the sale of this property. Those tickets holders who chose to purchase were guaranteed against loss under 50 percent, but those who did not were to run all the risks.

Several objections were raised by the ticket holders regarding the division of the profit as well as about the entire process of judgment to decide the claims of the tickets. The objections were dismissed by stating that

> "the objectors are not the original householders but speculators in tickets. No property of theirs was taken up for public purposes. The houses were destroyed long before they had any interest in the present case. They did not buy houses they bought tickets which gave them no right to property destroyed, but to whatever the ticket might fetch in the future arrangement. Therefore, they have no right to complain of the manner in which the houses were valued.

Even if the value put on them had been merely nominal the interests and rights of the ticket speculators would be in no way affected."

Mr. Thornton showed in his report that even if the arrangement of the objectors should be admitted, the total profit, which the ticket holders would receive would be only Rupees 1,51,559 instead of Rupees 1,76,410 which had been offered by the British Government.[33]

The entire process of confescation and compensation got so controvertial that its critism was raised within the official circles. The Officiating Advocate General J. Graham raised the question of whether the property, at the time of its appropriation belonged to the State by virtue of any act of Confiscation in war or did it remain in the hands of the former proprietor? Further, he argued, it was not improbable that all the inhabitants of Delhi, who had deserted the city at the time of its capture were not guilty of acts of rebellion.[34]

Total amount of ticket issued including reissues to cover mortgages etc.	8,77,000	
Value of property assigned in lieu of compensation		
1. Confiscated house property after reduction of estimate and including 1,24,000 Rs. Worth of forfeited compensation tickets for railway clearances	7,34,633. 12	
2. Fines on rebel villages in deposit	1,05,853.12.3	
3. Miscellaneous confiscated property sold to close account	36,512.7.9	
Total Rupees	8,77,000	
Profits Declared		
1. On selected property sold 3,12,336.12.0as per reduced estimate	47,726.7	Of this amount 18,947.3.0 were actual 28,779.4.0 imaginary
2. On Balance including I. Property substituted for the selected property, including the railway compensation tickets II. Property added when the 2nd batch of demolitions took place III. Fines on rebel villages IV. The portion of the selected property subsequently sold	1,25,683.11.7	Of this amount, 50,772.8.0 were actual profits the rest granted under Commissioner's sanction.
Total	1,73410.2.7	

The discriminatory attitude of the government towards the Muslims continued while decided on the compensation as well. While clearing the area of Darya Ganj, where most of the properties were in the possession of the Muslims owners and were eligible for the compensation, but as they were Muslims they were only allowed to claim the compensation after paying a fine for their 'treacherous' behavior towards the government. These discriminatory rules reduced the share of the Muslims in the payable amount of compensation drastically. The deducted amount was to be used to 'compensate' the Europeans who had suffered during the rebellion.[35]

All these policies and processes were being implemented in the city when most of its population was not even allowed to enter it. The Muslims were allowed to enter Delhi much after the others, as an additional punishment from the Government due to the assumption of the entire community as their enemy. When they came back they came to realize that it was no more the city they had called their own. Their businesses/jobs were gone, their houses were either demolished, sold or simply captured by the people who were allowed to enter the city before them. The harsh attitude of the Government directed at the Muslim inhabitants also left no other legal avenue for them to challenge any verdicts and actions against them, This group, therefore, took the longest time to get back to their normal life and even after decades, these nobles, traders, shop-keepers, artist and workers could not regain their original status and glory in Delhi.[36]

Notes

1. John Henry Yonge (ed.) (hereafter Yonge), *A Narrative of the Siege of Delhi with an Account of Mutiny of Ferozpur in 1857* by Charles John Griffiths, London, 1910, p. 226.
2. For a heart-wrenching account of the trial of the Bahadur Shah and its day by day proceeding ref. K.C. Yadav (ed.) *Delhi in 1857*, Vol. I The Trial of Bahadur Shah, Gurgaon, 1980.
3. Delhi Archives, Commissioner's office, Delhi Division, letter to the Secretary to Chief Commissioner, Punjab, from Major Grant, Commissioner of Delhi Field Force, dated 14th November 1857, file no. 11.
4. Delhi Archives, Commissioner's office, Delhi Division, letter from the Secretary to Chief Commissioner, Punjab to C.B. Saunders, Commissioner, Delhi, dated, 17th November 1857, file no. 11.

5. Delhi Archive, Commissioner's office, Delhi Division, letter from R. H Davies Esquire, Secretary to the Government, Punjab and its dependencies, to C.B. Saunders esquire, Commissioner and Supdt., Delhi Division, dated 9th May 1859, file no. 64. See also, file No. 18, dated 16th June 1858.
6. Delhi Archive, Commissioner's office, Delhi Division, letter dated 27thJanuary 1859, from R. H Davies Esquire, Secretary to the Government, Punjab and its dependencies, to the Secretary to Government of India, Foreign Department, 3rd March 1859, file no. 46.
7. Delhi Archive, Commissioner's office, Delhi Division, dated 9th April 1859, file no. 47.
8. Delhi Archives, Commissioner's office, Delhi Division, letter from the Secretaryto Chief Commissioner, Punjab to C.B. Saunders, Commissioner, Delhi, dated, 17th November 1857, file no. 11.
9. Central Report on the Administration of the Punjab Territories from 1856-57 to 1857-58, Inclusive together with a brief account of the administration of the Delhi Territory, from the reoccupation of Delhi, up to May 1858, Section XIII (additional) Administration of Delhi Territory, para. 128-130.
10. NAI, HDPB, 24th September 1858. Nos. 38-42, 67-71.
11. NAI, FD, Political Consultation, 2 July 1858, no. 145-153 & K.W., letter to G.F. Edmonston, Secretary to the Government of India with the Governor General, from Richard Temple, Secretary to the Chief Commissioner, dated 9th March 1858, Camp Delhi.
12. NAI, FD, Political Consultation, 2 July 1858, no. 145-153 & K.W., letter to G.F. Edmonston, Secretary to the Government of India with the Governor General, from Richard Temple, Secretary to the Chief Commissioner, dated 9th March 1858, Camp Delhi.
13. Memoranda on the Native States of India 1905, furnished by the Local Political Officers, Simla, 1905.
14. Yonge, p. 227.
15. The idea of unhindered looting was considered like a poison which only led to the corrupt practices in the army. In the initial years of Company in India, it used to fight wars with the collaboration of the native powers, therefore controlling the army became a necessity. Therefore, the army used to strictly observe the rule that Company's troops may plunder only in the cases of the actual assault of a place by storm, that as the fort or city in question had fallen, the army had no claim to any treasure contained in there. Due to the subordinate position in the initial years and due to the reasons to maintain the discipline in the army the officials tried to avoid the whole notion of Prize money. Therefore instant of prize money Company used to accept an amount to be distributed among the soldier by the authority *A Calender of Indian State Papers (Secret Series),* Fort William, 1774-75, Calcutta, 1864, Consultations, 1174 Volume H. 1, pp. 331, 334-5, 339, Vol H. 2 pp. 701, 707, Vol. H. 3, p 710.

16. After the order from the Governor General, a private soldier of the 60th Rifles, inspired by the most exquisite sense of humor as well as of bitter satire, wrote upon the walls of the palace "Delhi was taken and India saved for 36 rupees 10 *annas*. In reference to this order the *Times* had a leading article recommending Delhi army to bring an action against the Government for the payment of the prize. Yonge p. 230-1.
17. Yonge, p. 229.
18. Yonge, p. 238-9.
19. Yonge, p. 240.
20. Delhi Archives, Commissioner's office, Delhi Division, dated 31st December 1857, no. 2. Also see Delhi Archives, Commissioner's office, Delhi Division, dated 17th March 1858, no. 2.
21. The Commissioner of Delhi raised an objection to the distribution of the Hamid Ali Khan's property among his captors. Delhi Archives, Commissioner's Office, dated 1st December 1857, no. 6.
22. NAI, HDPB, 25th March 1859. No. 58, circular no. 51 of 1859, letter from E.C. Bayly, officiating Secretary to Government, NWP, dated Allahabad, 14th February 1859. See also, NAI, HDJB, 18th March 1859, no. 12, Circular no. 8 of 1859, from E.C. Bayly, officiating Secretary to Government, NWP, to Commissioners of divisions, Allahabad, dated, 11th February 1859.
23. NAI, HDJB, 8th October 1858, no. 12, a notification from Fort William, Foreign Department, dated 25th July 1854.
24. Delhi Archives, Commissioner's office, Delhi Division, dated 18th January 1859, no.1. See also Delhi Archives, Commissioner's office, Delhi Division, dated 22nd Jan 1859, no. 4.
25. Delhi Archives, Commissioner's office, Delhi Division, dated 28th July 1860, no. 75.
26. Delhi Archives, Commissioner's office, Delhi Division, dated 24th February 1860, no. 31. see also Delhi Archives, Commissioner's office, Delhi Division, dated 1st March 1860 File no 33, Delhi Archives, Commissioner's office, Delhi Division, dated 13th July 1860, no.72.
27. Delhi Archives, Commissioner's office, Delhi Division, dated 28th March 1860, no. 49A.
28. Delhi Archives, Commissioner's office, Delhi Division, dated 11th February 1860, no. 30.
29. Delhi Archives, Commissioner's office, Delhi Division, dated 2nd July 1860, no. 70.
30. Delhi Archives, Commissioner's office, Delhi Division, dated 24th March 1859, no. 7 and Delhi Archives, Commissioner's office, Delhi Division, dated 28th April 1859, no. 8.
31. Delhi Archives, Commissioner's office, Delhi Division, dated 3rd June 1860, no. 68.

32. Delhi Archives, Commissioner's office, Delhi Division, dated21st August 1863, no. 78.
33. For the entire detail on the ticket system and the objections raised by their holders see, Delhi Archives, Commissioner's office, Delhi Division, dated 15 October 1864, no. 92-B.
34. Delhi Archives, Commissioner's office, Delhi Division, dated 20th June 1864, no. 91.
35. Delhi Archives, Commissioner's office, Delhi Division, dated 21st May 1859, no. 15.
36. One Haji Qutabuddin resident of Delhi proposed to the Government in reference to the mosque at Daryaganj at present used for the Commissariat bakery. He had a sum of money at his disposal to be expended for religious purposes; and he wishes to apply part of this if he can obtain the sanction of the government, to the restoration of the above mosque. He was ready to supply funds, to a reasonable extent for constructing a new bakery entirely free of cost to the government if the government on their part cancels the confiscation under which the mosque became a property of the government and make the mosque over to him. *Delhi Archives, Commissioner's office,* Delhi Division, dated 1st February 1872, no. 25.

Chapter - 9

The Battle for Delhi, Meos and the Great Uprising:

A study of Anti-British Resistance during 1857

—Dr. Zakir Husain
Assistant Director,
National Archives of Infia

The spirit of resistance has been ingrained in the Meo community for nearly a millennium. The Meos of north India– one of the largest Muslim population in south Asia endured a succession of regimes from the Arab conquest in the eighth century to the establishment of Turkish rule, the Mughal Empire, the Rajput kingdoms and an era of British Imperialism. Interestingly, without abandoning their religious and ethnic identity, the Meos developed an independent tradition that enabled them to challenge state-formation for centuries through which they were able to successfully retain a degree of cultural sovereignty. However, their quest for autonomy was stigmatised, even criminalised as histories written by the ruling elite transformed ethnic prejudice into historical fact.'[1]

Although S.N. Sen in his work *Eighteen Fifty Seven* has asserted that with the exception of Awadh, the 1857 rebellion did not reflect national sentiments yet, in K.C. Yadav's words, 'perhaps such a great historian was unaware of Mewat otherwise he would not have argued, thus, as Mewat was equally imbibed with the feelings of national fervour where pitched battles from village to village and street to street were fought against the English'.

This spirit of rebellion that began from Ambala, subsequently spread from Meerut to Mewat on 13 May 1857. Mewat did not have *taluqdars* or *rajas* and the people had to rely on the *chaudhuris* of their 12 *pals,* among whom Sharafuddin was the leading figure. Firozpur Jhirka, Doha Rawli, etc., were controlled by Sa 'adat Khan who was one of the prominent leaders while Sadruddin played a pivotal role in Mahun, Tigaon, Pinangwan, etc. Firoz Shah Mewati was a very courageous *Chaudhuri* who exercised tremendous influence on Sohna, Taoru and Raisena. Since Delhi was the real centre of inspirational leadership where the Mughal emperor lived, Alaf Khan was the Meo Chaudhuri. Religious leaders also played a prominent role in the resistance, among whom was Maulana Mehrab Ali Khan Mewati who inspired the people to fight against the British by personally moving from place to place, enthusing them by distributing amulets *(tawiz)* of victory.

The Meo Chaudhuris fought in collaboration with people of different castes and religions, considering them of equal courage and determination.

Thakur, Mina, Meo aur Gujar, Jat, Ahir
Yan sab dharti pootan ki mardani tasir

Eventually, the revolutionary fervour spread to Gurgaon on 13 May 1857. Other than a few police stations, police checkposts and custom-houses here was little else for the town to boast of. Since the police stations, police check posts and custom-houses also had positions occupied by the English officials, these vacant places became easy targets of the Meo ire. They were set ablaze leaving no signs of the British Government by the end of May 1857.'[2] Although the Meo resistance against the British'[3] and its agents was quite strong'[4] yet the *khanzadas,* (who were originally Meos and since Humayun's time separated their identity and later served as English agents) or the British loyalists were defeated at Nuh.'[5]

The extreme active role of the Meos when the great uprising of 1857 began, placed the English on guard, eventually compelling them to admit their apprehensions.'[6] The situation was so favourable for the Mughal emperor that the Meos were able to establish an independent administration, which yielded opportunities for huge collection of revenues. Accordingly, the Emperor got General Mohammad Bakht Khan to issue a *shuqqa* to the *zamindars* of Mewat, ordering them to collect and gather the men for the expulsion of the enemies (i.e. the British). It was also reported that 80 horsemen marched to Gurgaon and were able to snatch from the English a cannon and four camels loaded with tents, killed about 25 Englishmen and seriously wounded 5-7 of them as they brought these items for their *morchas* (entrenchments). These *sawars* were dispatched by the Commander-in-Chief who, however, recorded their strength to be around 200 horsemen.'[7]

The loyalty of the Meos to the Mughal crown can be gauged from the contents of a representation written on behalf of the fighters of Mewat on 13 August 1857 to the Mughal Commander-in-Chief (in addition to several others) stating that hundreds of fighters of Mewat region for several months had been sacrificing their lives without receiving any thing in exchange. The representation also stated that if no justice was done to them, the fighters would return to their homes.

This is, however, an established fact that none of participants except for the Meos fought without yearning for a salary, as is evident from 8000 documents of the Press List of the *Mutiny Papers,* 1857, Imperial Records Department, Kolkata, 1921. However, a translation of the representation by their leader Alaf Khan of Raisena (Mewat) is given, for a better understanding of the position of the Meos in AD 1857 in Delhi:

Alif (i.e. God)

Submit to the Commander-in -Chief (titles omitted) that we hundreds of fighters of Mewat region who by leaving our families on the divine mercy for several months have been sacrificing our lives at the threshold of the servants of the emperor. While other people who are also present, get their salaries from him, we, instead of getting food are depending upon our own blood leaving many people martyred, hungry and thirsty. It is known to all and sundry that we have been making and utmost sacrifice. But in spite of assigning the allowance for the maintenance of a horse, i.e. ₹ 25 in cash which amounted to its sale price, it has been withdrawn due to the allegation of the irreligious Gujars. Notwithstanding several representations of Alaf Khan, the leader of our *qafila* (carvan) you have never paid any heed to it, merely due to the allegation that we are considered as fraudulent and were arrested unjustifiably on the way. You have made no investigations till date. This is extremely contrary to justice and fair play because everyone has to appear before the Almighty Lord on the Day of Resurrection. Since this temporary life is a God-gifted one, we are yearning for justice, otherwise after this representation and another one to you, we, shall leave to our respective homes. Our justice shall be done on the Day of Judgement. If you take cognizance (of the situation) this is all in short which we have represented to you was represented by the people of Mewat, dated 13th August 1857.

Post script: In a nutshell we do not receive our maintenance allowance. If justice is done to us then it shall be appreciated, otherwise, after representing to you, we, shall proceed to our homes.'[8]

The slogan to kill the Englishmen was raised at Ambala, subsequently at Meerut and also spread to Delhi from where it went upto Alwar. The Meo community, however, did not give up their struggle, striving to liberate Alwar, Delhi, Rewari and Mathura from

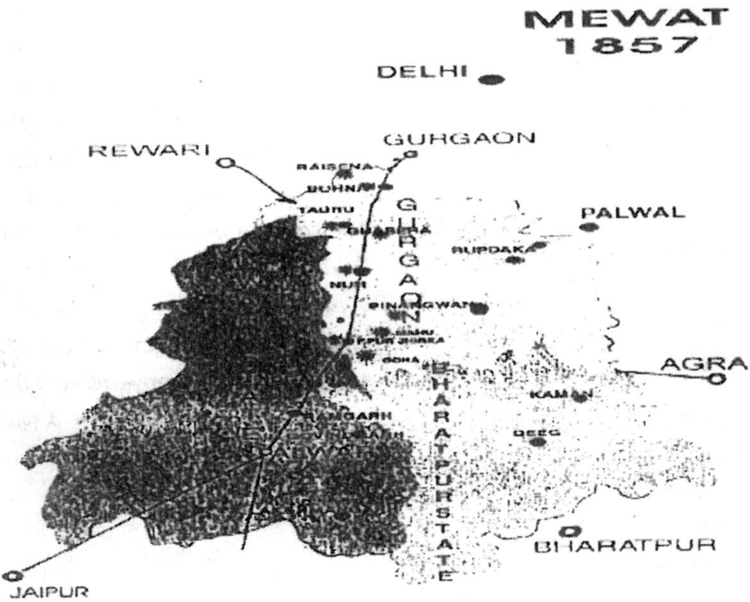

British. In retaliation, they were brought to the gallows and their lands were confiscated by the English.'[9]

The English oppression heightened 'national sentiment.' Their campaigns spread in the villages and towns of Mewat including Raisena, Tauru, Sohna and its surroundings, Nuh and its environs as also villages like Hatheen, Kot, Utawar, Roop Raka, Firozpur Jhirka (where emperor Babur stayed overnight and Nawab Shamsuddin Khan established his headquarters) Doha Rawli and Naugawan and its suburbs like Nageena, Pinangwan, Ponhana, Hodal, Mahun, Cheetora, Nihareeka, etc. Pitched battles were fought between the Meos and the English army and police. Surprisingly enough they occasionally also fought the military contingent of the Maharaja of Jaipur and the English army at Tauru. Meanwhile, Rao Tula Ram on the pretext of streamlining his administration was allegedly involved in their chastisement and complained to the Mughal emperor that the Meos were spreading lawlessness. At Nuh, the English army and the local *khanzadas* fought against the Meos in support of their English masters. The Meos also bravely fought the military contingent of the Maharaja of Alwar. A contemporary account reveals that the Meos even threatened to attack a particular village that was sheltering English officials.

Due to the mutiny of the sepoys of Bharatpur and Alwar, which perhaps largely consisted of Meos, the English officials had to flee from Hodal under the command of Ford who reached Sohna on 9th June 1857 and met Captain Eden's contingent who fought against the Meos at Tauru. They also destroyed Tauru, Sohna, Firozpur Jhirka, Ponhana and Nuh where the *khanzadas* along with the police fought the Meos, many *khanzadas* were put to death. Though Ford returned to Gurgaon on 13th October, yet the Meos continued to encounter the English for a long time. Ultimately the Meos were suppressed following the assassination of Ford after which Ghasera, Roop Raka and Mahun were put in order. However Raisena, Sohna and Nuh remained the chief centres of the freedom struggle. On the pretext of a complaint from his English supporters, Ford visited Raisena near Sohna and Bhandsi in the Aravali valley. Here too the Meos continued their fight, but many were left dead. It is also stated that Ford, the Deputy Commissioner of Gurgaon owing to the murder of his sister in Delhi set ablaze every village that came on his way upto Sohna, besides killing old and young near Raisena. Firozshah Mewati raised slogans to restrain such an oppression due to which a large number of people came forward and attacked Ford's forces. Stiff resistance took place in which two officers and numerous sepoys were killed. Villagers armed with staff, spears, etc., defeated forces carrying cannons and guns. A Meo poet has described the scene thus:

Raisena ke Meo ko bado jagayo deen
Khakkey marey dedso kursi khali kari teen

Since the struggle of 1857 was vehemently fought at numerous places, the Meos strove hard against the British at Raisena killing many Englishmen in this battle. A Meo poet has described this event:

Bangla mein man na lage suni dekhi sej
Raisena ka gor mein dekha bina sis angrej

Mirza Ghalib too has described the situation of Mewat as, 'In the land of Sohna and Nuh, the Mewatis have created such a disturbance that one can imagine that the mad have broken their chains'.[10]

In Nuh, which had become a centre of resistance, the Meos fought vigourously against the English army, police and *khanzadas*. After 1857, the *khanzadas* being strong supporters of the English complained against the Meos. Due to this in 1858, 52 Meos (out of which 12 hailed from Adbar, 4 belonged to Shahpur Nangli and the remaining 36 were inhabitants of Nuh, were hanged to death at the instigation of Khairullah alias Khaira, a *khanzada*. Simultaneously, all records were destroyed due to the vested interests of British authorities. However, a penalty of ₹ 3,500 was also imposed upon them and the *zamindaris* were given to their spies or traitors in 1858.

The resumption of the *zamindaris* with the details of re-allotment are given in the revenue settlement of 1877 of *qasba* Nuh under the title, *'Buniyad-i Husul-i Haqiqat-o Hal-i Taqsimi- Awwalin Arazi'*. However, Khairullah, *numberdar* of the *qasba* had stated that about a century ago 'we, the *khanzadas* had appointed their ancestor Prithi Meo and settled him as watchman by assigning him some land.' Thereafter, when the *khanzadas* became weak and helpless the Meos who inhabited this *qasba* controlled the land. Until 1857 the Meos controlled the *biswadari* (i.e. *zamindan).* In 1857 the Meos plundered this *qasba,* killing a large number of people. After suppressing the Meo tumultuousness the community was excluded from the *biswadari* in accordance with the order of the British Government and their *biswadari* awarded to the *khanzades.* The facts of the first owners of the land who had obtained it either by purchase or as a gift is given as follows: Out of half of the 42 shares of the Thakurs, the Brahmins, Jats, Meos and the *khanzadas* in *Samvat* 1405/AD 1348 (rectified *Samvat* 1413/ AD 1356) occupied it thus: *Patti* Brahmins (8 shares), *Patti* Jats (7 shares), *Patti khanzadas* (15 shares), *Patti* Meos (12 shares).

Till the time of Morrison the revenue was paid according to this division. After the Mutiny the rights of the Meos were resumed and granted to the *khanzadas* who were assigned 27 shares.

Consequent upon the re-establishment of British hegemony the village of Raisena and adjoining villages of Nunnerha, Mohammadpur, Sapanki, Haryahera, Bainsi, Harmathla, etc., which were under the *zamindari* of the Meos were resumed by the British Government. These were given as a reward to the Rajputs of Bhondsi and the Kayasths of Sohna where the Meos still serve as cultivators. The Gurgaon *District Gazetteer* furnished the British line of action adopted in regard to Mewat in AD 1857. We also come across certain official reports from camp Hatheen despatched on 19th November 1857 by Saundaras summarising the confidential reports received through the local officers of Sohna, Hatheen and Palwal that several thousand Meos, with several hundred horsemen had assembled at Kot and Roop Raka. They had been incessantly attacking Hatheen for three days so that by ruining that village of the Rajputs, who were supporting the English, they could attack Palwal so as to plunder the government treasury there. A considerable police infantry had been left in charge of Lt. Grant for the protection of Sohna whereafter he marched to Ballabhgarh. The Meo villages of Pachanka, Gohpur, Chilli, Malpuri, Roop Raka, Kot, Utawar, Mithaka, Khalluka, Guraksar and Jhanda were set on fire. Stiff resistance took place at Roop Raka. When the Meos bombarded the English, they repulsed the attack by killing 400 Meos out of 3550 soldiers of the Meo army. The British, according to their own assessment had fewer casualities than the Meos. Moreover, the villages and properties of the Meos were also set ablaze. However, some friendly

Jat villages came to the rescue of the English, saving them from the clutches of the Meos. Interestingly, the Meos were intelligent enough to give shelter to a Mughal prince and his family as a token of gratitude as was the case of Mirza Shahzor.

Fazl-i-Haq Khairabadi, the author of *Saur Hindiya* remained in Alwar district of Mewat region from 1855 to 1857 where he further revolutionised the Meos. In support of the Mughal cause, Major Hur Khan along with 300 Meo sepoys accompanied by Prince Mohammad Azim, after seizing the fort of Hissar and ₹ 1,70,0007 of the district treasury marched towards Delhi by defeating the English army stationed at Hansi and Rohtak. It was at Rohtak where Major Hur Khan died fighting the English while some of his Meo sepoys alongside Prince Mohammad Azim escaped to Rewari to join hands with Rao Tula Ram. At Rewari, Majlis Khan a Meo leader in collaboration with Rao Tula Ram was ready to fight the English. Even the celebrated gunner Kale Khan who hailed from Raisena was originally posted at Jhansi, from where he reached Delhi and was deputed at Kashmiri Gate which he vigourously defended for three days. From here he escaped to Raisena and died a victorious death while the English army was defeated at Raisena. An outline of Mewat in 1857 does indicate that Delhi and its neighbourhood Mewat region had become the most rebellious belt against the British onslaught.

In October 1857 Brigadier General Shower was despatched with a large force to supress the Meos. Armed with cannons, horsemen and infantrymen he encountered stiff resistance in each village. An English official writes about a brave Meo who was surrounded in a mountainous valley where he constantly strove to save himself from uninterrupted firing until he was hit by a bullet. Showers of bullets killed many Meos while Firoz Shah Mewati was also martyred. Though Brigadier General Shower left a trail of destruction in many villages, yet he could not demoralise the Meos. However, a few days later he returned to Delhi. In the beginning of November 1857 another military force was dispatched to Mewat under the command of Colonel Gerrard who oppressed the areas around Sohna for several days. He martyred 150 Meos at village Ghasera and destroyed it together with other villagers. hereafter he marched towards Ahirwal.'[11] A contingent under the command of Captain Durrmmund was sent to Hatheen towards the close of November 1857. The Meos fought against him under the command of Sadruddin, the Meo leader of Pinangwan, where due to heavy firing 400 of them were killed. Thereafter, the English under Captain Ramsay's command fought against Sadruddin who again courageously resisted them. However, the English emerged victorious and numerous Meos were martyred, including Sadruddin's son. The English forces faced heavy resistance in the village of Mahun where they could enter only after killing 70 Meos. An English officer expressed shock as to how so small a number of men could do so much. Notwithstanding the fact that Mahun was set on fire, the inhabitants of Mahun still remember their heroes thus:

Mero Mahun Tigaon gaon jahan ka beer ladaka
Kat diyo Angrej likha gaya naam salaka

A fierce battle was fought under the command of Sa'adat Khan who was martyred in the clash at Doha. Though several villages were ruined, yet apparently, no peace was established in Mewat till December 1857. At least 875 Meos sacrified their lives, out of whom 313 were identified while 30 villages were gutted.'[12] Since the Mughal emperor Bahadur Shah II was well aware of the sincerity and fidelity of the Meos he issued the following orders for the collection of revenues in Mewat:

> *Hukumnamah* to the *Chaudhuris*, revenue-contractors *Qanungos* and *Numberdars* of the villages of *parganas* Hodal and Ponhana: Since Saiyid Musharraf Ali has been appointed for the collection of revenues (*tehsildari*) of the townships of Hodal and Ponhana it is hereby written to them that they should wholeheartedly comply with the *tehsildar* (revenue collector's) orders and they should make utmost endeavour in the work of revenue collection and being well-wishers, they should consider it the cause of their favour as any carelessness shall be injurious to them. They should know injunction (in the matter). Written on 23rd *Zilhijja* AH 1273 (25th July 1857) *(Mutiny Papers,* Collection number 151, Serial numbers 4, 5).
>
> The emperor to Saiyid Musharraf Ali (titles omitted): Since he has been appointed for the realisation, etc., of *parganas* Ponhana and Hodal to the office of the *tehsildar* (revenue collector), it is

obligatory upon him that the administration of the *parganas* should be done so excellently that the work of the Government is done properly and the inhabitants of the *pargana* should not in any way become disheartened. They should help in streamlining the arrangement of *thanedari* (policing) for the revenue collection as no mismanagement should occur. In view of their well-wishing of the government, they should consider themselves worthy of favour and he can employ as much *sawars* (horsemen) as he deems suitable. He should engage them in government duty. He should remit their salaries from the amount of the revenue collections. He should despatch the balance of the revenues to His Majesty. He should consider injunction (in the matter). Written on 25th July 1857 *(Mutiny Papers,* Collection number 151, Serial number 6).

Instances, such as these indicate the mutual co-operation between the Meos and Rao Tula Ram. Rao Tula Ram succeeded in procuring an imperial *farman* (order) through the intercession of General Mohammad Bakht Khan, granting him Rewari along with two more *parganas* (translation given in the Appendix). However it was a political gimmick that on 17th July 1857 Rao Tula Ram represented to the Mughal emperor regarding certain villages, where according to him, miscreants frequently created disturbances. To chastise them, he had recruited 4000 to 5000 cavalry, yet in other areas adjoining his territory, the Meo and the Gujars continued to plunder. For this, Rao Tula Ram sought the imperial intervention by provision of 1000 muskets and 4-5 cannons from the English magazine, along with a platoon to put in place imperial administration there so as to check anyone indulging in tumultuousness and confrontational activities.'[13] Since the original *shuqqa* was sent to Tula Ram, we can refer for its contents only to an undated representation to the Mughal emperor sent by him wherein he acknowledged the *shuqqa* to the effect that since village Sidhrawli was among the *tuyul* (*jagir*) no one from the Meo community could plunder it. Furthermore when the *zamindars* of Sidhrawli were to collect the revenue they were supposed to deliver the collected amount to His Majesty. Tula Ram submitted that he was already well aware that since village Sidhrawli was the royal *tuyul* he did not occupy it, and in compliance with the royal orders stationed the officers of his army one kuroh (i.e. 3.60 kms.) away from Sidhrawli. He issued strict injunctions that none of the miscreants could seize and plunder the inhabitants of Sidhrawli, while strict instructions were issued to the *zamindars* to collect and escort the stipulated amount to the Mughal emperor.'[14] In yet another undated representation Rao Tula Ram also insinuated that the Meos had taken shelter on a mountain where they had made an entrenchment *(imorchei,)*'[15] This is however, identical to Mirza Asadullah Khan Ghalib's description:

> Tula Ram, a miscreant has created disturbance in Rewari, thereafter he has joined the Meos due to the devilish guidance. This gang is separately fighting in that desert and the mountain against the rulers of the world (i.e. the British government) as if the Indian soil has become everywhere a factory of wind and strong fire.'[16]

However, in an undated representation Rao Tula Ram not only submitted an account of the money on 10th May 1857 and the amount collected since but also pleaded to the emperor that he was uninterruptedly engaged in administering Mewat. He also stated that the administration of *pargana* Rewari, together with other annexed *parganas* yielding about ₹ 2,00,000 as revenues were an imperial gift by way of a *jagir* to his ancestors and that following the establishment of the British administration his forefathers were granted a *jaidad* (personal property) worth ₹ 1,00,000 in perpetuity. He also sought permission to streamline the administration of Tauro, Sohna, Nuh, Palwal, Hodal and Hatheen administering the above mentioned *mahals* (fiscal units) and collect ₹ 24,00,000 to remit to the imperial treasury as he had already raised an army of 4000-6000 and the cavalry and infantry according to Bahadur Shah's *shuqqa* of 1st *Shawal* AH 1273 which was sufficient for the annexed *parganas* together with the region of Mewat.'[17] In an undated entreaty Tula Ram recognised the civil rebellion of the Meos who were antagonistic to the assignment of some Meo villages in *pargana* Bhora to Tula Ram due to which they refused to accept his overlordship, declined to remit the revenues and even complained to the Mughal emperor. Their complaint against Tula Ram was seriously entertained as he was admonished for oppressing any victim by General Mohammad Bakht Khan.'[18] However, an in-extenso translation of the a document can clarify certain ambiguities in regard to the confrontation and collaboration of Rao Tula Ram and the Meos:

> Through the servants of His Majesty (titles omitted) thankfully acknowledging the receipt of the special *shuqqa* directing this applicant for streamlining the administration of District Mewat and waiting upon him presently. Submits that since the *khanazad* (son of a noble, i.e. Tula Ram) from the very day lawlessness and disturbance has spread is busy in administering this region while during this period the mischievousness of the refractory elements of the Meos and the Gujars has spread every where for the destruction of this region particularly the city of Rewari. But due to the labour and exersion of the *khanazad* (Tula Ram) who is gallantly facing them owing to the unfailing support of His Majesty's servants, has been able to protect Rewari in every way by the grace of the Almighty Lord. The aforesaid mischief mongers who are intentionally and forcibly indulging in plundering with impunity in the towns of Firozpur, Ponhana, Nagina, Pinangwan, Tauru etc. of District Gurgaon which they have desolated and they do not shun their uncalled-for activities and every day groups of 10-12,000 men armed with swords, guns, etc., gather from place to place. As soon as this situation is brought to the notice of the devotees they rush there and disperse those shortsighted ones and the miscreants and remain engaged in (such activities). There shall be no peace and calm so long as proper warning and chastisement is not meted out to such recalcitrants. Since the *khanazad* by spending a large amount has recruited 4000-5000 cavalry and infantry for their extermination it is not suitable to leave the city of Rewari unprotected. Assures that soon after the suppression of this tumultuousness he shall wait upon His Majesty. Prays for His Majesty.'[19]

As compared to four modern districts of Gurgaon, Faridabad, Mewat and Palwal, Gurgaon was the only district which encompassed all these others. Since it was also under British control it became the target of attacks of the Meos and other freedom fighters. Mirza Zaheeruddin, the Mughal Commander-in-Chief represented on 6th July 1857 to the Mughal emperor that he was sending a gun and other articles obtained by the plunder of Gurgaon which were to be kept in the storehouse as Mohammad Khan and Ilahi Bakhsh, *risaladars* had marched there with 200 horsemen. However, consequent upon their departure, the *zamindars* of villages of Basaee, Gurgaon, etc., represented to the emperor that the horsemen unjustifiably cannonized the village. The Commander-in -Chief pleaded that the aforesaid horsemen with the *risaladars* (had seized the booty) with extraordinary bravery and courage and by accompanying them with cannon and numerous other items known to them waited on His Majesty which were to be observed and kept in the stores and award them with whatever the emperor thought advisable.'[20] Although Firozpur Jhirka was annexed by the British and its ruler Nawab Shamsuddin Khan was hanged in AD 1836 on the charge of the assassination of the morally corrupt William Fraser, the British Resident at Delhi, his son Nawab Iftikharruddin was arrested in 1857 on the charge of inciting Bahadur Shah to proclaim his authority, for whose arrest even Mirza Ghalib was also accused of.'[21]

Dehli Urdu Akhbar, a weekly newspaper reported that someone who had come from Firozpur Jhirka stated that the Mewatis had created disturbance, had set to fire Nuh and plundered the villages of Nagina, Tauro and Firozpur Jhirka. While the highway was closed, only the poor could traverse the way.'[22] Through the British insinuation, the Raja of Alwar tacitly took over the control of Firozpur Jhirka contrary to the Meo control over Mewat as their tussle against the English was underway not only in Bhopal, Delhi, Haryana but also in Alwar. Alwar, like other areas of Mewat in Haryana formed part of the Mewat region together with Tijara and Bharatpur.'[23] That is why on 7th August 1857 Khwaja Bakhsh reported to Ahmad Husain Khan, Police Officer/ Revenue Collector of Firozpur Jhirka that the gates of Alwar were closed before dawn (probably due to the Meo freedom fighters).'[24] He also reported on 19th August 1857 that disloyal rebels (probably Meos) had again appeared at Badur (Bahadurpur) in Alwar region. He had already supplemented the information on 8th August 1857 that the rebels (i.e. freedom fighters) had arrived at Jaipur from where they intended to proceed to Alwar where no gates were opened except for a window. However, there was no disturbance till date.'[25]

Majlis Khan, (a Meo) along with his contingent had come to the suburbs of Rewari and then left the place.'[26] It is also reported that on 10th August 1857 the Raja of Alwar had arrested some persons whom he wanted to bring to Delhi. He was however, denied permission due to prevailing conditions in Delhi'[27] The Meos created a disturbance in Alwar.'[28] Surprisingly, the conditions of the disloyal (i.e. the Meo) at Jaipur, Tijara and Rewari could be known through such correspondence.'[29] In such a critical situation the Meos from Khanpur Ghasoli were summoned by the Raja of Alwar on 12th August 1857.'[30] There were numerous Meo (fighters) who were supporting the senior Rani while the inhabitants of Alwar were afraid of a backlash against the Muslims.'[31]

Plenty of information can be culled from the English records of the National Archives of India, New Delhi, with regard to the action taken against the Meos after the termination of the war of 1857 in Mewat region. This information not only relates to the confiscation of their *zamindaris* but also their imprisonment, and the unexpected release of some Meos by an English officer. However, since the Meos played crucial role in the events of 1857, they suffered tremendously as several of their villages were confiscated by the British-something which is also evident from the details of Doha that was acquired by Inamullah Khan, son of Aminullah Khan and Mohammad Barkatullah Khan an Alvi Shaikh for a sum of ₹ 2200. The AD 1877 revenue settlement of Doha does mention that it was taken away from the Meos.

Similarly the 1877 revenue settlement of village Raisena also tell us that previously this village belonged to the Meos. Consequent upon their rebellion against the British in 1857 it was resumed and auctioned (*vide* a letter of the Secretary, Government of Punjab, No. 112, dated 12th February 1862 received by the Commissioner, No. 52, dated 20th February 1862, in the public auction in the court of Gurgaon district) which was purchased by Gokul Singh for a sum of ₹ 10037. Accordingly the *zamindari* of the village was in his possession. If one goes through the numerous records concerning the Meos and Mewat, one comes to know about the details of the atrocities perpetuated by the English upon them both in the form of the resumption of their *zamindari* villages as well as in the burning of their villages, besides killing a large number of Meos in 1857.'[32] However, their contribution in the great freedom struggle has not been properly documented and analysed so far.

APPENDIX

[A]

Arzi (representation) of General Mohammad Bakht Khan to the Emperor

For two days the plenipotentiary of Rao Tula Ram, the Chief of Rewari, accompanied with a letter to the *khanazad* (son of a noble, i.e. Mohammad Bakht Khan) has been staying and pleading on behalf of his chief *(hakim)* that my client has procured and brought ₹ 45,000 as *nazr* (offering), for His Majesty as well as has solicited a *farman* (imperial order) for the region of Rewari, etc. Submits to His Majesty that verily this is the advisability of the situation, nay His Majesty has repeatedly stressed that there is no way of obtaining the money. Accordingly I request that he should approve and accept the offering of the aforesaid Rao and by adorning the draft of the *farman* with the big seal *(muhr-i kalan)* which Munshi Khairat Ali, *khanazad* is bringing to His Majesty, he should hand over it to the sincere Munshi while the (letter) of Rao Tula Ram enclosed with this representation shall be brought to His Majesty's notice. The three chiefs of Jhajjar, Neemrana and Patodi shall wait on His Majesty after the approbation and acceptance of the *nazarana* (offering) of the said Rao along with the above mentioned Rao. Submitted for the sake of information as there is a great apprehension in the event of disapproval of the offering of the abovesaid Rao and the grant of a *farman* to him failing which His Majesty shall be responsible (for the consequences). The plenipotentiary of the Rao has thus stated to the well-wishers of His Majesty. Rest is beyond the writer's preview. Petition of Mohammad Bakht, Lord Governor General, dated 31st July 1857 with his seal also calling him Commander-in-Chief of the armies.

[B]

Draft of the *farman* of Bahadur Shah II to Rao Tula Ram

During this auspicious time the sublime imperial order, worthy of compliance, of His Majesty was issued that parganas Rewari, Shahjahanpur and Bhora, all the *asli* (principal) and *dakhli* (additional) villages and the revenues and the transit duties of the city, *qasba* (town) except for the *imlak,* gardens, daily allowances and the perpetual revenues, free grants have been bestowed and gifted by us owing to the sincerity, endeavour, abundance of favour and kindness taking into consideration the oldness of the principality of Rao Tula Ram by the grant of the administration of the realisation of the revenues, settlement of the disputes of the peasantry and the right of the imposition of punishment and revenge. Thus, under the circumstances it is incumbent upon him that he should wholeheartedly comply with His Majesty's death-like order and make utmost efforts in administering and chastising the short- sighted malefactors, thieves and the highwaymen, render fair play and justice according to the sublime Islamic law (*shariat*). It is, therefore, obligatory on the renowned, victorious, noble lineage and sublime princes, powerful ministers, high nobles, kind potentates, revenue collectors effecting economy in government expenditure, clerks of the imperial affairs and administrators of the royal matters to allow the above-mentioned *parganas* permanently in his charge where after to his elder son and likewise forever and in any eventuality relinquish to the family of his ancestors whosoever is closer to him and they should perpetually remain busy in the continuance of the sublime imperial order and they should keep it exempt from any change and alteration. They should strive in strengthening and assisting him and they should consider him immune from *shikar* (hunting), bonded labour, *peshkhash* (tribute) *nazrana* (offering), *zabitana* (measurement party charges), including all imperial cesses on any pretext and never deviate from this august imperial order. They should, by considering extreme injunction and extraordinary restriction, act according to the written order.

Details of the *Parganas*

1. *Qasba* Rewari and *parganas* comprising 416 *asli* and *dakhli* villages	*pargana* Bhora Comprising 52 villages *asli* and *dakhli*
2. *Pargana* Shahjahanpur comprising 9 villages *asli* and *dakhli* villages	revenue of the transit Tolls of the town *(qasba)* and the city *(shehr)*

written on 20th *Zilhijja* 21 RY (30th July 1857)

(*Source:* Mutiny papers, Collection number 34, Serial number 3)

Notes

1. Shail Mayaram, *Against History Against Tradition,* Delhi, 2004.
2. Ct. K.C. Yadav, 1857 *Aur Mewat* is an illustrious chapter of the national movement which is based on the documents of the National Archives, Haryana State Archives, *The Revolt* of 1857 in Haryana etc., pp. 1-6.
3. National Archives of India, *Mutiny Papers,* Photographic reproduction in Hakim Abdus Shakur, p. 457 and from *Akhbaruz Zafar,* 5 July 1857 without citing its reference at p. 554.
4. Kanahiya Lal, *Tarikh-i Baghawat-i Hind,* 1857 as cited in Hakim Abdus Shakur, *Tarikh-i Meo Chhatri Mewat,* 1974, pp. 456-7.
5. Nahar Singh who embraced Islam at the hands of Shaikh Nasiruddin *Chiragh-i Dilli* in AD 1356 was designated as Bahadur Nahar with the title of Khan by Firoz Shah Tughlaq. Cf. Hameed Qalandar, *Khairul Majalis,* ed., K.A. Nizami, Department of History, Aligarh, Muslim University, Aligarh, 1959.
6. *Gurgaon District Gazetteer,* 1910.
7. *Tarikh-i Meo Chhatri,* pp. 461-3.
8. *Mutiny Papers,* Collection number 100, Serial Number 68.
9. K.C. Yadav, 1857 *Aur Mewat.*
10. Mirza Ghalib, *Dastanboo,* Aiwan-i-Ghalib, Delhi.
11. K.C. Yadav, *The Roll of Honour, Haryana's Martyrs of* 1857, HIPA, Gurgaon (Haryana), 2007.
12. The following place names are given in the description of Mewat and its surroundings in 1857 can be traced in lrfan Habib, *An Atlas of the Mughal Empire, Political and Economic Maps with Detailed Notes, Bibliography and Index,* Oxford University Press, 1982, Alwar (6A, 6B, 27 + 76 + 7) Dahora 6A Mewat, region (6A, 6B, 24 + 77) Tauru (4A, 6A, 28 + 76), Nuh (8A, 37 + 77), Sohna (4A, 4B, 6A, 6B, 8A, 8B), Firozpur Jhirka (6A, 27 + 76), Naugaon (6A, 27 + 76), Pinangwan (4A, 4B, 6A, 6B, 28 + 76), Mathura (6A, 6B, 8A, 8B, 27 + 77), Hodal (6A, 8A, 27 + 77), Ballabgarh, Ballamgarh, (4A, 6A, 8A,8B), Kot Qasim (6A, 27 + 77), Pataudi (6A, 27 + 77), Mandawar (6A, 28 + 77), Faridabad (28 + 77), etc.
13. *Mutiny Papers,* Collection number 34, Serial number 1.
14. *Mutiny Papers,* Collection number 34, Serial number 12 (Also its copy in Collection number 34, Serial number 16).
15. *Mutiny Papers,* Collection number 34, Serial number 10.
16. Mirza Ghalib, *Dastanboo,* Aiwan-i-Ghalib, Delhi.
17. *Mutiny Papers,* Collection number 34, Serial numbers 12 and 17.
18. *Mutiny Papers,* Collection Number 34, Serial number 4, which, without naming any victim simply stresses that Rao Tula Ram shall be warned not

to oppress any victim. Hakim Abdus Shakur does refer to Collection number 34 which was an acknowledgement and appreciation letter to General Mohammad Bakht Khan Bahadur's letter. However in Collection number 34, Serial number 11, Tula Ram assures Bahadur Shah Zafar that he will not interfere in the *jagir* of Ataullah Khan. Furthermore there was a dispute with the Saiyids and other inhabitants of Kathura for which the Commander-in-Chief issued a *shuqqa* for not molesting inhabitants thereof, especially the wife of Shaikh Murad Ali, Collection number 102, Serial numbers 50, 72 and 73.

19. *Mutiny Papers,* Collection number 34, Serial number 13. Since the powerful Jats of Bhora were afraid of the recalcitrant Meos they supported Tula Ram. Consequent upon their weakness, the Meos immediately attacked them in a two-day battle in which 111 Jats and Ahirs died and 80 Meos were killed. Cf *Gurgaon District Gazetteer,* p. 19.
20. *Mutiny Papers,* Collection number 188, Serial number 6, *Akhbarul Zafar,* Delhi, *Dehli Urdu Akhbar* statement already cited from Collection number 78, Serial number 180, which is a letter of the Mughal Commander-in-Chief to Mohammad Bakht Khan Bahadur of 15th July 1857 regarding a plunder in Basaee of District Gurgaon by Lucknow *sawars* from where they seized a cannon together with some English property.
21. Charles Ball, *History Of The Indian Mutiny,* pp. 458-69 as cited in *Rashtriya Sahara* (Supplement) 11 May 2008.
22. *Dehli Urdu Akhbar,* 5th July 1857.
23. *Mutiny Papers,* Collection number 199, Serial number 257 (A).
24. *Mutiny Papers,* Collection number 199, Serial number 257 (B).
25. *Mutiny Papers,* Collection number 199, Serial number 259.
26. *Mutiny Papers,* Collection number 199, Serial number 261 (B).
27. *Mutiny Papers,* Collection number 199, Serial number 263 (A).
28. *Mutiny Papers,* Collection number 199, Serial number 263 (B).
29. *Mutiny Papers,* Collection number 199, Serial number 272 (A).
30. *Mutiny Papers,* Collection number 199, Serial number 272 (B).
31. *Mutiny Papers,* Collection number 199, Serial numbers 291-2.
32. The *Ain-i-Akbari* does refer to pargana Bhora under the *zamindari* of the Ahirs while a manuscript of the *Ain-i-Akbari* in the National Archives records the Jats as the *zamindars* which indicates that there were different castes including the Meos. Mohammad Ahmad Ali Khan Bahadur, *Nawab* of Farrukhnagar used to complain against such activities of Rao Tula Ram, which were injurious to him, to the Mughal emperor that RaoTula Ram, through his brother had seized *pargana* Bhora on the strength of an imperial farman of 11th August 1857 which was originally in his *jagir* assignment. When the imperial *hukamnama* (order) was solicited for the perusal, RaoTula Ram's brother immediately stood against his men, who in view of the royal

orders avoided any confrontation whatsoever while his brother killed 15 men of the *Nawab* for which he sought a ransom from Rao Tula Ram.

The Nawab simultaneously alleged that RaoTula Ram had indulged in mischief and disturbance, cf. *Mutiny Papers,* Collection number 38, Serial numbers 2 and 3, dated 2nd September 1857. According to Munshi Jeewan Lal, the Mughal Emperor had granted the family of the Nawab a sum of ₹ 2 crore. RaoTula Ram had extended his sway over Rewari and Bhora, collected the revenue, strengthened his forces, and gathered ammunition from the Meos. Interestingly enough, there were four villages, including Binda whose Meo inhabitants migrated to Nanuka near Tauru in 1947, Uton (now in district Mewat) and Ghatal (near district Alwar), which were found to be part of *pargana* Bhora. This is contrary K.C. Yadav's assertion that there were no Meo villages in *pargana* Bhora. However, these Meo villages did not recognise RaoTula Ram's overlordship which caused bad blood among them as they refused revenues to him resulting in the desolation of their villages.

Chapter - 10

Communitarian Relations, Colonial Remodeling, and the British in Pre-Mutiny Awadh

— ***Dr. Heena Ansari***
Jamia Millia Islamia, New Delhi

The Nawabi kingdom of Awadh and the British East India Company had fairly good political relations since the Battle of Buxer in 1764, when the treaty of Allahabad was signed,[1] till the time of its annexation in February 1856. At no point Awadh had stood up against the British East India Company. But this is not to say that the years immediately before the revolt were uneventful. Rather, these years witnessed various serious incidents such as the religious/sectarian clash/es in 1855 around the Hanumangarhi issue and the annexation of Awadh in Feb 1856.

Scholars have examined aspects of Awadh's pre-Mutiny period. J.R.I. Cole analyzes the relations between Shia nobles and the rulers of Awadh.[2] While Rudrangshu Mukherjee focuses on the impacts of summary settlement, which violated the traditional norms and created conditions for peasants and *talluqadars* to unite against the British administration, which ultimately resulted in the revolt of 1857.[3]Veena Oldenburg examines the transformation of Lucknow between the years 1856-77: taking into account the decline of Nawabi city and the reorganization of the physical landscape by the British.[4] Works of Rosie Llewellyn Jones and Madhu Trivedi evaluate the making of Awadh culture and architecture.[5] These works have relied largely on the British imperial records and the normative indigenous material available in printed form. Though some of the scholars have used indigenous sources like *Awadh Akhbar,* but they have missed to take notice of *Tilism-e Lucknow,* a newspaper covering the phase from annexation till the revolt (25th July 1856 to 8th May 1857).[6]

It was late Professor Iqbal Husain, who introduced this newspaper for the first time way back in 1974 in his path breaking essay *Lucknow between the Annexation and the Mutiny*. The article covers the impact and effects resulting from the British occupation of palaces, the demobilization of Awadh army, economic impact of annexation and people's reaction to various measures of the government, the condition of *talluqadars* and *zamindars*, the social and religious life and finally the mutiny. However, being the pioneer one, this work provides a window for further detailed analysis of it.[7] The task is taken over by Prof. Zaheer Jafri in his, *Awadh from Mughal to Colonial Rule*, who has reconstructed the agrarian, economic and social life of Awadh during various phases of Mughal Empire, Nawabi regime, Colonial times and the revolt of 1857 by using the village records and private papers.[8] The present work is an attempt to elaborate further the line of his argument and to explore further the unused data from *Tilism-e Lucknow* to understand the pre-mutiny Awadh in a better way. The newspaper provides the psychic make up of people who developed commonalities with royal household and therefore, though there was no public outcry of the royal displacement, but a very hostile public opinion, which ultimately, prepared the ground for the outbreak in near future.

A

The Hanumangarhi incident at Ayodhya, 1855

There happened a brutal incident of a Hindu-Muslim conflict in 1855, despite the fact that the land of Awadh is very well known for the composite culture. Despite the secular and religious tolerant nature of the State and society, serious acts of communal violence sometimes tend to occur in society. One such dispute was at Hanumangarhi at the close of the *Nawabi* regime (in 1855), which has apparently destroyed (or had the potential to destroy) these inter-community relations in a big way. This case of Hanumangarhi Mosque/Temple has practically arrayed not only the Sunni Muslims against the Shia Regime, but also led to a deep divide between the Hindu and Muslim land owners in the rural society. It is remarkable that the leaders in this dispute were able to mobilize huge numbers of people in the name of religion. Also, the role of the Wajid Ali Shah and the play of Colonial forces in this disturbance and mobilization are interesting elements to study and understand the complex society of Awadh, which ultimately gathered again, keeping aside the religious differences, under the leadership of a Sufi leader [Ahmadullah Shah] against the Colonial rule in 1857.

The case is related to a very sensitive issue of the destruction of a *Qanati* Masjid,[9] which was said to have been created sometimes during the reign of Mughal Emperor Aurangzeb. Later on it was enclosed by a *bairagi*, who got the adjacent area as a grant by the second *nawab* of Awadh, Abul Mansur Safdar Jung (r.1740-54) in return for curing the *nawab* by his prayers. He was allowed to build a Hanuman temple, whom he had seen in his dream to be built. (*Qanati* Mosque and a *Shivala* were located near the temple). It was Raja Darshan Singh, the *Nazim* of the region in the first half of the 19th century who enclosed much larger area, fortified it and named it as *Hanumangarhi* of Ayodhya [in Faizabad district].[10] It is said that the said *Nazim*, being a favorite of the *nawab* had taken numerous measures at the local level, which could be seen as detrimental to the local Muslims.[11] It is also alleged that he tried to ban the practice of calling of the *azaan* [the Islamic call for prayer] and cow-slaughter around this complex. Further, it is said that during the reign of Wajid Ali Shah (r.1847-56), he even placed idols inside the premises.

The issue started when once a traveller named Ghulam Husain Shah, unaware of this situation came to perform *namaz* at *Hanumangarhi* Mosque and loudly called the *azaan*. The priests of *Shivala* and the local *zamindar* heard this and forcibly tried to stop him. They entered the mosque, thrashed the person and even said to have snatched the holy *Quran* from him, burnt it and throw him out of the mosque.

This had greatly affected Ghulam Husain Shah and he decided to liberate the Masjid from the control of Hindus. Thus he called for a *Jihad* and hoisted the Muhammadi flag across the Gomati. His call was successful in attracting many of the Muslims who came up to support him and followed him towards Faizabad. Agha Ali Khan,the *Nazim* of Sultanpur, tried to stop them turning them to Lucknow. However, some of them managed to reach Faizabad but they were also thrown out of the city by the *kotwal*, Nisar Hussain and Cap. Alexander Orr.

When the news reached to Wajid Ali Shah, he ordered Agha Ali Khan and *kotwal*, Munim Beg to investigate the matter and present the report. The investigation was thus made and the report was presented on 27Aug 1855 saying;

> "For the last 37 years I have held my present office under the Oude Government and during that period no Mohomedon has ever brought to my notice that a mosque existed within the Hunooman Gurhee, nor have I ever been directed by the Durbar to make any enquiries relative to such a building, having stood in such a locality. When the late Raja Darshan Singh was *Nazim*, I accompanied him through the fort, conducted by the Mahunts, but I saw no mosque. Had I seen it, I should have made due arrangements regarding it and should have reported the circumstances to the Government."[12]

The report worsened the situation and Ghulam Husain Shah now decided to go to Faizabad with some of his men. He managed to gather 100-120 men despite the efforts of Cap. Orr, Mirza Munim Beg and Mirza Agha Ali. The *bairagis* on the other hand, also prepared themselves to handle the situation and gathered support from people like Raja Man Singh, Raja Kishan Dutt Pandey and other Hindu *zamindars*, amounting in all to 10,000.On Wednesday 25th July 1855 (10th *Ziqad*, 1271), nearly 300 Muslims gathered to perform *namaz* at the *Hanumangarhi* Masjid. This alarmed the *bairagis* and they surrounded the Masjid from all sides. State officials (who were said to have been bribed) remained away from the case.

This caused great unrest among the Muslims and only after the intervention of the official infantry and cavalry the unfortunate blood bath could be prevented. However, the so-called negotiations took such a long time that the Muslims could not perform their prayers (as the time for the *namaz* got over by then). However, frequent skirmishes continue to occur.

One such clash happened when Ghulam Husain Shah and his followers were having dinner inside the Mosque on the assurance and insistence by Hearsay and Alexander Orr. At that time, a thousand of *bairagis* came in shouting out loud and began to shoot the *mujahidin.* Rajab Ali Beg Suroor says:

> "Seventy Muslims, 30-40 *Quran Sharifs* were martyred. Some of the *Qurans* were torn into thousands of pieces; some were burnt down while some others were used for blocking the drains."[13]

Bairagis killed Ghulam Husain Shah and his 296 companions.[14] The bodies of the *mujahidin* remained lied there till the *Kotwal*, Nisar Husain came for their burial the next day.[15]

The brutal news forced the king to take some serious action and thus, he ordered a committee[16] to go to Ayodhya and investigate whether there ever existed a mosque or not. On 25th August, 1855 (12th *Zilhij*, AH 1271), the committee went to Ayodhya and noted down the interview of a large number of people including those who talked in favor of the mosque, and presented the report to the King.[17] Qazi Yaar Ali Tabirah Habibullah even showed many *mahzars* proving the existence of the Mosque. The report (which was in favor of the Mosque) was thus presented to the Emperor. But the situation changed when some courtiers questioned the neutrality of this report. Resultantly, Ali Naqi Khan, the Prime Minister (who was in a pact with nobles & the elites) sent Raja Man Singh and Agha Ali again to look into the matter severely and neutrally. This new committee drafted a report for the non-existence of the mosque. The report was presented to the Emperor, who finally accepted it and rejected the orders for the construction of the mosque.

The situation of the Emperor was such that he sought measures to curb the issue, to appease both the groups-Hindus and Muslims. The reason was the pressure from the British government, who was alleging or was in search of the points to blame him for the mismanagement of the Empire. Thus he called a conference, and then he asked the opinion of the *Ulema* on *Jihad* and, finally when all his efforts to control the people failed, he ordered the use of force or army.

1. The Movement of Maulvi Syed Amir Ali, the State and the *Ulema*

The judgment of the Emperor angered the Sunni Muslims and one Maulvi Syed Amir Ali now took the lead organizing the Muslims. Maulvi Abdur Razzaq Firangi Mahali gave the call for *Jihad*. Both of them managed to mobilize a large number of Muslims in the name of restoration of Mosque. Thus, people from different places like Kheri, Rampur, Pilibhit, Rohilkhand etc. came to join the movement. In fact hundreds of *wilayati Pathans* became Amir Ali's followers and supporters. They all reached Amethi and hoisted the Mohammadi Flag. This mass mobilization greatly feared the authorities and ultimately Ali Naqi Khan (the Prime Minister) called Maulvi Mohd. Yusuf Firangi Mahali to stop the people from his institution from interfering into the movement. To further persuade the leaders, Ali Naqi Khan promised that the Mosque would be constructed again [within a period of one month] if the existence of it found. He managed to appease Maulavi Abdur Razzaq, who withdrew himself hearing the promise of Ali Naqi.[18]

However Maulana Amir Ali continued with his campaign and this way he became the prime target of Ali Naqi Khan. Ali Naqi Khan now managed to call Amir Ali in the court of Lucknow. Here many other contemporary *Ulema* were also called to discuss the conditions of *jihad*. Maulvi Khadim Ahmad Firangi Mahali was one of them.[19] However, they could not move Maulvi Amir Ali from his position and though Ali Naqi tried to imprison him but Bashiruddaulah[20] saved him and Maulavi Amir Ali went out to his place safely. This incident greatly threatened the authorities and Ali Naqi convinced people like Ramzan Ali Khan and Mir Safdar Ali to shushed the Maulavi.

As soon as the period of promise of one month (i.e 14th *Zilhij* to 24th *Muharram)* to reconstruct the mosque has come to end and the promise by the authorities was going waste, Maulavi Amir Ali took a stand and called for *jihad*. He preached a sermon to people and led them to Bansa and Dariyabad. In response to this, Ali Naqi too sent his forces (platoon of *telangs* and Gulabi platoon) under the commandership of Captain Barlow and Husain Ali. These forces were sent to stop the forward movement of Maulvi Amir Ali. Unfortunately for Amir Ali all his advocates and supporters had turned their backs by now and many of them issued a *fatwa* against him for calling off his *jihad*. The king too sought the sanction of religion to discredit the crusade by submitting the case of Maulana Saiyyid Muhammad, the highest Shia 'Alim[21]. All the leading *Ulema* delivered a sermon at the *Eidgaah* mosque to persuade people that this *jihad* against the will of ruler is incorrect. This group included famous *Ulema* and Maulvis like Maulvi Hais Ahmad Malihabadi, Maulvi Ghulam Jilani *wakil* at English court, Maulvi Mohammad Yusuf Firangi Mahali, Maulvi Fazl-e Haq Khairabadi, Maulvi Sa'adullah Muradabadi and various others.[22] They had even issued a *fatwa* for the killing of Maulvi Amir Ali. Many others wrote that even during the fight with *Kafirs*, Muslims are not allowed to go against the *Hakim-i waqt* i.e. the king. In all the *fatwa* of the leading *Ulema* of the time, no point went in favor of Maulvi Syed Amir Ali.[23]

On 7th November, AD 1855 (26th *Safar*, AH 1272) Maulvi along with his 300 followers moved to Mohammadpur. Haji Mirza Husain Ali was sought to be a trustworthy person by Maulvi Syed Amir Ali, but he also cheated and backstabbed the *Mujahidin* in favor of Major Barlow. Four platoons, two cannons and Gulabi platoon was sent to deal with Amir Ali under his headship only. Mirza Husain Ali, on the plea of Major Barlow went to Amir Ali and stopped him from moving to Muhammadpur and asked them to halt near Shuja'tganj. From this place Mr. Barlow managed to turn them to other direction. This gave Mr. Barlow a chance to use cannon. Hearing the voice of cannon and facing smog everywhere, the horse of Maulvi Amir Ali lost its control and threw away Amir Ali.[24] Now, Amir Ali stood up and ordered *Mujahidin* to move forward and fought bravely and captured the cannons. This actually was the trap of Mr. Barlow; as soon as the *mujahidin* reached at the cannon, the hiding cannons at the back were blasted and killed the entire fighters. At this time a knife brutally hit the shoulder of Amir Ali. Despite this fatal wound, he continued to encourage his remaining force. But the army of Thakur Singh came from the back and attacked *mujahidin*. This dual attack completely devastated all the *mujahidin*.

The dead body of Maulvi Syed Amir Ali remained lay there, only the head was taken to Captain Barlow at Lucknow. However, fearing a big unrest Barlow immediately ordered to take it back. The same threat prevented the army to take the head back and they threw it somewhere on the way. Few women also participated in this incident as *mujahid.* The rest of the bodies of the *mujahidin* were buried by the nearby Muslim *zamindars*, the next day.

2. The 'Cult' around Maulvi Syed Amir Ali

The communal strife generally results in the emergence of new heroes and few personalities; whether dead or living. Likewise within a year of the martyrdom of Syed Amir Ali, he received a wider following and there emerged a sort of cult around him, which grew at the place of his burial or his shrine. The burial place of Syed Amir Ali,soon became important enough for the masses. People from both religions began to visit his *dargah. Tilism-e Lucknow* quotes a detailed report of his annual *Urs* festival. The graphic description provides information about the various legends, which grew by the time and various miraculous healing qualities were sought to be associated with his tomb. The presence of Syed Amir Ali's *dargah* had turned the atmosphere of the area into paradise-like an area which was earlier only a *jungal*, inhibited with the wild animals and vultures. The people come from far away places got their wishes fulfilled; *Tilism* mentions detailed description of two instances. On 26th October 1856 (26th *safar*, AH 1273), a blind man came to visit the *dargah* of Maulvi Amir Ali and got his eyesight back. The incidence turned the heart of evil-doers (*munkarin*) too. Similarly, a servant named Gulab came to the shrine to find a life partner for himself. He was committed not to leave the *dargah* until he got his wish was fulfilled, though people were laughing at him for his stupid wish and act. Next day, however, a girl came to him and asked him to keep herself as she had no one to look after her and to live with. He felt pleased to see her and took her with him. His fellow men told the girl by telling about the abject poverty of him. But nothing could move her from her position and thus the man got his wish fulfilled.[25] Such events took place daily at the shrine and thousands of people cure themselves simply by visiting the *dargah* of Maulvi Amir Ali.

3. The 'Revenge' for Maulvi Syed Amir Ali, Maulana Ahmadullah Shah and the Making of the 'Revolt of 1857' in Awadh

The assassination of Maulavi Amir Ali was an event which shook the imagination of the people especially the Sunni Muslims and in the whole episode the needle of suspicion was invariably pointed towards Ali Naqi Khan, the then prime minister of Nawab Wajid Ali Shah. The poets and writers composed a number of chronograms lamenting his death and cursing the government of Wajid Ali Shah[26]. However, we see that this time the communitarian relations in the kingdom of Awadh were at its lowest ebb.

This was exactly the time when Maulavi Ahmadullah Shah, the famous rebel leader had also arrived in the city of Lucknow. His arrival in the city was reported in *Tilism,* the weekly newspaper of Lucknow on 21st Nov. 1856 in the following manner:

> These days a person called Ahmadullah Shah in disguise of a *faqir* but having all paraphernalia of royalty has arrived in the town and stayed in the *sarai* of Mutammad-ud Daulah, now has shifted to *Ghasiyarimandi*...People of the town visit him in a large number on Mondays and Thursdays to take part in the mystic gatherings (*majalis-i-hal-o qal*). A number of feats are performed in midst of these gatherings...such display takes place every morning and evening for the viewing of the masses....[27]

The impact of these gatherings on the population of Lucknow can be gauged by the next report of *Tilism,* which appeared two months later. On 30 January 1857 it was reported that:

> Ahmadullah Shah in Ghasiyarimandi is very fearless in saying whatever he wishes to say and a large crowd is always there, often Maulvi Amiruddin Ali is remembered. Although he is unable to do anything, orally he always pleads for *jehad.*[28]

Ahmadullah Shah left Lucknow apparently for Bahraich but he made a stop at Faizabad where he stayed at Chowk Sarai and once again he started preaching for *jihad.* His companions used to visit the graves of the companions of Maulvi Amir Ali who supposedly died fighting for *jihad.* Seeing the changing mood of the people, English authorities arrested him and he was put in the district jail. At the time of the outbreak of mutiny the gates of the prison were opened and all the prisoners were freed. Ahmadullah Shah was elected as the leader of the people. It is reported that on assuming leadership he issued orders for the destruction of temples of Hanumangarhi. But on realizing that such an attempt will ultimately alienate the Hindus, he gave up this idea and left for Lucknow. At the time of final reckoning, forgetting all these apprehensions the sepoys joined Ahmadullah Shah's forces and at the Battle of Chinhat, on 30th June 1857, he emerged the leader of the people as well as the sepoys, Hindus and Muslims both.

This is indeed an important turn of events when somebody who visits Faizabad to avenge the death of Maulvi Amir Ali and to rebuild the *Hanumangarhi* mosque, is invariably chosen as the commander of the Hindu and Muslim sepoys. The temporary nature of worsening of community relations is quite apparent. People were ready to forget such differences at the hour of the crisis perhaps this entire episode brings out the deep rooted and a very strong nature of the elements of composite culture of the region. During the course of 1857 the British forces made definite attempts to highlight Hindu -Muslim differences; even they tried to play the sectarian Shi'a- Sunni divide but up to little use. It is not for nothing that a large number of *talluqadars,* majority of them were Rajputs were still siding with Begum HazratMahal, now fugitive in the Nepal *terai* with no authority of her own!

B
The Impacts of Annexation and the City of Lucknow

1. The Decline of the Economy

The impacts of the annexation of Awadh were disastrous for every section of the society. The foremost problem before the people of Awadh was economic. There was a disastrous increase in the prices of essential commodities, which caused great hardship for citizens. Atkinson tells us that in 1826 wheat, barley and *bajra* were being sold at 45.5 *sers*, 66.9 *sers* and 53 *sers* respectively for a rupee, which in 1858 had increased considerably to 37 *sers*, 60 *sers*, and 35 *sers* for a rupee.[29] There was also a stagnation or decline in the wages. F. H. Fisher presented a table to show the decline in wages for the Ruhelkhand and sees it as applicable over the Awadh as well. Thus, the people were at the mercy of moneylenders and were facing acute hardships.

Decline in the wages of peasants and Daily wage earners over the period 1826-1858[30]

Peasants anddaily wage earners	*1826 (earnings per month)*	*1858 (earnings per month)*
Field Laborers	Rs. 2-Rs. 6	Re. 1-14 annas
Herdsman	Rs. 2-Rs. 6	Re. 1-14 annas
Barbers	Rs. 4- Rs.8	Rs. 2- Rs. 13 annas
Blacksmiths	Rs. 5- Rs. 20	Rs. 2 -13 annas
Carpenters	Rs. 5- Rs. 20	Rs. 2- 13annas
Beldar	Rs. 4- Rs. 5	Rs. 3

The class of *talluqadars*, who had been the holder of much power and authority, were reduced to a state of bankruptcy. Sleeman wrote: "in 1801 when the Oude territory was divided and half taken by us and half left to Oude, the landed aristocracy of each was about equal. Now hardly a family of this class remains in our half, while in Oude it remains unimpaired. Everybody in Oude believes those families to have been systematically crushed".[31] On assuming power, the prime purpose of the British Government was to extract as much revenue as possible. But the local system of assessment and collection [i.e the *kists* system] was thought a major problem. The matter was solved by declaring that the first 41/2 *kist* [i.e. from *Kooar* to the 15th Maugh (Feb- March)] will belong to Awadh and the rest 71/2 will go in the account of British Government.[32] But, the situation worsened when the British authorities began to ask for the 41/2 *kists* i.e. arrears, resulting in great dissatisfaction for the *zamindars* and the *talluqadars*. The *talluqadars*, in response, denied paying the dues, which led the revenue collector to use force.

To resolve the issue permanently, the British authorities came with the introduction of Summary Settlement, 1856-7, which was a great blow to the power of *talluqadars* and *zamindars*. The Settlement, now, was to be made for three years, village by village with the parties actually possessing the land. It was to be based on the detailed information and statement of

1. The past five years' *Jama*

2. The *nankar* grants
3. Rent free villages, namely *ma'afi*, *jagirs* etc.
4. Religious grants and
5. *Patwaris* and *chowkidaris* of the old system.[33]

The Settlement was made to curb the powers of *talluqadars*. However, the execution of this settlement was not so simple because the details of previous five years assessments were scarcely available. It could be accrued only from the *jamabandi* accounts kept by the *talluqadars'* servants, where the English authorities faced concealments and corruptions. Further, there was difficulty in dealing with the lands held at a favorable assessment and cultivated by the landholders himself or by hired labour. Thus, there were many serious slips.[34] Initially, the *zamindars*, too, did not came forward, either they mistrusted the English officers or the *talluqadars* had enough control over them to keep them away. It was only gradually that they came to know that the actual settlement was to be made with the *zamindars*, who will be considered the 'actual proprietors of the soil'.[35] Though the Government had tried to eliminate the intermediaries from the system, but what it actually resulted in was an alliance between *talluqadars* and the peasants against the British rule, which acted strongly in the Revolt of 1857.

The result of Summary Settlement was the large scale decline in the population of some of the towns of U.P. between 1834-1868. The following table shows that densely populated areas in the pre-annexation Awadh witnessed large scale migration after the hold of Colonial rule.[36]

Names of the town	*Population in 1834 (Donald Butler)*	*Population in 1868 (First Census, 1872)*	*Remarks (Composition)*
Amethi	10,000	7,128	Muslim dominant area
Bihar	10,000	2,242	Both Hindus and Muslims
Dalmau	10,000	1,382	Both Hindus and Muslims
Ghatampur	4,000	1,809	Hindu dominant area
Hindaur	3,000	1,109	All Hindus
Khiron	5,000	3,480	Muslim dominant area
Nain	10,000	827	Mostly Hindus
Partabgarh	10,000	3,743	Both Hindus and Muslims
Ranjit Purva	50-60,000	2,132	All Muslims
Terha	6,000	2,755	———

2. The 'Remodeling' of Nawabi Lucknow: The 'Politics' and Development

On assuming power, British authorities started the drive for the 'beautification' of the city. The new planning envisaged an almost complete 'over-haul' of the *nawabi* town. They began to plan new houses, buildings, roads, railway lines and other standing structures to create an image of improved state of affairs and also to present a picture of grandeur of the British Empire. But this decorative drive came at the expense of previous glory i.e. in order to give way to new structures old heritage of the city was destroyed, especially those standing contrary to the British image of beauty.

> "Apart from the deliberate trashing of the Qaisar Bagh palace, [as it had been the headquarters of the opposition] huge areas of houses and gardens were destroyed over the next twenty years.[37] Many of the old medieval residential *mohallas*, that pre-dated the arrival of the *nawabs*, were demolished to make space for broad military roads that cut through the middle of the old city. Important religious structures were taken over by the Company soldiers, who stored cannons and ammunition in the Bara Imambara. A mesh of palace out buildings around the Chattar Manzil complex was demolished, leaving the original palace building standing denuded of the intricate entrances, pavilions and gardens that had given them a real sense of importance and dignity. The Qaiser Bagh palaces were emasculated by main roads cut through the fairy-like buildings and fantasy garden follies, ruining the architectural axes."[38]

In Faizabad also, three royal houses, which were underneath the wall of *Pa'ain Bagh* and were used for the prisoners of *Kachahri wizarat* and *Diwan khana* were fallen down. And a wide road was to cut out from there.[39] The destruction was such that Russell found it hard to recognize the magnificent and intricate city that he had seen twenty years earlier, then in its entire bizarre splendor.[40]

a. Dislocation of Royal Household

The process of beautification of the city of Lucknow resulted in the destruction of the old royal palaces. The 'royal ladies' too were forcefully asked to vacate the palace and to move to the non-significant dwelling places. This was done in just one day so that no complaints could be made or actions could be taken against the Colonial officials. Similarly, the royal storehouse containing arms and ammunition of state were seized in a most blatant manner. The protest by the officials was paid no heed and when Wajid Ali Shah wrote a letter to the Chief Commissioner protesting against this loot, a most sweet quoted reply was sent to him- "the royal buildings are the specimens of the past; they will be protected and repaired by Colonial administration if we occupy them". The message was loud and clear; these buildings belonged to the State and shall remain to the State. It was started with *Macchi Bhawan,* whose bungalows were ordered to be emptied, forcing people of royal blood to move to the local areas. *Tilism* records the order issued by the British government, whereby various *Begums* of the royal household were moved away from the palaces to the city areas, as per following details.[41]

Begums displaced by the Administration	***Newly Allotted places for Residence***
1. Nawab Khurshid Mahal Sahiba	Inside the Shah Burj
2. Nawab Dilruba Mahal Sahiba	Inside the Shikoh Manzil
3. Nawab Waqar Mahal Sahiba	Inside the Waqar Manzil
4. Sultan Nawab Zohra Mahal Sahiba	Inside the Akhtar Pasand
5. Nawab Khurd Mahal Sahiba, Nawab Sultan Jahan, Nawab Sayyida Mahal Sahiba	Inside the Mahalsara of Munna Moti
6. Nawab Farkhanda Mahal Sahiba	Inside the Sadar Mubarak
7. Nawab Imtiyaz Mahal Sahiba	Inside the Yemen Manzil
8. Nawab Hazur Mahal Sahiba 9. Nawab Umrao Mahal Sahiba	In Taskin Bakhsh In Padshah Manzil
10. Mallika Meher Tan Afasarun Nisa Nawab Nishat Mahal Sahiba	In the house of Munshi Muzaffar Ali
11. Nawab Yasmin Mahal Sahiba	In the mahalsara of Darogha Haideri

The well-known Hindi poetess Subhadra Kumari Chauhan [1904-48] lamented the situation in case of Rani Laxmi Bai and she says:

रानी रोई रानिवासों में, बेगम ग़म से थीं बेज़ार
उनके गहने कपड़े बिकते थे कलकत्ते के बाज़ार

सरे आम नीलाम छापते थे अंग्रेज़ों के अखबार,
'नागपुर के ज़ेवर ले लो लखनऊ के लौ नौलख हार'।

[Queens wept in their quarters, the Begums were sick of the situation,
Their ornaments and royal clothes were being sold in the markets of Calcutta
The advertisements for the sale of the royal stuff were being published in the daily newspapers of the British Government
"Buy the ornaments of Nagpur, Buy the Naulakha locket of Lucknow"]

Thus, those who used to have a luxurious life under Wajid Ali Shah were now reduced to a condition of utter misery. *Tilism* reports:

"At last, all the houses along with its material were removed in the single night. The things, which were left because of the darkness of night, were brought in the morning by the *thanadar* of Chini bazaar[42]. English *barqandaaz* were placed on security of first door of Sultan Manzil and the rest cavalrymen were placed on second door near Nusrat Bagh."[43]

However, there were some buildings, which were so strong that even blasting failed to pull them down. For such buildings, the authorities decided to use bombs (these buildings according to them were waste and should be destroyed as these can be used by locals against the authorities during resistance) for demolishing them. The case of Sultani Kalan Kothi is very much revealing: sixteen earthen pots (big containers) of bombs were put inside and fire was shown. Pots and bombs got burst but not a single brick of the wall moved from its place. This angered Mr. Thornhill[44] and he look for other ways. Then, laborers were called to dig the place for the whole day but that too of no avail. Thus, all efforts of authorities including spades, axes ended in failure before the strength of this building.[45]

b. The Royal Library Store houses and Zoo after the Annexation

Libraries and books are the means of dissemination of knowledge and source of accumulated wisdom of the past. The Indian ruling elite was very much concerned in acquiring books on a variety of subjects. They have encouraged the translations from other languages. The *nawabs* of Awadh were also the patrons of art and culture and their personal libraries containing books on each and every subject were very well maintained. When Wajid Ali Shah has left for Calcutta to represent his case, apparently he was in a hurry and has little realized that his absence from the city will give the Colonial officers a free hand to deal with his personal collection of books, and artifacts in the manner they think fit. Similarly, he has never realized that the officers in whose care and in whose in-charge he is leaving these valuables will not be able to exert their position in view of the pressure by the Colonial authorities.

Thus, the most obvious case relates to the royal libraries of Wajid Ali Shah. It said to have contained around 2, 00,000 volumes and under the care of officer of *nawabi* times. The library of Wajid Ali Shah was maintained after great search throughout and outside the Empire. But after the annexation Major Hayes ordered to move all the books from Husain Baksh Kothi to Kothi Martin[46] while Carnegie ordered to throw away all the books, which were settled in the shelves of library of Farah Baksh[47]. Hisamuddaulah tries to protect this priceless collection but his protests were not heeded. They simply ordered all these books to be moved away from the royal building to an individual house.

'By orders of the Chief Commissioner the royal library at the palace of Hossain Bukhsh was removed to the Kothee (residence) of General Martin, although Hissamood Dowlah Bahadur wrote a letter to the authorities stating that the library might be removed with sanction and knowledge of your Majesty, and that the kothee of General Martin is neither the property of your Majesty nor belongs to magazines, and when Hissamood Dowlah Bahadoor perceived that his apologies were not accepted he said that the library was entrusted to his care by your Majesty, at the time of departing from Lucknow, and he therefore requires a receipt from the person who remove the books, or from those who would take charge from them, that such may serve as a release to him, yet his request was declined, as your Majesty will see by the correspondence on the subject. The authorities give their replies in such a harsh and severe manner, that every person is in fear of being degraded. If anything is done contrary to the orders of your Majesty, Hissamood Dowlah and others would be held responsible for disobeying them, and if they disobey the Commissioners, they will be degraded them.'[48]

Worse was the fate of King's zoo; all the animals of the zoo were auctioned for nearly about Rs.70,000.[49] All the valuable stud horses of Arabian, Persian and English horses, his fighting, hunting, riding and luggage elephants, camels, dogs and cattle were sold by public auction at prices scarcely more than what their hides and skin would have fetched.[50] However, only passing reference and less sympathy to this treasure of Wajid Ali Shah has been shown in *Tilism,* which reflects that these things were less symbolic and less important of the Wajid Ali's rule as compared to structural remains.

Here it would not be wrong to say that people were not very much concerned with the destruction of the city as a whole, especially of Empire's glory until their personal houses and lives were not attacked. They did not actively react to the dispossession of Wajid Ali Shah, or digging of his palace or destruction of his zoo and library or ruining the fate of his close relatives, except for crying with him and following him during his departure to Calcutta that too was more ceremonial than expression of any true loyalty.[51]

c. Destruction of Houses of Elite & Common Citizens, The 'façade' of Compensation

What is more strongly focused in *Tilism* was the destruction of the local houses of the city. The establishment of English Hospitals forced people of the area to shift to some other places, leaving their houses. All the *kaccha* and *pakka* houses were ordered to be raised to the ground and the nearby pond was also to be filled up and paved. Few people reached Tare Wali Kothi[52] to complain to Commissioner Major Bunks and Deputy Commissioner Simson of their plight but that was of no use.

In Faizabad, the plan to make a new road from *Lohe wala pul* to *Nahar ka pul* also led to demolition of thousands of *kaccha* and *pakka* houses. One road is made from Tripolia to Dilkusha and demolished the building called *Naqqarkhana*. On that occasion only the houses of Darab Ali Khan were spared. Another road from the house of Zafaruddaula to *Khwaspura* of Darab Ali Khan was made, removing all the houses of that area too.[53]

There was even a plan to construct a new city which filled people with further fear as the plan for the new city would have invested more destruction that has been taken earlier for smaller things like roads or canals. It will eventually leads to destruction on a larger scale.

> "Government had accepted the need to rebuild the ancient land, a new city is planned to be made. Layers of houses and shops are to be made. Every type of thing is to be available there. Rs. 40,000 were to be spent on this project. Mr. H. Wilson and Governor General visited the place and approved it as they liked it. Let us see, whose and how much land gets destroyed."[54]

Further, there was a suspicion that few of the ordinary houses had the doubt of having gold or other jewels and thus on promising compensation, the Company ordered to blow them down and dig them. What is to be noted here is the matters of compensation: there was no fairness shown by the British authorities. They had promised for higher amount prior to demolishment, but when it came to get the actual payment, the amount was drastically reduced. For example a man asked for Rs.500 for his house, but the government approved a compensation of Rs.71 only. Another problem in the cases of compensation occurred due to the illiteracy of local people; to demand compensation one has to file written complaint and most of the people of the Empire were unable to do so.[55] The drive of destruction became acute after the Revolt of 1857 and the authorities were aware of the impact of their policies on people. The Chief Commissioner of Awadh implied in a memorandum that these demolishment disrupted normal life and spread chaos in the city. The memo described how the demolishment squads arrived in an area destined for clearance and proceeded to engage in their work, often without taking even the elementary precautions of making sure that the houses about to be razed were empty.[56]

The project of destruction even included the religious places. Mosque near *Seekchi Wali Astabal* and the two mosques in *Chaupad* were destroyed and a platoon of English soldiers has been stationed there. The Buland Mosque was turned into a residence by a commander of English platoon: he put up shutters on the three arched gates. The Qanati Mosque was filled with so much lime that the entire mosque got covered by it and only the back wall of it indicates that there had been a mosque here.[57]However, where the situation was at risk and the threat of religious riots prevailed, the government turned itself to the safe side and brings flexibility in the decisions. Thus in Faizabad, when a mosque came on the way of road, it was spared from removal due to the fear of religious riots.[58] There was also a plan to dug Hanumangarhi[59], but the idea was not accepted in the discussion of the Council. However, this softness went away after the Revolt of 1857 and sparing religious places was seen as the heaviest loss. Thus Muslim religious places especially, the Jami Masjid and Asafi Imambara became the prime targets of the government.[60]

The government also carried out a sanitary and improvement drive. On AH.16th *Zul Hijjah* 1272 [18 August 1856] orders were given to the *thanadars* to shut all the toilets with the help of *chaukidars*. Mr. Carnegie asserted that those toilets, which are open towards streets (*kucha*) lead to spread of huge dirt and intolerable smell through roads and streets. Thus, it is not correct to keep them. But closing of these toilets will cause problem for locals and therefore, he ordered to cover and connect them with main sewer [which was supposed to remain close except for during the time of cleaning] or to built their toilets inside their homes & connect them with sewer. He strictly denied the presence of open toilets between streets.[61]

The editor of *Tilism* further mentions the socio-economic problems coming up with the enforcement of newer and newer policies of the Company. We saw dissatisfaction with the prevailing justice system of the English rule. There was also a sense of biasness in justice provided to English and Indian citizens. Many of the officials of high rank were found guilty of bribing such as Mr. Rawerty[62], Captain Bacch[63], Major Deckfield[64] and Major Ricard who ultimately managed to remove all the charges and get their jobs back. However, the case was different for Indians, who were caught only on the basis of doubt. They got imprisoned for years and had to bear the insult as well. They were removed from their official position and had to face unemployment and miseries.[65] *Dafa'dar* Ja'afar Husain and *chaukidars* named Makka Singh & Ganga Singh all were removed from their positions on the charge of bribing. They were imprisoned and insulted.[66] To further substantiate this point, the newspaper presents a case of accident in

Madras, where a woman got died by an Englishman's cart. No one cared about this incident. Had the incident been done by any Indian, he would be hanged without any hesitance and that too on the very next day.[67]

It were these Colonial policies which resulted in the dissatisfaction and ultimately to the rebellion of 1857. Mr. L.E.S. Rees, an eye witness of the event of 1857 at Lucknow showed the acute dissatisfaction among people as the reason behind the revolt.

> "That the Lucknow people should rise against us [the English] was a very probable event, notwithstanding the false reports which we received of their universal contentment. We had done very little to deserve their love and much to merit their detestation. Thousands of nobles, gentlemen, and officials, who during the king's time [before the Annexation, 1856] had lucrative appointments, and who were too idle to work, were now in penury and want, and their myriads of retainers and servants thrown out of employ of course. Then the innumerable vagabonds, bravos and beggars, who under the native rule infested the city and found bread in it. The native merchants, shopkeepers and bankers, who, while Wajid Ali was on the throne, made large profits from supplying the luxurious wants of the king, his courtiers and the wealthy ladies of the thronged harems, found no sale for their goods, and the people in general, and especially the poor, were dissatisfied because they were taxed directly and indirectly in every way."[68]

Notes

1. Concluded on 16th August 1765, the treaty of Allahabad was signed between Mughal Emperor Shah Alam II, Nawab of Awadh Shujauddaulah, and British EIC after the Battle of Buxar. As per the provision, Awadh was returned to Shujauddaulah, who had to pay Rs.53 Lakhs as war indemnity to the EIC and the regions of Kara and Allahabad were separated from Awadh, to be given to the Mughal King Shah Alam II. cf. S Z H Jafri, *Awadh from Mughal to Colonial Rule: Studies in the Anatomy of a Transformation*, Delhi, 2016, pp. 25-27
2. J.R.I.Cole, *Roots of North Indian Shi'ism in Iran and Iraq: Religion and State in Awadh,* 1722-1859, 1989.
3. Rudrangshu Mukherjee, *Awadh in Revolt1857-1858: A Study of Popular Resistance*, Orient Blackswan, 1984.

4. VeenaTalwar Oldenburg, *The Making of Colonial Lucknow.*
5. Rosie Llewellyn Jones, *A Fatal Friendship: Nawabs, the British and the City of Lucknow*, OUP, 1986; MadhuTrivedi, *The Making of the Awadh Culture*, Primus, 2014.
6. All 42 issues have survived in Centre of Advanced Studies, Department of History, Aligarh Muslim University. It has been published recently (2012) by National Council for the Promotion of Urdu with an introduction by Prof. Iqbal Husain. The first issue of this weekly newspaper was published on 25th July, 1856. It was printed at Mohammadi Press by Maulvi Mohammad Ya'qub Ansari of *Firangi Mahal*, its editor.
7. Iqbal Husain, 'Awadh on the Eve of 1857: Evidence of Urdu Newspaper *Tilism'*, in *Images of Lucknow*, RoshanTaqui, New Royal Book Co. Lucknow, 2005; 'The Rebel Administration of Delhi' S. Z. H. Jafri (ed). *Delhi in 1857: Studies, Images and Documents,* Souvenir published by the Department of History, on the occasion of 70th session of Indian History Congress, Delhi, 2010; 'Lucknow Between Annexation And The Mutiny' in *Religion and Ideology of the Rebels of 1857*, Primus Books, 2013; 'Primitive Newspapers: The Eighteenth Century *Akhbarat'* in *Studies in Polity, Economy and Society of the Trans-Gangetic Valley, Fifteenth-Nineteenth Centuries*, Primus Books, 2013.

   The newspaper has been available effectively from 1974 and its full text was published later in 2012. Yet historians working on the revolt of 1857 in Awadh have not used it. I have had the good fortune to undertake a detailed study of the newspaper while working on my M.Phil dissertation under the research supervision of Professor S Z H Jafri; see, Heena Yunus Ansari, *Indigenous Discourse Of The Great Uprising Of 1857: A Study of Urdu Weekly Newspapers From Delhi And Lucknow (Dehli Urdu Akhbar & Tilism-e Lucknow)*, M. Phil Dissertation, Department of History, University of Delhi, 2014.
8. S.Z.H.Jafri, 'Co-existence and Conflict in pre-1857 Awadh: Societal pulls, Cultural Practices & State', in N.R.Farooqui & S.Z.H.Jafri ed. *Understanding the Past: India in the Mirror of History*, Delhi, 2014, pp.17-43, reproduced in S.Z.H.Jafri, *Awadh From Mughal to Colonial Rule: Studies in the Anatomy of a Transformation*, pp. 245-276.
9. *Qanati* Masjid is an open space enclosed with a canvas.
10. *Sanad and parwanas issued by Safdarjang & Shujauddaulah*, cf. Najmul Ghani, pp.199-200.
11. There were reports relating to the disobedience of *zamindars* to the orders of the local authorities in several districts and especially so in the large district farmed by Raja Darshan Sing, See. Foreign Dept. Pol. Cons. 26th November, 1832, No. 34.

12. Foreign Dept. Pol. Cons. December 28, 1855, No.380, cf. G.D. Bhatnagar, *Awadh under Wajid Ali Shah*, p.125; this is the major modern writing (in English) which has given most of the details of the incident. He seems to have based himself mainly on the official writings and the English archival records. Hence, he represents the official point of view.

    While in the recent times Ayyub Qadari, in his *Jang-e Azadi: Waqiyat wa Shakhsiyat* (in Urdu), Karachi, 1976 has discussed the matter in the most detailed manner. He has mainly used *Hadiqat-us Shuhuda* of Mirza Jaan, the principal source for the incident, in the most exhaustive manner.
13. *Ibid,* p. 24.
14. Kamaluddin Haider, *Qaisarut Tawarikh*, Vol. II.
15. Ram SahaiTamanna, the author of *Afzalut Tawarikh* wrote a chronogram of the event

    Pay salash cho kamar himmat dast *ilm-e ghayb guft 'yaft shikast' (AH 1271)*
    (Looking for the chronogram [of the event] *I was enlightened that he was 'ultimately defeated')*
16. The members included Maulvi Nihaluddin, Darogha of Faizabad Adalat Hafizullah, Maulvi Syed Mohammad.
17. *Hadiqat us Shuhuda* carries a list of those eyewitnesses and their interviews.
18 *Hadiqat-us Shuhuda,* pp. 22-23.
19. *Ibid,* p. 5; Foreign Dept. Pol. Cons. 28th December 1855,Nos. 360-366; 415-18; 435-441.
20. He was a relative of Maulvi Amir Ali and was blamed by Ali Naqi to have incited Syed Amir Ali to start a *jihad*. Ali Naqi and he were rivals in the court politics and it was only with the help of Bashiruddaulh that Syed Amir Ali was safely let out from the court. Since, it was on the plea of Bashiruddaulah only, that Syed Amir Ali went to the Court to participate in the discussion.
21. For. Dept. Pol. Cons. December 28, 1855, No.414, Appendix A, No. 1, cf. Bhatnagar, op cit; also see *Afzal-ut Tawarikh*, p. 111.
22. NajmulGhani, *Tarikh-e Awadh*, vol. V, pp.222-23
23. *Ibid,* pp. 19, 222, 223
24. For. Dept. Pol. Cons. December 28, 1855, No. 453
25. *Tilism-e Lucknow,* dated 14th November 1856, vol. 17; This aspect has been highlighted by S.Z.H. Jafri, *Awadh From Mughal to Colonial Rule: Studies in the Anatomy of a Transformation* pp. op.cit.
26. *Ba zikr-e haq sarapa gosh daram;* *maey hubb –e 'Ali dar josh daram*

    (In remembering the Truth I pay utmost attention; intoxicated by the love for Ali I get enthusiastic)

    Suno tarikh-e man qabl az shahadat; *sar-e maidan kafan bar dosh daram*

    (AH 1272/AD 1856)

(Before martyrdom I write this chronogram; on the battle field I carry the shroud on my shoulder) See, *ibid,* p. 113.

27. *Tilism,* dated 21 Nov. 1856, No. 18; see S. Z. H. Jafri, The Profile of a saintly Rebel: Maulvi Ahmadullah Shah in *The Facets of the Great Revolt of 1857;* (ed.) Shireen Moosvi, Tulika; New Delhi; 2008; p. 41.
28. *Tilism,* dated 21 Nov. 1856, No. 18.
29. Atkinson, vol. V, p. 632; F. H. Fisher, Statistical, Descriptive and Historical Account of the N.W.P, Vol. IX, pt. II, pp. 129-30, cf. Iqbal Husain, *Religion and Ideology of the Rebels of 1857,* Primus, 2013, pp. 3-4.
30. Atkinson, Vol. V, p. 632 cf. Iqbal Husain, op. cit, pp. 3-4.
31. Sleeman to Colvin, 28 Dec 1853: Sleeman, Journey, II, p.415, cf. Rudrangshu Mukherjee, op. cit. p. 37.
32 Gubbins to Couper, 11th March 1856: For. Dept, Political Proceedings, 13 June 1856, No. 317, cf. *ibid,* pp. 38-9.
33. Barrow, 'Memo on former administration', BROG File No. 305, cf. *ibid.*
34. *Ibid.*
35. *Ibid.*
36. Irfan Habib presented this decline in the population of Lucknow, which continued till 1911, through a table of censuses. Chiding the editors and contributors of *Cambridge Economic History of India, Vol. II* for ignoring these aspects, he has strongly argued for the negative impact of the Colonial Regime in India

    Population of Lucknow, 1869-1911, as provided by Irfan Habib

1869	284,779
1881	261,303
1891	273,028
1901	264,049
1911	259,798

    See, Irfan Habib, *Essays in Indian History: Towards a Marxist Perception,* Delhi, 1995, Tulika Books, p. 349.
37. See map A and compare this map of [Qaisar Bagh] Baradari with the late 19th century map of the region.
38. Rosie Llewellyn-Jones, *Lucknow Then and Now*, ed. Marg Publications, Mumbai, 2003, pp. 13-14.
39. *Tilism*, dated 31th October 1856, No. 15; dated 7th November 1856 No. 16.
40. W.H.Russell, *The Prince of Wales'Tour: A Diary in India*, London, 1877 cf. Rosie, p. 10.
41. *Tilism,* No. 7, dated 5th September 1856.
42. It was a sort of market where English and Chinese merchandise were sold Chinese jade and clay pottery along with glass items of decorations were

the special attractions here, R.R.Kidwai, *Lucknow: The Lost Paradise*, p. 52.

43. *Tilism*, dated 5th September 1856, No. 7.
44. Mr. Thornhill was the Assistant Commissioner of Lucknow before mutiny and was present in Lucknow throughout the siege.
45. *Tilism*, dated 10th October 1856 No. 12.
46. *Tilism*, dated 22nd August 1856 No. 5.
47. Kamaluddin Haider, *Qaisarut Tawarikh*, p.182;

    The fate of the royal libraries after the annexation of Awadh is unclear. Nearly 200,000 volumes of rare books and manuscripts of immense value were reputedly destroyed by the Company when it annexed Awadh. There are suggestions that some of the books went to the La'Martiniere School Library, and were destroyed during its occupation by sepoys in 1857-8. Other seem to have formed the nucleus of the Aminud Daulah Public Library, built in 1882 on the site of one of the garden follies, but the majority, like the royal portraits, have probably found their way to collections in Britain and America; *The Residency, Lucknow,* Archaeological Survey of India, 2003.
48. 'Report of the officers of His Majesty at Lucknow' cf. Masihuddin Khan, *Oude: Its Princes and its Government Vindicated*, John Davy & Sons. London, 1857, ed. with an introduction by Safi Ahmad, British Aggression in Avadh, Meerut, 1969 p. 158.
49. *Koh-e-Noor* dated 19th April 1856 cited it from the 'Eastern Times' newspaper.
50. Masihuddin Khan, op cit, p. 154.
51. However for some historians, Wajid Ali Shah was so intensely loved by the people that the departing emotions of general public took the shape of folk songs and therefore, the destruction was done to destroy the popularity of the king. Roshan Taqui, *Lucknow 1857: The Two Wars at Lucknow- The Dusk of an Era*, New Royal Book Co., 2001, p. 3; Kamaluddin Haider mentions that the day of annexation was the day of *Qayamat* for locals and the declaration of dispossession was as if that Hazrat Israfil is about to blow the world with his mouth.
52. It was supposed to be an astronomical laboratory, having at least 4 telescopes, barometers, thermometers, magnetometers and various electrical and galvanic gadgets. Kamaluddin Haider was employed in the observatory, who translated 17 books and scientific journals from English. Seven other Indians were also employed here. However Colonel Low opined that no Indian would get any benefit from this scientific facility and for Indians this is just a showpiece. During the Mutiny, it was used as an assembly hall for the fighting Rajas and *ta'lluqdars*. Maulvi Ahmadullah Shah used to held meetings here and conducted the revolt from here, R.R.Kidwai, *Lucknow: The Lost Paradise*, pp. 56-8.

53. *Tilism*, dated 31th October 1856, No. 15; dated 7th November 1856 No. 16.
54. *Ibid,* dated 12th December 1856 No. 21.
55. *Tilism*, dated 8th August 1856 No. 3, dated 22nd August 1856 No. 5.
56. Memorandum of Chief Commissioner, Civil Organization of the City of Lucknow, Foreign Political Consultations, 23rd July 1858, no.186, NAI, New Delhi, cited in Veena Talwar Oldenburg, *The Making of Colonial Lucknow*, Delhi, OUP, 1989, p. 34.
57. *Tilism*, dated 25th July 1856 No. 1.
58. *Tilism*, dated 7th November 1856 No. 16; 14 November No. 17; 28th November No. 19; 23rd January 1857 No. 27; 30th January 1857 No. 28.
59. see the following sections.
60. Veena Talwar, in this regard argues that this policy of demolishing religious places had a long lasting negative impact on the Muslim community as a whole. The absence of a grand central mosque restricted the intermingling of Shia and Sunni and thus created a rift between the two principal Muslim sects. Veena Talwar Oldenburg, op cit, pp. 28-37.
61. *Tilism*, dated 29th August 1856 No. 6.
62. He was the Assistant Commissioner of Multan.
63. He was the Assistant of Rao Ram Singh Kothe Wala.
64. The Joint Magistrate of Myanmer platoon.
65. *Tilism*, dated 3rd October 1856 No. 11.
66. *Ibid,* dated 5th December 1856 No. 20.
67. *Ibid.*
68. L.E.S. Rees, *A Personal Narrative of the Siege of Lucknow*, London, 1858, pp.33- 34, cited in Irfan Habib, 'Coming of 1857' in Shireen Moosvi ed. *Facets of the Great Revolt, 1857,* Tulika Books, 2008.

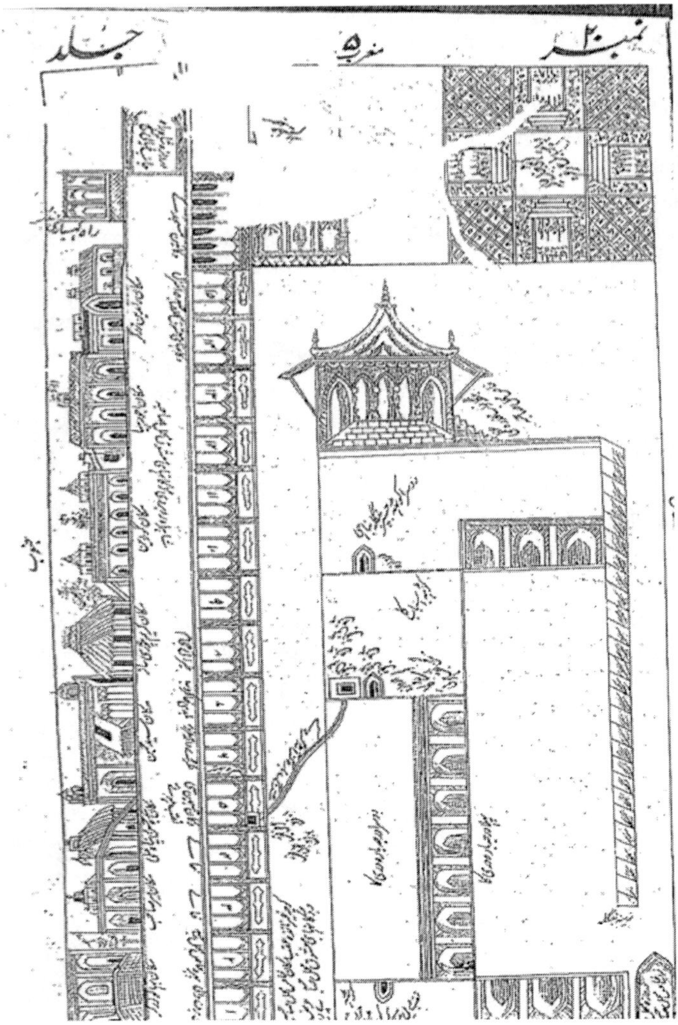

Source: Tilism-e Lucknow.

Map A: ***The Pre-Mutiny Map of [QaiserBagh] Baradari and other adjacent buildings in the vicinity***

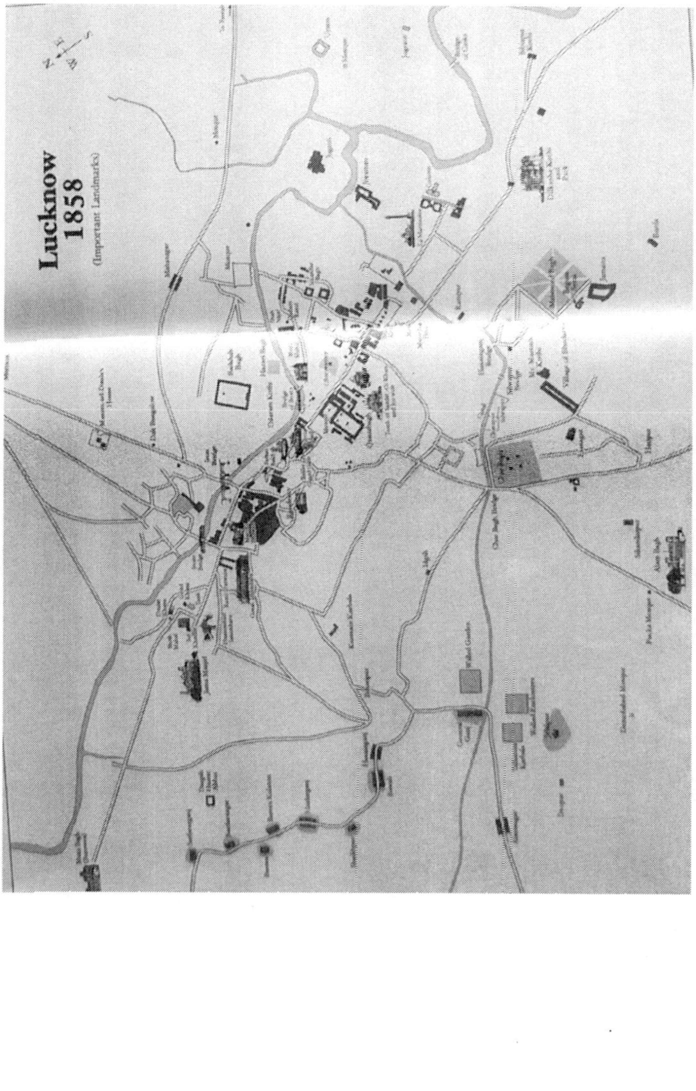

Map B: The City of Lucknow After the Revolt
(Lucknow City of Illusion The Alkazi Collection of Photography, *ed.* Rosie Llewellyn Jones 2006)

Ideologues and Commanders

Chapter - 11

Fazl-e Haq of Khairabad:
A Scholarly Rebel of 1857

— Professor Iqbal Husain

While the Rebellion of 1857 has been described in much details and variously interpreted, the rebels themselves still remain elusive. It was their victors and not they, who have left the bulk of our records on the Rebellion. This is why any document produced by the Rebels of 1857 is always fraught with interest.

An interesting feature of the rebellion was that a considerable number of Muslim scholars (*ulema*) took part in it. One of them was Maulana Fazl-e Haq of Khairabad (Awadh) who has left a very interesting account of the rebellion in Arabic under the title *As-Saurat al Hindiya* (hereafter *As-Saurat*). The work was translated into Urdu by Muhammad Shahid Khan in 1947.[1] It was also noticed by Ghulam Rasul Mehr who has written several historical works in Urdu.[2] Mahdi Hasan has also utilized portions of *As-Saurat* in his monograph on Bahadur Shah II.[3] Nevertheless *As-Saurat has* escaped notice of most of the historians working on the history of the Rebellion of 1857. In this chapter, an attempt is made to sketch the career of Fazl-e Haq, and his role in 1857, with reference to extracts from *As-Saurat* concerning some of the interesting and significant events of the rebellion.

Fazl-e Haq was born in 1796 at Delhi where his father held the office of *Sadr-us Sadur.*[4] He belonged to a very distinguished family of *ulema*, which was also quite prosperous owing to the *madad-i ma'ash* grants which it had received from the Mughal Emperors and the Awadh rulers from time to time.[5]

Fazl-e Haq acquired his early education from his father and some of the renowned *ulema* of the period like Shah Abdul Qadir and Shah Abdul Aziz of Delhi.[6] Completing his education at the age of 13 he began his career as a teacher in 1809. He is said to have excelled in many oriental sciences. It is not difficult to speculate on the impact that the recent British conquest had on the young scholar's mind. Shah Abdul Aziz's reaction to the fall of Delhi in 1803 reflects his religious decree, where he declared that Delhi ceased to be a *Dar-ul* Islam.[7] Fazl-e Haq then a student in the *Madrasa-i Rahimiya* (founded by the father of Shah Waliullah) might have been inspired by Shah Sahib's political ideology. Around the same time Syed Ahmad of Rae Bareli (Awadh) acquired education from Shah Abdul Qadir and Shah Abdul Aziz. His reaction to the British rule is implicit in his letter to Hindu Pat Rao where he says, that he was planning a movement directed against the British.[8] We get an echo of the same attitude in Maulana Fazl-e Haq's later writings.[9] The Maulana however, did not initiate any movement. like that of Syed Ahmad Rae Barelvi. Rather, he began his career as *Sar-rishtadar* in the office of the Resident at Delhi in 1825. Good work and sound knowledge soon brought him close to the Resident as well as to King Akbar Shah II.[10] In 1828, he was elevated to the position of *Mufti* in the Department of *Qaza.* Upon the abolition of this department, he was appointed as a government pleader and sent to Allahabad.[11] When and how he came back to Delhi is not known. It seems that he resigned from the service.

Due to lack of evidence we are not in a position to say whether the resignation had any link with the death of Syed Ahmed at Balakot in 1831, or there was some other reason apart from the attitude of high officials towards him. From Allahabad, Fazl-e Haq came to Delhi where he came into contact with Prince Mirza Abu Zafar (later on Bahadur Shah). From Delhi, he went to Jhajjar,[12] from there to Alwar, Shaharanpur, Tonk and finally, Rampur where he remained in the service of the Nawab for eight years.[13] From Rampur, the Maulana went to Lucknow where he was appointed *Sadrus Sadur* in 1848. He served in this capacity till 1856.[14] The year (1856) is a turning point in Maulana's career. The annexation of Awadh was a severe blow to Indians, specially for the people ofAwadh. It seems that Fazl-e Haq also came into contact with Ahmadullah Shah the determined opponent of British rule, during this period at Lucknow, and most probably under his influence, he resigned.[15]

The abolition of the Department of *Qaza* also seems to be one of the reasons of annoyance to the Maulana as it adversely affected a large number of Muslim families whose subsistence came through employment in this Department. In these circumstances, he left Lucknow on a mission to persuade persons of influence and power to do something to overthrow the British from India. His endeavours in persuading the Maharaja of Alwar, however, bore no fruits. Fazl-e Haq was actually at Alwar when the rebellion took place. He now openly preached *jihad* against the British. Many responding to his call joined under his banner as *jihadis*. He appeared before Bahadur Shah on 16 August 1857, presented a gold muhur in *nazr and* held a discussion with him for some time on the current situation.[16] Hereafter, he appeared before Bahadur Shah frequently. At Delhi the rebels were, however gradually losing grip and British reoccupation of Delhi was imminent.]iwan Lal says that at this juncture the Maulana proposed to Bahadur Shah 'to devise such means to induce the sepoys to cease their opposition to the English, for they cannot prevail against the English'.[17] Maulana's career and anti British feelings, however, do not conform to this statement, and there may be some error in Metcalfe's translation. Since Jiwan Lal's original Roznamcha is not available with us, we'can only infer from the subsequent lines that the Maulana must have advised contrarily, since Bahadur Shah directed him as follows: 'Look to your troops, go out yourself to fight, and lead them against the British.'[18] It is significant that the Maulana had some troops under his command-probably the *jihadis* from Alwar, Mewat and Delhi. Most of them were poor and armed with traditional arms. Their determined fight against the British in 1857 earned them the derisive designation 'fanatics' by the victors.[19]

In order to provide subsistance to the troops, Bahadur Shah allowed Fazl-e Haq to collect revenue from the villages. On 18 August 1857, Fazl-e Haq's son Abdul Haq and Faiz Ahmad left for Gurjawan for collecting revenue while the Maulana got busy in persuading the people of the fort as well as Delhi to come forward for the *jihad* (28 August 1857).[20]

It seems that the *jihad* movement by Fazl-e Haq was paralleled by another movement for the same objective by the pandits. Zakaullah, the Urdu historian of the nineteenth century himself a resident of Delhi and an eyewitness of 1857 thus says:

> The Hindu Pandits were not behind the Muslims in harbouring enemity to the English. On several occasions the Pandits consulting their *patras* told the *Tilangas* (sepoys) of auspicious moments to fight against the British, assuring them of victories.... A strange feature was noticed in Chandni Chowk and other markets that the *pothi-wielding* Pandits were communicating commandments from the *Shastras* that they should fight the English *malechchas*.[21]

By the end of August 1857, the position of the rebels worsened in Delhi. To keep the morale of the sepoys high, Maulana Fazl-e Haq, in consultation with the rebel General Bakht Khan, issued a *fatwa* signed by almost all the leading *alims* of Delhi. Consequently a force of 90,000 men was raised.[22]

Fazl-e Haq could not stay at Delhi for long owing to the growing differences between Prince Mirza Mughal and General Bakht Khan.[23] As events proceeded, Delhi fell on 19 September. Fazl-e Haq kept himself concealed in a house for five days. On the night of 25 September he along with his family members fled to Awadh. On his way he stayed at Bhikampur (Aligarh) for eighteen days with Nawab Abdul Shakur Khan.[24] From Bhikampur he moved towards his home-Khairabad. Leaving his family there he rejoined the rebel Prince Firuz Shah.[25] After the departure of Firuz Shah, the Maulana joined Ahmadullah Shah.[26] He accompanied Ahmadullah Shah to Pawayn, where the latter was treacherously killed.[27] After the fall of Lucknow, Fazl-e Haq retired to some unknown place. He was arrested in 1859 and brought to Lucknow. He was prosecuted for issuance of a *fatwa* of *jihad* and seditious activities and sentenced to transportation for life.[28]

Maulana Fazl-e Haq suffered unbearable humiliation and torture in the Andamans. He had so far lived a decent life. Rigours of jail life injured his self-respect. His inner feelings are reflected in his two *works-As-Saurat* and *Qasaid Fitnat-ul Hind.* These works were compiled in the'Andaman prison. *As-Saurat* is, however, of great interest so far as the rebellion of 1857 is concerned. It presents an account of the

Rebellion from a rebel's point of view. *As-Saurat* has been written in lucid and simple Arabic. The selection of Arabic as the medium seems to have been made purposely so as to keep the work as far as possible unintelligible to ensure its safety. The original manuscript of *As-Saurat* was written with pencil and coal on small sheets of papers. The author took care not to cite any names in *As-Saurat.* He meticulously uses metaphors which makes the identity of the people clear. *As-Saurat* was smuggled out of India by another rebel convict Maulvi Inayat Ahmad of Kakori who was released from jail for his good work.[29]

As-Saurat begins with the traditional prayers to God and praises for the Prophet. Thereafter, the author writes in a touching way, 'My this book comes from the pen of a broken hearted, injured, grief-stricken and unfortunate person, who now does not possess the least strength to withstand little hardships'.[30] After giving an account of hardship, suffering and his failing health, Fazl-e Haq gives the causes of discontent leading to the Rebellion of 1857:

> The Christians from Britain whose hearts were full of malice and enemity after the occupation of villages and cities of India and its contiguous regions; they humiliated all those who enjoyed power and honour so that they were rendered powerless to raise their heads. They (the English) chalked out a scheme to convert to Christianity all the inhabitants of India irrespective of their positions. They thought that the Indians who have no friends would not dare to defy except submission. All this was with the purpose to making Indians heretic and irreligious like themselves and to make them of one community with them.... They understood well that the differences in religious faith between the ruler and the ruled would be of great difficulty for their rule and occupation of the country, and it would lead to revolution. Therefore, on various pretexts they began to destroy the religion and faith (of Indians) with full vigour. They began to impart education to the children and the illiterate, in their own language by establishing schools in cities and villages to preach their own religion. They exerted vigorously to destroy the oriental learnings, sciences and the learned and their centres of learnings.[31]

It is significant that what Fazl-e Haq alleges in *As-Saurat* found prominence in almost all the Proclamations issued by the rebel during the rebellion.[32] Even Syed Ahmad (later Sir Syed), a loyalist, boldly argued that one of the causes of the rebellion was the activities of the Christian missionaries which annoyed both the Hindus and Muslims.[33]

Fazl-e Haq did not simply see the British rule as an attack on Indian religions, he saw the economic aspect as well, though his perception was undoubtedly hazy, 'They (British) adopted a second method to contain different groups of people by purchasing all the foodgrains from the cultivators, paying them in cash, depriving these poor people of any right of purchase and sale. In this way they became the only source of supply of grains to the markets and raising or reducing its prices'.[34]

Maulana Fazl-e Haq makes it clear in *As-Saurat* that the majority of the rebel sepoys consisted of Hindus. The British attempted to spoil their religion forcing them to take the fat of cows while the Muslims being in a lesser number were forced to take lard. This caused the sepoys of both faiths to rebel.[35] Fazl-e Haq is not unmindful of the atrocities committed by the rebels and he sees that the cause of the rebels' humiliation was their own excesses:

> Their restlessness turned into disorder and (the sepoys) killed the Christians, committed dacoities and attacked their sardars and commanders. Some of them excelled in hardness of hearts and madness by not sparing even small children and women from their murderous assaults. Murders of small children and innocent women caused (their own) humiliation and disrepute. Settling scores with their officers, all the rebel groups of sepoys came out of their cantonments disrupting civil and revenue administration. Highways become disturbed and insecure, riots and disorders spread among the people of God, villages and towns fell into the grip of tensions and horrors.[36]

As we are aware Fazl-e Haq had taken an active part in the rebellion at Delhi. His close contact with Bahadur Shah enabled him to know the real position that prevailed in the Red Fort. Referring to the assembling of the rebel forces he writes:

> Many of the rebel troops reached the residence of the descendants of Timur, the capital of the kingdom, Delhi. There they installed

> the person who had been previously their ruler and had his own ministers and advisers. But he was himself very weak, afflicted and inexperienced. Having passed several stages of life he had entered the valley of old age. Honestly speaking instead of being an independent ruler he was subordinate to this own wife[37] and the *wazir.*[38] The *wazir* was in fact an ally of the Christians and sunk in their loyalty. He strongly opposed those who were enemies of the Christians and (their) Sovereign. Similar was the attitude of the family members of the ruler (Bahadur Shah). Some of them were very close and trusted by the King. They did whatever they liked and acted according to their own will, expressing only loyalty to the King. And that the King was so fickle-minded and inexperienced that he knew nothing. He exhibited unusual gestures. He could not do anything following his own opinion. He had no capacity to discern between the good and the bad. Neither could he give any order openly or secretly nor do any good or harm to anyone.
>
> While all this was taking place, a group of brave Muslims, having obtained *fatwa* of *jihad* from the *ulema* and interpreters of religion came forward from villages and towns to fight the Christians. On the other hand, the inexperienced *sardar* (Bahadur Shah) made some of his cowardly unscrupulous, licentious and treacherous sons leaders, of the sepoys.[39] They hated honest and wise men.[40] They had neither any knowledge of battle nor experience of using swords and spears, They had made friends and companions from the street. In this way these untried people indulged themselves in the pursuit of pleasure, extravagance, luxuries and mischief mongering.[41]

As-Saurat thus frankly describes the real situation prevailing in Delhi at the beginning of the Rebellion. Having assumed authority, the Princes unabashedly misused their powers in exacting money from the rich people of the city specially the *Sahukars*.[42] So we note in *As-Saurat.*

> They were paupers and now became rich. With prosperity they fell into pursuits of pleasure. On the pretext of raising equipment for the sepoys, they collected considerable money. They did not

> spend even a grain on the sepoys and utilized the amount for themselves. Even this was tolerable. But they were prevented from leading the scouts owing to their company of the maidservants in the night.... Consequently the army of the Christians pounced upon them.[43]

As-Saurat's narration of the rebels resistance to the British forces besieging Delhi provides an insight into the actual condition of the sepoys. 'Condition of the rebel sepoys, morally and economically, was also not satisfactory. They were divided and some of them had no resting place and some were rendered useless owing to hunger and fatigue. Some of them had already retired after plundering the people.... Only one group kept on fighting bravely against the Christians.'[44] However, despite divisions and weaknesses among the rebels, they continued to fight. Fazl-e Haq refers to this situation somewhat in a general way:

> When the Christians got tired and demoralized from fighting, they sought help from the Hindus of the West.[45] The Hindus within a short time provided them with considerable troops, money and war equipment enabling the Christians to fight with determination. They planted a strong army on the Ridge. The army consisted of the white faced-men, the accursed Hindus and unfortunate Muslims of bad characters.[46] who had sold their faith to the Christians and had become heretic.[47]

Mounting British pressure on the rebels at Delhi followed by continuous exactions of the Princes from the bankers, and sepoys, plundering activities had adversely affected the people, particularly the Hindu traders. Many of them became secret allies and informers. Fazl-e Haq in *As-Saurat* says, 'Thousands of the citizens turned friendly to the Christians and all Hindus became their followers. Muslims were divided into two groups. One was an uncompromising enemy of them (British) while the other was so deeply sunk in pleasure that it tried its best in destroying the Indian army and humiliating the *Jihadis.* They were active to create disunity among the *jihadis.*[48]

Fazl-e Haq praised the *jihadis* for their determined and gallant role in resisting the British occupation of Delhi. When their number declined (owing to hunger, deaths and illness) they could not provide a guard to protect the city wall. 'Unfortunately one night, a luxury loving and negligent body of troops was posted to guard the front facing the Ridge. They went to sleep putting off their arms. Taking advantage of their carelessness, the enemy attacked and left them in eternal sleep.'[49]

As-Saurat gives some startling details of the British attack on Delhi, their war tactics and the help that they received from some of the inhabitants. 'So they reached the houses of those who had become their allies. They made arrangements for their protection and entertained them with sumptuous food.... Closing doors of their houses, they opened holes in the walls so as to defend themselves against the rebels. They shot to death the sepoys and citizens who happened to appear there. Their opponents had no defence against thern.[50] General Robert who reached Delhi with the British forces largely supports *As-Saurat*. He found about 40 to 50 terror striken banias huddled together.

> After considerable hesitation and consultation amongst themselves they agreed to two of their party guiding Lang and me.... Our trembling guides conducted us through houses, across courtyards, and along secluded alleys, without our meeting a living creature, until we found ourselves in an upper room of a house looking out on the Chandni Chowk, and within 50 yards of Lahore Gate. From the windows of the room we could see beneath us the sepoys, lounging about, engaged in cleaning their muskets and other occupation.... I could see from the number on their caps that these belonged to the 5th Native Infantry.[51]

At a time when the British were tightening their grip on Delhi from all sides, there remained no place of safety for the rebels nor was there any ruler or leader to guide them. The rebels at Delhi began to suffer from lack of food supplies. The situation was created by the loyalist, Mirza Ilahi Bux and like-minded men. *As-Saurat* describes the situation as follows:

> The baniyas and other Hindus friendly to the Christians; and the managers[52] of the King who were enemical to the *jihadis* adopted a new way to kill the citizens and the sepoys. They concealed all the foodgrains available with the baniyas and stopped supplies from the villages. This step worked effectively. The sepoys and citizens had to pass days and nights with hunger, thirst, restlessness and inflammation. At last having no alternative, they retired.

Consequently the Christians seized the gate of the city, its wall, fort, palace and markets.[53]

As-Saurats account of the rebellion in Delhi concludes with the arrest of Bahadur Shah and executions of his sons, followed by indiscriminate killings particularly of Muslims, plunder of people, suicides by innumerable women and girls to save their honour and other hardships suffered by the Delhi populace.[54]

Fazl-e Haq's exit from Delhi and journey to Awadh with his family members is also of considerable interest. In Awadh the rebels had installed Birjis Qadr under the care of Begum Hazrat Mahal. Awadh was also not free from internal conflicts. Fazl-e Haq's account of the state of affairs prevailing in Awadh is vivid. Birjis Qadr 'had not the ability to understand the intricacies of the administration, nor was he capable of issuing orders and leading the army. All of his nobles and ministers were incompetent, lazy, cowards, foolish, licentious and dishonest. A majority of them was mean and slave of money.... Most of them were supporters and allies of the Chnstians.[55]

As-Saurat gives some interesting details of the war in Lucknow, the weaknesses of the rebels, Begum Hazrat Mahal's patronage to the Delhi rebels, the rebel's defeat and the escape of the Begum from Lucknow.[56] It holds Mammo Khan responsible for the defeat of the rebels in Lucknow because he was incompetent, evasive to good counsel, foolish and coward. Out of conceit he did not meet the gentle and wise advisors and appointed his own relatives as companions and administrators who were foolish and ignorant.[57] As a result of this, the rebel forces were headed by incompetent and corrupt persons.[58]

Fazl-e Haq's praises in the *As-Saurat* for Ahmadullah Shah are not entirely owing to his having entertained the same ideology. Even Holmes[59] and Malleson[60] pay tributes to Ahmadullah Shah for his determined resistance. Fazl-e Haq had accompanied Ahmadullah Shah to Pawayan where the latter was killed. *As-Saurat* says that it was a treacherous murder by the Raja of Pawayan as Ahmadullah Shah had proceeded there with a few supporters to negotiate with him for the expulsion of some pro-British elements and securing help for waging the war against the British.[61] The treachery of the Raja of Pawayan towards Ahmadullah Shah greatly embittered the rebels and some of the pro-rebel *zamindars* of the area who made several attempts to destroy the Raja but the presence of British troops saved him.[62]

The last pages of *As-Saurat* are mainly concerned with the sufferings of the author who is bitter that, despite their victories the British did not stick to the promises made in the Queen's Proclamation. Believing that he was not involved in any murder, he came out of his hiding place. But he was captured, prosecuted, and sentenced for transportation of life. He remained as a cônvict in the Andaman Islands until his death in 1862.

Notes

1. *Baghi Hindustan,* Bijnor, 1947.
2. 1857 *Ke Mujahid,* Lahore, 1957.
3. *Bahadur Shah II, and the war of* 1857 *in Delhi,* Delhi, n.d., pp. 381-92. My colleague Professor Iqtidar Alam told me that *As-Saurat* has since been translated into English by Professor Moin-ul-Haq, Karachi. Unfortunately despite my best efforts, I could not procure a copy of it at Aligarh.
4. Intizamullah Akbarabadi, *Moulana Fazl-e Haq Khairabadi,* n.d., p. 1. Maulana Shahid places his birth in 1797, *Baghi Hindustan,* p. 11.
5. Maluvi Mustafa Ali gopamauvi, *Tazkirat-ut Ansab,* p. 1. *Baghi Hindustan,* pp. 26-7.
6. *Ibid.,* pp. 29-30.
7. *Fatawa-i Aziziya,* vol. I, Mujtaba-i Press, p. 17.
8. Abul Hasan Nadvi, *Syed Ahmad Shaheed,* vol. I, pp. 388-94.
9. *As-Saurat,* pp. 356-7.
10. Intizamullah Akbarabadi, p. 5; Mohammad Husain, *Abe Hayat,* p. 512.
11. Intizamullah Akbarabadi, p. 8; *Baghi Hindustan,* p. 41.
12. Mirza Ghalib, *Yadgar-i Ghalib,* p. 355.
13. *Intikhab-i Yadgar,* pp. 291-2.
14. Intizamullah Akbarabadi, p. 8; *Intikhab-i Yadgar,* pp. 291-2. He also looked after the work of *Huzur tahsil* established by Hardinge . See Najmal Ghani, *Tarikh-I Awadh,* vol. IV; Newal Kishore, p. 72.
15. 1857 *Ke Mujahid,* p. 131.
16. Jiwan Lal, p. 196; Abdul Latif, 1857 *Ka Tarikhi Roznamcha,* ed. K.A. Nizami, pp. 162-3; *Jasuson ke Khutoot,* NAI, p. 97.
17. Jiwan Lal, p. 198.
18. *Ibid. Jasuson ke Khutoot,* p. 87 refers to Maulana's efforts to persuade the people of Delhi for jihad.

19. Roberts, *Forty One years in India,* London, 1897, p. 202; Jiwan Lal, pp. 178-9; For the role of *jihadis* in Delhi, See K.M. Ashraf, 'Muslim Revivalists and Revolt', in *Rebellion* 1857, ed..P.C. Joshi, New Delhi, 1957, pp. 71-102.
20. *Jasuson ke Khutoot,* p. 89.
21. Zakaullah, *Tarikh-i Uroj-e Saltanate-d Englishiya,* p. 676 (hereafter Zakaullah).
22. Zakaullah, p. 676.
23. See my paper, 'Bakht Khan, a leading sepoy general of 1857', *PIHC, 1985.*
24. *Baghi Hindustan,* p. 158n.
25. For career see 1857 *Ke Mujahid,* pp. 120-9; *Bengal Past and Present,* August December 1969 and January-June 1970.
26. For life and career see, Abrar Hasan Faruqi, *Masir-i Dilawari,* Hardoi, 1966; *Freedom Struggle in UP,* vol. II, pp. 13, 18, 42-4, 81, 102, 104, 141, 419; *Tilism,* Lucknow, nos. 18-19, 28, 33.
27. *Freedom Struggle in up,* Vol. V, p. 149.
28. *As-Saurat,* p. 417.
29. *Baghi Hindustan,* pp. 173-4.
30. *As-Saurat,* p. 353.
31. *Ibid.,* pp. 355-7.
32. *Freedom Struggle in UP,* vol. I, pp. 442-4; Mahdi Husain, *Bahadur Shah II,* Appendix B, pp. 328-32; *Eighteen Fifty Seven,* pp. 382-4.
33. Hali, *Hayat-i Javed,* Lahore, 1957, pp. 892, 897-901.
34. *As-Saurat,* pp. 357-8.
35. *Ibid.,* pp. 358-60.
36. *Ibid.,* pp. 360-1.
37. A reference to Zinat Mahal.
38. Hakim Ahsanullah Khan.
39. Mirza Mohammad Jawan Bakht and Mirza Mughal were appointed wazir and cammander-in-chief. Other princes also got military assignments. See *The Press List of the Mutiny Papers,* No. 1, Vol. 13, 16-22 May 1857; Jiwan Lal, p. 58 and Sen, *Eighteen Fifty Seven,* p. 74.
40. *Jasuson Ke Khutoot,* pp. 9-10; Zakaullah, p. 682.
41. *As-Saurat,* pp. 363-4.
42. *The Press List...,* no. 146, SN 109, no. 199; SN 359, 1857; 1857 *ka Tarikhi Roznamcha,* p. 124.
43. *As-Saurat,* pp. 363-5.
44. Jiwan Lal, p. 100; *As-Saurat,* p. 366.
45. Maharaja Patiala and others.

46. Balauch and Afghan British soldiers.
47. *As-Saurat,* p. 368.
48. Zakaullah, pp. 675-6; *Sadiq-ul Akhbar,* Delhi, 6 July 1857; Jiwan Lal, pp. 134-5.
49. *As-Saurat,* pp. 370-1.
50. *Ibid.,* pp. 373-4.
51. *Fourty One Years in India,* London, 1897, vol. I, pp. 245-6.
52. Mirza Ilahi Bakhsh and his supporters.
53. *As-Saurat,* pp. 376-7.
54. *Ibid.,* pp. 380-8.
55. *Ibid.,* 'pp. 390-2.
56. *Ibid.*
57. *Ibid.,* p. 402.
58. *Ibid.,* p. 403.
59. Holmes, p. 506.
60. G.B. Malleson, *The Indian Mutiny of* 1857, Vol. IV, p. 381.
61. *As-Saurat,* pp. 109-10. .
62. *Freedom Struggle in UP,* vol. V, pp. 545-6, 553,. 569-70, Malleson, op. cit., p. 1-91.

Chapter - 12

Bakht Khan:
A Leading Sepoy General of 1857

— Professor Iqbal Husain

Soon after the fall of Delhi (11th May 1857) to the mutineers from Meerut, a serious problem of maintaining law and order arose.[1] Delhi remained under the mercy of the unruly elements throughout the months of May and June despite vigorous attempts made by Bahadur Shah to restore order.[2] At this juncture, Bakht Khan with his Bareilly forces appeared on the scene and assumed a leading position among the rebels until Delhi fell to the British forces on 19th September 1857. In this essay, an attempt is made to reconstruct the career of Bakht Khan and his role in the Rebellion.

Though many of the historians writing in Urdu ascribe to Bakht Khan an origin from the Ruhelas,[3] none of them give a clear account of his family background. One of the Military Officers who participated in the suppression of rebellion says sneeringly, that he belonged to a 'family of Hindu extraction, but converted under temptation of territorial acquisition'.[4] Munshi Jiwan Lal a spy of the British and stationed at Delhi during the rebellion refers to Bakht Khan, first meeting with Bahadur Shah on 2nd July, says, Bakht Khan claimed to be of Mughal descent and the 'same family' to which the king belonged. Khwaja Hasan Nizami says without quoting any authority that Bakht Khan was related to the Awadh rulers maternally and to Ghulam Qadir Ruhela's family paternally.[5] One of the modern writers in Urdu, quoting the evidence of one Chanda Begum, great grand daughter of Dundey Khan, the Ruhela Chieftain of Bissauli says that Bakht Khan was very closely related to Ghulam Qadir Ruhela.[6] Chanda Begum claimed that

Bakht Khan's father Abdullah Khan shifted to Sultanpur (Awadh) where he was married to one of the princesses of the Awadh family.[7] The claim that Bakht Khan belonged to the family of Najib-ud Daulah is, however, fully substantiated by the genealogical table where his father Abdullah Khan is mentioned as the son of Sultan Khan—a brother of Najib-ud Daulah.[8] Bakht Khan was, therefore, a cousin of Ghulam Qadir Khan Ruhela. Bakht Khan's Ruhela origin in itself is quite interesting as after the destruction of the Ruhela power in 1774, the Ruhelas had not reconciled themselves with the new regime of Awadh (up to 1801) and the British thereafter. They made attempts to overthrow the new governments as and when they got an opportunity.[9] Bakht Khan may, therefore, have imbibed an anti-British feeling from his Ruhela antecedants.

He appears to have joined the Bengal Army and served the artillery branch for over 40 years with distinction.[10] He served under the command of Sale in 'the Anglo-Afghan war and fought at Jalalabad.[11] On the termination of war, he was promoted to the post of *subadar* in the artillery branch, and posted at Nimach.[12] Bakht Khan was posted at Bareilly when the rebellion took place.[13] Initially, he expressed loyalty to the British and was not willing to join the rebellion until his Pir Maulvi Sarfaraz Ali prevailed upon him.[14] Bakht Khan then joined the rebel leader Khan Bahadur Khan, grandson of Hafiz Rahmat Khan, the Ruhela Chief of Bareilly.[15] He was designated as Brigadier General and soon became a trusted associate of Khan Bahadur Khan.[16] On 11th June, Khan Bahadur Khan asked Bakht Khan to proceed to Delhi with his sepoys to support the king.[17] Bakht Khan thereupon marched to Delhi adopting a longer route, collecting revenue and raising troops in Badaun and Farrukhabad.[18]

Bakht Khan arrived with his force within the vicinity of Delhi on 1st July.[19] He found Delhi in a practically anarchical condition. Many ruffians were committing atrocities in the guise of sepoys. Some of the Princes notably Mirza Khizr Sultan were active in exacting money from the bankers.[20] Bahadur Shah lived under a constant fear of being overthrown by two different groups of sepoys who wished to raise Mirza Mughal and Mirza Abu Bakr to the throne.[21] His attempts to maintain law and order through the princes or the sepoys were of no avail.[22] The nominal Emperor therefore saw a ray of hope in the arrival of Bakht Khan. He sent a delegation of notables to welcome him.[23]

On 2nd July, Bakht Khan appeared before the king.[24] He was conferred many honours and appointed as commander-in-chief of the rebel forces.[25] By an imperial proclamation, all earlier arrangements, were cancelled and all the military officers in command of regiments, were placed in subordination to General Bakht Khan. Prince Mirza Mughal was elevated to the position of Adjutant General. Bakht Khan was given sweeping powers; he could even severely punish the Princes for plundering activities.[26] Bahadur Shah gave the following orders to Bakht Khan:

1. To destroy the enemy's positions and defeat them;
2. The sepoys and troopers intruding the fort should be provided alternative accommodation outside the city and they should be asked to desist from plunder and causing hardships to the people:
3. Suitable steps be taken to disburse salary of the old and new servants;
4. Collection of revenue and arrangements of the *thanas* be made through the army; and
5. Ruffians intruding the houses of the city in the guise of sepoys and plundering them be dealt with properly.[27]

The tasks assigned to Bakht Khan would have daunted anyone, but, as we can see from Jiwan Lal's account, Bakht Khan was fully confident of carrying these out.[28] Without wasting time he decided to launch an attack on the British forces in the morning of 3rd July. The plan was however, deferred presumably because it was rather premature. In order to tone up the city administration, Bakht Khan made the Kotwal of Delhi fully responsible for law and order failing which he could even face death punishment.[29]

The plundering acts of the sepoys and the Princes had greatly demoralized the bankers and shopkeepers in Delhi. In protest, most of them had drawn their shutters and hid themselves in their houses. To restore confidence Bakht Khan, by the beat of drums, directed all the shopkeepers to keep arms, and those who did not possess these, could obtain the same from the army headquarters. He also issued stern orders for punishing the plundering sepoys and directed the police officers to ask the respectable inhabitants of Delhi to attend his levee—a step which was largely misunderstood and resented by them.[30] Perhaps realizing the necessity of satisfying the apprehensions of *jagirdars* and *ma'afidars* (*madad-ma'ash* holders) and the pensioners of Delhi and its neighbourhood, assured them of their possessions and payment of arrears of grants for the period of disturbance when peace had been restored.[31]

It seems that throughout the day (2nd July) Bakht Khan remained engaged in issuing instructions and making other important arrangements. In the night he visited the king. What transpired between them is not very clear. It, however, seems that the princes were the central theme of discussion, for the next day (3rd July), by an imperial order, the 'Princes were relieved from all further duties connected with the army'.[32] These measures seem to have considerably improved confidence of the people in Delhi. Bakht Khan was greatly praised by one of the leading newspapers of Delhi for his control over the administration and his success putting a check on the lawless elements in the capital.[33]

It may be recalled that when Bakht Khan arrived in Delhi, he had 100 *jihadis* with him.[34] The number of *jihadis* naturally began to increase as they found a friend in Bakht Khan in Delhi. The active interest of the *jihadis*, also termed *Wahabis* in some of the contemporary works, is of great interest as it indicates that the movement initiated by Saiyid Ahmad Barelvi still had strong influence on the Muslims in north India. Zakaullah, the historian of the nineteenth century, says sarcastically that with the arrival of Bakht Khan, the cry of *jihad* against the English greatly increased. Preachers delivered inflammatory speeches in the mosques to persuade Muslims to join the crusade to protect their religion and their family members from being slain by the infidels, if they won.[35] Apart from Bareilly, a large number of *jihadis* arrived from Hansi, Hissar,]aipur, Nasirabad, Bhopal and Tonk.

It may again be noted that Hansi, Hissar, Bhopal and Tonk had a considerable population of the Ruhela Afghans. The leaders of these crusaders were Maulvi Abdul Ghaffar and Maulvi Sarfaraz Ali, Imam

Khan Risaldar and Ghaus Mohammad Khan. Maulvi Sarfaraz Ali, was elected *Amir-ul Mujahidin* ('leader of the crusaders') and Bakht Khan their patron.[36] Most of these crusaders belonged to the poor class as Zakaullah sneeringly described them 'ill dressed' and Ill-fed, hungry' people who lived on the charity of the well-to-do citizens of Delhi; but they were fully equipped with conventional arms.[37]

Theoretically, the king had conferred all powers on Bakht Khan but in practice the latter's strength lay in the support of his own brigade, wrongly alleged to have been paid six months salary in advance.[38] The presence of the crusaders within his camp understandably also helped to improve the morale of the troops.

Bakht Khan, unlike his predecessors in Delhi, made operations against the British forces strongly entranched on the Ridge, by attempting to intercept their supplies (4th July).[39] On 9th July, Bakht Khan with a strong force supported by the *jihadis* attacked the English position and captured Tihari Hazari (Tis Hazari).[40] The victory, first since the rebels entered Delhi seems to have a serious repercussion causing jealousy among the other rebel forces from Meerut and Nimach.[41] The princes were already unhappy owing to the sudden eminence of Bakht Khan. A forged letter from the King, censuring Bakht Khan, was circulated. Bahadur Shah, however assuaged Bakht Khan's feelings denying by authorship of the letter (11th July).[42]

Bakht Khan's main concern was to keep the army satisfied and united. To raise their morale, he prevailed upon the Emperor (11th July) to agree that wounded sepoys should receive pension as well as grant of land. Next day (12th July) under his advice, the king ordered the withdrawal of levies on sugar so as to ensure its regular supply to the army.[43]

Administrative reforms and efficiency in controlling the army, however, had little effect on the hatred of the princes and a hord of conspirators among the courtiers.[44] Mirza Mughal always flouted Bakht Khan's orders and constantly poisoned the ears of Bahadur Shah. He appealed to the king to issue an order to Bakht Khan not to interfere in the affairs of his troops.[45] Despite such efforts, Bahadur Shah remained unmoved. To keep the opponents of Bakht Khan silent, he increased his favours to the former by sending presents and expressing his satisfaction in public.[46]

Bakht Khan's success in the battle of Tis Hazari, did not force the English to vacate their positions from Sabzimandi, Alipur and Mubarak Bagh. The presence of enemy forces so close to the city was very dangerous for its security, and Bahadur Shah issued orders to Bakht Khan to seize these places. But Bakht Khan's own forces were quite incapable of achieving any success without support of other forces present in Delhi. Of the rebel forces, the Nimach force had a reputation for bravery but their Generals, Ghaus Khan and Sidhari Singh, were constantly in disagreement with Bakht Khan. 'Moreover, some of them charged Bakht Khan of complicity towards the English.[47] Consequently no joint action could be taken for sometime to the great advantage of the English forces.[48] Bahadur Shah then, intervened and brought about a reconciliation between Bakht Khan and Sidhari Singh.[49] But the reconciliation was only on the surface. Bakht Khan's opponents, continued their efforts, to alienate Bahadur Shah. Not surprising, most of the officers from Nimach showed their hostility to Bakht Khan, once their equal, and in a commanding position. On 5th August Bakht Khan's differences with General Sidhari Singh came to a head after their joint failure in capturing the English positions at Alipur, the Ridge and Mutali Bridge. What precisely led to the defeat of the joint Bareilly Nimach forces is not very dear. If factional feuds have some influences on such joint enterprises, it may be recalled that the Nimach forces under General Sidhari Singh were adherents of Mirza Mughal-and supported his succession to the kingship. It is not surprising that in the joint attack the Nimach forces gave only a show of fighting and left Bakht Khan high and dry. Moreover, on return, they loudly made allegations of Bakht Khan's relations with the English. Bahadur Shah once again succeeded in securing a reconciliation between the two factions.[50]

Bakht Khan's failure to capture Alipur on 5th August, did not demoralize him. Indeed, he now decided to attack the Ridge on 7th August with his own force. But heavy rains forced him to postpone the assault, causing great annoyance to Bahadur Shah.[51] The disappointment shown by Bahadur Shah considerably encouraged the opponents of Bakht Khan and they began to defy his authority. Bakht Khan responded by a warning.

As time passed Bakht Khan's difficulties increased. His primary responsibility was to keep the army satisfied, but his differences with the Nimach Generals placed him in an awkward position. Moreover, the financial position already stringent, became increasingly critical. Although the king sent appeals to numerous chieftains around Delhi[52] to supply money, the immediate suppliers of money were the bankers. But they were quite annoyed owing to the past conduct of the princes. Factionalism within the army and intrigues against Bakht Khan began to affect administrative efficiency. Bakht Khan complained before the king that the Princes were collecting money from various 'bankers for the pay of the troops but the troops had not received a pie. Mirza Khizr was forced to surrender all the money so realized and orders to the bankers were issued to negotiate directly with Bakht Khan in future.[53] But when under the pressing circumstances Bakht Khan summoned the bankers to secure more money, he drew a blank. After ten hours of confinement two of the bankers Devi Singh and Saligram managed to secure their release by paying Rs. 6,000.[54]

On 20th August another attempt to subvert Bakht Khan's position was made by General Gauri Shanker (a spy of the British) and Talyar Khan by producing a Sikh witness before the king who alleged that Bakht Khan was in secret communication with the English. Bahadur Shah, knowing of the links of Nimach officers with Mirza Mughal, dismissed the witness as an enemy agent. Nevertheless, Bakht Khan's position had become so vulnerable on this account that he had to clear himself of these charges on 23rd August in the presence of the principal army officers and Mirza Mughal.[55]

Bakht Khan's plan to launch an offensive against the British positions in the morning of 21st August, therefore, could not again materialize owing to internal dissensions.[56] Availing the opportunity, Mirza Mughal charged him for withholding his forces till the English received adequate reinforcements. He and the Nimach officers, therefore, induced the king to prohibit Bakht Khan's entry in the palace and to disarm the Bareilly force. The king, however, abstained from such a rash measure.[57] Moreover, any action against Bakht Khan might have risked his own existence as Mirza Mughal had grown very powerful with the support of the Nimach forces. Later in the day, the king, issued orders to all officers forbidding them to obey the commands of either Mirza Mughal or Bakht Khan. In order to look after the administration, he appointed a Court of Administration, consisting members out of which four were to be appointed by the king and six by the army.[58] (We are not in a position to discover who the framers of the rules governing the newly formed Court were.) Evidently the formation of the Military Court of Administration was the work of persons with some background of service in the British army. Naturally, one thinks of Bakht Khan himself. The composition to the Court of Administration was neither purely Indian nor Western in Character.[59] It was obviously devised keeping in view the prevailing conditions in Delhi. The Military Court of Administration was to function under a set of 12 rules. After coming into being, the Court held two kinds of sessions, viz., ordinary sessions for five hours each day in the Red Fort; and special sessions at any time of the day and night according to the exigencies of the situation.[60] Future events, however, indicate that the Court of Administration too, did not prove to be a very effective body; since the differences between the Nimach and Bareilly forces continued.

On 24th August, Bakht Khan marched with his forces towards Alipur via Najatgarh.[61] The Nimach forces also marched the same evening to Alipur. Their common target was to attack the enemy positions at the Ridge. The two forces, however, did not have any common plan of action nor were able to achieve much coordination with one another. While Bakht Khan was camping at Alipur, the Nimach brigade arrived there. Since the English forces were close at hand Bakht Khan suggested caution and proposed to the Commanding Officer of the Nimach force that they should attack the enemy jointly the next morning. His advice was ignored, resulting in a complete rout of the Nimach force, who suffered a loss of a thousand dead and wounded.[62] Bakht Khan returned to Delhi without risking his own army to the onslaught of the enemy fire. The Nimach officers and Mirza Mughal made the old king to believe that the defeat was caused by the passivity shown by Bakht Khan.[63] Fed up with regular accusations Bakht Khan decided to keep himself concerned with his own troops. But the King once again intervened, assuaged his feelings, and restored him to his position.[64]

By the end of August, the British forces in Delhi had become quite strong, with constant reinforcements from Punjab. The plight of the rebels in Delhi took a new turn when essential materials for the war such as regular supplies of rations and sulphur were affected. [65] Now the bankers, too refused to pay further money to the Court of Administration.[66] Even in this grave condition, the rebels remain disunited. Palace intrigues for succession intensified. A section of the rebel sepoys, hard-pressed for non-receipt of their salary, threatened to enthrone the Taj Mahal Begum in place of Zinat Mahal unless they were paid within fifteen days (3rd September).[67] Another faction of the sepoys conferred on 6th September in Daryaganj proposing to remove all the princes and to raise Prince Jawan Bakht as heir apparent. After victory over the Ridge, he was to be declared king. They hoped to obtain salary from Zinat Mahal upon this assurance.[68] Delay in salary payments seems to have also created discontent in Bakht Khan's army (4th September).[69] The same day Bakht Khan held a private conversation with the King, probably on the alarming situation arising out of the imminent danger of an enemy's attack.[70] A larger meeting was held on 5th September where Bahadur Shah enquired from Bakht Khan of his plan to defend the city and remarked that if he could not oppose the enemy, it would be better to open the gates of the city.[71] Bakht Khan firmly favoured a fight and explained his plan of action.[72] Bakht Khan's measures were, however, easily communicated to the English through their spies.[73] On 6th September one of the spies informed the British that 'Now the army (of the rebels) is absolutely demoralized. There will be no fresh attack unless they received re-inforcernent'.[74] By 6th September, Bakht Khan seems to have lost much of his hold on the army. Jiwan Lal tells us that the sepoys complained to the King that there was no chief official to command or issue orders. A broken Bahadur Shah had only to answer: 'You alone have the power to act. Whatever, you think, you are able to accomplish, do that.'[75]

From the beginning of September, the rebel forces, despite all differences, factionalism and heavy odds, gallantly resisted the British attacks. But the fall of the city was only a matter of time. Bakht Khan with his troops had been guarding Ajmeri Gate since 31st August.[76]

As the British increased their pressure and attacked the city from all sides, Bakht Khan with his brigade seems to have fought bitterly and to have inflicted heavy losses on the British force attacking at Delhi Gate.[77] When resistance became hopeless, Bakht Khan begged the Emperor, to accompany him to Lucknow as the entire open country was still with the rebels.[78] But Mirza Ilahi Bux foiled his attempts.[79] Bakht Khan collecting his army, vacated Delhi and proceeded to Lucknow on 19th September.[80]

It was to Bakht Khan's credit that he managed to take his entire infantry unharmed along with several leading families of Delhi.[81] Crossing over Miranghat he visited Bilgrarm and Farrukhabad. Perhaps Prince Firoz Shah also accompanied him as Kamaluddin Haider tells us that Bakht Khan arrived in Lucknow with 200 horses and 500 infantry.[82] They were welcomed by Sultan Bahu Sahiba and lodged in the Khuld Manzil.[83]

When Bakht Khan arrived in Lucknow, the rebels were still fighting against the British. Bakht Khan seems to have been present with his forces when the British army launched an attack on Alam Bagh (Lucknow) on 16 March under Brigadier Franklyn. Bakht Khan and his forces fought gallantly here; the gallantry was praised by Malleson though he failed to recognize the real person behind the tough resistance.[84] In the battle, Bakht Khan lost his guns and a number of men.[85] Bakht Khan was commended by Hazrat Mahal for his gallant fight and assured that the loss of the guns would be made good.[86]

Not much is known about the subsequent events in Bakht Khan's life. Mehr says that after the fall of Lucknow he moved to Shahjahanpur with Maulvi Ahmadullah Shah and from there crossed over Nepal via Mohammadi.[87] But there seems little substance on this. Sen says on the basis of Foreign Political Consultations, that Bakht Khan was killed in an action on 13th May 1859.[88] He was not a man who would easily give up the cause.

Notes

1. Abdul Latif, 1857 *Ka Tarikhi Roznamcha,* ed. K.A. Nizami, Delhi, n.d., p. 123 (here after *Roznamcha);* Moinuddin Hasan Khan, tr., C.T. Metcalfe, *The Two Native Narratives of the Mutiny in Delhi,* repr., Delhi, 1974, pp. 41-57 (hereafter Metcalfe).

2. *Roznamcba,* pp. 23-5; Metcalfe, pp. 55-8, 85-7, 91-2; Garret, *The Trial Bahadur Shah,* 1932, pp. 256-82; *Delhi Urdu Akhbar,* 17 May 1857; Charles Ball, *The History of Indian Mutiny,* vol. I, p. 495; *Press List of the Mutiny Papers,* National Archives of India (hereafter*NAI),* no. 1, Vol. 13, 16-22 May 1857.
3. Ghulam Rasool Mehr, 1857 *Ke Mujahid,* Lahore, n.d., p. 104; Intizamullah Shahabi, *East India Company aur Baaghi Ulama,* Delhi, Ist edn, n.d., p. 73.
4. Frederic Cooper, *Crisis in Punjab,* 1st pub. 1857, repr., Chandigarh, 1977, pp. 108-9.
5. *Ghadar Ki Subh* o *Sham,* cited by Anis Fatima, *San Sattavan Ke Hero* (hereafter Fatima), Aligarh, 1949, pp. 65-6.
6. *Ibid.*
7. *Ibid.*
8. Genealogical Table provided by Sir Saiyed Ahmad Khan as Appendix 1 (a) *Sarkashi Zila Bijnore;* ed. Sharafat Husain Mirza, Delhi. Also see Saiyed Altaf Ali's note, in *Al-Ilm,* Karachi, *Jang i-Azadi number.*
9. Kaye, vol. III, pp. 274-5; Marques Hastings, *the Private Journal* ..., Allahabad, 1907, pp. 250-1; Atkinson, vol. V, pp. 677-8.
10. S.N. Sen, *Eighteen Fifty Seven,* pp. 677-81.
11. Metcalfe, p. 133.
12. 1857 *Ke Mujahid,* p. 106.
13. Kamaluddin Haider, *Tarikh Salatin-i Awadh,* vol. II, p. 425; Malleson, Vol. I, p. 303n; Fatima, pp. 69-71.
14. Kamaluddin Haider, vol. II, p. 425; Shahabi, p. 73; 1857 *Ke Mujahid,* p.106.
15. Malleson, vol. I, p. 317; Kaye, *A History of Sepoy War India,* Vol. III, 1880, p.277.
16. *Ibid.*
17. Kaye, Vol. III, p. 277 and Malleson, Vol. I, p. 317 say that Khan Bahadur Khan apprehensive of the presence of Bakht Khan with his brigade, persuaded him to proceed to Delhi.
18. Shahabi, p. 73; 1857 *Ke Mujahid,* pp. 107-8; Fatima, p. 72.
19. Jiwan Lal gives the strength of Bakht Khan's force: 4 Regiments of foot, 700 cavalry, 6 horse artillary guns, 3 fieldpieces, 14 elephants, 300 spare horses, 100 jihadis; Metcalfe, p. 134. Zaheer Dehlavi says that Bakht Khan arrived with 14,000 troops, and two or three regiments of cavalry, etc. *Dastan-i Ghadar.* Lahore, 1955, p. 135.
20. *Roznamcha,* p. 124; *Debli Urdu Akhbar,* 12 July 1857; Zaheer Dehlavi, pp. 73-108.
21. Ch Zakaullah, *Tarikb-i Urooj-i Saltanati EngLishia,* Delhi, 1904, p. 683 (hereafter Zakaullah).

22. *Roznamcba;* pp. 59-64, 78; Metcalfe, p. 133.
23. The nobles deputed to receive Bakht Khan included Nawab Ahmad Ali Khan (father-in-law of Bahadur Shah; Hakim Ahsanullah Khan, General Samad Yar Khan, Ibrahim Khan and Ghulam Ali Khan). Metcalfe, pp. 133-4; Zakaullah, p. 681. Also see *Delhi Urdu Akhbar,* 12 July 1857,
24. Metcalfe, p. 134; Zakaullah, p. 681. Abdul Latif shows Bakht Khan's presence on 26th May at Delhi—a mistake as he wrote his *Roznamcba* much after the suppression of the Rebellion. See *Roznamcha,* pp. 45, 65; Zaheer, p. 135.
25. Crisis in Punjab, op. cit., 1st pub. 1857, repr., Chandigarh, 1977, p. 107; Metcalfe, pp. 133-4. Spear, perhaps, basing on Jiwan Lal's account gives a graphic picture of Bakht Khan's first appearance before the king. *the Twi Light of the Mughals,* London, 1957, p. 214.
26. Metcalfe, pp. 134-5; Kamaluddin Haider, Vol. II, p. 445; *Delhi Urdu Akhbar,* 12 July 1857; *Sadiq-ul Akhbar,* 11th August 1857.
27. *Delhi Urdu Akhbar,* 12th July 1857; Metcalfe, pp. 133-4, 136-7 with slight variations.
28. Metcalfe, p. 135.
29. *Ibid.*
30. *Ibid.,* pp. 135-6.
31. *Delhi Urdu Akhbar,* 12th July 1857.
32. Metcalfe, p. 137.
33. *Sadiq-ul Akhbar,* 6th July 1857.
34. Metcalfe, pp. 134-5.
35. Zakaullah, pp. 675-6.
36. *Ibid.,* p. 675. Kamaluddin Haider, vol. II, p. 445 says that Maulvi Sarfaraz Ali paid 2 annas daily to the crusaders for their subsistence.
37. Zakaullah, p. 675.
38. Metcalfe, p. 135; Zakaullah, p. 678.
39. Malleson, vol. II, pp. 425-6 claims that the attempts were foiled by Major Cock. Jiwan Lal, however, says that Bareilly force returned victorious with booty. Metcalfe, p. ·133; *Sadiq-ul Akhbar,* 6th July 1857 reports: '300 horse and several carts loads of foodgrains' were captured by Bakht Khan; *Delhi Urdu Akhbar,* 19th July 1857.
40. Metcalfe, p. 145; Kamaluddin Haider, vol. II, p. 445; Fatima, p. 74.
41. *Jasuson ke Khutoot,* NAI, p. 5 (Photograph copy in the Research Library, Department of History, AMU) (hereafter cited as *Khutoot).*
42. *Ibid.*
43. *Ibid.,* pp. 149-52; Zakaullah, p. 687.
44. *Roznamcha,* p. 87; Metcalfe, pp. 161-2.

45. *Khutoot,* pp. 9-10; Zakaullah, p. 582; *Crisis in Punjab,* op. cit., 1st pub., 1857, repr., Chandigarh, 1977, p. 112.
46. Metcalfe, pp. 160, 167. He was made Governor.
47. Zakaullah, p. 683; *Khutoot,* pp. 65-6; Metcalfe, pp. 160, 171.
48. *Crisis in Punjab,* op. cit., 1st pub., 1857, repr., Chandigarh, 1977, p. 109.
49. *Khutoot,* pp. 65-6.
50. *Khutoot,* p. 17; *Crisis in Punjab,* p. 110; Metcalfe, p. 184; Gauri Shankar's letter to the English officers, dated 8th and 10th August 1857, NAI, *Press List of Mutiny Papers,* nos. 5, 15, 19. .
51. Metcalfe, p. 177.
52. Zakaullah, p. 689 gives a list of the chieftains.
53. Officers of the court's petition to Bahadur Shah, 20th August 1957, *Press List of Mutiny Papers,* no. 57, SN 352, NAI; Metcalfe, pp. 197-8, 203.
54. Metcalfe, pp. 199,200-1.
55. *Ibid.,* p. 205.
56. *Ibid.,* pp. 205-6.
57. *Ibid.*
58. *Press List of Mutiny Papers,* Bundle no. 57, no. 539-51, NAI. Jiwan Lal says that the court consisted of 12 members. Metcalfe, pp, 205-6. For a detailed discussion of the Court of Administration see *The Great Rebellion of* 1857, ed. P.C. Joshi, pp. 37-40.
59. Spear, *The Twilight of the Mughals,* London, 1957, p. 206.
60. *The Great Rebellion of* 1857, p. 39.
61. *Khutoot,* p. 63.
62. Metcalfe, pp. 26-8. Zaheer Dehlavi says that the Nimach force was sandwitched between the British forces and Bakht Khan's army.
63. *Kbutoot,* p. 30; Metcalfe, p. 209.
64. Metcalfe, p. 212.
65. *Ibid.,* p. 213.
66. *Ibid.,* pp. 214-15.
67. *Ibid.,* p. 218.
68. *Khutoot,* p. 98.
69. *Ibid.,* p. 48. Jiwan Lal records that on 4th September, Bakht Khan was asked by the King to pay the troops a sum of Rs. 26,000. This he could not do on grounds of his own difficulties. See Matcalfe, pp. 211-24.
70. Metcalfe, p. 219.
71. *Ibid.,* p. 222.
72. *Ibid.*
73. James Leaser, *the Red Fort,* London, 1956, p. 145.

74. *Khutoot,* p. 102.
75. Metcalfe, p. 223.
76. *Khutoot,* p. 89.
77. Malleson, vol. II, pp. 71-2; Kaye, vol. III, pp. 592-3.
78. *Ibid.;* Kaye, vol. II, p. 644.
79. *Ibid.*
80. Kamaluddin Haider, vol. II, pp. 311-12; Telegram from Fatehgarh to the Governor General dated 12th February 1858 cited in *Insurrection in the East Indies,* 1857, p. 104.
81. G.B. Malleson, *the Indian Mutiny of* 1857, 1887, p. 307.
82. Kamaluddin Haider, vol. II, pp. 313-14.
83. *Ibid.,* p. 314.
84. Malleson, vol. II, pp. 402-3.
85. Kamaluddin Haider, vol. II, pp. 311-12. Sen apparently missed this account.
86. *Ibid.*
87. 1857 *Ke Mujahid,* p. 118.
88. S.N. Sen, *Eighteen Fifty Seven,* p. 371.

Chapter - 13

Maulavi Liyaqat Ali

— Professor Iqbal Husain

The First War of Independence, 1857 had been-a turning point in the History of Modern India. Peoples' sufferings of a century, erupted into a rebellion: In a short time, the British rule disappeared from north India. Significantly the rebellion was not started by the serving nobility of former Mughal regime. Majority of the rebels against the British Raj were poverty-stricken consisting of peasants, teachers, government servants, weavers, artisans and daily wage earners. Indeed soon after the beginning of the rebellion some descendants of the old ruling houses not only extended their support but also led them. For example, Bahadur Shah Zafar, Maharani Lakhshmi Bai, Kunwar Singh, Nana Sahib, Begum Hazrat Mahal may be cited by way of illustration. However, it were the sepoys who rebelled on 10th May 1857. It is noteworthy that these people remained firm and made a frantic effort to expel the alien rulers from India. In their desire to expel the British they suffered heavily. Of the common men, there was a class of people identified as Maulvis and Pandits, Imams of the mosques, considered to be influencial in the society, who also plunged into the war against the English. Their anger against the British rule could be traced from the confiscation of the *madad-i-maash* land granted to them by the previous regime for the maintenance of *Pathshalas, maktabs, madrasas,* mosques, etc. The activities of the Christian missionaries provided them enough cause to launch a counter propaganda against the British. In Allahabad, Maulvi Liyaqat *Ali,* a *madarsa* teacher and an *Imam* of the mosque emerged as the leader of anti-British faction in 1857.

Maulvi Liyaqat Ali was a resident of village Mahagaon, *pargana* Chaile and enjoyed considerable respect of the people.[1] An article published in the daily *National Herald,* Lucknow on 1st September 1957 refers that he held the office of *Qazi* in Mahagaon. Intizamullah Shahabi provides some more information: 'Maulvi Liyaqat Ali Sahib belonged to the Qadriys sect and a large number of people of Allahabad and Chaile were his disciples.[2] It appears that Liyaqat Ali obtained his early education in Arabic, Persian and Qoran. From his writings and interpretation of Qoranic verses, one may discern that he must have obtained higher education.[3] According to the British records, Maulvi Liyaqat Ali began his career with the English army. He was later on removed from the service for stirring anti-government ideas.[4] Having lost the job, Liyaqat Ali returned to Mahagaon where he moved to a mosque as an *Imam* and teacher. From here his reputation as a pious man spread to other parts of the district of Allahabad and soon a large number of people became his disciples.[5]

On 10th May 1857, the sepoys at Meerut broke into rebellion. Soon the rebellion spread to many parts of north India. Restlessness against the British rule was manifest in Allahabad from the beginning of May 1857. The British apprehending danger shifted their families to the Allahabad fort. Considering that the danger had disappeared, they returned to their houses in the first week of June 1857. They were, however, disillusioned as on 6th June 1857, Ram-Chandra an officer of the sixth regiment posted at Allahabad revolted against the British,[6] followed by the entire district of Allahabad.[7] Maulvi Liyaqat Ali had been actively preaching for *jihad* and propagating against the British.[8] His *jihad* cry was responded quickly by his followers, sepoys and others. Within a short period people of Shamsabad, Rasoolpur and adjoining areas joined him.[9] The unity among the people was great. Kanahyya Lal tells us: 'A Musalman *jihadi* whose name is still not correctly known but was popular as Maulvi, raised the standard of rebellion against the Government by collecting a majority of ruffians. It has been widely known that Maulvi Liyaqat was teaching in a *madarsa*. But the ungrateful and killers of their benefactors, the sepoys rose in rebellion when the English forces were not present to punish them. However, two things were important. First the unity among the Muslims is well known, and second that they (Muslims) detested the "English".'[10]

It appears that Maulvi Liyaqat Ali's call for *jihad* mobilised a large number of people. The Maulvi chose Khusrau Bagh (Allahabad) as his headquarter. Ram Chandra, a rebel sepoy officer and other sepoys supported him.[11] On the suggestion of Ram Chandra, Maulvi Liyaqat Ali was declared ruler ofAllahabad on 7th June 1857.[12] A strong body of the Mewatis supported the Maulvi.[13] On 6th June 1857 the Guyn regiment including the cavalry had already revolted along with the Maulvi.[14] They plundered the treasury. The people of Shamsabad, Rasoolpur, Baily, Baghra, Shadibad, Johnhul, Seori, Fathpur, Bichwa, Katra, Colonelganj, Mahadpuri, Bakhtiara, Bakhtawari, Minhajpur, etc., joined the rebellion. After Maulvi Liyaqat Ali's arrival at Khusrau Bagh, people from Rasoolpur and Shamsabad joined him. Maulvi Liyaqat Ali organised the administration appointing his own men as *Kotwal*, *Thanadar*, *Tehsildar* and officers in the army.[15] Gradually people from Koilha, Mahagaon, Sarai Saleem, Seodha, Fathpur, Barmuhar, Chile Khas, Kashiya, Baragaon, Shaikhpur, Angur alias Kathgaon, Shaha alias Behgaon, Mohiuddinpur Ghaus, Begam Sarai, Odani, Imraoti, Chak Raj pur, Lohra, Korai, Amar Chaha, Bakhiyara, Baghira, Chitpur, Nemibagh, Rasoolpur deh, Minhajpur, Rohi, Ghayasuddinpur, Kasmanda, Sarai Moja (or Sarai Meja), Umarpur Sayan (or Umarpue Niwan), Mau, etc., gathered around the Maulvi Sahib increasing the number of his followers.[16]

Maulvi Liyaqat had to face numerous problems. The most important problem was to keep the Muslims united as a section of them argued that the call for *jihad* could only be given by the Prophet or *Imam*. A small section of the Sunni Muslims led by Hafiz Rahmatullah declared that the war against the British was political. They opposed to the *jihad* cry.[17] To face the situation, Liyaqat Ali issued two Proclamations one is versified and the other unversificd to forge unity among the Muslims explaining virtues .of the *jihad*. These Proclamations, claims Kanahyya Lal, were sent to Birjis Qadr and circulated extensively in the district of Allahabad.[18] Through the Proclamations Liyaqat Ali invited the people to take part in the *jihad*. The unversified Proclamation while emphasizing the dignity of *jihad*, surveys the misdeeds of a hundred years of British rule.[19] In this Proclamation Liyaqat Ali has cited the peoples grievances such as widespread killings, setting places on fire, lynching innocent persons, destruction of houses, raids, ill-treatments with the *ulema* and disrespects shown to the holy scripture. Liyaqat Ali succeeded in his efforts. A number of respected and influential people of the society such as Nizam Ashraf, Ghulam Ismail, Mohd. Husain, Chaudhari Miran Bakhsh, Maulvi Syed Ahmad Ali, Maulvi Ghulam Haider, Maulvi Amjad Ali, Husain Ali Khan, Sher Khan, Shaikh Lutf Ali, Shaikh Najaf Ali the Naib (Deputy) *Kotwal* responded to Maulvi's call.[20] After forging unity, Liyaqat Ali addressed himself to the re-organisation of the administration of the district. Shafiullah Khan and Saifullah Khan were appointed *Tehsildar*.[21] Qasim Ali Khan was appointed as *Kotwal*. Chaudhari Shahabuddin was made *Naib Kotwal*. Hadi and Faizullah the *zamindars* of Bhukka were assigned army positions.[22] These arrangements had salutary effects in controlling the ruffians bringing peace and order in the city and the neighbourhood.[23]

Maulvi Liyaqat Ali faced a great challenge from the formidable English who had shut themselves in the fort with sufficient arms and provisions. Contrary to this, despite having more adherents to his side they were not acquainted with the warfare. The Maulvi was in possession of a large number of modern weapons which he had seized from the English. However majority of his men could not use them as they were untrained unlike their opponents. Despite this weakness Maulvi Liyaqat Ali attempted to capture the fort. But he failed. In the meantime Lt. Arnold arrived on 7th June 1857 with an auxiliary corps. The English received another auxiliary corps on 9th June 1857 through the boats. The leaders of the rebels concentrated themselves in the city and the bridge of boats at Daraganj. They were probably not in a position to besiege the fort. Moreover Lord Canning anxious to recapture Allahabad deputed one of his most experienced officers Colonel Gorden Neill.[24]

Neill's arrival on 11th June 1857 with enforcement changed the situation. Peoples' anger against the British army can be seen from one of the letters sent on 14th June 1857 by a British officer which indicates the hardships on the besieged and the excessive work they had to do for survival.[25] In another letter the English acknowledged that the entire country was up in arms and hinted to a possible desertion by the Indian sepoys in the fort.[26] It is interesting that about 400 Sikh sepoys present in the fort had become insolent and violated army discipline and rule. Colonel Neil handled them intelligently.

The rebels in Allahabad now began to attack the residences of the English and their properties. Their main targets were now the *tehsils*, thanas and stations considered to be the symbols of the British rule.[27] While the Maulvi's adherents were busy in the city, their influence on the people across the Yamuna was negligible due to the Raja of Munda, a loyalist, to the English. He suppressed the peoples revolt. Rajas of Dayaja and Bira also supported the English.[28] However, close to Yamuna, Dhakan Singh, the *zamindar* of Dharawal and some other *zamindars* supported the rebels. For the capture of Dhakan Singh and Hanumant Singh, the British announced a reward of Rs. 1,000 each. The rebels activities in Allahabad district were alarming. Specially the English singled out the Muslim *zamindars* of Doaba for the fury to fight a religious war.[29] In the north-east of Allahabad, people under the command of Tej Mall Singh *Taaluqadar*, Fakir Bukhsh *Taaluqadar pargana* Jhusi had also taken up arms against the British.[30] Ishwari Bukhsh and Chatrarpati Singh were also actively involed to expel the British. In Allahabad, perhaps independently, Rao Gulab Singh was fighting against the British. Although, almost the entire district of Allahabad was up in arms, yet it seems that there could not be a close rapport between various rebel groups. Every area had been under the command of a separate rebel leader. Since there could not establish a central leadership, the rebels remained split and scattered. Maulvi Liyaqat Ali was in difficulty due to the scarcity of supply as appears from his Proclamation (see Appendix). In that situation the Maulvi could neither take offensive nor continue armed struggle for long. The English, contrarily, received reinforcements regularly. Colonel Neill had his sikh contingent commanded by Captain Braseyr and Lt. Baily destroyed Qadirganj, Mawahaganj and its neighbourhood through artillery fires from the Fort.[31] Neil now resolved to destroy the villages around Allahabad as the rebels were getting support from there.[32] On 14th June 1857, Neill attacked on the lines of Maulvi Liyaqat Ali but a stiff resistance foiled his attempt. The success raised the morale of the Maulvi and his supporters for the time being.

Neil, according to his plan, began military actions around the villages of Allahabad. The Pathan population of Shamsabad and Rasoolpur was his first target. Kanahyya Lal tells us that the British slaughtered the people teaching a good lesson to the Muslims.[33] Colonel

Neil in rage destroyed the Jama Masjid at the western end of the fort turning the place of worship into a barrack.[34] Maulvi Liyaqat once again tried to reorganize his men but could not succeed due to lack of arms and trained men. He returned to Khusrau Bagh with a small body of 3,000.[35] Soon he was besieged by Colonel Neil.

In the conflict between the British and the Maulvi, rumours, probably at the instance of Neil that the English were going to destroy the city by artillery fire, caused panic. Atrocious acts of the British army at Shamsabad, Rasoolpur and, other places were heart-rending. Now the Maulvi had only two options, either to continue fighting endangering life of the city people on retreat.[36] The Maulvi mysteriously disappeared from Khusrau Bagh. The English and Indian historians are silent as to how the Maulvi breaking the siege disappeared. Liyaqat Ali 's disappearance apparently baffled the British. Proclamations were issued for his arrest offering rewards. From Allahabad, the Maulvi reached Kanpur to continue his mission joining the ranks of Nana Sahib's army. By the time Nana Sahib's position has weakened. He was unable to sustain the British pressure and crossed into Awadh. Maulvi Liyaqat Ali also left Kanpur. It is not known from Kanpur where did he go. The later events indicate that he did not stay at one place and kept on wandering from place to place for years. After twelve years he was captured at Bombay. He was prosecuted for sedition against the British government. Despite years of sufferings Maulvi Liyaqat Ali remained firm to his cause and confessed in organising people to revolt. He took pride in his act of rebellion and predicted that the British rule would come to an end from India. Maulvi Liyaqat's confession made the prosecutor's job easy who sentenced him to transportation for life to the Andman Islands. Maulvi Liyaqat Ali there died after some time.[37]

We do not know much about the descendants of Maulvi Liyaqat Ali. The *National Herald* daily, Lucknow on 1st September 1957 published an article under the title "The Hero of Mahagaon' referring to three of his surviving grandsons, Qazi Ali Ahmad, Qazi Ayyub and Qazi Hafiz Abu Ahmad. At that time Qazi Abu Ahmad was of 70 years of age. In recognition of Maulvi Liyaqat's sacrifices, the government granted a monthly pension of Rs. 200 to Qazi Abu Ahmad. While talking with the correspondent of the *National Herald,* Qazi Abu Ahmad revealed that Maulvi Liyaqat Ali had been maintaining a diary which was under his possession. It was taken away by one of his friends and probably lost. Apparently with the evidence from Qazi Abu Ahmad, the correspondent of the *National Herald* reported that Maulvi Liyaqat wàs photographed with the Amir of Afghanistan. The photograph was available in the Peshawar Museum. It is quite possible that Liyaqat Ali while wandering reached Afghanistan where he met the Amir. This, however, needs investigation.

Notes

1. Intizamullah Shahabi, *East India Company and Baghi Ulama:* Delhi, p. 91.
2. Intizamullah Shahabi, *Ghadar Ke Chand Ulama* (hereafter *Ghadar Ke Chand Ulama),* p. 126.
3. Shahabi tells us that Liyaqat Ali belonged to a family of scholars and received education from the *Ulama* of the age. See *Ghadar Ke Chand Ulama,* p. 128.
4. *Liyaqat Ali Mutiny Basta,* no. 5, file no. 16, Allahabad Collectorate. See also Jafri in *Role of Muslims in the Freedom Struggle of India,* Aligarh, 2007, p. 149.
5. *Ghadar Ke Chand Ulama*- p. 128.
6. Pandit Kanahyya Lal, *Maharba-i Azeem,* Nawal Kishore, Lucknow, 1861, p. 166; John Kaye, *A History of Sepoy war in India,* vol. II, pp. 256-8 (hereafter Kaye).
7. Kaye, vol. II, pp. 256-8.
8. *Ghadar Ke Chand Ulama,* p. 128; Kaye, Vol. II, pp. 256-8, 261.
9. Rizvi, *Freedom Struggle in UP* (hereafter Rizvi), vol. IV, p. 55.
10. Kanahyya Lal, p. 198; Kaye, vol. II, p. 261 endorses this statement.
11. *Ibid.*
12. *Ibid.,* Abdul Qadir Jafari without any source says that on the suggestion of Ram Chandra, Bahadur Shah appointed Liyaqat Ali as ruler. *Role of Muslims in the Freedom Struggle...,* p. 151.
13. Rizvi, vol. IV, pp. 348-9.
14. *Ibid.*
15. *Ibid.,* p. 549.
16. *Ibid.,* p. 550.
17. *Ibid.,* p. 551; *Ghadar Ke Chand Ulema,* p. 129.
18. *Maharba-i Azeem,* p. 199 (translation of the unversified Proclamation is given as Appendix).

19. See Proclamation, Appendix.
20. *Allahabad Mutiny Basta,* no. 5, file no. 16.
21. *Foreign Proceedings* (Secret), 31 July 1858, p. 94.
22. Rizvi, vol. IV, p. 550.
23. *Ghadar Ke Chand Ulema,* p. 129.
24. Kaye, vol. II, p. 261 gives credit to the English artillery which foiled the rebels attempts.
25. Rizvi, vol. IV, p. 639.
26. *Ibid.*
27. Thompson, F. *Official Narrative of Allahabad District,* no. 376, p. 6 (hereafter Thompson).
28. Thompson, p. 94.
29. *Ibid.,* Rizvi, vol. IV; p. 612.
30. *Ibid.*
31. Neil to the Secretary to the Government of India, 17th June 1857, cited in Rizvi, vol. IV; p. 639.
32. *Allahabad Mutiny Basta,* no. 4, file nos. 4, 16.
33. Kanahyya Lal, p. 198; Kaye, vol. II, p. 266 says that due to the terror of the Sikhs of the English army, village after village became desolated.
34. *Allahabad Collectorate Mutiny Basta,* no. 4, file no. 16.
35. Kanahyya Lal, p. 198; *Allahabad Mutiny Basta,* no. 4, file no. 16.
36. Kanahyya Lal, p. 198.
37. 1857 *Ke Mujahid,* p. 144. Prof. Abdul Qadir says that Maulvi Liyaqat Ali escaped from Kanpur to Gujarat and stayed at Lajpur 10 km. off Surat. Nawab of Lajpur informed the British officer. Consequently the Maulvi was arrested at Bombay. He died in the Andaman Islands on 17th May 1872. See for details, *Role of Muslims in The Freedom Struggle,* p. 156.

APPENDIX

'In the name of the beneficent God, the absolver of sinners.' 'All praise to the Great and Merciful God, May the Merciful God and Preserver shine upon the great Prophet, his Descendants and his companions, that have carried courage to the highest pitch. May the mercy of God alight upon the Votaries of the Great Religion of Islam.'

After praising God, and praying for blessings upon the Prophet, I Leeaqat Ali of Allahabad, a servant of the students and humble among the mendicants, conveys some very essential doctrines after a deep research, to be followed by the faithful Muslims in the light of the ordains of the Holy Koran and well proved by the sayings of the Prophet that the innovations, oppressions and mischief throughout the government of Hindustan specially in Allahabad have been inflicted upon by the accursed non-believing Christians generally on the Muslims after plundering, murdering, lynching, digging and burning of their houses, raiding and executing the ulema and *mashaikhs* and dishonouring the holy book Koran, *ahadis* and *fiqh* which is as clear as the shining sun. In this state of affairs every Musalman is bound to be ready for *jihad*.[1] And according to the sayings of the Prophet: 'Every Prophet had his duty assigned to him the duty allotted to me is that I should make *jihad*.' Undoubtedly he who ignores profession he would suffer from humiliation, misery and poverty.

You should act according to the following precepts: 'The real paradise lies beneath the strokes of swords'.[2] You will then obtain salvation and the honour of martyrdom, which is eternal life. You will then obtain the blessings of paradise, and get Elysian Nymphs for your wives. You should never entertain in your minds any kind of fear or doubt. In the present cause, you should devote both your life and property and give every kind of assistance as far as it is in your power. God forbid that you should fail to avail yourselves of the present propitious days and to unite in this cause, and that you should afterwards repent.

He who heads the undertaking regard him[3] as your *Imam* (Leader), he be good or bad.[4] Our holy Koran is full of promises and blessings attainable by undertaking *jihad*, and they are also mentioned in several places in the chapter designated 'Sooreh-i Tobah'. I trust my friend will not wait for separate letters and addresses to them but regard this proclamation as enough intended for all friends and acquaintances. One important point to be observed by men engaged in *jihad* is that they should place the sole reliance upon God, the Creator of the Heavens and Earth, who will certainly get help from the unknown.[5]

Musalmans of India being destitute of resources, and having no ammunitions, guns, or army, have been all along in a helpless condition, but the Gracious God who has strengthened the religion *of the Prophet Ahmad*[6] internally, has *externally*[7] for the encouragement of weak creatures like ourselves, furnished with us the resources formerly enjoyed by the unsuccessful and unprincipled Christians without any attempt being made by us. Our being backed by a large army of infantry, cavalry, and artillery, our having obtained an immense treasure, the arrival of the letter from the King of Delhi, *the king of Hindostan*[8] who is the shadow and representative of God (May his dominions ever extend) the assistance given to us by the army of Birjis Qadr, Ruler of Lucknow (May God always bless him with prosperity), our alliance with the rajas of the province of Oudh and the states adjacent to Allahabad, and the union which prevails throughout Hindoostan, notwithstanding the people are of different persuasions and tribes, are clear proofs that the people are determined to extirpate these rebel Christians now. 0 my Mussulman brothers! as soon as you hear the above glad tidings prepare yourselves for *jihad*, come to Allahabad, subdue and put to sword the besieged Christians there, and try to expel the remnant of their body from the country, and then rule the country according to laws and institutions of *Islam.* 'Now fearing that my writing may have become lengthy, I quote for your perusal some lines from the Koran with translation in the vernacular: 'The Great and Holy God has said in that chapter of the Koran which is designated "Sooreh-i Tobah" that

he who believe and emigrate
And strives with might
And Main, in Allah cause,
With their goods and their persons,
Have the highest rank

In the sight ofAllah
They are the people who will achieve (salvation).

Their Lord doeth give them
Glad tidings, of a Mercy
From Himself of His good pleasure.
And of Gardens for them,
Wherein are delights
That endure:
They will dwell there in
For ever, verily with Allah
Is a reward, the greatest (of all).

o ye who believe! Take not
For Protectors your fathers
And your brothers if they love
Infidelity above Faith:
If any of you do so,
They do wrong.

Say: If it be that yours fathers,
Your sons, your brothers,
Your mates, or your kindered,
The wealth that ye have gained:
The commerce in which ye fear
Maulvi Liyaqat Ali

A decline: or the dwellings
In which you delight
Are dearer to you than Allah
Or His Messenger: or the striving
In His Cause;-then wait
Until Allah brings about
His Decision: And Allah
Guides not the rebellious

O ye who believe! what
Is the matter with you,

That, when ye are asked
To go forth in the cause of Allah,
Ye cling heavily to the earth?
Do you prefer the lift
Of this world to the Hereafter?

But little is the comfort
Of this life, as compared
With the Hereafter.

Unless ye go forth,
He will punish you
With a grievious penalty,
And put others in your place;
But Him ye would not harm
In the least, For Allah
Hath power over all things.
Go ye forth (whether equipped)
Lightly or heavily, and strive
And struggle, with your goods
And your persons, in the Cause
Of Allah. That is best
For you, if we (but knew).

Allah ordains in the Sooreh-Saff:

Truly Allah loves those
Who fight in His Cause
In battle array, as if
they were a solid
cemented structure

O ye who believe!
Shall I lead you
To a bargain that will
Save you from
A grievous chastisement?

That ye believe in Allah
And His Messenger, and that
Ye strive (your utmost)
In the Cause of Allah,
With your wealth
And your persons:
That will be best for you,
If ye but knew!

He will forgive you
Your sins, and admit you
To Gardens beneath which
Rivers flow, and to beautiful
Mansions in Gardens
Of Eternity? that is indeed
The Supreme Triumph
And another favour
(Will He bestow), which ye
Do love-help from Allah
And a speedy victory.
So give the Glad Tidings
To the believers.[10]

Notes

* A misleading translation. *Jihad* is not confined to the Christians. It is equally applicable to the Muslims violating the *shariat*, non-Muslims if the religious freedom of the Muslims is forbidden, the self to control the evil desires including lust for power, etc.

1. Originally translated: 'I Leeaqat Alee o f Allahabad a poor scholar, and a mendicant, with a view to save by my readers from the trial of the Judgement Day, beg to publish some of my observations, based upon precepts extracted from the sacred Koran and the Holy Book of our Prophet, and trust that the faithful Musalmans will attend to my appeal, as I am only discharging a great religious duty, viz. inculcating the doctrines of our sacred scriptures. Every Musalman well knows and it is a notorious fact that the accursed Christians have been awe fully tyrannizing over the whole country of Hindoostan, especially over the district of Allahabad. These Christians have been guilty of the crimes of massacring, plundering and hanging human

being burning and destroying our houses, attacking us unawares, killing innocent learned men of our country, and burning our sacred scriptures. Accordingly it is our duty incumbent upon every faithful Musalman to prepare himself for *jihad* as our Gracious Prophet has said: "Every Prophet had his duty".'

2. The translator adds 'quoted from Koran' which does not occur in the text of the Proclamation.
3. In translation 'regard him' omitted.
4. 'You should comply the following precept quoted from the Koran', 'Consider jihad as your duty and engage in it under a leader whether he be good or bad'. There is no such reference in the Koran.
5. 'get help from the unknown' omitted in the translation.
6. Italics omitted in the translation.
7. Italics omitted in the translation.
8. Italics translated as 'the bonafide ruler'.
9. Italics translated 'Mohammad'.
10. The original translation of the Proclamation is slightly different to the above which has been taken from Abdulla Yusuf Ali for its distinguishing characteristics, such a highly elegant style, a choice of words close to the meaning of the origin al text. The original translation may be seen in Foreign Political Consultations, no s. 749-53, National Archives of India, New Delhi. Also see Mutiny Basta no. 7, Trial of Mammo Khan, Lucknow Collectorate Record Room.

Chapter - 14

Indigenous Discourse and Modern Historiography of 1857: The Case Study of Maulavi Ahmadullah Shah

— ***Prof. S. Zaheer Husain Jafri***

I

1. The events of 1857 and the causes of its failure have largely been studied from the point of view of the victors. This is not to say that this is wrong in itself. It, however, has not created a complete historiography of the events of the years between and 1859, as in this approach, the aspirations of the rebel leaders as well as the causes of the failure of the rebellion remain secondary. Consequently, only those mutineer's records and literature, which have a direct bearing on the events and circumstances affecting the British suppression *of* the rebels have been utilised. This remain s true even for works like S. N. Sen's *Eighteen Fifry-Seven* which, in fact, aimed at correcting this bias. By way of an exception, Syed Moinul Haq's *The Great Revolution* of 1857 has tried to utilise much of the available indigenous literature (of course, he had little access to material in Indian archives and libraries). Since Pakistani books were not available in India in the 1960s and 1970s, Indian students and scholars could not make use of this exceptionally well-researched work. Haq's work has remained the most underutilised study of 1857 in India. Similarly, there have been a few scholars in India who were able to use monographs written in Urdu by scholars from India as well as Pakistan. The scholars writing in Urdu have also made every effort to make use of English works. Therefore, the works of Intizam Ullah Shahabi, Ghulam Rasul Mehr, Abrar Husain Farooqi,

Ayyub Qadri and a host of other Urdu writers, whose work, incidentally, *is* easily available in all the major libraries, were simply ignored by modern authors writing in English due to their linguistic handicap. This has, unfortunately, led to a **vertical divide** between the perceptions of the English reading public and the Urdu reading public about the events, causes of failure and the heroes of 1857. Surprisingly, mainstream historiography, with all its arrogance, does not bother to correct such a growing divide and has never thought of utilizing indigenous discourse to balance the picture.[1]

2. Contrary to the popular perception that the mutineers had spread their "fanatical" and "religion-centered" appeal against the British by word of mouth, I come across a large number of printed proclamations, appeals and pamphlets issued by rebel leaders in the various centres of the uprising. Documents of this nature were seized by the East India Company's troops and officers and were not destroyed and most of them passed into private and public collections. An analysis of this documentation yields enough data for an understanding of the motives of the rebels, the means used to mobilise the rebels and the classes, and strata that were mobilised. Such printed data also helps us to examine the question of how far the appeals remained within traditional frameworks of communication and how far sepoys' background as members of a modern army helped them use the new medium of the printed word. Modern ideas and technologies that-germinated under the influence of the British might have played a greater role in the course of events than what has been recognised so far in modern historical writings. Answers to questions like the conflicts between the sepoys on the one hand and more traditional elements on the other, and the kind of polity or the polities that the leaders of the rebellion envisioned can also be sought in such data.

3. That Maulavi Ahmadullah Shah was one of the central figures in the popular Uprising of 1857 in Awadh and Rohilkhand becomes clear when we reconstruct his life and his activities in the context of the course of events in this region during 1857-59. British officers and military commanders have at times praised his military qualities and organising skills. He is said to have evaded Sir Colin Campbell (hero of the Crimean War) twice in pitched battle. Along with his tactical

skills, the nobility of his character and his chivalry and humanism have also been praised by British officers. His modesty was amply proved when he thanked the jailor at Faizabad, who was to send him to the gallows, for having allowed him use of a *hookah* while he was in prison. Ahmadullah Shah has won universal praise from modern writers who have studied this short but heroic phase of India's resistance against colonial domination. Historians like R.C. Majumdar and V. D. Savarkar described him as a hero, while Tara Chand, S. N. Sen, Syed Moinul Haq, Abrar Husain Farooqi, Ayyub Qadri and Ghulam Rasul Mehr, and a host of other Urdu writers have praised his leadership qualities.

4. There is a significant amount of material in Urdu on this period. Fateh Mohammad Taib, a disciple of Ahmadullah Shah and a small *zamindar* of the Lucknow region composed a biography in verse of Shah. The biography is divided into forty sections and the main discussion about the activities of Ahmadullah Shah is confined to section numbers 11-35. Section 18 (Verse Nos. 1243-88) is the most important section, which sets out Shah's arguments about the questions of *imamat* (leadership), the necessity of *jihad,* and the role of the *mujahedin.* Another important source is a proclamation issued from Lucknow, the capital of the erstwhile kingdom of Awadh, by a group closely associated with Maulavi Ahmadullah Shah. This is in the form of a pamphlet that was translated by British officers as "A Cry of *Jehad* in Oudh" (originally, *Futteh Islam/Fateh-i-Islam)* and was used as evidence of the religious bigotry and "holy nature of the war" waged against the Christians. The pamphlet was also used to argue that the *Wahabis* and *jihadis* played a crucial role during the course of rebellion.[2] While in Subaltern historiography this has been singled out as a representative document showing the extreme hatred that Indians had for the British because of the insulting language used to describe Queen Victoria, it has also been chided for its condemnation of the chain of British authority. But, when one compares this pamphlet with the British dispatches and reports sent through the course of 1857-59, one finds that it is the British who use abuse in describing the rebels and their leaders as scoundrels and *badmashes,* and the *mujahedin* as a "debased class of the people and fanatics." They employ the most abusive language for the rebels, which they never did for Irish rebels or Australian convicts.

Apart from the purportedly "fire and sword" nature of the pamphlet for which it has been rather harshly criticised by all modern writings, there is enough material to be culled from it to examine the vision of people participating in a battle unto death. The pamphlet reveals what they felt about the ongoing struggle and the strategies that had been worked out under the circumstances. The document also reveals that they were conscious about the death of English women and children as something that was totally unacceptable under the tenets of any religion. Besides making a strong plea for Hindu Muslim unity, it underlines the importance of firearms and canons, which were now available to the sepoys.

Fateh-i-Islam was issued some time between 5-17th July 1857 (the date has been worked out by S. A. A. Rizvi on the basis of the references in the text) after the Battle of Chinhat on 30th June 1857. Maulavi Ahmadullah Shah had defeated the British there and had emerged as the most powerful military commander at Lucknow. His group was seriously contemplating appointing him *amir* (leader) to control indiscipline among the troops and to restore law and order' In the preamble of the document, the atrocities committed by the British have been highlighted in great detail and thus, the people, Muslims as well as Hindus, have been asked to unite and wage a holy war against the "inhuman and ungodly Christians." It also talks about British attempts to deprive the troops of their religion by "applying impure substances" to the cartridges and forcing troops to use them, which ultimately, would result in the destruction of the British. There is a warning to the people that in case the British succeed in re-establishing their authority, great misfortune would befall the Hindus, Muslims, the sepoys, the kings and the *vazirs*. Finally, the document gives a call to unite, fight and annihilate the British without delay. Interestingly enough, the deadly impact of artillery has been praised and the document says that since the sepoys now possessed guns, what "the people of Hindustan needed" was now in the possession of the kings of Delhi and Lucknow. Hence, it becomes very clear that for the rebels, it was this deadly weapon that had tilted the balance in favour of the English earlier. Now that weapons were at the command of the rebels, they were deployed and used as effectively and as quickly as possible. This reference in the document is probably to sepoys joining the rebel army in large numbers with artillery and large guns.

The endeavor here is to utilise the available indigenous discourse on the life and activities of Maulavi Ahmadullah Shah in order to study how modern historiography has treated him and how his biography has been reconstructed by reading (or by *not* reading) crucial documents, and how this has affected the approach of many modern historians. This exercise is not only limited to highlighting the value of indigenous discourse but also seeks to show how the ultimate interpretation of events has been distorted by not cross-checking the victor's narrative with that of the vanquished, which is in languages like Urdu. During recent debates, it has been pointed out that since Ahmadullah Shah had very strong *sufi* antecedents, being a *qadri pir,* his sympathies could not have been with the *Wahabis*. Hence, his movement is seen as being independent of the *Wahabi* movement. But, it is very difficult to separate the sufi antecedents of a person from that of the orthodoxy. In fact, all the *Wahabi* leaders and their followers enrolled themselves in one or more *sufi* orders. Their campaign was never against the *tassawuf* (Islamic mysticism) *perse*, they were only trying to purify *tassawuf* from what they considered to be corrupt practices. So, such an argument has little strength and Ahmaduallah Shah's antecedents as a *sufi pir do* not make him any different from those subscribing to *Wahabi* ideas. *His* camp was *Wahabi* and he was, in a way, dependent on their support and strength.[4]

However, on the basis of the study of indigenous discourse, along with reports in contemporary newspapers and the despatches of British officers, a picture of Maualvi Ahmadullah Shah emerges, which is quite at variance with the projections of modern scholars. In the section below, I will try to reconstruct his biography using indigenous discourse.

II

Most of the studies on Maualvi Ahmadullah Shah rely heavily on the reports of British officers who had crushed the uprising in the provinces of Awadh and Rohilkhand. No doubt, they speak in respectful terms of his personal qualities and organising capacity, yet, they don't offer a complete picture of the person and his movement. Apart from these memoirs, the despatches of British officials on the day-to-day occurrences, which bear out his exceptional courage and valour have also been used.[5] Most modern studies tend to rely heavily on these accounts.[6] Little attempt had been made to utilise his biography[7] in Urdu to have a substantive idea of his career during the uprising. Similarly, reports in contemporary newspapers and short notices in the lesser known works of Shah's contemporaries have also escaped the notice of mainstream historians.[8]

From the documentary and literary evidence available in Arabic and Urdu, one can reconstruct an account of Ahmadullah Shah's life, and obtain many details, not otherwise known, of his role in the rebellion. This will also be of nelp in understanding the character of the popular uprising.

Saiyid Ahmad Ali Khan, alias Ziauddin, titled Dilawar Jang, was a son of Nawab Muhammad Ali Khan of Chinapattan (Madras). Born in the second decade of the 19th century, as a prince, he received the best education of his time. During his childhood, he was noticed for his exceptional memory, intelligence and industry. After completing his study of classical languages and traditional Islamic sciences, he received extensive training in warfare.[9] He seems to have acquired some knowledge of English at this stage. As an enterprising young prince, his fame travelled far and wide. He visited Hyderabad as a guest of the Nizam in connection with a marriage proposal. Though the proposed marriage' did not occur, he stayed on in the city for quite some time. According to Taib, Shah undertook an expedition on behalf of the Nizam to coerce a rebellious raja into submission. The details of the expeditions reveal his preference for deceptive methods of warfare.[10] But such spectacular success earned a number of enemies for him. In a surprise move, the jealous courtiers of the Nizam are said to have planned an attack on his person, but fortunately, Shah escaped unhort.[11] The British officers at Hyderabad then formally requested his father to allow him to visit England. Thereafter, Shah went to London and met the king as well as a few notables. His biographer, Fateh Muhammad Taib has not provided too many details of his stay in England, except that Shah displayed his skill in the use of arms there.[12] On his way back to India, Shah stopped at Mecca[13] and Medina, then passing through Iraq, reached Iran, where the king wanted him to join his service. But Shah declined the offer and proceeded to India.[14]

By the time he was back in India, he became inclined towards mysticism and after an intense search for *a sufi* guide, became a disciple of Saiyid Furqan Ali Shah, a saint of the *qadri* order at Sanbhar (Rajasthan).[15] He remained with his *pir* for some time to get initiated into the doctrines of the order. From here, he was directed by his *pir* to proceed to Gwalior. From now on, he was called Ahmadullah Shah by Saiyid Furqan Ali Shah, a name by which he became widely known later.

At that time, Gwalior happened to be in the *wilayat* (spiritual jurisdiction) of another *sufi* saint of the *qadri* order, Mehrab Shah Qadri. After some initial hesitation, Ahmadullah Shah was initiated by him into the creed for the second time. In the company of the new *pir,* he spent at least four and a half years, roaming in the vicinity of Gwalior because the initiation entailed practical training in the propagation of *Jihad.* As part of strategy, he was directed to go to Agra. Mehrab Shah gave him a new name, Waliullah, but this name did not gain much currency.

In Agra, *qawwali* or audition parties were often arranged to attract crowds to preach the call for *Jihad.* Although the *qadris* were averse to the very idea of audition parties, sermons were delivered after these parties were over, calling upon people to be ready for *jihad.* Another contemporary testimony about Shah's activities in Agra is worth reproducing.

> ...(Ahmadullah Shah) arrived at Agra with a large number of *murids* [disciples]. He took a palatial house at rent, kept *naqqaras* [large musical drums; often used as a sign of royalty] at the gate and the drums were beaten five times a day. As his popularity grew, many more people became his *murids.* Audition parties *[majalis-i qawwali]* were arranged. I also became a frequent visitor at his place...[16]

During the course of these audition sessions, Shah often practiced meditation for long durations by holding his breath-a technique called *habs-i dam.* It was on one such occasion that Shah apparently told Faiz, "From this date after six months, there will be great disturbance in the territories of the government."[17]

From Agra, Shah left for Aligarh to meet Raja Mursan. He stayed in the *sarai* of Ratan Lal and the raja made in offering *(nazr)* of two hundred and fifty rupees in cash, one highly prized horse and two hunting dogs. According to Faiz, this is when he had the opportunity to meet Shah. Shah apparently told him about his intention to go to Lucknow, "where he will sit on the throne and issue his own coins, the whole army will obey him and the treasure will also be under his control."[18]

It seems that at Agra, Shah was very vocal in pleading *for jihad,* so much so that complaints were lodged with the British authorities to the effect that, "He is a *derwesh* only in name, actually he is a prince and is preparing the masses to wage a war against the government." No action was, however, initiated against him![19]

Sometime afterwards, he again went to Gwalior to discuss the future course of action. By this time, the incidents at Hanumangarhi and the assassination of Maulavi Amir Ali had became widely known and this might have influenced Ahmadullah Shah. In any case, he decided to proceed to Lucknow, the capital city of the recently annexed kingdom of Awadh, where he arrived in November 1856. His arrival in the city was reported in *Tilism* on 21st November 1856:

> These days a person called Ahmadullah Shah in the disguise of a *faqir* but having all the paraphernalia of royalty has arrived in the town and stayed in the *sarai* of Motamad-ud Daulah...he has now shifted to Ghasiyarimandi. People of the town visit him in large numbers on Mondays and Thursdays to take part in mystic gatherings *(majlis-I hal-o-qal).* A number of feats are performed in midst of these gatherings...such a display takes place every morning and evening for viewing.[20]

The impact of these gatherings on the population of Lucknow can be gauged by the next report of *Tilism,* which appeared two months later. On 30th January 1857, it was reported:

> Ahmadullah Shah in Ghasiyarimandi is very fearless in saying whatever he wishes to say and a large crowd is always there. Often, Maulavi Amiruddin Ali is remembered. Although he is unable to do anything, he always pleads for *jihad.*[21]

It appears that in January 1857, along with a group of chosen followers, Shah decided to make a surprise attack on a Christian gathering (in a church?) on a Sunday. But Shah's supporters could not adhere to the time schedule and the plan failed; even as the news of the planned attack leaked to the British.[22] A *kotwal* was sent to him to ask him to give up his call for *jihad* and to surrender his arms. But Shah is said to have replied,

> Since you (kotwal are also a Muslim and if you follow the *shariat,* then *jihad* is obligatory even for you. Likewise, I also consider *jihad* obligatory for me, but for want o f means (to carry on the struggle) I have not been able to undertake it. Otherwise I am quite ready for it.[23]

The *kotwal* was not convinced and the British administration thought it necessary to post some sepoys to check the inflow of visitors for Shah and even to record their names.[24] At the same time, orders were issued to the *thanadar* of Chinibazar for curbing his activities. Finally, Shah was forced to leave town and was asked to go wherever he wanted with his arms.[25] Such an order was not resisted by him, although we are told by Taib that "thousands of *telingas* (sepoys) used to come there (in the audition parties) and had discussions with him and went away.[26]

Ahmadullah Shah left Lucknow, apparently heading for Bahraich, with ten or twelve men (in some reports, only with five or seven men). A halt was made at Faizabad, where he stayed in the *chowk sarai.* Here, again, he started preaching Jihad.[27] About three days after he began delivering his sermons, a *chuprasi* informed the magistrate of the dangerous tendencies of this man's doings and accordingly, the officer in-charge of the city issued orders for his arrest. The principal terms demanded from Shah were that he and his armed followers, numbering about seven, should give up their arms, which would be kept in safe custody. Further, the British authorities demanded that all this preachings and distribution of money were to be entirely stopped. Shah refused to accept these coercive terms and, the next morning, an infantry company attacked them.

Ultimately, Shah was arrested and placed under guard in the cantonment as, "He seemed too dangerous a character to be kept in the city jail."[28] After a brief trial he was imprisoned in the district jail at Faizabad.[29]

With the outbreak of the mutiny at Faizabad on 8th June 1857, the gates of the prison were broken open and Ahtnadullah Shah was chosen by the mutineers as their leader and the notables of the town presented themselves before him and offered *nazr.* On assuming their leadership, he issued orders for the destruction of the temples of Hanumangarhi, reportedly built by the order of Wajid Ali Shah, the deposed king of Awadh at the site of a destroyed mosque. The *mahants* of Hanumangarhi reportedly offered assistance to the British and "exerted them to keep the troops steady."[30] It was natural for the Hindus to feel alienated, therefore they thought of withdrawing their support for Shah as "Just now he is planning for the destruction of *garhi,* nothing can be predicted for the future." The difference of opinion among the officers of the sepoys over the question of leadership was also made known to Shah. Therefore, he left for Lucknow. Nevertheless, the sepoys, at the final reckoning, forgot these apprehensions and joined Ahmadullah's forces. Consequently, at the time of the battle of Chinhat, he commanded both the Hindu and Muslim sepoys of Faizabad.[31]

With the battle of Chinhat began the second phase of Shah's career. He was now a busy commander, planning attacks on British positions and strengthening his defences. Since most of these details are well researched and since Syed Moinul Haq has used this information from Taib's *masnavi* (biography in verse), there is little need for repetition. Still, here are quite a few aspects that should be highlighted in order to understand his mission.

Shah's first engagement with British forces took place at Chinhat when the British made a surprise attack on him on the morning of 30th June 1857.Though the columns were hurriedly organised, Ahmadullah Shah and his contingent distinguished themselves in hand to hand fighting and even captured many assault guns. In inflicting a crushing defeat on the British, the Shah had a very significant role. He had wanted to take full advantage of the confusion in the British camp, but other mutiny leaders failed to realise the importance of such a strategic move. Shah's contingent was left alone to pursue the enemy. Taib bitterly complains that for want of joint action at the decisive moment, the English again consolidated their position. In any case, Shah led an assault on the English fortification (Residency) and suffered a bullet injury. He remained undeterred, yet "there was need for the cannons and the balls, not for the lances and swords; therefore, Shah had to beat a hasty retreat and fixed his quarters at Tara Kothi, This continued to be his headquarters for quite some time.[32]

Taib also discusses the reasons for the estrangement between Shah and the prince, Birjis Qadar. He records that as a result of the military victory against the British, the sepoys as well as the army commanders had become very arrogant, causing much hardship to the inhabitants of the city. People were being plundered indiscriminately. This lawlessness on the part of the sepoys was objected to by the *mujahedins* who raised the matter before Shah. Shah decided that a leader should be chosen to check the indisciplined and disorderly conduct of the sepoys. Quite contrary to his expectations, the army leaders decided in favour of Birjis Qadar. Shah sharply reacted to this. His plea was that since *jihad* could only be conducted under the leadership of an *imam,* it was necessary that the creed of the *imam* be the same as that of the *mujahedin.* Moreover, *jihad* is not obligatory for the *shias,* and by declaring the *shia* Birjis Qadar as the leader, according to Shah, the most important ingredient of *jihad was* missing. Therefore, for him, the fight against the British was no longer a battle for religion. Hence, the *mujahedin* could fight only for self-defence. Further, since the *mujahedin* had offered the stiffest resistance to the British, they also had an inflated sense of importance. Shah felt that since he had arrived to fight at the behest of his *pir,* the leadership should have been conferred on him.[33] However, this seems to be only a theoretical position taken by Shah, as practically, he lent full support while attacking the Residency. At the request of Barkat Ahmad, his disciple and the commander of the Faizabad contingent, he personally participated in an assault on the Baily Guard. In this attack, a bullet pierced his right hand.[34]

Taib broadly confirms the general impression that at Lucknow, the British position was strengthened by the two separate factions having conflicting and even contradictory interests, and hence the military leaders frequently changed sides and quite often shifted their loyalties from one camp to another. But, after the British captured Lucknow, the main rallying point of the anti -British forces was Shah and a joint venture to fight the British was proposed by prince Birjis Qadar. Shah readily agreed to this proposal. In the ensuing fight, the prince's forces withdrew half way, leaving the *ghazis* (fighters with a cause) to face the cannon fire of the British. Ultimately, Shah was forced to retire to the palace at Gaughat. In this battle too he was severely wounded.[35]

The occupation of Gaugh at probably gave some strategic edge to Shah over his rival camp and, consequently, Shah's forces were besieged by the prince's forces, but Shah refused to fight these "new adversaries as he never wanted to fight Indians, since he thought of himself as their leader and guardian. The siege went on for ten days without affecting the morale of the *mujahedin.* The prince's army commander made a plea to Shah that a treasure was buried in the palace and that unearthing it would provide the salaries of the soldiers. Shah readily conceded to this request, though, needless to point out, the treasure story was a hoax.[36]

According to Taib, common soldiers had the utmost respect for - Shah and whenever he thought of going somewhere else, they prevailed over him to change his mind. At the same time, it must be conceded that the unruly mob of the sepoys was hardly under anyone's control. Sharafud-Daulah, the one time prime minister of Awadh, was suspected of treachery. So the sepoys arrested him and wanted to execute him. Shah did not approve of this and the prime minister was put into prison. But, he was killed here. Taib absolves Shah of any responsibility for his murder and says that had this been Shah's intention, none of the conspirators would have escaped.[37]

Soon, a murderous assault was made on Shah during his morning walks. However, the assassin missed his target and against Shah's wish, the assassin was killed by his bodyguards.[38] Unable to hold his ground at Lucknow, Shah decided to withdraw with his small following towards Sitapur and establish his quarters at Bari. Hazrat Mahal (Birjis Qadar's mother) also joined him there. Although Shah's initial response was cautious, he ultimately agreed to her staying. Taib insists that after reaching Bari, prince Birjis Qadar offered his *bay 'at* (spiritual allegiance) to Shah. This put the management of the rebel forces in Shah's hands and he forced the officers of Begum to part with their wealth. This would have certainly caused resentment. Therefore, when the Shah decided to make a surprise attack on the Gorkha army of Nepal returning after much plunder, his new allies did not help him. As a result, the *Mujahedin* were left alone in the assault.[39]

After suffering considerable losses at Bari, Shah was forced to retire to Muhammadi. Here, he made a last bid to take a firm stand against the British. Although his health was deteriorating very fast, he was the guiding spirit behind the planning and execution of the designs of the rebel army. Taib says that despite his power, he demanded the total support of the sepoys and the army commanders before deciding on any course of action. He also sought to arrange the supply of ammunition for his forces. Accordingly, he sent an envoy to Nawab Bahadur Khan of Bareilly for the supply of lances. Although, the envoy was received courteously, lances could not arranged as they were needed by the Bareilly regiment.[40]

It was at Muhammadi that Shah declared himself an independent ruler. The coronation is said to have taken place on 15th March 1858 and coins were also struck with the legend,

> The slave of Mehrab Shah struck his
> Coins in the seven countries;
> A supporter of the faith of Muhammad is
> king Ahmadullah.[41]

No such coins have survived. This measure was probably announced to boost the sinking morale of the fighting forces. At Muhammadi, according to Taib, Shah received many rebel leaders like Azimullah Khan, prince Firoz Shah, Nawab Bahadur Khan of Bareilly, and one Ismail Khan. Besides these generals, some sixteen thousand sepoys are also said to have gathered there.[42]

Many details of the military campaigns of Ahmadullah Shah in Rohilkhand region have been included in Taib's bibliography.[43] Finally, we have a first hand account of Shah's death at Pawayan by Maulana Fazle Haq Khairabadi, who was an eye witness.

> With the innocent amil[44] (Ahmadullah Shah) a most treacherous game was played by an infidel *(kafir)* rustic *zamindar.* On oath, he had promised that when both the armies came face to face (Shah's army and the British forces) he would support Shah along with contingent of four thousand brave soldiers. As a result, the guns

> and cannons sprayed fire from the front, while the soldiers were stabbed on their backs by the treacherous, hypocrite *zamindar* and his contingent. In fact, they were acting at the behest of the Christians. They had become friends with the devil. Consequently, that god-worshipping *amit* attained martyrdom in the battlefield itself, and many of his supporters followed suit. After the martyrdom of these (brave men), the cowardly supporters fled from the battlefield only to be slaughtered by their Christian pursuers. Hence, all the inhabitants became obedient to Christian rule. Two faithful commanders gave a very tough battle in spite of the fact that they did not possess sufficient war material, still the enemy was killed in thousands...This was the last of the saddest incidents, and heralded the end of the war...[45]

A large number of documents have been reproduced by Abrar Husain Farooqi relating to the assassination of Shah by the raja of Pawayan. From the reports of British officers, one gains an impression of the sense o f relief they felt after receiving the news of Shah's death. The raja received a cash reward of fifty thousand rupees.[46]

Before the outbreak of the mutiny, Maulavi Ahmadullah Shah carried out systematic propaganda to emphasise the need *for jihad* in the United Provinces and in Awadh. This call for waging a religious war had a considerable popular impact. At least we know for certain about Agra, Aligarh, Lucknow and Faizabad. At the same time, Shah cannot be considered a lone preacher as significant roles must have been played by people like Saiyid Furqan Ali Shah and Mehrab Shah Qadri, but, unfortunately, very little is known about these people. Such intense propaganda bore the desired result as all the English officers were unanimous in saying that the most fierce resistance was from the "fanatics" or the *jihadis,* who entered the battlefield crying *"deen! deen.*[47]

Notes

1. This attitude is reflected in recent historiography where writers of modern works seem to be totally unaware of the writings on Maulvi Ahmadullah Shah. Most scholars depend on an article by Late Professor Iqbal Husain, where he had used information from an extremely important newspaper of Lucknow, *Tilism.* The said article is "Lucknow between Annexation and

Mutiny," and was published in *UP Historical Review,* Vol. No. II (1983). It was on this article alone that both Rudrangshu Mukherjee and Gautam Bhadra wrote about the early career of Maulvi Ahmadullah Shah. As late as 2003, Rajat Kanta Ray, in his otherwise important work, seems totally unaware of any of modern writings on Ahmadullah Shah-what he used was the typescript of an article I had presented in a seminar at Aligarh in 1988. Ray is totally unaware that a revised version of the same article was published in 1998 in *Social Scientist,* No. 296-99: 39-52. See Ray, R. K., *The Felt Community: Commonality-and Mentality before the Emergence of Indian Nationalism* (Delhi, 2003): 370, 474n, 487n, 517n.

2. It was a widely-held belief among the British that it was mainly due to a Muslim conspiracy against British rule that such a catastrophe occurred. This suspicion further increased when it was found in 1863 that the *Wahabis* were still active in the North-west Frontier as they were now in direct confrontation with the British after the collapse of the Sikh kingdom there. Here, they regularly received money and recruits from areas as far as Bengal and Bihar. A series of "Wahabi Trials" followed during 1863-72. In the context of this witch-hunt, W. W. Hunter wrote in his famous *Our Indian Musalmans* (London, 1871) that the notion of *Jihad* had historical continuity from the time of Shah Waliullah (d. 1762) and his son Shah Abdul Aziz (d. 1824) to Syed Ahmed of Balakot (who died in action 1831). This became the most important interpretation of *jihad* in the Indian nationalist discourse of the 20th century when Maulana Azad reaffirmed this theory of the origins of the idea of *jihad.* This interpretation got full-fledged support when Maulana Ghulam Rasul Mehr, who served as the secretary to Maulana Azad as well, developed this interpretation in his monumental Urdu biography of Syed Ahmed Rae Bareilley. This understanding remains the most dominant trend in modern writings, especially in Urdu historiography. See Gaborieau, M., "The 'Forgotten Obligation': A Reinterpretation of Sayyid Ahmed Barelwi's *Jihad* in the North-West Frontier. 1826-1831," in *The Resources of History: Tradition, Narration and Nation in South Asia,* edited by J. Assayag (Paris-Pondicherry, 1999): 297-98.

3. Contrary to Shah's expectations, the army leaders and the notables decided in favour of Prince Birjis Qadar, the minor son of Wajid Ali Shah, the ex-king of Awadh, who was on a forced exile in Calcutta. The differences between Birjis Qadar and Shah are referred to in the biography of Shah composed by Maulana Fateh Muhammad Taib. See the couplet numbers 1261-88, where some of the arguments given in *Fateh-i-Islam* are reflected. See, Farooqi, A. H., (ed.), *Tawarikh-i Ahmadi of* Fateh-i-Muhammad Taib *as Mirat-Ahmadi* (Hardoi, 1973): 239-42.

4. It was argued by K. M. Ashraf, as early as 1957, that the *Wahhabis* had a crucial role to play during the events of 1857. It was generally believed that their anti-British feelings had made them one of the most important opponents of the Company's regime-a line of argument that was accepted

in nationalist historiography. However, recently Professor Iqtidar Alam Khan has questioned the validity of this argument as he has argued that the rank and the file of the Wahhabis might have participated as individuals in fighting during 1857, but the same cannot be said o f their leaders. Moreover, he says that most of the organisers of the revolt had *sufi* antecedents rather than Wahhabi antecedents. It is very difficult to make such a distinction when identities and loyalties were sharpened and yet overlapped so much to make it very difficult to make a distinction between the two. See Khan, 1. A., "The Wahhabis in 1857 Revolt: Brief Appraisal of their Role," presented at the 'National Conference on the *Historiography of 1857: Debates in the Past and the Present State of Knowledge,'* December 2006, ICHR.

5. See, for example, Melleson, G. B., *A History of the Indian Mutiny,* Vol. III (London, 1878-80): 541-44; Kaye, J. *W, History of the Sepoy War in India,* 1857-8 (London, 1880); Innes, *Lucknow and Oude in the Mutiny* (London, 1896); Hutchinson, G., *Narratives of the Mutinies in Oude* (Calcutta, 1859).
6. Sen, S.N., *Eighteen Fifty-seven* (Delhi, 1957); Mukherjee, R., *Awadh in Revolt,* 1857-1 858, *A Study of Popular Resistance* (Delhi, 1984). A biographical sketch of Shah has been attempted by Gautam Bhadra in "Four Rebels of Eighteen-fifty Seven," in *Subaltern Studies,* Vol. IV, edited by R. Guha (Delhi, 1985): 263-75. But. like Rudrangshu Mukherjee, Bhadra too seems unaware of the biography in verse of Shah.
7. Taib, F. M, *Tawarikh-i Ahmadi* (Lucknow, 1925). Taib, the author of *this masnavi* (composed in A.H. *1280; A.D.* 1863), was a landed aristocrat of Lucknow and had become a disciple of Ahmadullah Shah in 1856. On the instructions of Mehrab Shah Qadri of Gwalior, the spiritual guide of the author's *pir,* he composed this *masnavi.* The work is divided into 40 subsections and the main discussion on the activities of Ahmadullah Shah is confined to section numbers 11- 35, but the verses are numbered in continuation. For the purpose of precise reference, the numbers of the verses have been cited here. I have used Abrar Husain Farooqi's edition, which has been reprinted with copious notes and a useful introduction as *Mirat-i Ahmadi.* Although in English works Ahmadullah is invariably referred to either as Maulvi or as the Maulvi of Faizabad, to be in tune with Taib, he has been referred to as 'Shah' in this article.
8. By way of an exception, S. M. Haq's *The Great Revolution of 1857* (Karachi, 1968) made full use of Taib's account, but, unfortunately, he had no access to the weekly newspapers of 1857 in Indian archives and libraries. There are a number of important Urdu works that discuss Shah. See, for example, Shahabi, 1., *East India Company our Baghi Ulema* (Delhi, n.d.); Mehr, G. R., *Atharah Sau Sattalvan ke Mujahid* (Lahore, 1957); Shahabi, M. 1., *Ghadr ke Chand Ulema* (Delhi, n.d.); and Farooqi, A. H., *Masir-i Dilawari* (Lucknow, 1965), all of which utilise material in Urdu on Shah with a

number of photo plates of rare documents. See also, Qadri, M. A., *Jang-i-Azadi 1857*: *Waqiat aur* Shakhisiyat (Karachi, 1976): 525-40, for a fairly comprehensive account of Shah's activities.

9. Taib, *Tawarikh-i Ahmadi:* Section 7, 551-67.
10. Ibid.: Section 8, 580- 96. It is said that on nearing the territory of the defiant chieftain (the name of the raja and area cannot be ascertained), Shah left the soldiers in a neighbouring forest, crossed the river and entered the territory of the raja in the disguise of a wondering ascetic. Soon, the fame of the 'holy man' reached the raja, who paid a number of visits to him. Thus, Shah was able to persuade him to go for an outing in the neighbouring forest, where the army was camping. The raja was made captive here and could secure his release only after submitting to the Nizam's demands.
11. *Ibid.:* Sectio n 8, 597- 632.
12. *Ibid.:* Section 9, 644-66.
13. *Ibid.:* Section 9, 674-90.
14. Saiyid Furqan Ali Shah belonged to a family of *madad-I maash* holders of Sanbhar since the Mughal period. For sometime, he was in the service of the *maharaja* of Jaipur, Ram Singh. He was initiated into the mystic order of the *qadris* by one Shah Hafizullah of Khatav, Nagaur, who, in turn, was a disciple of Shah Habibullah Qadri of Lahore. (This information was obtained by Mirza Abdul Hafiz Beg, Superintendent, Rajasthan Waqf Board during a field survey conducted in November 1969.) See A. H. Farooqi, *Mirat-i Abmadi:* 323-27.
15. Mehrab Shah Qadri was a soldier in the contingent of a Maratha *sardar.* But due to strong mystic tendencies, he resigned after a while and retired for meditation and contemplation. Shah's biography also states that he preached *jihad* against the British to all his disciples. The special favours shown to Ahmadullah Shah were due to the fact that he had extensive training in warfare and hence was thought quite capable of leading a *jihad* in reality. However, it is not known whose disciple Mehrab Shah Qadiri was. The *Shajra-i Manzooma* of Ahmadullah Shah, reproduced by Farooqi, is of no help in this respect due to its rather in coherent nature. The *dargah* of Mehrab Shah still exists and is located at Jiwajiganj, Laskar, Gwalior. See A. H. Farooqi, *Masir-i Dilawari:* 284-92.
16. M. Akram Faiq, *Khwariq-i Mastan* (Agra, A. H. 1317): 29. The author's ultimate sympathies are with the victors as he praises the British for "providing stability" and for having "established the tenants of justice for high and low." Also, for him, they were unmatched as, "... they possessed an excellent army." Further, he says that at Aligarh, Shah had made him an offer of appointing him as the *imam* of the army, but realising "the futility of the cause" that Shah was engaged in, Faiz had apparently refused the offer. Ibid.: 32.

17. *Ibid.*: 32.
18. *Ibid.:* 32-33. Faiq further says that after Shah left for Lucknow, he (Faiq) went to Moradabad. The reports of the mutiny seemed to confirm all the predictions Shah had made. Although he showers praise on Shah for his bravery and valour, he hastens to point out the "futility" of Shah's venture.
19. Taib, *Twarikh-i Ahmadi:* Section 14, 1 016- 29.
20. *Tilism,* No. 18 (21 November 1856). This paper was edited by Maulvi Mohammad Yaqub Ansari of Firangi Mahal, Lucknow, during 1856-57. The last issue of this paper was published on 10 May 1857. For a discussion on the importance of this newspaper, see Husain, I., "Lucknow between the Annexation and the Mutiny," *UP Historical Review* Vol. No. II, 1: 40-51. Mukherjee and Bhadra have both used this article to sketch the early career of Ahmadullah Shah.
21. *Tilism,* No. 28, 30 January 1857: 1.
22. Taib, *Tawarikh-I Ahmadi:* Section 14, 1034-47. In fact, one verse clearly states that as Shah had been ordered (by his *pir)* to fight the Christians, he preached *jihad* to everyone. Sec S. M. Haq, *The Great Revolution of* 1857: 592.
23. *Tilism,* No. 28, 30 January 1857: 1; see also, Taib, *Tawarikh-I Ahmadi:* Section 14, 1047-57.
24. *Tilism,* No. 29, 30 January 1857: 1.
25. *Tilism,* No. 32, 27 February 1857: 1-2.
26. S. M. Haq, *The Great Revolution of* 1857: 60.
27. *Tilism,* No. 32, 27 February 1857, explicitly asserts that while leaving Lucknow, he made it known to all the visitors that he was leaving for Bahraich and that his stay at Faizabad was simply as a traveller. For details of the Faizabad happenings, see Taib, *Tawarikh-i Ahmadi:* Section 15, 1065-97.
28. See G. Hutchinson, *Narratives of the Mutinies in Oude;* S. M. Haq, *The Great Revolution if* 1857: 61. The incident of Faizabad became widely known and all the leading newspapers reported it in detail. See *Tilism,* No. 33 (4th March 1857); *Dihli Urdu Akhbar,* No. 10 (8th March 1857): 3; and *Sahr-i Samiri,* No. 17th March 1857).The editor, Raghubir Narayan *Aysh* notes that "He is the same person who had established himself at Ghasiyarimandi, but considering him a dangerous person, the *kotwal* had expelled him... earlier Maulvi Amir Ali had also led *a jihad* and in spite of the opposition of the king, he was able to enroll many followers, but in the end, everybody met destruction. They were beheaded when they came face to face with the soldiers."
29. Taib, *Tawarikh-i Ahmadi:* Section 15, 1065-97. Shah was not just roaming from place to place aimlessly. In fact, his preaching and sermons had a consider able impact on his disciples. The testimony of Hutchinson is worth noting: "This man [Ahmadullah Shah], after passing through a vast number

of cities and stations under our rule, in all parts of India, and establishing his disciples therein reached Fyzabad in February 1857, subsequent investigations elicited that everywhere he had preached *jehad,* or religious war against the *kafirs,* or infidels, as the Europeans were politely designated. From some places he had been summarily ejected, but in others evaded expulsion, meeting with no real check until he came to Fyzabad" (G. Hutch inson, *Narratives of the Mutinies in Oude*: 292).

30. Nevill, H. R., *Fyzabad: A Gazetteer* (Allahabad, 1920): 165. See also, Fisher, M. H., *A Clash of Cultures: Avadh, the British and the Mughals* (Delhi, 1987): 231-32.
31. Taib, *Tawarikh-i Ahmadi:* Section 16, 1135-55.
32. *Ibid.:* 1170-236.
33. *Ibid.:* Section 18, 1243-88. The arguments set out by Taib on the question of *imamat,* on the role of *mujahedin* and on the necessity of *jihad* find strange corroboration in the arguments on these issues in a pamphlet called *Risala-i Fath-i Islam.* Although the authorship of the pamphlet is yet to be determined, one can conclude that it is the most representative piece of writing on the ideology and organisation of the *mujahedin.* It is divided into two portions. The first portion contains a highly academic discussion on the necessity of *jihad,* the role that the *mujahedin* and the *ghazi* are to play *in jihad,* the difference between plunder and the distribution of *ghanimah* (the war booty), the need for appointing an *amir* and the necessity of offering him *bay 'at* for *jihad,* the wisdom of the sages behind the theory of the Quraish descent of *imams* and its impracticability in the prevailing circumstances of 1857, and last but not the least, an appeal to Hindus for joining the *jihad* against the common enemy. Apart from this, certain practical measures were also suggested to continue the struggle. While the second portion of the pamphlet is in the form of an *ishtihar,* "meant for the Hindus and the Muslims of India, so that they should think over, and should prepare themselves for the slaughter of the English in order to protect their *din* and *dharma:"* This call was intended to be popularised among the masses by the *maulvis* and the *pundits.* By its very nature, the *ishtihar* was meant for public consumption in the form of propaganda literature for the rural poor.

    In fact when one compares the British describing the rebels and their leaders as scoundrals, *badmashes, shuhda,* and riffraffs, and the *mujahedin* as a debased class of fanatics, one can understand why this pamphlet uses, "the most insulting language to describe the British, especially Queen Victoria." See R. Mukherjee, *Awadh in Revolt.* 148; also see Gautam Bhadra on the "abusive condemnation of the whole chain of British colonial authority from the crown to the common soldiers and administrators" (G. Bhadra, "Four Rebels of" 1857": 271).

The *mujahedin* and their leaders had offered such stiff resistance to the British that after the suppression of the events of the 1857 Revolt, the entire class of the *maafidar* had become a suspect in the eyes of the British. As happened during the course of the first regular settlement, each confirmation of the *maafi* was based in the notion of the disputed loyalty of the *maafidar* during 1857. Those who were hostile toward s the British, those who supported the rebels and even some who remained neutral, all had their grants summarily confiscated or drastically reduced. For the role of the *mujahedin* in 1857, see Ashraf, K. M., "Muslim Revivalists and the Revolt," in *Rebellion, 1857- A Symposium,* edited by P. C. Joshi: 71- 102.

34. Taib, *Tawarikh-iAhmadi:* Section 19, 1293-311.
35. *Ibid.:* Section 21,1377-418.
36. *Ibid.:* Secti on 23, 1553-70.
37. *Ibid.:* Section 25, 1737- 49.
38. *Ibid.:* Section 25, 1724—27.
39. *Ibid.:* Section 26,1 766-812.
40. *Ibid.:* Section 28, 1883-909. See this section for an account of the *farman* despatched to Nawab of Bareilly and also section numbers 1910-40 for versions of the *'arzdasht* of the Nawab in reply to the *farman.* See also, Farooqi: 133- 36.
41. See Taib, *Tawarikh-i Ahmadi:* Section 30, 2024-65 for details on coins and the despatch *of farman* to various rulers, See also S. M. Haq, *The Great Revolution of* 1857: 544.
42. For Shah's activities in the Rohilkhand region, see Taib, *Tawarikh-i Ahmadi:* Section 29, 1941-2023 and also Section 31, 2066-145. Company officers were also equally concerned about his movements and they too kept themselves informed about every thing Shah was doing. In this connection, a letter from the Chief Commissioner of Awadh to the Secretary, Government of India is worth mentioning: "The defeat of the rebels at Bareilly and Shah jahanpur drove Moulvi Ahmadullah Shah with his followers back into Oudh, where he was joined by Nurput Singh of Rohia. After reconnoitering Palee with a strong body of sawars, the Moulvi with nine guns and seven thousand men made a movement on the Thane of Palee, which he entered on the 22nd instant. From hence he marched on to Sandee, and immediately threatened the position of the Commissioned Colonel Clarke at Dhurmpur.... The circumstances in which Colonel Clarke found himself thus suddenly placed, fully justified him in withdrawing all his civil officers to Putah Gurh at once before their retreat was cut -off" (Letter No. 373 [1858], dated 29th May 1858, *Foreign Secret Consultations,* Nos. 56-57 [25June 1858], National Archives of India).
43. The best account has been provided by S. M. Haq, who used Taib's account. See S. M. Haq, *The Great Revolution of* 1857: 544-50.

44. It is quite interesting that Shah was designated *amil* by one of his chief supporters. Does it mean that the claim of independence by Shah posed no challenge to the authority of Birjis Qadar?
45. Fazle Haq Khairabadi's. *Al Thaurat-al Hindiya* (written in Arabic), edited with comprehensive notes and a useful introduction by Abdul Shahid Khan Sharwani was published as *Baghi Hindustan* (Bijnore, 1947). The Urdu translation of the text has also been provided. See especially page numbers 409-13; also compare Haq, S. M., "The Story of the War of Independence, 1857-58," *Journal of Pakistan Historical Society,* Vol. No. V, I (January 1957): 21—57.

    Maulana Fazle Haq of Khairabad (1797-1862) happens to be one of the most fascinating and a multifaceted persons of his times. Belonging to a well-known family of scholars of Khairabad, after studying traditional and rational sciences at his father's *madarasa,* he came to Delhi, where, during this period, some bitter theological controversies were being debated, resulting in a vertical division within the *sunnis:* on hypothetical issues such as the question of the intercession of Prophet Mohammad *(shifa'at)* and the finality of his prophethood *(imtina un-nazir)*. A man of Khairabadi's genius could not remain a mute witness to such debates. He proved to be one of the most bitter critics of Maulvi Shah Ismail of Balakot fame on the question of *jihad.* But strangely enough, during 1857, he changed his position and caused the leading theologians to issue a *fatwa for jihad.* A detailed study of his intellectual environment is worth analysing in order to understand the ideological trends of this period. For details on his role during 1857, see Husain, I., "Fazle Haq of Khairabad-A Scholarly Rebel of 1857," *Proceedings) of the Indian History Congress,* 48th session (1987): 355-65; and Malik, Jamal., "Letters, Prison Sketches and Auto biographical Literature: The Case of Fadl-e Haqq Khairabadi in the Andaman Penal Colony," *Indian Economic and Social History Review),* Vol. No. XLIII, 1 January-March 2006): 77-100. It is interesting to note that Malik has used S.M. Haq's translation of *Risala as Saurat al Hindiya* throughout his work, with a few comments either on the manuscripts or about the history of the document as it has been traced by Shahid Khan Sharwani.
46. See Abrar H. Farooqi, *Masir-i-Dilawari* 192-243, for the photographic reproductions of various applications, reports and orders along with their transcripts.
47. It is strange that the scholars working on this period have seldom touched upon this important aspect. This is in spite of the fact that there is no dearth of material giving the point of view of the vanquished. These proclamations, letter s and intelligence reports *give* an insight into the rebels' point of view. Apart from S. Muinul Haq and K. M. Ashraf, in recent years. Professor Iqbal Husain has studied this subject seriously. For his important contributions, see Iqbal Husain, "Fazle Haq of Khairabad-A Scholarly Rebel of 1857": pp. 207-219 of this volume.

'Suppression and Reign Terror'

Chapter - 15

William Hodson and the Abduction of Bahadur Shah 'Zafar'

— *Professor Amar Farooqi*

As is well known, the revolt of 1857 began as a mutiny in the East India Company's Bengal Army, and soon became a popular uprising. The mutiny broke out at Meerut on Sunday, 10th May 1857, when Indian *sipahis* stationed in the city rebelled. The *sipahis* then as a body marched to Delhi, where they arrived the next morning. They put an end to the East India Company's administration in Delhi, and assumed control of Shahjahanabad and its immediate outskirts. They sought the blessings of the Mughal emperor, Bahadur Shah II (r. 1837–57). This gesture was an indication of the symbolic political importance of the emperor. The Company too had reluctantly recognized the *de jure* authority of the Mughals, even though by the middle of the nineteenth century they had made the emperor completely powerless and irrelevant.

Delhi was governed by the *sipahi* regime from 11th May to the middle of September, 1857. Throughout this period of a little over four months, Bahadur Shah continued to reside in the palace, and was nominally the 'constitutional' head of the *sipahi* regime. Several princes of the royal family played an important role in both the civil and military administration set up by the *sipahis*. On 14th September the British launched a major military offensive to capture the city. The attack on the walled city was carried out by the Delhi Field Force which had been constituted by the British to recapture Delhi. By 20th September the entire city had been taken over and the rebels were defeated.

The Red Fort, headquarters of the *sipahi* regime, fell on the 20th, and immediately became the headquarters of the Delhi Field Force.[1]

When the British occupied the palace they discovered that Bahadur Shah had already vacated it along with his family. They were not exactly surprised as rumours had been afloat since the previous day that he had sought shelter in the shrine of Hazrat Nizamuddin Auliya.[2] Mahdi Husain, who carefully collated what different sources have to say about the emperor's movements in the last few hours before the fall of Delhi, suggests that he left the palace on the night of 19/20th September, halting initially at the shrine.[3] The important point here is that the emperor stayed on till the end, and did not 'slip out' earlier as has at times been alleged.[4] There is evidence to suggest that he was actively assisting with the defence of the Red Fort on the day he is supposed to have, according to some later accounts, abandoned the *sipahi* cause.[5] We do not have any definite information about the emperor's movements after he departed from the palace. S.N. Sen pieced together the following account from available sources:[6]

> The King had at first gone to the Qutb. Mirza Ilahi Baksh[7] persuaded him to come to Humayun's tomb. Maulavi Rajab Ali of the British intelligence service informed [William] Hodson of the whereabouts of the fugitives. Hodson went to General Wilson[8] and obtained his permission to negotiate for the King's surrender through Ilahi Baksh on the sole condition of sparing his life. This was a political business which was normally the responsibility of the civilian officer attached to the Camp, Hervey Greathed [who had been appointed commissioner of Delhi]. But Greathed died of cholera on the 20th, and was succeeded by [C.B.] Saunders. Hodson verbally told him that he had obtained the General's authority to treat for the King's surrender and to guarantee his life.

William Hodson, who handled the intelligence wing of the Delhi Field Force, had been able to put together a network of spies to gather information about the activities of the rebels in the final weeks of the *sipahi* regime's control over Delhi. To this network may be attributed the deliberate spread of misinformation about 'secret' contacts between Bahadur Shah and the British. These rumours were intended to discredit the *sipahi* regime, demoralize the rebels and engineer defections. There is no reliable evidence whatsoever to suggest that the emperor colluded, or tried to negotiate, with the British. As we have noted earlier, he remained firmly committed to the struggle of the *sipahis* right till the end.

While the British troops were establishing their control over the city, following the occupation of the Red Fort, Hodson was busy pursuing the emperor and his family. It is not clear what personal interest he had in this. Quite possibly he was after the treasure that Zinat Mahal was carrying with her.[9] All the evidence we have about what transpired relative to the emperor in the forty-eight hours before he was taken prisoner on 21st September at Humayun's tomb can be traced back to Hodson and his gang, of which Rajab Ali, Mirza Ilahi Bakhsh, and Jeevan Lal (*munshi* in the Company's Delhi establishment) were key members.[10] In view of the spymaster's extremely dubious role, and his reputation of being financially corrupt, this evidence is of little value. Ilahi Bakhsh (whom the emperor never trusted) and Rajab Ali were creatures of Hodson, and cannot be relied on either. Greathed had conveniently died on the 19th (midnight). Saunders, who had just assumed charge as officiating Commissioner, reportedly relied on Hodson's word in the absence of any documents. Correspondence on the subject of the 'guarantee' given by Hodson to the emperor that his life would be saved if he were to 'surrender' is revealing. Extracts from this correspondence were first published by Mahdi Husain in 1958.[11] The 'guarantee' issue is quite irrelevant, and distracts the historian from Hodson's own agenda. The British were in no mood at this time to respect any assurances or 'guarantee'. It was therefore immaterial whether Hodson had any authorization to give the 'guarantee'. Bahadur Shah could easily have been eliminated, with or without any guarantee. His 'trial' was an afterthought.

When enquiries were made by the Calcutta authorities about the circumstances in which the emperor had been taken into custody, and about the author of the 'guarantee', no categorical answer was forthcoming from the officers at Delhi. Hodson had consistently lied, misleading both Wilson and Saunders. Saunders was taken aback when he learnt that he was being held responsible for sanctioning the 'guarantee'. He 'emphatically denied any personal role in granting the guarantee of the King of Dehlee of his life'. Seeking to clarify his position he stated that he 'did not receive until after the Ex-King had been made over a prisoner to me any of the official documents in the possession of Mr. Greathed at the time of his decease'. Saunders asserted that it was 'not until *after* the person of the King had been on the strength of the guarantee secured that I can be said as stated by the General [Wilson] to have approved of the measure' (emphasis added).[12] Saunders reminded Wilson 'that I was not present on the occasion when Captain Hodson applied for and obtained your permission to guarantee the King his life but was at the time absent at Mr. Greathed's funeral'. 'On my return from the funeral', he continued, 'I met Captain Hodson outside the city near the Cashmere Gate cantonments. As he passed me he checked his horse and called out that he was off to make arrangements for securing the King's person through Ilahee Bukhsh as he had received your permission to guarantee the King his life'.[13] Wilson was 'quite sure' that Hodson had not sought his approval, though he was willing to concede that he might not recollect with accuracy everything that had occurred 'on such a day of excitement' as 20th September. He concluded his reply to Saunders by observing that 'as Mr Greathed is dead and I have no evidence of my conversation with him on the subject and you object to taking any responsibility on your part you are perfectly at liberty to throw the whole on my shoulders'![14] Hodson had taken advantage of the prevailing confusion to create the impression that he had orders from above to deal with the emperor in the manner he did. He could go ahead with his own scheme without any interference. Significantly his action was never closely scrutinized, nor was anyone certain as to what orders Hodson had actually received. A military official named W.M. Stewart who had been present when Hodson spoke to Wilson about the emperor later recalled,

> I did not hear all that passed in the *Diwan-i Khass* [Wilson's office in the Red Fort] between the General and Hodson as I continued writing at my own table for some time after Hodson began talking. Having occasion to speak to the General I went up to him and found him engaged with Hodson upon the guarantee question. ... There was no one with the General during Hodson's interview. In fact, there was no one in the verandah except myself and I was at my own table which was ... at some distance from the General.[15]

The suspicion about Hodson's motive is confirmed by his act of assassinating several princes who were captured from Humayun's tomb on the 22nd. They were shot dead on their way to the Red Fort under military escort.[16] Why Hodson should have killed the princes before they could be presented to his superiors remains a complete mystery. However, we do have one clue. The bodies of the princes were stripped by him 'of their signet rings and turquoise *bazubands* (armlets)', as well as 'their bejewelled swords', objects that were immediately 'pocketed' by Hodson.[17] The solution to the mystery might be very simple—robbing the princes of the possessions they had on their persons. This was Hodson's private loot. Most historical accounts of the episode refer to the killing of three princes: Mirza Mughal, Mirza Khizr Sultan and Mirza Abu Bakr. These princes were the principal leaders of the *sipahi* regime from amongst the royal family. It is almost certain that several other princes were slain by Hodson at the same spot. In his well-known memoir of the revolt, Sayyid Zahiruddin Zahir Dehlvi mentions 'sons, sons' sons [*pote*], daughters' sons [*navase*], and sons-in-law [*damad*]', altogether *thirty* princes (*shahzadgan*), all of whom had been identified by Mirza Ilahi Bakhsh, being killed on 22nd September outside Delhi Gate while they were being escorted from the shrine of Hazrat Nizamuddin to the city.[18] Colonial historiography was successful in concealing the extent of Hodson's brutal slaughter by suppressing the actual figure. Standard textbook accounts continue to repeat the much reduced figure—just three princes, killed because they were part of the leadership of the *sipahi* regime.

Surprisingly Zahir Dehlvi did not name Hodson as the perpetrator of this slaughter. Rather, the main actor in his narrative is Saunders. According to him, Saunders (assisted by Rajab Ali) persuaded the emperor to return to the city; Saunders then rode out to dargah Nizamuddin to apprehend the princes (assisted by Ilahi Bakhsh); and it was Saunders who ordered the execution of *thirty* princes whose heads were then severed and sent to the emperor.[19] Whether Zahir Dehlvi deliberately avoided mentioning Hodson's involvement or whether he made an inadvertent error we do not know. Chances are that the former explanation is the right one. Zahir Dehlvi's family was beholden to Rajab Ali who had given a job to his brother as a *katib* in the large library he maintained on his estate in Jagraon (district Ludhiana, Panjab).[20] Rajab Ali in turn was indebted to Hodson. There was another link which connected Zahir Dehlvi's family with Rajab Ali. Zahir Dehlvi's maternal grandfather had studied Arabic under Rajab Ali. Many of the stories about the revolt that form part of Zahir Dehlvi's memoir were based on what he had heard from his maternal grandfather, who in turn would have picked up many of them from Rajab Ali's personal reminiscences.[21] Zahir Dehlvi would not have wished to remind his readers of Rajab Ali's association with the doings of the hated Hodson.[22] William Dalrymple has used Zahir Dehlvi's memoir extensively in *The Last Mughal*, assuming that it is unbiased. It seems Dalrymple overlooked the close connection between Rajab Ali and the family of Zahir Dehlvi. This makes the memoir somewhat unreliable, especially since Rajab Ali was a key player in the British reconquest of Delhi.

Bahadur Shah's so-called 'surrender' was more an abduction, carried out by Hodson in collaboration with his band of spies and informers. Four months after the reconquest of Delhi, the abducted emperor was put on 'trial'. This sham show, lasting from 27th January to 9th March 1858, was conducted by a military commission. From where it derived its constitutional authority we do not know. In terms of international law it could not have sat in judgement on the actions of the emperor to whom the East India Company, which constituted the commission, was legally subservient. The juridical framework of the commission too is suspect as the evidence placed before it had nothing to do with its predertermined verdict. To designate the proceedings of the military commission as a trial is absurd. The East India Company, through the commission, was exercising the right of a victor in war to deal with a captured enemy in whatever arbitrary manner it chose to, as a prisoner-of-war. At the end of the 'trial' Bahadur Shah was con-victed of 'treason', and for having allegedly abetted the killing of some Europeans. The *Diwan-e Khas* was chosen as the venue of the 'trial'. Pramod Nayar in his introduction to a recent edition of the proceedings of the 'trial', for which he has supplied a lengthy introduction, points out that, 'The fact that the trial of the Mughal emperor was held *in his own palace* hall is a significant feature. The palace of the emperor, where he gave special audiences and received visitors, is re-inscribed as a space where British authority reigned.

At stake here is the re-appropriation and transformation of space itself: from the site of the Mughal emperor's power—such as it was... to one of his criminalisation'.[23]

Notes

1. Surendra Nath Sen, *Eighteen Fifty-Seven*, Delhi, 1995 (first published, 1957), p. 104.
2. 'The report is that the King and all his family have gone out to Nizamoodeen's Tomb ... there is a large *serai* there, and lots of room to accommodate a very large party'. Henry W. Norman and Mrs. Keith Young, ed., *Delhi 1857: Extracts from the Correspondence and Diary of Colonel Keith Young*, reprint, Delhi, 2010 (first published, 1902), p. 296.
3. Syed Mahdi Husain, *Bahadur Shah Zafar and the War of 1857 in Dehli*, Delhi, 2006 (first published, Delhi, 1958), pp. 280-81.
4. Cf. William Dalrymple, *The Last Mughal: The Fall of a Dynasty, Delhi, 1857*, New Delhi, 2006, p. 369.
5. Norman and Young, *Delhi 1857*, p. 290.
6. Sen, *Eighteen Fifty-Seven*, p. 105.
7. Father-in-law of the recently deceased heir-apparent Mirza Fakhru.
8. Archdale Wilson commanded the Delhi Field Force from mid-July onwards.
9. Cf. Sen, *Eighteen Fifty-Seven*, p. 105.
10. 'The late Major Hodson [Hodson was killed in March 1858] entered into correspondence with the Mirza immediately after the assault of Delhie in order to effect the capture of the Ex-King through Maulvi Rajab Ali and Turab Ali [another spy]...'. Saunders to Govt. of Panjab, cited in Mahdi Husain, *Bahadur Shah Zafar and the War of 1857 in Dehli*, p. 355.
11. Mahdi Husain, *Bahadur Shah Zafar and the War of 1857 in Dehli*, Appendix E, pp. 345-356.
12. Saunders to Govt. of India, 27th December 1857, cited in Mahdi Husain, *Bahadur Shah Zafar and the War of 1857 in Dehli*, pp. 345-47.
13. Saunders to Wilson, 28th December 1857, cited in Mahdi Husain, *Bahadur Shah Zafar and the War of 1857 in Dehli*, p. 349.
14. Wilson to Saunders, 29th December 1857, cited in Mahdi Husain, *Bahadur Shah Zafar and the War of 1857 in Dehli*, pp. 350-51.
15. Stewart to Saunders, 29th December 1857, cited in Mahdi Husain, *Bahadur Shah Zafar and the War of 1857 in Dehli*, pp. 352-53.
16. Sen, *Eighteen Fifty-Seven*, p.106; Dalrymple, *The Last Mughal*, pp. 393-98.
17. Dalrymple, *The Last Mughal*, p. 398.

18. Sayyid Zahiruddin Zahir Dehlvi, *1857 ke Chashmdíd Halat*, Delhi, 2011 (originally published with the title *Dastan-e Ghadar*, Lahore, 1912), Delhi, 2011, p. 117.
19. Zahir Dehlvi, *1857 ke Chashmdíd Halat*, pp. 116-17.
20. Zahir Dehlvi, *1857 ke Chashmdíd Halat*, p. 116n1.
21. Zahir Dehlvi, *1857 ke Chashmdíd Halat*, p. 116n1.
22. Zahir Dehlvi, *1857 ke Chashmdíd Halat*, p. 116n1.
23. Pramod K. Nayar, ed., *The Trial of Bahadur Shah Zafar*, Hyderabad, 2007, p. xxxiv (emphasis in original).

Chapter - 16

The battle for Delhi: Myths and the Construction of the Raj

— Dr. Ms. Madhu Prasad

On the morning of 11th May 1857, the rebellious sepoys and sawars from Meerut entered the city of Delhi and were joined by their counterparts in the city. One of the early targets of the rebels was the Delhi College located in the Residency buildings. The rebels sacked the library of the college and killed its British principal. Their anger was said to have been fuelled by the fact that the college provided European learning and promoted the study and use of English. Widely reported in the local press and in British reports, this incident epitomised British portrayal of the 'Mutiny' as a fight between ruthless, unlettered natives and a civilising British power.

However, in this as in many other instances, conditions in Delhi, and most of north India, during and after the Revolt of 1857 tell quite a different story. Reports by British officials, and accounts by Indians who supported their growing power, provide enough evidence to conclude that facts were neither as simple as the constructs of the victors, nor were they particularly flattering to the British.

In the first place, the college was a unique institution where both oriental learning and European sciences had been enthusiastically studied for three decades as they were taught in the vernacular Urdu medium. Arabic, Persian, and Sanskrit were also studied and English was also taught. James Thomason, Visitor to the Delhi and Agra

Colleges and later Lt Governor of the North-Western Provinces, recognised that the Delhi College occupied 'a prominent part in the eyes of a large and influential section of the native community, whom it is most important to convince of our liberality and sincerity'. He complained about changes in the official educational policy, implemented after Macaulay's Minute of 1835 but already articulated in an 1830 despatch of the Company's Directors, of downgrading and discouraging the study of the classical languages, literature and sciences of the east by withdrawing student stipends and, in the case of the Delhi College, of trying to promote an 'education in English' by fraudulently siphoning off funds from the oriental institution's large private endowment. Second, although it was stated at the end of June that 'English books' from the sacked library 'are lying in the streets still'[1] it was equally significant that 'many of the Oriental works were recovered after the outbreak was quelled'[2] Finally, many students and teachers of the college supported the rebels and were sympathetic to their cause. Consequently, the college was shut and ultimately closed down by British authorities. During the weeks of terror that followed the defeat of the revolt, many students and prominent scholars were either exiled or killed by British forces, including the renowned Persian scholar Imam Baksh Sehbai who was shot along with his two sons in the infamous Kucha Chellan incident in which 1400 persons lost their lives.[3]

Dual purpose in Targeting the College

The rebels had targeted the college not because they were unlettered but because it was part of the Company's complex of public buildings in the Kashmiri Gate area that one of the first columns to enter the city was required to disable. The rebels were, of course, opposed to British domination and the promotion of English as an instrument in that policy of domination. It served the dual purpose of rendering the learned elite redundant, while at the same time aimed at creating a class of lower level native functionaries to occupy the subordinate posts open to them in the British administration. In fact, the rebel attitude towards Christians also requires to be understood within this complex framework and not simplistically interpreted as evidence of 'fanaticism'. 'Christians were allowed not only to preach but to found religious establishments in India and Persia, before their faith became a formidable political power in the hands of alien and usurping races from the West.[4] The Mughal state comprised a reliable and professional imperial elite at the centre, and co-operating regional aristocracies elsewhere. The Mughals observed a ruling ethos that led to the emergence of a cross-communal service class. Akbar's descendants continued with his legacy of drawing upon differentiated symbols of legitimacy. Standards were aristocratic rather than communal. Among the elite, communalism was regarded as bad manners.[5] Consequently, there was a tradition of well-informed debate about non-Islamic religion and culture among the learned elite which had a significant effect on the socio-political environment of the city.

This was much in evidence during the period when the rebels held the city. 'Though the great majority of the parties (27 of the leading officers of the rebels at Delhi) were Hindus, it is worthy of remark that they style the King of Delhi as their "spiritual as well as secular' leader": The king and the leaders of the rebellion consciously nurtured this unity. The celebrated incident when the Emperor banned the sacrifice of cattle at Iduz Zuha, and the troops and administrators were able to enforce it totally, was the source of great demoralisation for the British camp on the Ridge. In an apparent move to dampen the over-zealous ardour of a section of extremists, 'some of the 3rd Cavalry made the fanatics in the Jama Masjid take part in the fight today. Many were killed and wounded.[6] Renowned mathematician and early Christian convert, Professor Ramchandra of the Delhi College, bore witness to this unity, contrasting it with British racism, in his complaint to the military authority after the city was taken by British forces: 'there is hardly any comfort remaining, when a native Christian is in danger from Christian officers themselves merely because he was not born in England and had not a white skin. This was not the case even among the rebels in Delhie who were professors of false religion. A Mahomedan or a Hindu was received as a brother among them:

Unparalleled Devastation

Even the myth of rebel 'excesses' pales in comparison with the unparalleled murder, plunder and loot with which British forces, who occupied Delhi on 20th September 1857, devastated a city that had rivalled Baghdad as a centre of intellectual and cultural life.

A communication from 'Sunt Nana', dated Mhow, 21st November 1857, refers to 'a letter from my father (which) gives an insight into the miserable and wretched condition the inhabitants of Delhi have been put to…A general plunder of the town seems to have followed a general bombardment, and the news formerly received were that the whole townspeople were allowed one rough night to escape barely with life….families scattered over the face of the country-mothers separated from children, husbands from wives and so on….no one ever thought the capture of Delhi by Englishmen would be attended with more cruelty than that by a Nadir (Shah):

Ghalib bemoaned the fate of Delhi. 'When the raging lion-hearts set foot in the city, they held it lawful to slaughter the helpless and burn the houses, and indeed, in every territory taken by force of arms these are the sufferings that people must endure. At the naked spectacle of this vengeful wrath and malevolent hatred the colour fled from men's faces, and a vast concourse of men and women, past all computing, owning much or owning nothing, took to precipitate flight through these three gates (the Ajmeri, the Turcoman and the Delhi gates which were still held by the rebels).[7]

> 'In the city no man's life was safe', said Moinuddin Khan, 'all able-bodied men who were seen were…shot.'[8] The Delhi Commisioner's wife, Mrs Saunders, corroborates this in a letter dated 25th October 1857 (Saunders Papers): 'For several days after the assault every native that could be found was killed by the soldiers; women and children were spared.' However, CJ Griffiths writes that Clifford, Assistant Collector at Gurgaon, personally informed him that at the fall of Delhi, 'he had put to death all he had come across, not excepting women and children'.

Professor Ramchandra, who had refused the post of native headmaster at Thomason College, Roorkee, several months before the rebellion because of a 'constant and sincere wish to remain in Delhi', now gratefully accepted the opportunity to escape from the city, as 'there is no power in Delhi and natives of every description are suffering and are in danger every moment'.

The people of Delhi had expiated many times over, the 'crimes' of the rebels. Tens of thousands of men, women and children were wandering, for no crime, homeless over the country. What they had left behind was lost to them forever; for the soldiers going from house to house and from street to street, ferreted out every article of value, and smashed to pieces whatever they could not carry away. A Military Governor had been appointed; but he could do little to restrain the passions of those who surrounded him. Natives were brought forward in batches to be tried by a Military Commission or by Special Commissioners, each one of whom had been invested by the Supreme Government with full powers of life and death. These judges were in no mood to show mercy. Almost all who were tried were condemned; and almost all who were condemned were sentenced to death. A four-square gallows was erected in a conspicuous place in the city; and five or six culprits were hanged every day. English officers used to sit by, puffing at their cigars, and look on at the convulsive struggles of the victims.[9]

William Russell, an early war correspondent who arrived in India in January 1858 on a year's assignment for *The Times,* made the following entry in his diary on 5th June 1858, 'I found myself in the ruined streets of a deserted city, in which every house bore the marks of cannon or musket shot, or the traces of the hand of the spoiler....I could scarcely believe that I was in a city which is described by an old traveller as being "of the bigness of London, Paris and Amsterdam together, and of an incomparable greater population and riches"[10] Returning from a picnic to the Qutab Minar four days later, Russell saw 'in the full glare of the morning the miserable sheds, in which the outcast population of the city, forbidden to return to their homes, are now forced to live,...For miles they stretch along the roadside. More squalid and vile nought can be, save the wretched creatures who haunt them-once perhaps rich bunneahs, merchants and shopkeepers.'[11]

When they were allowed back, it was 'decided that every citizen who desired to return should pay a fine, but there should be a discrimination in the rate on a communal basis. While the Muslim had to pay a fine equivalent to 25 per cent of the value of his real property, the Hindu was required to pay 15 per cent less.'

The Prize Agents held that the whole city had by conquest become the property of the army and hence legitimate 'prize'. This extraordinary doctrine, despite some feeble protests and appeals for limitation, held for three full months! Suggestions that 'no parties be employed by them, without consent of Col. Burn (Military Governor of Delhi) and that such parties should be furnished with a license by that officer; serve only to emphasise the impunity with which the city was being ransacked. Burn himself complained to General N Penny, commanding the Delhi Field Force, that '...several parties under European Commissioned officers have, during the last few days, been searching for plunder within the city....Even the Sabbath brings no rest to either plunderer or plundered.' On 24th October 1857 Burn reports that 'loss of property from plunder by our soldiers or from its wanton destruction is estimated at the large sum of two crores of rupees', yet even by 15th January 1858, 'not more than 15 lakhs have been, or will be realised by the Prize Agents'. Penny, in a telegram dated 25th November 1857 to John Lawerence in the Punjab, reports that 'prolonged search (for treasure) by digging is continued to the danger of houses'. On 12th December, Lawrence enquires from Delhi Commissioner, Saunders: 'Is private plundering still allowed? Do officers still go about shooting natives?' (Saunders Papers).

Incredible Plunder

The myth that plunder was the work of native troops doesn't stand up to evidence. Even the property of Englishmen, retrieved from rebels and local bad characters, was not spared and thousands of rupees were said to have been pilfered from the government treasury by English soldiers of the 60th and 61st Rifles while on guard duty. 'Had you seen their wives come to Church, dressed in the most gorgeous of silks...with French bonnets you would have known they never bought them out of their husbands pay."[12]

> That many of the private soldiers of my regiment succeeded in acquiring a great quantity of valuable plunder was fully demonstrated soon after our arrival in England. An unusual number of non -commissioned officers and men bought their discharge, having during three years kept possession of the plunder acquired at Delhi awaiting a favourable opportunity for the sale of the articles. Many jewellers shops in the town we were quartered exposed for sale in the windows ornaments and trinkets of

unmistakeable Eastern workmanship...The plunder daily being found in the city...is almost incredible. I fancy every officer present at the siege might be able to retire at once."[13]

British officers also used their servants to acquire and transport plunder of value. Russell sardonically comments that 'this is better than the way in which another officer is said to have got some precious stones...as a result of a sharp fight with one of our own Sikhs.'[14]

Among the prize were manuscripts, rare and valuable manuscripts that any power with claims to a 'civilising mission' should have been careful to exempt from prize property in order to protect and preserve them. Instead, the following advertisement appeared in the newspapers on 29th July 1858:

> By Order of the Prize Agents, Delhi Field Force will be sold by auction at Delhi on the 1st September 1858, 17,000 volumes in Vernacular, many of them illuminated. Comprising works on Theology, Medicine and General Literature. The above have been carefully assorted and catalogued and may be viewed any day prior to the sale at the house of BHAWANEE SUNKER, Chandney Chooke. J H KERR INNES, Prize Agent. Lieut. W N Lees, Secretary to the Board of Examiners at Kolkata, drew the attention of the Governor General to the advertisement, stating that it 'adverts to the very great value set upon oriental manuscripts by the European nations, England being the sole exception, and begs that the Governor General maybe moved to purchase for the state any manuscript of value which the above collection may contain or the whole.'

Some 4,700 Mss' were eventually acquired. The services of a good scholar were required to classify and catalogue them. As always, 'the cheapest and most expeditious means of accomplishing the task...(was) to direct the Arabic Librarian of the (Kolkata) Mohamedan College, with the assistance of 2 of the senior students, to attend at the College for 3 to 4 hours...(for) six months'. Approval for a 'trifling and reasonable' payment, covering only *palki* fare both ways for the librarian and one way for the students, did not fail to carry the warning that Lees should personally ensure that none of the manuscripts were stolen in the course of the cataloguing!

Lees was apparently one of that small but rapidly diminishing group of administrators, somewhat derisively termed the 'orientalists', who did not always go along with the then prevalent official denigration of an ancient and still vibrant culture. The early 'orientalist' strategy adopted by the Company in the late eighteenth century when the Kolkata Madrasa for instruction in Arabic and Persian was established by Warren Hastings in 1781, and the Benaras Sanskrit College by Jonathan Duncan in 1791, reflected the fragile base of British presence in India. Hastings had preferred to rely on an elite corps of acculturated British officials, who through their knowledge and sympathetic understanding of Indian institutions, laws and customs, would exercise power in the manner of traditional rulers. 'The early servants of the East India Company perfectly understood their position; and when they first took over the Provinces, they left the Muhammadan administration absolutely undisturbed. They retained the Mughal code as the law of the land and appointed Muhammadan law officers to carry it out, and in the smallest matter, as in the greatest, acted merely in the name of the Mughal Emperor of Dehli.'[15]

However, the first half of the nineteenth century saw a concerted assault from evangelists, on the one hand, and utilitarian reformers on the other, that resulted in a deep contempt of Indian sensibilities and culture. It coincided with attempts by the Company, which had so far functioned within traditional forms of governance and recognised the authority of the Imperial presence at Delhi, to shed the shackles of this dependence and establish itself as an independent power. As a result, beginning with the Vellore incidents of 1806, a chain of disaffected, mutinous actions occurred in the Bengal Army across the country. 'Almost all mutinies of India...have been more or less produced.... There has usually been some departure from contract, some disregard for the feelings, health or convenience of the native soldiers, when at the same moment the utmost care was lavished on a European regiment,"[16] They were usually put down with brutality.

The major stumbling block to British ambitions was not the growing disaffection in the Bengal Army, but the continuing legitimacy of the Emperor at Delhi. They chaffed against it and were pressurising the royal family to leave the Red Fort and their claims to sovereignty after the death of Bahadur Shah....although the Delhi Sovereign had long been deprived of all real power and dominion.

> ...almost every state, and every class of people in India, still continue to reverence his nominal authority. The current coin of every established power is still struck in his name and the princes of the highest rank still bear the titles and the insignia, which they or their ancestor derived from this source;...The universality of this impression maybe further inferred from the conduct of the Tamburetty or Princess of Travencore, a Hindu state situated near Cape Comorin, the southern extremity of the region, and at no period of its history subject to the Mughal, or to any Mohammedan superior: yet in 1813, she applied to have a dress of investiture for her son, the infant Raja, although he was under the special guardianship of the British government, to which he was indebted for the tranquility of his accession.[17]

'All persons conversant with Indian history must be aware of how much moral importance attaches to the possession of Delhi in the eyes of the inhabitants of India generally.'

For this reason, the outbreak at Meerut was 'seized upon as the real starting point of the Indian Mutiny; for the weakness of Hewitt and Wilson (who failed to contain it) allowed the mutineers to seize the Imperial city...and to enlist the influence of the Mughal's name on their side, and thus yielded to them an immense moral and material advantage at the very outset of their operation....They could confidently appeal to the discontented who had hitherto longed but feared to rebel.'[18]

Calculated Barbarism

> Delhi is not a city...that we may hold or abandon at our pleasure. The possession of Delhi is a tower of strength to us politically and morally.

Delhi was the focus of the rebellion, and the vital point upon the recovery of which was staked the very existence of British aspiration to empire. This accounts for the ferociousness with which control over the city was established by the victors after the defeat of the rebellion. The myth that the barbarism was caused and justified by the desire for revenge following the massacre of a group of European men, women and children in the Palace on 16th May though it reached exaggerated proportions in the popular imaginati on, diverted attention from the fact that it was, in fact, calculated policy.

The manner in which the Punjab was quelled from 12th May onwards, following the receipt of the telegraph message from Delhi, and troops raised for the assault on Delhi, already displayed a ruthlessness that was explicitly seen as essential to securing British supremacy. Col. Sydney Cotton compelled troops to witness the executions of deserters and suspected leaders. The method was simple and horrible. According to an eyewitness account of executions ordered by John Nicholson, later lionised as the 'hero' of Delhi, 'the first ten were picked out, their eyes were bandaged and they were bound to the guns-their backs leaning against the muzzles, and their arms fastened to the wheels. The port fires were lighted, and at a signal from the artillery major, the guns were fired. It was a horrid sight...a regular shower of human fragments of heads, of arms, of legs appeared in the air through the smoke... fragments of Hindoos and fragments of Muslims, all mixed together-were all that remained of those ten.'[19] The news of these executions and the mode adopted in carrying them into effect, 'spread far and wide, and even in the city of Kabul itself, were the subject of discussion and astonishment...and the Afghans,...on finding that the supremacy of the British government had prevailed, were themselves deterred from an aggressive movement'.[20]

This conduct was not atypical; it constituted the policy with which the mutinous rebellion and conditions of general insurrection were to be brutally crushed. 'Our object is to make an example to terrify others', John Lawrence, Chief Commissioner, Punjab wrote to the then commanding officer of the Delhi Field Force, General Sir Herbert Edwardes in June 1857, advising that 'I would select all those against whom anything bad can be shown-general bad character, turbulence, prominence in disaffection, or in the fight, disrespectful demeanour to their officers....I would then add to them the oldest soldiers. All these should be shot or blown away from guns....The sepoys will see that we punish to deter, and not for vengeance.'[21]

The promise of plunder was also held out to pre-empt the spread of the revolt. A proclamation authorised 'anyone who found a deserter to kill him, and take possession of his personal property'.[22] Likewise, the police of the states with loyal rajahs, like Patiala, Nabha and Jind, 'scoured the country, and assured of indemnity, slew every criminal upon whom they could lay their hands. Highway robbers and plunderers were in many cases hanged on the nearest trees as soon as they were caught....It is needless to say that severity like this proved to be the truest mercy in the end.'[23]

Following these 'severities', Secretary to John Lawrence informed Maj-General Wilson, then in command of the Delhi Field Force, that the 'Chief Commissioner cannot conceive that any danger can now arise at Dehli from the people of the country... they will now be thoroughly overawed....[Olur troops may now do almost anything ... no one dare raise his head. All are our devoted servants.'

Atrocities imposed by British officers on civilians in the North-Western Provinces, which led to suicides in many instances, became embarrassingly public in 1859 when the Lt-Governor of the Province placed written reports by serving officers, without reprobation or rebuke either from him or their senior officers, before the Legislative Council. Officers declared that in order to govern the Indian people, 'they must not be treated as civilised or intelligent beings' and advocated 'the maintenance of a foreign mercenary army so that we may be in a position to pass what laws and what taxes we chose "without the slightest regard for the opinion of the whole native world'.

Ruling by Force

At the end of his Diary in 1859, William Russell explicitly stated: 'I am deeply impressed by the difficulty of ruling India, as it is now governed by force, exercised by a few who are obliged to employ natives as the instrument of coercion. That force is the base of our rule I have no doubt; for I see nothing else but force employed in our relations with the governed.'[24]

'I protest against meeting atrocities by atrocities...instead of bowing before the name of Jesus, we were preparing to revive the worship of Moloch.'[25] Such protestations notwithstanding, it was clear that the British regarded their own conduct in India as being above morality and not bound by any civilised codes. 'It is necessary in all

Eastern lands to establish a fear and awe of the government. Then and not till then, are its benefits appreciated.'[26] Neill's cruelty and perverted vindictiveness, and he was by no means an isolated figure, found few contemporary critics. Queen Victoria would award him a posthumous knighthood. John Nicholson believed in flogging Afghan tribesmen and cultivated the myth of their hero-worship on this barbarism-a myth treated with skepticism even by British officials although none opposed his behaviour.

Deep-seated Racism

Brutality was grounded in a deep-seated and carefully cultivated racism: the Muslim as bigot; the Hindu as dishonest and servile. The unreliable, superstitious and corrupt Asiatic as opposed to the civilizing British resulted in the converging of both the 'vulgar' and the 'refined' racism. The retreat of Englishmen, women and children, accompanied by droves of native domestics, from the Flagstaff Tower to Karnal and Ambala, is 'that piteous flight, the first of many such incidents which hardened the hearts of the British to inflict a terrible revenge, not more for the physical sufferings of their kindred than for their humiliation by an inferior race.'[27]

Racial discrimination marked the personal behaviour of British soldiers ; commissioned officers appeared to be little better. 'The sepoy is estimated an inferior creature. He is sworn at. He is treated roughly. He is spoken of as a nigger.'[28] 'Subalterns fresh from school, often called natives "niggers"....He is addressed as a "suar" or pig', it being regarded as a 'praise-worthy sense of superiority over the sepoy to treat him as an inferior animal'.[29]

General Wilson who took over command of the Delhi Field Force on the Ridge after 17th July 1857, resolved 'above all...to protect the camp-followers, whom in their unthinking hatred of the coloured races, they (English soldiers) had treated with unthinking cruelty....[I]gnorant soldiers too often repaid the camp-followers, without whose services, given at the risk of their lives, they could'nt have existed for a day, with brutal words and savage blows; and few of their officers cared or ventured to restrain them.'[30]

Russell records with disgust what counted as acceptable behaviour towards natives: 'I was very much shocked to see in this courtyard two native servants, covered with plasters and bandages, and bloody, who were lying on their charpoys and moaning....[T]hey were so and- so's servants who had just been "licked" by him. It is a savage, beastly and degraded custom. I have heard it defended. But no man of feeling, education or goodness of heart can vindicate or practise it.'[31] I believe', he wrote, 'that we permit things to be done in India, which we would not permit to be done in Europe, or could not hope to effect without public reprobation; and that our Christian character in Exeter Hall, will not atone for usurpation and annexation in Hindustan, or for violence and fraud in the Upper provinces of India.[32]

The convergence of political ambitions and racial arrogance combined to ensure that the treatment meted out to the Emperor and members of the royal family was astonishingly crude. 'I saw that broken-down old man-not in a room but in a miserable hole of his palace....He showed me his arms, which were eaten into by disease and by flies...he said, in a lamentable voice, that he had not enough to eat! Is that a way in which, as Christians, we ought to treat a king?'[33]Two sons and a grandson of the Emperor, leading figures of the rebellion, were shot without trial by Col. Hodson. 'I also saw the dead bodies of the three princes...exposed to public view for two days at the Kotwallie....Some days later I was present when two more princes of the royal house were shot by a platoon of European soldiers...and their bodies afterwards thrown into the river.'[34] Twenty-one princes of the royal family were 'all condemned, hanged and carted off the same day.'[35]

It would be argued after the trial of Bahadur Shah that it was the East India Company, and not the Emperor, who should have been tried for treason, for at no time had the Company formally renounced the position of feudatory it had accepted after the Battle of Plassey in 1757. However, power was the supreme legality for realising Britain's imperial ambitions, and Christian values, laws, and even 'natural tenderness', were easily overcome to attain this singular end.

'The struggle we have had has been more like a national war than a local insurrection. In its magnitude, duration, scale of expenditure and in some of its moral features it partakes of the former character.'[36]

The term 'mutiny', which would afterwards be officially used to refer to this 'national war', was the final myth which converted the subjugation of India into a purported return of peace with 'the cause of loyalty, humanity and rightful authority vindicated.'[37]

However, the real history of that period found its reverberations during the freedom struggle. In 1944, in a ceremony held at the tomb of Bahadur Shah in Rangoon, members of the INA took an oath to free the country from British colonial domination. In the call to arms given by Subhash Bose, the slogan of the heroes of 1857 was recalled: The road to Delhi is the road to freedom. And finally, in 1947, it was at the Red Fort, acknowledged in that Red Year by courageous rebels across the country as the symbol of India's pre-colonial unity and sovereignty, that the flag of an independent India was raised.

Notes

1. *Annals of the Indian Rebellion,* p. 216.
2. *Punjab Gazetter,* Delhi District, 1884, p. 152.
3. Zahir Dehlavi's '*Dastan-e-Ghada*r' in SN Sen, *Eighteen Fifty-Seven,* Publications Division, Government of India, New Delhi, 1959, p. 116.
4. WH. Russell, My *Diary in India in the Year* 1858-59, Vol. 2, p. 269.
5. Henny Sender, 'Kashmiri Pandits and the Culture of Delhi' in *Delhi Through the Ages: Essays in Urban History, Culture and Society,* ed. R.E. Frykenberg, p. 322.
6. Translation of Delhi News, Futteh Mohumed, 12th September 1857.
7. Quoted in Ralph Russell and Khurshid ul lslam, *Three Moghul Poets,* pp. 67-8.
8. Sir T. Metcalfe, *Two Native Narratives of the Seige of Delhi from Outbreak* at *Meerut* to *the Capture* of Delhi
9. T. Rice Holmes, *A history of the Indian Mutiny and of the disturbances which accompanied it among the civil population,* pp. 397-8.
10. WH. Russell, 1860, Vol. 2, p. 53.
11. *Ibid.,* p. 77.
12. 'Statement of Capt. Tytler', in *An English Woman in India: Memoirs of Harriet Tytler* 1828-1858, ed. Anthony Sattin, p. 171.
13. Report of an Assistant Surgeon, Sir William Muir: Records of the Intelligence Department, Government of *North-Western Provinces of India during the Mutiny of* 1857, ed. Coldstream, Vol. 1, p. 239.
14. WH. Russell, 1860, Vol. 2, p. 39.

15. WW Hunter, *The Indian Musalmans: Are they bound in conscience* to *rebel against the Queen?,* London, 1871, pp. 185-7.
16. *The Mutiny in the Bengal Army by* a *Retired Officer,* London, 1857, p. 4.
17. Walter Hamilton, *Description of Hindoostan and the Adjacent Countries,* 1820, (rpt. 1971), pp.422-3.
18. T. Rice Holmes, p. 111.
19. 'Letter by a British officer from Peshawar who witnessed 30 executions on a single day', printed in *Blackwood's Magazine,* Edinburgh, November 1857.
20. General Cotton, *Nine Years on the North-Western Frontier of India,* pp. 174-175.
21. Micheal Edwardes, 1973, Appendix 2, p. 157.
22. *Punjab Mutiny Report,* p. 67.
23. T. Rice Holmes, 1898, pp. 337-8.
24. WH. Russell, *The Diary:* My *India Mutiny Diary,* ed. Michael Edwardes, p. 34.
25. Benjamin Disraeli, Speech at Newport Pagnell, September 1857.
26. Letter to Henry Tucker from Col. James Neill, July 1857, Edwardes, 1973, Appendix 2, p. 159.
27. Letter from an officer of 38th Native Infantry to *The Times,* 6th August 1857, T. Rice Holmes, p. 110.
28. *The Rebellion in India by* a *Resident in the North-Western Provinces of India,* p. 34.
29. Captain. J G Medley, *A Year's Campaigning in India from March* 1857 to *March* 1858, p. 197.
30. T. Rice Holmes, pp. 351-2.
31. *Ibid.,* p. 129.
32. Russell, ed. Edwardes, p. 114.
33. Mr Layard, MP for Aylesbury, 'Speech at a public meeting in London', May 1858. Quoted in C. Ball, *History of the Indian Mutiny,* Vol. 2, p. 169.
34. Col. E. Vibart, *The Sepoy Mutiny as seen by* a *subaltern from Delhi* to *Lucknow,* pp. 149-50.
35. 'Memo of the Seige of Delhi' by E Hare. Quoted in Sen, p. 111
36. Governor-General and Viceroy, Charles Canning to Sir Charles Wood, Secretary of State, 8th August 1859.
37. Notification of the Kolkata Gazette Extraordinary, No. 1237 of 1857, announcing the fall of Delhi.

Chapter - 17

The concept of Booty, Revolt of 1857 and Delhi as a 'Prize'

— ***Dr. Shaheen Islamuddin***
Bhagini Nivedita College
Delhi University

Delhi was not simply a city- a garden it was. What shall I say of this peace that it had!
They have erased of its repute; now it is simply a place laid waste[1]

In the nineteenth century Indian history, the event of 1857 is one of the most important episodes. Since then, it has occupied a good space in the academic and non academic spheres where efforts have been made to study, understand, and explain its nature, meanings and significance. Scholars have been highlighting its various untouched aspects with rich and critical analysis, resulting in its constantly extending and surpassing boundaries. The uprising was a major challenge to the company Raj that had suddenly uprooted its existence from a major part of India. It was a result of a long series of unrest spread among the Indians under the British domination. This long series of exploitation and interference in the life of the common people constituted the past of the uprising while its suppression can be associated to its future[2] proved a turning point in colonial India. Attempts were made to suppress the revolt brutally and never allowed the people to raise their arms against the colonial government in future. At the same time, focus was also given to rebuilt the injured image of the colonial supremacy (it was a long process that can be seen in the enactment of the various acts, changing policies and giving new definitions to the relation between the rulers and the ruled especially in the second half of the nineteenth century) caused by it. The almost lost Indian Empire was recovered but the first phase of recovering the empire began with the fall of Delhi and spreading terror of the victors immediately after the rebellion in 1857. This brutal suppression of the uprising was the first step in the process of retracing and re-establishing their erased presence, prestige, and position as a dominant supreme power. This exercise kept colonial administrators busy, hectic and dizzy for a long time.

The impact of the suppression of the revolt was so widespread and far reaching that it not only turned the life of the people around but gave no space to the voices of the sufferers that were enclosed with many layers of torture, pain, loss and distress that had turned the event into awful memories in the minds of the vanquish class. Delhi was one of the important centres of the uprising. The history of re-establishing the British rule coincided with violence. British reoccupied Delhi on 20th September. Though, they were not able even to re-capture the area beyond the Kashmere gate until 16th September as their mortality rate had suddenly increased.[3] In the meanwhile, fear of losing life led the inhabitants to leave the city as soon as possible. Army's slow but advance steps coincided with terror and bayonet created a background in their favor where soldiers roaming through the narrow streets, were entering the houses 'from which the fire was more than usually severe and putting to death without mercy all who were found inside.'[4]Most of the people died in this upheaval. Revengeful spirit, hostility, desire of plunder, power of life and death was in the hands of British army and dominated the screen where Delhi had become unsafe for its people. Within few days, city was forcefully vacated and reserved for looting. This legalised plundering enhanced the terror of the victors more, as the properties of the people were being targeted. In short, this aspect was very shocking and destructive in its nature.

An attempt is made here to explore this untold story when Delhi was turned as a prize for its victors and loot was permitted in an imperial town immediately after the revolt. Households of the escaped people and those who had been permitted (few in numbers) to stay within the city were indiscriminately pillaged. However, properties belonged to 'rebels', 'Muslim' and 'disloyal inhabitants' were mainly targeted. Loyal and disloyal all were treated alike. Attack on private properties must have turned the whole environment with uneasiness and tension for the subordinate subject. How much did it affect and augment the distress of those days of turmoil? To what extent, turning Delhi as a prize affected the common life of the people? Was this deliberate policy connected to the suppression or the 'punishment'? Was this concept of the prize was an innovative or an old? Was there any pro perception in searching the riches of Delhi? Was Delhi the only city, where they operated? These questions will be dealt in the subsequent pages of this paper.

The concept of the 'prize money' and 'prize' connected to the war was equal to the booty. It was an old and well-established concept at universal level. In western countries, it developed since the late fifteenth and early sixteenth century when the ships had been looted and its proceeds considered as 'prize'.[5] In this period, different European powers traded with the East world, tried to dominate the sea routes. Wars between them were very common that had been created a concept called 'prize'. In this regard, conquering party was given a full right in the war to loot the properties of the defeated party and distributed among them. Thus, at initial level, it developed at the naval stage[6] and gradually expanded and implemented territorial level. It was a 'recognized law' in both the spheres. Navy and the military prize money shared the same rules in theory.[7] But in practice, they were dealt differently especially in the context of India. In India, this concept was developed by the East India Company in the middle of the seventeenth century while fighting with the French and the Nawabs of Bengal. It is a well-known fact that before the treaty of Allahabad, concluded between the Mughal Emperor Shah Alam and Robert Clive in 1765, the political career of the East India Company was not very clear in the Indian subcontinent. Company had limited financial sources. Clive remarks on the position of the company after concluding the treaty of Alinagar with Siraj-ud-Dowla in 1757.

> they (the opponent of the treaty of Alinagar) never considered that, with a war upon the coast and in the province of Bengal at the same time, a trading company could not exist without a great

> assistance from the Government and, last of all, they never considered that a long war, attended through the whole course of it with success and many great actions, ended at last with the expense of more than fifty lacs of rupees to the Company.[8]

Company relied on its Home government. Gradually increasing control over Bengal made the officers of the company able to buy the seats of the parliament that had created an anxiety not only among the members of parliament but also among the class of entrepreneurs. Therefore, parliament came into favor to limit the increasing influence of the company's officers by making Acts. 'Home' surveillance over the company's policies in India for sharing the profits of India is interesting to note. England government never wanted to empower the company's traders with full right over the property and the profits of India. In the late eighteenth century, rules regarding the company's 'military booty' were established. According to them, three institutions were given right to decide the disputed cases of the company's officers related to the 'Indian prize money' or 'military action' and its distribution among them. These were- the treasury, the Horse Guards and the India Office. Final decision was of the Lords of treasury after recommendation of His/ Her majesty. According to the rule of constitution, distribution of the 'booty of war' rested upon the sovereign (Crown). But, in practice, the Horse Guards returned the name of the officers and men who were entitled to share the royal bounty (after 1858, the Secretary of State of India was also consulted) then, the lists went to the Lords of Treasury for the final order. In between, rare cases were transferred to the court of admiralty.[9] This process was considered long to finalise the disputed case in comparison to the navy booty. Sometimes, long waited trial and contested distribution created uneasiness among the company's military. Final order used to come after a gap of few years. Delay was common in disputable claims. As the amount of booty sometimes far exceeded than imagine therefore question of sharing between the officers occurred. After 1857, the demand to change the rules was raised and emphasize was given to the right of the actual captors. Suffix is to say that prize agents at 'naval' and 'military' level were not dealt equally that had been created 'jealousy' and 'embarrassment' among company's officers against the navy rights. According to an English officer,

> It may be objected that principle deduced from decision of the admiralty Court on the question of naval prize do not necessarily regulate the distribution of military booty. There must, however, be to some extent a similarity and analogy between the rights of the army and of the navy with regard to their respective capture. And this more obviously in the present day, since the Court of Admiralty, by the Act 3 and 4 Victoria, c. 65, can now entrain questions respecting booty captured either on sea or land. But judicial decisions on disputed cases of purely military booty, though very rare, are not altogether wanting.[10]

It was a common characteristic to hold a 'council of war' before any military expedition in order to fix the amount of loot earlier especially when the joint efforts of navy and military took place against any Indian state. This rule was followed from Anglo-Carnatic war to the subsequent battle where requirement occurred. Let's see one of the earliest examples of formation of the council of war in May-June 1756, against the French.

> Clive and Admiral Watson (Captain of navy), having received the sanction of the authority of the Bombay, determined to extirpate such a noxious swarm of outlaws; and it is characteristic both of the men and of the theatre on which they operated, that a council of war was held previously to the departure of the expedition, in order to fix the proportions according to which the spoil which they counted securing was to be divided. For this it is which casts its darkest shadow over the entire series of events which led forward the East India Company from its original state to that in which we now find it. Plunder seems to have been the one great object sought by leaders of armies and fleets throughout the whole of our earlier wars in the East; and it not infrequently came to pass that, having achieved conquests and gained honour in the field, they ran of losing at least the latter in squabbles over the booty.[11]

Looting and plundering constituted an important part of the Company's territorial expansion.[12] This method had become more important for the company future because it reduced the risk of losing the battle too. To have something after the war could easily stimulate the soldiers in the field of battle. Thus, it could be more than 'incentive' as the question of political and military expansion connected to it.[13] There are instances where agents were appointed and loot was reserved for the army or the victor party. The name of Lieutenant General Gordon who had served in India from 1788 to1811 AD connected to the loot of Seringapatnam. In his whole career, he was appointed prize agent only for two times. The battle of Seringapatnam in 1792 gave him a chance to be selected as an agent while second in 1793, he became agent during the capture of the French fortress of Mahé, on the Malabar Coast.[14] In 1803, Delhi booty was amounted 10 Lakh rupees (excluding many articles) in which Lord Wellesley acquired a good amount of it.[15] Likewise, the name of Lord Hastings, the governor general (1813-1823) connected to the 'Deccan booty'[16] after the third Anglo- Maratha war as a constructive captors but Lords of the treasury favored to Sir Thomas Hislop, Commander-in- Chief of the Deccan army in Deccan booty case. Sir Thomas Hislop was the actual captor and presented his case strongly against the Lord Hastings where he was allowed the portion of 'the property taken in the daily operations of the troops' while Lord Hastings was offered all the money extracted from the 'forfeited revenues accruing to the state' in other words 'that part of the booty which consists of the produce of arrears of tribute rent, &c.,'[17] In the series of military successions one after another, the amount of loot increased and the position of the officers of the company had been stronger. Therefore, career in the eastern empire for any person belonged to the ruling race was advantageous. Though, military was dealt as a unit but in practice, individual officers were promoted to show their valour and expertise in the military tactics.

The issue of military prize money became little complicated only after the revolt of 1857 in India. In the process of suppression, almost all the centres of the revolt witnessed the same fate of legalized plunder.[18] Consequently, the amount of booty was very large and excited the hearts of the British. British troops considered their right as legal over the booty and wanted to have it all without sharing to the civil authority at local level. However, the then Governor General, Lord Cunning's announcement against the military demand turned the whole situation for some time. This decision came for Delhi booty. Delhi was recaptured on 20th September. But with the capture of Bahadur Shah Zafar, the Mughal emperor and some other royal members, complete victory was announced officially on 23nd September.[19] In the meanwhile, measures had been taken to secure the city. Various regiments were instructed to occupy the principle and comfortable havelies and palace was turned into the army's headquarter where General and his staff resided. British soldiers were appointed on the few entrances of the city and license system was approved under the supervision of magistrate of the city.[20] Within few days, the people who did not leave the city were forcefully turned out except few. Old men, women, and children all half starved and wretched were treated alike.[21] The pass system was followed more than two years. It had scrutiny and restrictive tendency as it prevented 'dangerous characters' to enter the city. John Lawrence writes to General Wilson that 'this and other regulations of a police nature,' would give them more security and suggests debarring the people from leaving their houses after a given hour at night and before dawn.[22] Government declared military authority as a 'sole judge' to seize the property of those who had acted again the British or against whom there might be reasonable ground of suspicion and retained them until further order issued.[23] However, these measures not only secured the control of the army over Delhi but helped to spread the news of their victory to the other parts of India too. At the same time, this step also favored the desire of the army to collect booty in Delhi without any interference. For some officers, it was a 'novel' and 'just punishment' that ought to be given to the people of Delhi. William Muir, a secretary of North Western Provinces was one of them, appreciates this 'new method' by saying that

> The idea is novel of subjecting a city for above a month to plunder and its inhabitants to temporary exile, and then requiring them to pay down the value of their property. For people or class of people who had connected themselves with the rebellion confiscation of property to the state is of course a just and reasonable punishment.[24]

Background for the episode of loot had prepared earlier.[25]Therefore, soldiers were allowed to loot for first three days after the end of a hectic war. In a dead city, accumulation of many people in various form of properties were opened before them. Army who had daytime dream to possess the wealth of the city had come true. Mughal had become a mine of treasure. Empty grand *havelies, shops, godowns, temples,* filled with oriental luxuries were searched for jewels, pearls and valuable articles. In isolated streets and houses, every soldier was looking to possess a 'Delhi memento'.[26] In the words of William Ireland, 'The shops and warehouses in the Chandni Chowk were full of costly goods. Those containing jewellery were entered and cleaned out in a few minutes. A great deal of valuable spoil fell into private hands... The European soldiers went about selling the things. They had plenty of money in their pockets, which they spent with the recklessness common to their profession. Some private soldiers kept their carriages for a week or two. The temptation now and then proved too strong even for officers. Some of them carried away, and even presented to their friends, valuable jewels and costly shawls.[27] City witnessed a general air of damage and ruin. Soldiers from high to low succeeded in acquiring wealth in different form of loot. Griffiths states that, 'To my certain knowledge many soldiers of the English regiments got possession of jewellery and gold ornament taken .....and I was shown by men of my regiment string of pearls and gold *Mohur* which had fallen into their hands.'[28] Furniture, articles, cloths, pots, coins, and ornaments were either broken or battered into fragments or carried away by them. This 'individual anarchy' of the armed force ceased after some time and replaced with the team of official plunderers, called prize agents who began a systematic search for unearthing the remaining hidden treasure of the city.

In this second round of search, individual loot continued. No discrimination is going to be made, argues Colonel Burn, 'between the property of friends and foes up to the present time all treated alike.'[29] He further states that 'the loss of property from plunder by our soldiers or from its wanton destruction is estimated at the large sum of two crores of rupees.'[30] To put a stop on this individual searching was necessary otherwise the commercial life of the city could be ended as many incidents had occurred of threatening and looting the wealthy merchants and other people who were allowed to stay together with British servants and those who had possessed a cover of protection from the loyalist Rajas.[31] Major General Penny felt much 'delicacy' to stop prize agents from random search but strongly believed that all the houses of 'known rebels should be justly subject to search' and that the house and property of friends of the government 'of which there can be but few should be respected.'[32] From November onwards, licensed based search began but in vain.[33] In 1859, it was clearly mentioned that it was out of the power of the lieutenant governor to stop the prize agents in searching the houses. In the words of R. H. Davies, the secretary to the government of Punjab 'the lieutenant governor has taken it upon himself to prohibit the civil authorities from assisting in such inquisitions. But it is not in His Honor's power to retrain the action of the Prize agent.'[34] The unoccupied houses were comparatively easy target but the owners of the occupied areas were threatened 'with execution and blank cartridge fired or to be fired' upon them until they ransomed.[35] At the same time, Army was dispersed for eliminating the surrounding Nawabs such as Nawab of Jhajjar[36], Farrucknagar (Farukhnagar), Ballubgarh and Bahadurgarh all were arrested and hanged except Nawab Bahadur Yar Jung of Bahadurgarh whose property was looted and then was allowed to survive not in Delhi but in Lahore.[37] 'We neither kill them nor forgive them' writes John Lawrence in his letter to one of his friend.[38] Ghalib under distressful condition after witnessing the loot of his brother's property too writes that during the time of searching of Nawabs' havellies 'not a penny was left behind', each and everything, from gold to cloths and pots were taken away by the agents.[39] Even the grain belonged to the late Raja of Ballubgarh was sold in public auction and prices around more than eleven thousands were transferred to the Delhi prize fund[40] besides it, in the district of Panipat, Karnal, from needle to cloths, dishes, copper pot, calf and pony were collected and sold in the auction held from 30th November 1857 to 16th July 1858 amounted around twelve thousands rupees.[41] For unearthing the hidden treasure secreted in the *teh-kahana* (underground room) or saved in the walls, some artistic manners had been adopted such as pouring water on the ground and tapping the walls as their sound would give them hint, and from there, they could start search. They searched until they satisfied to leave one house for another. As an 'excited pursuit'[42] Saunders, the Commissioner of Delhi informs that 'the city was thoroughly ransacked and plundered and the parties were not willing to pay much for their effects.'[43] Army had turned the whole city as a 'prize' and suggested that this difficulty might be got over if the people could get the service of millionaires or *seth* to ransom them sufficient amount which was not difficult to understand to W. Muir who considers it rational that the whole booty should be of state rather than the army.[44] Prize agents claimed their right over all the property seized by both military and civil authorities within and without the city including, horses, arms, personal properties, household articles, chattels and above all the king's jewels. John Lawrence argues against the army claim and asked the government to place a limitation on the right of captors otherwise 'the whole of the inhabitants of Delhi, whether guilty or innocent will be reduced to pauperism, the trade of the country paralyzed.' In addition to it, he favored to use looted material in maintaining the civil administration. Therefore, when C.B. Saunders asked him 'are the prize agent entitled to claim horses and other valuable property taken from rebels by the civil authorities at a distance from Delhi..' he answered him that 'horses required for the police should be brought up by you'.[45] But it was not an easy task before defining the right of the prize agents. Therefore, the question had become very important to decide what ought to be counted as prize property in Delhi.[46] Government limited the right of the prize agents and instructed the military officers to form a committee for taking an account of all loot and put them all on auction and investigate the claim if made by anyone to the best of 'the satisfaction of the committee' [47] where the claimants had to prove their 'active assistance' rendered to the British government during the mutiny otherwise all proceeds would be send to the nearest treasury in the prize fund.[48]Agency was formed in January 1858 and only two claims after deep investigations were approved. The nature of the unsold booty had already assured the officers that no former owner would be able to recognize his looted objects as it 'consist of clothing, furniture, paper and other miscellaneous articles of a perishable nature and deeming it next to impossible that any former owner could recognize. Further, it was also stated that 'the bulk of the prize was taken from the houses of Musalmans and their owners being excluded from the town as put laws have no opportunity of claiming their property.' However, one member of the committee admits that, 'a great many cases are under the consideration of the committee but only one which has as yet been fully established till 3rd February of 1858 is that of a man Ram Sahai.' Ram Sahai was the brother of Umed Singh and Gunisha Lall. He received only 62000 rupees[49] after producing three guaranteed letters from the English officers before the Agency. These three were arranged from Captain William of the artillery, Captain Bruce Superintendent and Mr. Thorton. Captain Bruce Superintendent and Mr. Thorton were saved by Gunisha Lall during the outbreak of revolt and last letter was from A. Hamilton, the resident at Indore. Later on, one more case came under their consideration. It was the case of Krishee Lall, a native banker 'a wealthy man' of the regiment's irregular cavalry. Krishee Lall demanded compensation of 22,000 rupees. The effects of his house were taken away, on the order of the prize agent by the military officers on 20th October of 1857. Prize agent refused to refund all money except 9000 rupees. His plea was not considered as strong until he showed his 'strong certificates of good character' approved by Mr. Leptroll and Captain Hocking of the 17th irregular cavalry along with Mr. Paske letter, secretary of the Chief Commissioner of Punjab. Remaining sum was requested to reimburse from the government treasury. It is not clear to us whether he got the full amount of his property or not but lucky enough to be considered by the committee.[50] Though, officially, the operation of 'spoliation of private property' was prohibited by John Lawrence in December of 1857 and approved by government in January 1858[51] but still empty houses and 'attached properties' were opened before the army. Another incident of agent search recorded in the British records is of February 1859. This incident occurred subsequently after the queen proclamation.[52]Lawrence accepts that 'all classes whether friends and foes were despoiled with equal impartiality'.[53]

This wide-scale damage and destruction of the city extended to its academic and intellectual field also. Delhi, as a centre of learning possessed the scholarly strength and treasure of rich personal libraries prior to the uprising. Most of the private libraries had the rare collection of manuscripts on the different subjects such as maths, science, history, theology etc. Even fourteenth fifteenth centuries' Arabic manuscripts had been preserved in these libraries. One such example was of Mufti Sadruddin Azurda's private collection. Mufti Sadruddin Azurda was one of the prominent scholars of Delhi. He contributed in enhancing the learning capacity of the society through teaching that helped him to maintain rare collection. Austrian origin academician, Aloys Sprenger, the principal of the Delhi College and his friend, William Muir, who later became the Lieutenant Governor of North Western Provinces and wrote his most controversial book on the life of Prophet, named *life of Mahomet*, used this rare collection for their writings. After the fall of Delhi, these rare manuscripts were targeted and reduced to dust or collected as the 'Prize' property for sale. Muir also saved some Arabic manuscripts of fourteenth century for his use, and later deposited them to India Office.[54] Seventeenth thousands books were counted in the prize property after the revolt.[55] This treasure of the Prize consisted most of the rich private libraries of the descendants of Shah Walli Ullah, Mufti Sadruddin Azurda,[56] Zahir Dehlavi, Professor Ram Chandra[57] and the Mughal Imperial works. Zahir Dehlavi bemoans on the destruction of his personal collection, which included twenty very remarkable copies of the holy Quran along with seven copies transcribed by his grandfather, which were further copied by his own father on the expensive paper made at Yazd and Kashan, and numerous volumes of other exceptional and precious books on various disciplines. His father also purchased for him some history books of three hundred rupees namely *Rauzatus Safa, Tarikh-i-Farishta* and *Shah Namah.*[58] The library of Nawab Ziauddin Ahmad Khan of Loharu had manuscripts from which Sir Henry Elliot (Resident of Delhi (1823-1825) had compiled his eight volumes of translated excerpts on the history of India.[59] This rich library also consist Ghalib's precious verses and prose written in Persian and Hindi before the uprising that led him to mourn on its loot where he mentions the end of his own previous writings too.[60]

These manuscripts formed a valuable part of the prize collection. The government seemed very interested in preserving these 'priceless' and 'valuable oriental manuscripts' in the library of Calcutta which had been posted for the sale by the agents. The sale of these books had started in February 1858. Ghalib testifies this fact by refusing to his friend Saqib's request to go out and buy some books. He says 'loot has been sold off in holes and corners and even if it had been sold in the street, where would I have had the chance to see it.'[61] Advertisements had been put up for marketing the books and allowed to be publicized as much as possible. This business accomplished under the supervision of some agents, one of them was W. H. Marshall. Though, we are not sure about these auctions whether these had been held on weekly, fortnightly or monthly basis but it was quite clear that Delhi had shifted to a market place where its inhabitant's generation old property had been sold on very less prices. In which, buyers were those who had a cash, among them Europeans were obviously first in the list, followed by outsiders who were allowed and those who had *kothies* in the city but resided to the various parts of India. Tarachand Gunsam Doss and twelve other native shroffs, bankers and merchants temporary resided at Calcutta asked permission to secure their interest in the certain property under the charge of prize agents.[62] With regard to the sales of the books, four thousands seven hundreds Persian 'rare' manuscripts were transferred from Delhi to Calcutta on the government order in 1859.[63] More valuable and selective manuscripts were required to be preserved which was a hectic and laborious task. W. N. Lees, the Secretary of the board of examination at Calcutta presidency was selected for this work. It was supposed that under whose supervision this undertaking will be satisfactorily completed as at Delhi 'no European officer competent to pass a trustworthy opinion on the value of oriental manuscripts and as the duty of selection cannot be entrusted with confidence to any native'.[64] Lees accepted the proposal being an expert in Indian languages but suggested government to purchase whole the collection of 'rarest books' as it would be impossible to carry out this duty within a limited time.[65] Government agreed and instructed to C.B. Saunders to purchase and dispatched whole set of unprinted oriental manuscripts to Calcutta.[66] The whole undertaking took place under the supervision of Deputy Commissioner with the help of few trustworthy inhabitants.[67] In July 1859, forty one cases of books reached to Calcutta.

This paper can be concluded here by saying that every war brings a destruction and devastation to the properties and the lives of the people. 1857 was not distinct in these terms too. The concept of prize was not new but 1857 rebellion created a space where whole cities or the residential places were turned as prize and looted mercilessly. Delhi was turned as a prize too which was not only harmful for its people but also for its reputation. Delhi faced many atrocities committed by the controlling power aftermath of the revolt of 1857. One of the most important retributions was to legalise the loot in which most of the houses and possession of the people were targeted indiscriminately. The voices of sufferers listened but rarely who could prove their 'loyalty' at that time. Very few people who could save their possession also remembered the event with distress and destruction. Thus, the revolt of 1857 was one of those episodes, which had shook the very common life of the people. In other words, severe impact of mutiny on the city of Delhi can be characterized in those destitute people who were known for their wealth, learning, respect and manners.

Notes

1. Souvenir of Indian History Congress, Seventieth Session, *Delhi in 1857: Studies, Images and Documents.* Published by Department of History, University of Delhi 15th -17th May 2010.
2. Biswamoy Pati talks about the past and the future of the revolt that had began from 1830s and ended around 1870s which was not free from the peasants and tribal's resistances. (ed.) Biswamoy Pati *The Great Rebellion of 1857 in India: Exploring Transgressions, Contests and Diversities*, Routledge, New York, 2010.
3. In this struggle, the British had to fight for every inch of land resulted in a good amount of mortality. English lost their sixty six high ranked officers, and eleven hundred and four men killed and wounded in less than six hours of this fighting. Kaye, John, & Malleson, Col. G.B., *History of the Indian Mutiny of 1857,* Vol. IV, London, 1878, p. 37.
4. Griffiths, Charles John, *The Siege of Delhi with an Account of the Mutiny of Ferozepore in 1857,* reprinted Delhi, 1995, pp. 160-61.
5. In the Western countries, its history can be traced from the earlier times. It developed as a 'legalised institution' only during the mercantile phase. In different countries, various rules and regulations were formed to stabilize this institution. See for more detail, thesis submitted by Philip Quincy Wright, *Prize Money,* University of Illinois, Chicago, 1913.
6. Government had many rights in proceedings of the navy loot, such as, to lesser the number of prize courts, limit the fees payable to it, oblige the agents to pay into the office of government of the net proceed of the prizes sold by them etc. At the same time, bill motives was to give more value to the right of the actual captors rather than constructive captors. See for the debate on the prize agency bill in the Parliament of England. Cobbett's *Parliamentary Debate*, Peterborough- Court, Fleet Street, London, 1812, pp. 403-404, 541-543, 860-863.
7. *Ibid.,* p. 102.
8. Gleig, G.R. *The Life of Robert, First Lord Clive*, John Murray, London, 1869, p. 60-61.
9. See for more detail, *Case of 'Banda and Kirwee booty, Extracts from returns of papers relative to the Mutiny in India. Nos VI, VII, VIII, presented to*

Parliament, Harrison and Sons, St. Martin's Lane, London, 1865 p. xxiii; This case had published earlier in 1862, 1864 too.

10. *Ibid.*, p. 29.
11. Gleig, G.R. *The Life of Robert, First Lord Clive*, p. 49.
12. It is difficult to mention the appointment of the prize agents by the British army in India at the first time. Bengal witnessed the loot in a different way by extortion of money as 'prize money' during the war of Plassey. Without storming any town, Robert Clive received 300,000£ sterling including legitimate share of 'prize money' (28,000£ sterling) after the battle of Plassey 1757. It is interesting to note that till then issue of distribution of the prize money was decided by the war committee. As later on, Clive and the company's other individuals had become the source of jealousy in their home country because of their 'acquired wealth from India' then the decision of distribution of any prize might be transferred to the Crown. Mostly, distribution of the prize money remained the issue of disputed claim between His / Her Majesty's troop and the army of the company. Ibid., pp. 91-94, 128; Colonel Wilson, *Sir Charles Lord Clive*, Macmillan & Co. London, 1890, pp. 64-73; Philip Quincy Wright explains its beginning from the period of the Mughal Emperor Aurangzeb. Philip Quincy Wright, *Prize Money*, pp. 54.
13. Llywellyn-Jones, Rosie, *The Great Uprising in India 1857-58: Untold stories, Indian and British,* viva books, Delhi, 2008, p. 132, she argues that prize money won by the army was an incentive and a reward for them.
14. *The Gentleman's Magazine*, Vol. XV, January-June, by Sylvanus Urban, John Bowyer Nichols and Son, London, 1841, p. 97, (He was one of the twenty-one General officers receiving reward pensions for their distinguish services.)
15. Farooqui Amar, *Zafar and the Raj: Anglo-Mughal Delhi c. 1800-1850*, Primus books, Delhi, p. 33.
16. Deccan booty included the spoil of war taken at Puna, Nagpoor and Mahidpoor. For the case of 'Deccan prize money,' see John Henry Barrow, *The Mirror of Parliament: Second session of the tenth parliament of great Britain and Ireland*, Vol- IV, Abingdon street Westminster, London, 1832, pp. 3579-3583; Accounts and Papers, vol. xxvii, 1833, pp. 1-7.
17. Besides it, control over Multan and Bharatpur witnessed the legalized plunder by the army. The only difference was that, at that time, they did not capture the property of the individuals and the innocents as had been done in Delhi during the suppression of the revolt of 1857. Case of '*Banda and Kirwee booty*, pp. xliv ; INA, Foreign Department (Secret), 26th March 1858, no. 8.
18. For Jhansi, Kanpur and Bithur loot, see Nagar, Amrit Lal (trn.)., *Ankhon Dekha Gadar*, It is a translated version of a Marathi account, named *Majha Pravas* written by Vishnu Bhatt Godse. (first printed in 1907) Rajpal &

Sons, Delhi, reprinted 1986; Its English translation is also available. For Lucknow and Delhi loot, Sen, S. N. *Eighteen Fifty Seven*, Publication Division, Delhi, 1957; and for Banda and Kirwee loot and many previous examples see *case of Banda and Kirwee.*

19. NAI, Foreign Department, (Secret), 18th December 1857, No. 438.
20. Theophilus Metcalfe, son of Thomas Metcalfe who had escaped from the rebels attack became the first Chief Magistrate after the revolt of 1857. His vindictive and revengeful act against the inhabitants of the city was to such an extent that a formal appeal was made by John Lawrence to the government for removing him and replaced by P. H. Egerton (Nov 1857-March 1860). P.H. Egerton was became first deputy commissioner of Delhi district.
21. 'For many days', hundreds of old men, woman and children, half starved, wretched and lamentable sufferers were turned out. Griffiths strangely comments on the callous behaviour of the authorities with regard to human suffering and accepts 'I fear that many perished from want and exposure.' Griffiths, Charles John, *The Siege of Delhi,* p. 200.
22. NAI, Foreign Department, (Secret), 18th December 1857, No. 440-452. Owing to the failure of health, General Wilson was replaced by Major General Penny as a Commanding officer of Meerut division and Delhi field force in October 1857.
23. From Government to Chief Commissioner of Punjab, NAI, Foreign Department (Secret) 29th March1858, No. 827, p. 1650.
24. NAI, Foreign Department (Secret Progs.) 29th Jan 1858, No 825.
25. See for detail, Griffiths, Charles John, *The Siege of Delhi*, op. cit. Griffiths had worked as an assistant of the prize agent after 1857, told his experience with full of excitement and counted those days as fairy-tale or unforgettable experience of his life. To what extent he encountered unimaginable treasury by digging the houses of the rich merchants, money changer, painter, temples and noble families can be read in his account.
26. Wilberforce, G. Reginald, *An Unrecorded Chapter of the Indian Mutiny: Being the Personal Reminiscence of Reginald G. Wilberforce, Late 52nd Light Infantry*, reprinted, Delhi, 1976, p. 213 (Wilberforce asserts that he was amongst others who had a desire of having something as a 'memento' of Delhi).
27. Ireland, William., *A History of the Siege of Delhi,* p. 275.
28. Many such examples can be traced in the eyewitness accounts. *Ibid.*, p. 232,Griffiths., *The siege of Delhi*, p.232, 240-242; Wilberforce, G. Reginald., *An Unrecorded Chapter of the Indian Mutiny*; Mrs. Muter, *My Recollection of the Revolt,* London, 1911.
29. For limiting the search to the houses of rebels, Burn divides the whole society into three classes. According to him, first class belonged to the rebel's class, whose property should be justly searched and confiscated; second

class included bankers, merchants and *sahukar* should be entitled to ransom as they were ready to ransom for their property. While, third and final class was of those people who had actively supported the government should be spared from any kind of search. John Lawrence agreed to Burn's statement and passed the order to limit the search to the property of the 'rebels'. NAI, Foreign Department (Secret), 26th March 1858, No. 827, p. 1642; NAI, Foreign Department, (Secret), 26th March1858, no. 827; still, the property of loyalists who had played an important role as spy during the siege were looted and treated badly. Hamid Ali Khan case study can be seen in the Delhi State Archives along with Ilahi Bakhsh whose role to convince the Mughal emperor, Bahadur Shah Zafar for surrendering was important. See the petition of Umed Singh, brother of Ram Sahai, an influential merchant of the city to Hamilton, the resident of Indore for protecting his property, the houses of Krishee Lall, Salig Ram, Ram Chandra were similarly attacked along with the majority of Muslims. Undoubtedly, the grand houses must have been attracting the agents but the people who had limited things were also not spared, see the example of Ghalib's lunatic brother, Mirza Yusuf who was shot dead while walking unconsciously in the street and whose house was looted harshly.

30. NAI, Foreign Department (Secret), 26th March 1858, No. 827, p. 1642.
31. On the request of Raja of Patiala, a whole lane of Ballimaran was guarded because of Hakim Mahmood Khan's services given to the Raja before the revolt. In this particular lane, Ghalib also lived who tell us about coming of agents in spite of Sikh guards posted on the doors of the Mohalla. Though, Ghalib did not mention that Hakim Mehmood Khan was forced to give ransom but another indigenous account tells us about this fact. Nizami, Khawaja Hasan. *Delhi Ki Jaankuni,* (ed.) Chughtai, M. Akram., *1857: Mujmua-e Khwaja Hasan Nizami,* Sang-e-Meel publications, Lahore, 2007, p. 511.
32. According to the rules of the prize agency, nobody could interfere into the affairs of the agents until and unless he directly participated into the war. Therefore, General Penny could not take any action as he was not present during the period of war. From Commanding officer, N. Penny to the Secretary to the Chief Commissioner of Punjab, NAI, Foreign Department (Secret), 26th March 1858, No. 827, p.1643; See for the rules of prize agents, *Case of 'Banda and Kirwee booty.*
33. Lieutenant Butler, 1st B.F. and Colonel Edward Vibrat received pass for searching the shops at Chandni Chowk where they found 'some thirteenth and fourteenth wooden boxes filled with all kind of gold and silver article, coins and precious stones of more and less value. Vibrat, Edward., *The Sepoy Mutiny: As seen by a Subaltern, from Delhi to Lucknow*, Smith Elder & Co., London 1898. pp. 151-153.
34. NAI, Foreign Department, Genl. A, May 1862, File no. 69/72.

35. *Neel ka katra* was one such area very well known example where bankers ransomed to save their property. Hakim Mehmood Khan in Ballimaraan, Shaikh Turab Ali in the *Kucha* of Mir Ashique, Rai Sudha Singh at Turkman Gate and Diwan of Maharaja Patiala Nihal Chand along with a few other Hindus and Muslims's houses also followed the same path. There were instances of tipping the agents by some people as informers.
36. Nawab of Jhajjar's personal property was of nearly fifteen lakhs of rupees. Army was willing to claim that property. NAI, Foreign Department (Political),15th February 1858; According to another account, 'Four to five forts, including those of Kanaud and Jhajhar, about sixty guns, seven or eight lakhs of rupees, and plenty of other prizes fell into the brigadier Shower's hands who went to arrest the Nawab.' Trotter, Captain Lionel James, *The Life of Hodson of Hodson's Horse,* J. M. Dent & Sons. LTP, London, 1910, p. 213.
37. Khan, Muinuddin Hasan., *Khadang-e-Ghadar: Surguzisht-e-Inqilab 1857,*(ed.) Ibn Kanwal, Kitabi Duniya, Delhi, 2008. p. 105.
38. Smith, Bosworth, R. *Life of Lord Lawrence,* op. cit.,
39. Ghalib, Mirza Asadullah Khan., *Dastanbu,* (ed.) Qasemi, Sharif Husain., Ghalib Institute, New Delhi, 2007, pp. 104, 112-113.
40. NAI, Foreign Department (Genl.-A), November 1862, No. 69-70.
41. DSA, Residency Record, 31st October 1857, file no. 15 (See the list of articles sold in auction)
42. Mrs. Muter, *My Recollection of the Revolt, op.cit.,*
43. NAI, Foreign Department (Secret), 29 January 1858, No. 524.
44. NAI, Foreign Department (Secret Progs.), 29 January 1858, No. 825.
45. NAI, Foreign Department (Secret Progs.), 26th March1858, No. 827, p. 1615-1616.
46. NAI, Foreign Department (Secret Progs.), 26th March1858, No. 827, pp. 1610, 1615, 1640-49.
47. NAI, Home Department (Public), 14 May 1858. No. 97; The Committee consisted three members, Burn, Wriford and Edward Campbell.
48. Ibid.; Calcutta Gazette October to December 1857, imperial Record Department p.1866. Notice no.1499 of 1857. Government notification of 28th November of 1857 declared the state as the only owner of the booty but promised to pay the soldiers six months *batta* in recognition of their services. For Europeans reaction against this order, see, William Ireland, *A History of the Siege of Delhi,* op. cit., p. 277.
49. Umed Singh had already appealed to Hamilton and supposing his loss more than two lacs rupees as he had got a list of things from his servant that had taken away by the officers.
50. NAI, Home Department (Public), 14 May 1858. No. 97.

51. The hardship and oppression inflicted by the military on the people of the city and their properties was brought under knowledge of government by submitting the petitions of Umed Singh and Saunat Nana (?) that led governor general to give his assent against the loot of the 'private property' especially with reference of Umed Singh. See for government response NAI, Foreign Department (Secret progs.) Part I, 29th January 1858, pp. 37-39.
52. The queen proclamation was issued on November1858, in which full assurance was given to the people of India on the issue of their safety and security. But, subsequently to this proclamation, a house of a merchant of Delhi, named Shamsooddeen, Punjabee was searched and the property amounted of 7535-6-0 was looted by the officers of an agent on the pretext that he used to entertain a number of *jihadees* during the rebellion. Later on, his property was divided among Captain Nieoll, the prize agent, (1883-13-6 rupees), informer (2500 rupees) and the army (3,116-2-6 rupees).For some people, Queen proclamation was a hope of reclaiming their properties, Among them, a brother and the son of the deceased Shamsooddeeen can also be listed who appealed against the search and filed a case for refunding their properties. Since 1859, they had been petitioned four times (in February and November 1859 and in January and November 1860), when they filed the same petition to the Governor General of India received a reply that an order would be sent through the Punjab Government only. Only after January 1861, order was given in their favor. Prize agency and Captain Nieoll were ordered to refund the looted amount and rest that was related to informer was made out by the government. NAI, Foreign Department FC (Part A) Progs. April 1861, No 102-107; NAI, Foreign Department, F.C. (Part.-A), November 1862, No. 69.
53. NAI, Foreign Department, (Secret Progs.) 19th January 1858, Part A, pp. 37-39
54. Powell, Avril A., *Scottish Orientalists and India: The Muir Brothers, Religion, Education and Empire*, Boydell Press, UK, 2010. pp. 131, 189; Powell, Avril A., 'Reciprocities and divergences concerning religious traditions in two families of scholars in North India', pp. 188-222, (ed.) Malik, Jamal., *Perspectives of Mutual Encounters in South Asian History 1760-1860*. Netherland, p. 202
55. Prasad, Madhu., 'The Battle for Delhi: Myths of the 'Mutiny' and the Construction of the Raj', *Delhi in 1857: Studies, images and Documents*, IHC, 70th session Department of History, University of Delhi, 15-17 May. 2010, p. 45, meanwhile collected booty had been stored in havelies or *godaams* of the employed and trustworthy inhabitants like Professor Ram Chandra *kothi* and Mansoor Ali Khan's *havelie* which were used for accumulating copper, silver vessels and pots, whereas *havelie* of Bhawanee Sunker, located at Chandni Chowk was chosen to store books.
56. Mufti Sadrudeen Azurda was one of the famous and well known personalities of Delhi before the Uprising. He had devoted himself fully to spread learning

within the city. Though, he was a colonial servant and worked as *Sadre Sudur,* still he was able to spare time for the Delhi College and his own *madrasa,* called *Dar ul baqa* which he had purchased from Bahadur Shah Zafar, few years before the rebellion. After the rebellion, Mufti's properties were also confiscated and his *madarsa* was demolished. Only after 1860, he was returned less than half of his property. This loss of his property and distress of losing of his relatives and friends depressed him to such an extent that he was paralyzed him at the last stages of his life. Islahi, Abdur Rehman Pervaz, *Mufti Sadruddin Azurda: Hayat, Shakhsiyat, Ilmi aur Adabi Karname,* Delhi, 1977, p. 83.

57. Ram Chandra was a mathematician and teacher in the Delhi College prior to the uprising. He embraced Christianity in 1852. As one of the prominent teachers, he had his private library which witnessed the same fate like others libraries after the rebellion. Still, he was able to save some of them as he requested to Colonel A Becher, Quarter Master General for this. Colonel A Becher wrote a letter to Colonel Burn arguing to give some favor to Ram Chandra as 'he (Ram Chandra) had a larger library of religious and scientific works in his house at Chandni Chowk though many of them have been plundered....He is most anxious to get them I am sure under these circumstance you (Colonel Burn) will assist and allow him to do so.' NAI, Home Department (Education-A) 5th November 1862, No. 1-3.
58. Saiyid Zaheer Husain Jafri, 'Education and Transmission of Knowledge in Medieval India' presented as a symposium in 71st session of Indian History Congress, Feb 2011, pp. 21-22.
59. Francis Robinson 'The Muslims of Upper India and the Shock of the Mutiny: *Rutkhez-i-beja'* in *Indian's Colonial Encounter: Essays in the memory of Erick Strokes* (ed.) Hasan, Mushirul and Gupta, Narayani. p. 265;
60. Nawab Ziauddin Ahmad and Nazir Husain Mirza used to collect his writings in their libraries as a token of love and respect towards him. But with the fall of Delhi, these libraries had also fallen into the hands of agents and looted by them mercilessly. Muinul Rehman, Syed., *Ghalib and Inqlab sattawan*, Ghalib Institute, New Delhi, 2007, p. 332.
61. Ralph Russell and Khursheed Alam, *Ghalib Life and Letters*, OUP, 1994, p. 161.
62. NAI, Home Public Progs. February 1858, No.577- AI, order no. 1087, 1504; The demand of Delhi loot was not in India only, England shopkeepers were willingly ready to give high price of Delhi objects. See, Griffiths, the siege of Delhi, last chapter on prize agent.
63. After receiving the books, W. N. Lees, the Secretary of the board of examiner at Calcutta proposed to hire one Arabic librarian from the Mohammedan College with the two senior students for classifying, arranging and cataloguing these brittle manuscripts, some without beginning and some without ending under his supervision. He further suggested that only twenty

rupees monthly for a librarian and ten rupees each for two other senior students would be better as their remunerations. According to Lees, it was a 'lowest possible rate' as 'the college is nearly two mile from *madarssah* and 10 rupees a month will only suffice to cover *palki* hire one way i-e coming or going.' Government accepted his plan. NAI, Home Department (Public), 5th August 1859, No.1-2; For Lees respond regarding not receiving books in April 1859, See NAI, Foreign Department (Branch C), 22 April 1859, No.18; While, Lees allowances increased according to government rules. See, NAI, Home Department (Public progs.) 28th August 1858,No. 601, pp. 529, 744-745.

64. NAI, Home Public Consultation 10th September 1858, No. 41-44.
65. Lees also mentioned that unnecessary manuscripts could easily be sold to the *mawlvies* of Calcutta as they seemed ready to purchase them on good prices. NAI, Home Public Consultation 17th September 1858, No. 2-4.
66. NAI, Home Public Consultation 17th September 1858, No. 32-37.
67. People who collected the books were some loyalists and had proved their loyalty during the mutiny, these were Munshee Sheodial and Guneshee Lall, (see above mentioned case of Ram Sahai) who purchased books of more than ten thousand rupees. Mahesh Dass, Raja Lall and Rung Lall bought books of 3454, 366 and 283 rupees respectively. The total amount of four thousand seven hundred books was nearly fifteen thousand rupees including packing charges. NAI, Home Department (Public) 29th April 1859,No. 72-74; For the bill of the purchasing books see, NAI, Home Department (Public) 5th August 1859,No. 23-24; NAI, Home Department (Public) 2nd August 1859, No. 3-8.

Chapter - 18

Masjid-e Jahan Numa of Shahjahanabad During and after the Uprising of 1857

— ***Ms. Sadia Aziz***
Ph.D. Scholar
Delhi University

Context

Political dynasties in the Islamic-east have their own motives in constructing the grand religious structures in their capital cities as the important statements of their political authority. Prophet's mosque at Medina (*Masjid-e Nabawi*) became the first such example that the later dynasties followed in their respective capitals like in Damascus (during Umayyad rule), Baghdad (during Abbasids), Cordoba and Delhi among several other dynesties. These mosques catered and enriched the communitarian life of the Muslims in different Imperial Capital Cities in the Islamic world. The Indian subcontinent saw the establishment of the numerous congregational mosques built by the royal houses to fulfil and meet the requirements of the newly established/emerging Muslim communities. Therefore, the imperial mosque was not only centrally located but also had the massive contemporary structure representing best architectural traditions of the times.

The political statement of sovereignty through the weekly Friday sermons (*khutba*) was invariably made from the pulpit every Friday.[1] Francois Bernier, who visited India in the seventeenth century describe the importance of *Masjid-e Jahan Numa* or *Jama Masjid* for the Emperor through the processions made by the Emperor and his retinue to the Masjid every Friday which reflect that the Emperor must have considered this masjid as a sacred and an important structure.[2] Hence, the prayer leader (*Imam*) of the central mosque was carefully chosen: besides his being a renowned scholar of theology and law, he was supposed to be a personal noble descent also.

The city of Delhi served as the capital (*Dar-ul khilafa*) during the time of the Delhi Sultanate and later during the rule of Mughal emperors and had numerous massive mosques which served as the congregation mosques during various regimes. Some notable examplesare *Qubbat-al Islam, Masjid-e Qilu Garhi, Firoz Shah Kotla, Khair-ul Manazil, Kalan Masjid* and several others. All the above examples of grand mosques are from the pre-Mughal dynasties and therefore it was natural for the fifth Mughal emperor Shahjahan (1628-1657) to visualise the new city of Shahjahanabad with a centrally located Mosque, and gave it a lofty title of *Masjid-e Jahan Numa* (mosque, commanding the view of the world). Its construction was synchronised with the royal fort, the Red Fort. The management and all the expenses of the mosque were borne by the Emperor from the royal treasury. Hence, he was the *de facto mutawalli*, if one uses the term '*mutawalli*' in the modern context. Thereafter, the Mughal emperor and the Delhi based imperial household invariably offered the two *Eid prayers* and Friday prayers in this *masjid* only. Likewise, it continued to evoke strong communitarian sentiments among the people.

The masjid remained symptomatic of Mughal imperial grandeur in the city even after when Delhi was taken over by Lord Lake in 1803. After which the British became the actual power blocks that handled the administrative matters and attempted to penetrate into the civic society by addressing the administrative and bureaucratic needs of the city till the uprising of 1857. Even the repair work of the beams and minarets of the Jama Masjid that were damaged by lightning were done by the British in 1817 and 1829 respectively.[3] The main focus of this article is to study *Masjid-e Jaha Numa* or Jama Masjid of Delhi in the context of the turbulences it underwent under the colonial regime in the nineteenth century.

The Contested Interface of *Masjid-i Jahan numa* and the Colonial State in Delhi during the Uprising of 1857

The study of any building should not be done only in terms of its architecture or utility, but also in the context of the history of the political situations that shaped the very existence and survival of that building. Places of worship under the custodianship of any state are targeted by the regime that replaces it. Similarly, the reuse of the pillaged material like pillars, columns and carvings has also been a well-known phenomenon or a tool of establishing new political might. Following somewhat the similar historical pattern, the city of Delhi was taken over by the British Colonial State in 1803 in a *de facto* manner while the Mughal emperor remained the ritual imperial head. This dyrarchy provided enough space to the East India Company to expand its base in civil society. The efforts like repair of the abundant canal, waterworks, undertaking repair and even renovation of the Mughal Masjid were the attempts through which the Colonial authorities were trying to give a message that they are in a process of replacing 'the Mughal authority' in an altogether different manner.

This phase of 'camaraderie' ended abruptly during the uprising of 1857. The British authority was totally uprooted from the city of Delhi where their families were butchered to death by the rebels.The uprising of 1857 and the cataclysmic events following it resulted in complete disorder and chaos.When British authority was restored in mid-September 1857, a reign of terror was unleashed against the people of the city. The whole city was driven out after witnessing the devastation of the city as well as of the people, as no single man in the city was safe.[4] Percival Spear by quoting Mrs. Sanderson (wife of the then Commissioner of Delhi) stated that she had mentioned in her letter dated 25th October, 1857 that each and every house in the city was plundered and destroyed; the natives of this city died daily due to the starvation and in the need of shelter.[5]

Ghalib, the renowned Urdu poet who was at Delhi at the time of uprising woefully describes the condition of Delhi. He says that the City was flooded with blood before his eyes and none of his friends were survived to mourn him and shed tears on his death. Zahir Delhvi writes in his book *Dastan-i-Ghadar* that "sometime innocent persons are killed along with the sinners". This is what exactly happened after the uprising of 1857 as the English soldiers began to shoot whomsoever they met on their way and some of the people who resided in the *Kucha Chelan* (near present Daryaganj) area were shot dead and their dead bodies were thrown into the Jumna.[6]

Delhi from the very beginning had been a paragon of the cultural, social as well as economic activities since the time it became the capital of the Mughal Empire. For the British, regaining Delhi was the most important objective of crushing the rebellion. Strategically also, once Delhi would be seized and Mughal Emperor arrested, the rebellion at other locations would be demoralised automatically and hence it could be brought to a stall. During the course of four months of the revolt in Delhi -May to September- the British targeted the most important landmarks of the city.

The Muslim population was specifically targeted as the British perceived the uprising of 1857 as a 'Muslim conspiracy' against them. Consequently, numerous masjids- Jama Masjid, being the largest mosque- in the city of Delhi were targeted as being the centres of the rebel activities. The 1857 rebellion was perceived by the British to be masterminded by the Muslims of the city and they believed that the *Ulema* of the city had a special role to play in the uprising of 1857. During the course of the revolt Jama masjid also became the site of the actual military encounter between the British army and the Muslim inhabitants.

According to Khwaja Hasan Nizami, a battalion of soldiers under the control of Thomas Metcalf- who had been the Collector and Magistrate of Delhi and hence knew the city well- reached Jama masjid during the revolt.[7] According to him around thousand people inside the mosque who had gathered there for prayers got the news that the British forces had been stationed outside to destroy the mosque. On being given the option to fight the soldiers or to escape, almost all the civilians decided to encounter the British army with their swords during the course of which two hundred civilians were killed facing the bullets of the British army.But despite the initial failures, the civilians were successful in thrashing away the British army from the Jama Masjid.[8] From this description of Khwaja Hasan Nizami it appears that the war did not remain contingent to merely the rebels and the British army but the local Muslim population became active participants when it came to the prestige of their Jama Masjid.

At certain times directly and at other times indirectly the masjid continued to be the major target of the British army during the course of the revolt. Attempts were made to militarily attack the masjid. During this atmosphere 'some freelance Jihadis, militant Naqshbandi *faqirs* and pious Muslim civilans' started setting up camps in the courtyard of Jama Masjid and Zinat-ul Masjid.[9] These kind of activities increased the hatred of the British against the Jama Masjid manifold and capturing it became their most important goal. One of the British officials stated in a telegram dated 20th September (Sunday Evening) that 'One mortar battery continued to fire during the night towards the south of the Palace, in the direction Durreoogunj; we have now turned them towards the Jumma Masjid'.[10] Consequently within short span of time they had the possession of the Palace, Jama Masjid and Ajmeri Gate leading to the fall of the rebels and the Mughal Empire on 20th September 1857.[11] The indigenous people had no alternative left with them and as a result, unfortunately they have to succumb to the British power.

As a result, during this period after the city's recapture by the British, all the masjids in the city of any significance were confiscated by the colonial state and prayers were stalled. It is believed that the British out of their hatred after the uprising of 1857 had initially considered bringing the entire city to the ground leaving only 'the cathedral mosque, converted in to a Church, to remain a grim memento of Christian prowess.'[12] Various options were discussed in higher official circles as far as the fate of the Jama Masjid was concerned. Plans ranging from its demolition to converting it in to a Church or a more 'secular' college, floated in the bureaucracy. But finally, the plan to make it as barracks for the Sikh soldiers from Punjab, who in turn deliberately desecrated its sanctity by undertaking prohibited activities, was agreed upon by the colonial officials.

After this initial plan of action/reaction, the Colonial state tried to use this Masjid as a monument to bargain with and to win over the support of the Muslim citizenry of Delhi. Over the period of time we find enough data from the Colonial records at the National Archives of

India and Department of Delhi Archives which indicate that the slow process through which the Masjid was returned to the Muslims was not spontaneous and smooth but it was a protracted and a well calculated move by the Colonial administrators to make it as an object of their bargain with the Muslim community and to perpetuate control over the management of the Masjid.

Masjid-e Jahan Numa: Confiscation and the 'idea of demolition'

The British after their victory in 1857 took over the management of the masjid like other institutions of the city and from time to time the colonial administration in Delhi would use this mosque as a bargaining tool to negotiate with the Muslim inhabitants of the city. Other smaller masjids of the city were still spared from the proposal of being demolished by the British but Jama Masjid, having become the symbol of the rebel Ulema, was time and again considered to be demolished. However, the idea that at least the Jama Masjid should be demolished as a symbol of the British victory was abandoned and it was felt that there was a need for some other symbolic actions.[13] As a result of a conscious policy of insulting the emotions of the Muslim inhabitants, the British soldiers danced inside the Jama Masjid and Sikhs lit victory fires close to the masjid's holy *mihrab*.[14] It became the cantonment of the European guards and the Sikh regiment of the Colonial army.

Along with Jama Masjid the other magnificent public buildings that became the barracks of the European guards were *Diwan-e-Aam*(hall of Public audience), Eidgah etc. Governor General suggested devoting the southern half of the Palace fortress enclosure to the troops and the Northern half to officer's quarters and to the guards of the different departments and also suggested for the removal of the of the street running north from the Delhi Gate to the arcades between the Lahori Gate and the *Diwan-i-Aam*. The fort palace was used as quarters for a British garrison 'but instructions were given to preserve isolated buildings of architectural and historic interest and in this matter it would be best for the departmental officers to err on the safe side, referring for orders to lieutenant Governor whenever there is the slightest ground for hesitation. On the other hand one of the British officials, Lord Canning was prepared to make concessions to the Hindus, when he argued that 'small temples' which were within the area to be cleared for the stay of the soldiers be allowed to remain.[15]

In the following years of the stay of the soldiers inside the Jama Masjid, several contestations regarding the convenient stay of the soldiers which was against the basic tradition of the mosque arose. Some contestations can be substantiated by the correspondence between the chief engineer of the Punjab and Chief Commissioner of Delhi regarding the removal of the ablution tank which was located at the centre of the square of the Jama Masjid at Delhi for the conveniences of drilling the thirteenth Punjab infantry who were quartered there. In reply to this, Chief Commissioner Punjab wrote to the chief engineer of the Punjab on 11th November, 1858, that he could not authorize this measure as the Government did not intend to appropriate the Jama Masjid permanently. He further stated that this is also the view of Lieutenant Beville as it would damage the future use of the tank by the Muslims; for in this ablution tank contained the water with which they perform their ablution before prayers.[16]

In another correspondence from Military Secretary to Chief Commissioner of Punjab to Chief Engineer of Punjab, an estimate was submitted amounting to Rs. 433 of the expanse incurred in blocking up arches of the courtyard of the Jama Masjid in the city of Delhi which was required to accommodate shelter for the thirteenth Punjab infantry. However, Chief Commissioner was averse to the continued occupation of the masjid by colonial troops and he desired to relocate the troops to another place. After the assault and capture of the city it was obvious to occupy the masjid but the Chief Commissioner mentioned in the letter that the occupation of the masjid should be a temporary arrangement rather than permanent occupation of the troops as its continued occupation is objectionable.[17] Permanent occupation of the Masjid could not have been rightly proposed for the fear on invoking anger of the remaining Muslim population of the City. Hence, there was a power play at work by the colonial state to play with the sentiments of the Muslims and create a demoralising effect in them by threatening them from time to time to demolish the masjid or to block the arches or to break the ablution tank.

Consequently, several proposals ranging from the permanent occupation of the Masjid by the troops to converting it into a Delhi college or others wanted that a Christian cathedral to be built in its place came up from time to time and became the subjects of diverse debates within the colonial bureaucracy, but these suggestions were not materialized. The then British Prime Minister Palmerston wrote a letter dated 9th October 1857 to the then Viceroy of India Lord Canning that every civil building connected with 'Mohammadan' tradition should be levelled to the ground 'without regard to antiquarian veneration or artistic predilection'.[18] In reply to this letter Lord Canning, in a letter dated 21 November, 1857 wrote:[19]

> I am opposed to touching the Jama Masjid- which is a religious building- I will do nothing which shall stamp this rebellion as being in the estimation of the British Government and people a religious one............... If we destroy or desecrate Mussalman Mosques or Brahmin temples we do exactly what is wanting to band the two antagonist races against ourselves...........As we must rule 150 million of people by a handful of Englishmen, let us do it in the manner best calculated to leave them divided (as in religion and national feeling they already are) and to inspire them with the greatest possible awe of our power and with the least possible suspicion of our motives..........But I do wish to leave both religions alone and to treat them with indifference in the real sense of the term.

However, giving the Masjid back to the Muslims was also one of proposals but in the immediate circumstances, this idea was against their political agenda. In fact, the restoration was not only an administrative or a political issue in fact for the British, Jama Masjid symbolised their 'lost' prestige. And restoring the same to the Muslims meant a further blow to their already feeble prestige after the revolt of 1857 among the indigenous population.

They wanted to play with the basic religious identity of the Muslims through this Masjid. This can be substantiated by a letter from financial Commissioner Punjab to the secretary of the Punjab government in which he stated that the Jama Masjid, Eidgah (congregational masjid which was used specially for Eid prayers usually located at the outskirts of Delhi), the tombs of Humayun and Safdarjung and apart from these several other buildings should be considered as State buildings.[20]

As the Jama Masjid was occupied by a regiment of Punjab infantry, he suggested converting Jama Masjid into Delhi College as he believed that it would make a magnificent location for this institution.

The British troops stationed in Delhi having earlier faced a military encounter with the rebels had their own anguish against the ex-King and everything that symbolised his rule that included the city of Shahjahanabad, its landscape, its buildings-especially mosques and *madrasas*- and also its people. Bringing Delhi and its people to dust seemed their prime motive. Hugh Chichester, one of the military officers stationed at Delhi after the revolt wrote in his letter:

> 'There are several mosques in the city most beautiful to look at, but I should like to see them all destroyed. The rascally brutes desecrated our Churches and graveyards and I do not think we should have any regard for their stinking religion...'[21]

Charles Raikes, another military officer had other plans for the this mosque, where he wanted that Jama Masjid should be saved, but converted into a Church, each stone of it should be named after a Christian martyr that would continue to remind the people of the city about the supremacy of the British.[22] In fact, to flatten Delhi to grounds was a well-planned campaign on the part of the British officers and the same campaign was also being popularised in the local English magazines of the time such as *Lahore Chronicle*, where the editorial articles initiated the campaign of deserting Delhi to dust. Moreover, such magazines also brought out the mood of the local English people towards Delhi, its ex-King, and also its people. In reply to the editorial of this magazine which initiated the campaign to bring Delhi to dust, one of the readers wrote to the editor:

> 'Having just seen your issue of the 18th instant, in which you most properly, as in most of your late issues, uphold the necessity for the destruction of Delhi 'in toto' and no sparing of the Jumma Masjid etc for fear of offending the Moslem, I consider it a duty to my country, as it should be of all Englishmen, to assist you in the national cry of a "A bloody revenge" and "Down with Delhi".[23]

Converting Jama Masjid to Delhi College were not merely a practical step or administrative steps, in effect it signifies the attempts of the British to negate the religiosity and piety attached to the building and impose a 'secular' character to the building. There is a letter which proves this fact from A.H.L Fraser, Secretary of Government of India to the Chief Secretary of Government of Punjab by quoting the Commissioner's letter dated 20th March 1860, stating that the Jama Masjid was not only a popular place of worship for Muhammadans, but was also undoubtedly a great national monument. Before the Mutiny when it was in the hands of the King of Delhi and was exclusively under Muhammadan control, it was open to all comers subject to no restriction. Since then it has remained an object of interest to visitors from all parts of the world.[24] A.A Roberts, an official who had worked in Delhi in the 1840s did not want the Masjid to be returned to the Muslims: "Let us keep them as tokens of our displeasure towards the blinded fanatics……."[25]

Restoration of these institutions continued to garner contestations; at times among the colonial officers themselves and at times between the new colonial administrators and the Muslim inhabitants of the city. Financial Commissioner of Punjab also opined that under any circumstances neither Jama Masjid nor the Eidgah would be restored to the Muslims. He intended to make them as grand but silent monuments of the success which was conferred on them in September 1857 A.D. He made the episode of confiscation as a matter of dignity and a token of displeasure towards the blinded fanatics as he believed that these blinded fanatics along with their bigoted King made conspiracy in the masjids for British failure. On moral, political and religious grounds, he argued that no Muslim should ever be permitted to enter the Jama Masjid and worship there again.

He stated that there were several masjids within the city and in its suburbs,which were sufficient for their worship and would supply their demands without affecting the prestige of British. Further he also argued that the rent of the shops under and around the masjid is Rs. 345 and the income of the stalls on the steps of the masjid was Rs. 92 per month which formed the endowment of Jama Masjid. Since, they had been confiscated and without this endowment they would not be able to support and maintain masjid.

He recommended that none of the state places of worship be ever restored to the Muslim population and asked civil and military officers to concert measures for removing the troops from the Jama Masjid to more suitable residences and when the masjid be vacated it would convert into Delhi College. This letter evidences the fact that British tried to demolish the sanctity and piousness of the religious institutions of the city as well as to destroy the religious emotions and sentiments of the Muslim inhabitants of the city.

Restoration of the Masjid to the Muslims

In response to this kind of attitude of some of the colonial officers, the Muslim notables and Muslim inhabitants of the city petitioned the colonial state on the occasion of the Viceroy's visit to Delhi in 1860 and requested for the restitution of the masjid and to allow them to resume prayers in the masjid.[26] It was also done to cease the 'impure' practices that became common in the vicinity of this 'pious' establishment. The petitions were not considered favourable by the colonial administrators as they claimed that the signatures on the petitions were forged. They also claimed that if any time 'respectable Muhammadans' of Delhi would ask for the restoration of the Jama masjid and they were equipped 'to make proper arrangements for keeping it in repair', their request could be granted and the Masjid would be restored to the Muslims.[27]

The Government insisted that the condition for the release of the Masjid would be the presence of unanimity among different sects of the Muslims. They recommended that the new managing committee which was about to elect for the management of the Masjid shall fairly represent the different Muhammadan sects. In 1860, the Government of Punjab wrote to Commissioner Delhi Division that it was considered desirable that the Government should interfere in the regulation of the masjid as little as possible and only through the managing committee.[28]

An *Iqrarnamah* or agreement was then signed on 24th November 1862 between the ten members as managers of the Jama masjid managing committee who have signed the petition and the British administration embracing the following points:[29]

(1) Preserving the peace within the Masjid and its precincts.

(2) If any question should arise in connection with the masjid or religion they will state it privately between themselves.

(3) No act should be committed inside the masjid which may tend to show contempt of or disloyalty to Government. If any such thing took place and which might be beyond their power to check or control, they should bring the matter to the notice of the Deputy Commissioner.

(4) They would do repairs to the buildings of the Masjid, whenever it was necessary to do so and should keep up regular accounts of shop rents and of the endowed property.

(5) If a vacancy caused among the managers for any reason, they would appoint successor by agreement among themselves.

(6) If anything done or act committed contrary to the wishes of the Government, they recognized that Government should be at liberty at all times to close the Masjid or make other arrangements for its management.

There is no information in the sources available as to how the members of the managing committee were appointed. The observation that they were 'elected by the majority of the Musalman inhabitants'[30] was not something that was true as it did not follow any formal procedure of election.

British consulted those people whom they considered suitable representatives of the Muslim community, but we find no records and sources available for these discussions. Mirza Ilahi Bakhsh who was an ally of the British, became the Chairman of the Managing Committee. Other eminent Muslims in the Managing Committee were Sadr Uddin Azurda, who was a judge (*Qazi*) and famous poet of Delhi before the rebellion of 1857; Mirza Isfandiar Beg, a relative of the prince of Loharu, and Saiyyad Ahmad Khan. Munshi Turab Ali who was also a spy of the British during the siege of Delhi, also became a member.

Some of the members were probably Punjabi traders including Shaikh Qutb Uddin, Shaikh Mahmud Bakhsh and Shaikh Barkat Ullah. The members were usually appointed for life but if someone died, the vacancy was filled by co-option. The Managing Committee had to advise the British of their choice that was made, but the British did not assert the right of confirmation.[31] According to Margrit Pernau, before the Managing Committee was established, the Masjid's administration was regulated by the *mutawallis*, but later with the Managing Committee it worked as a kind of collective Mutawalli.

The Masjid was then finally returned to the Muslim inhabitants to worship on 28th November 1862 A.D which was comparatively less problematic than other masjids like the Fatehpuri masjid, which was sold to a Hindu merchant. The Masjid was restored in an unostentatious and informal manner by the colonial state with the employment of several rules and regulations to be followed by the worshippers. The rules were not favourable to them as the European officers and gentlemen, civil and military were allowed without a pass and not required to put off their shoes while entering the Masjid and on the other hand the Hindu inhabitants could enter without a pass in the Masjid. These rules were revised by the British Government in the pressure of the petitions filed by the Muslim inhabitants and new rules were made in 1886 A.D.

All these rules made by the British reflect their negative character towards the religious building of Muhammadans as they considered these buildings as a symbol of their dignity, religiosity and also their erstwhile political stature. So, in order to hit their conscience, they hurt the sentiments of the Muslims by imposing these rules because they were well informed of the fact that entering the Masjid with shoes is prohibited and it would destroy the piousness of the Masjid. These rules and regulations again were followed by several petitions from the Managing Committee which made this Masjid a site of contest. Finally, the revised rules were hung up at the gate of Jama Masjid in Persian and English Language which were as follows:[32]

(1) No one is permitted to remain in the Masjid at night except the appointed *Khadims*, the *Muazzin* and individuals specially authorized by the Managing Committee.

(2) All European officers, gentlemen and ladies are required before entering the Masjid to put on over their shoes covering which were provided by the Committee at the door.

(3) European soldiers are not allowed to enter the Masjid without a pass from their Commanding Officer or from the brigade officer.

(4) Non-Musalman Asians were not allowed to enter the Masjid without a pass from the Deputy Commissioner or from the Managing Committee. The *darwans* will indicate where such passes can be obtained.

(5) No smoking is allowed in the Masjid. Visitors are forbidden to take inside the Masjid- dogs, Hukkas, musical instruments, bottle of liquor or any other articles prohibited by Muhammadan doctrine within the Masjid. It was expected by the European ladies and gentlemen that they would observe the religious etiquette of the Masjid. Persons who desired to take photograph within the Masjid must obtain special permission from the Managing Committee.

(6) Visitors must not pass or stand in front of Muhammadans engaged in prayer and are required to remain in the eastern portion of the Masjid during the hour of prayer.

(7) No benches or chairs can be taken into the Masjid without the special permission of the Managing Committee and if any such item is taken in, with the permission, it must be removed as soon as the ceremony for which they were allowed has ended.

(8) No religious discussion is allowed in the Masjid nor is any assemblage allowed except for the purpose of prayer. Preaching in the Masjid is forbidden except with the permission of the Managing Committee.

(9) Two constables were detailed for duty at the North and South gates that were responsible for seeing that the above rules were observed.

After the finalization of these rules they were again took up for consideration in 1899 A.D as some officers in the British Government were not satisfied with the above revised and final rules. This consideration of rules can be seen in a letter from the Secretary of Government of India to Chief Secretary of Punjab Government, in which he stated that it was unreasonable in requiring European visitors to a Musalman place of worship to put shoe coverings over their boots if the Muhammadan worshippers desire this.[33] He stated that there were portions of the Jama Masjid which were not used for purposes of worship and were frequented by visitor's i.e, the quadrangle, staircases, terraces, minarets etc. He further stated that the proposed rule should have applied only to the domed building which is used as the prayer chamber. This correspondence shows us the true colour and the negative attitude of the British Government towards the religious institution of the Muslim population.

The Repair, Maintenance and Management of Jama Masjid after the uprising of 1857

As the political power shifted to the British from the Mughals after the revolt of 1857, the masjid after it was given back to the Muslims in 1862 A.D. was maintained, managed and repaired by the Managing Committee formed after a series of petitions from the Muslim inhabitants of the city. The masjid has been repaired since its construction time and again. The repairs of the masjid were undertaken by the same Managing Committee. Due to the lack of funds and income they were not able to undertake complete repairs and carry out large scale renovations of Jama Masjid. The minor repairs were made through the Masjid funds but for the large renovations and repairs the authorities had to depend up on the Muslim ruling chiefs and other influential persons.

Then later in the period of 1875 A.D some necessary repairs to the ceilings and to the northern dome were carried by money endowed by one Muhammad Shafi. Again in 1875 A.D the *Nawab* of Rampur Kalb-Ali Khan donated a sum of Rupees one and a half lac for the general repairs of the Jama Masjid placed in the charge of the Deputy Commissioner. This donation can also be substantiated from the archival record available in the Delhi State Archives,in a correspondence from the Chief Secretary of Government North Western Provinces and Oudh to the Secretary of Punjab Government forwarded a copy of a letter dated 24th December, 1885 and an enclosure (translation of the *khat*) received from the Commissioner of the Rohilkhand Division in which the Nawab of Rampur offered the munificent donation of Rupees 15,5000/- for the repair of the Jama Masjid at Delhi. Translation of a *khat* from the Nawab of Rampur furnishes us with the following details that Jama Masjid at Delhi required repairs as its domes were cracked in consequence of which there was an apprehension of it falling down.

In 1894 A.D the southern minaret of the masjid was struck by lightning and got damaged, and was repaired and restored by the *Nawab* of Bahawalpur. He presented a small amount of Rupees 14,000/- as a donation for the repairs of the Jama Masjid and the money was sent to the agent of the Bank of Bengal, Delhi to open a current account in the name of Deputy Commissioner, Delhi under the heading of "Bahawalpur Masjid Grant". This donation for the repairs of the Jama Masjid can also be substantiated from the archival file named 'Grant by the Nawab of Bahawalpur for the repairs of the Jama Masjid'. On the request of the Nawab of Bahawalpur an estimate for repairs to the minarets of the Jama Masjid was prepared through the Municipal Engineer of Delhi.In later periods also,Jama Masjid received several other donations and presents from the *Nawabs* and *Nizams* of the various states for necessary repairs and other requirements as they were unable to bear the responsibility of the management of the Jama Masjid.

Conclusion

The perceptions, notions and emotions that are attached to monuments in course of time and the human reaction that these buildings can generate are all marked by the historical occurrences. They are culturally constructed bearing direct interference from the contemporary state and power centres. As the centres of power shift from one regime to another regime, these perceptions also change.

To trap this shift was the key consideration behind the decision to use the building of *Masjid-e Jaha Numa* or *Jama Masjid* of Delhi to tell the story of how the mosques in India underwent a serious blow with the transfer of power from the Mughals to the Colonial rule. An attempt was to trace the historical overview of this mosque from its construction in A.D. 1656 till its confiscation by the British in 1857 and its subsequent restoration to the Muslims in 1862, a long period of more than two hundred years. This has provided a varied and layered history of this monument beginning from the sacred identity of it as the *Masjid-e Jahanuma* or *Jama Masjid* to an architectural marvel celebrated by art historians to a symbol through which the Muslim Community was 'disciplined and controlled' in the aftermath of the revolt of 1857.

As a part of their vengeful program after the revolt, the colonial authorities identified the main culprits who conspired against them during the revolt and punishments- death penalties, imprisonments, confiscation of properties, resumption of grants and destruction of the city- were inflicted on them recklessly. The Muslim class, especially the Muslim Ulema, scholars and intellectuals among them were the worst affected as the British assumed them to be the prime conspirators of the revolt against them, and the mosques were the places, according to them, that were used to mobilize people against the British by these conspirators. Similarly, the mosques of the city and Jama Masjid being the most prominent among them were confiscated and restrictions on the performance of prayers were put. Jama Masjid became a site of contest between the Muslims of Delhi and the colonial state in the wake of the former's involvement in the revolt against the latter in 1857 A.D. The memories of the violation of this monument did leave a deep impact on the minds of Muslims for whom Jama Masjid was a symbol of their piety and moral prestige. This paper attempts to study how a Mughal monument was used by the British authorities to assert their hegemony and discipline a particular community of faith.

Since these mosques were the symbols of the erstwhile ruling classes, and reminded the British of their predecessors, it became a prestige issue for them to desecrate these structures. However, the outright desecration was not possible because of the possibility of another popular revolt, and hence to at least keep a strict control over them was important for them to justify their ego. In all this, the masjid that was once the pride of the erstwhile ruling state was merely reduced to the structure that could be persecuted repeatedly. As far as the British were concerned, for them the confiscations of the mosques and other buildings was just a part of the 'sanitary' program that they introduced to change the urban landscape of the city that would be militarily more convenient for them.

As has been evident from the above discussion, the masjid remained closed for a period of five years till it was finally restored to the Muslim inhabitants of the city in 1862 after a series of litigations from them.The Jama masjid was restored to them but with strict conditions- regarding the performance of prayers, *aza'n*(call for the prayers), and gathering of devotees and admission into it with and without shoes- were imposed.

Along with these restrictions, it was to be managed by a Managing Committee, whose members were also selected by the British. The process of litigations on the part of the Muslim inhabitants regarding relaxation of these conditions continued for several decades. In all this, the masjid that was once the pride of the erstwhile ruling state was merely reduced to the structure that could be persecuted repeatedly.

Translation of the agreement dated the 24th November 1862, made by the Managers of the Jama Masjid, Delhi.

We the undersigned, ten Members, appointed by agreement among ourselves as Managers of the Juma Masjid, thankfully enter into the following agreement of our own free will with Government:-

1. We are responsible that there shall be no disturbances, disagreements or quarrels within the Mosque premises.

2. If any question should arise in connection with the Mosque or religion we will settle it privately between ourselves.

3. No act shall be committed inside the Mosque which may tend to show contempt of, or disloyalty to, Government. Should, however, any such thing take place and which may be beyond our power to check or control, we shall bring it to the notice of the Deputy Commissioner.

4. We will do repairs to the buildings of the Mosque, when ever it is necessary to do so, and shall keep up regular accounts of shop rents, tah bazari &c., of the endowed property.

5. If a vacancy is caused among the Managers for any reason, whatever, we will appoint a successor by agreement among ourselves.

6. If any thing is done or act committed contrary to the wishes of the Government, we hereby recognise that Government shall be at liberty, at all times, to close the Mosque or make other arrangements for its management.

Sd/- Mirza Ilahi Bax.
Sd/- Md: Ibrahim.
Sd/- Nasir Uddin.
Sd/- Hafeiz Daood.
Sd/- Mahboob Bax.

Sd/- Md: Sadruddin Khan.
Sd/- Md: Hussain.
Sd/- Turab Ali.
Sd/- Md: Tafazzul Hussain Khan.
Sd/- Hafiz Mir Mohammed.

Written on 24th November 1862.

Figure 1: Translation of the original agreement in English language made by the managers of Jama Masjid Managing Committee dated 24th November, 1862. (File No. 11/1860, Deputy Commissioner Vol. I, Delhi State Archives).

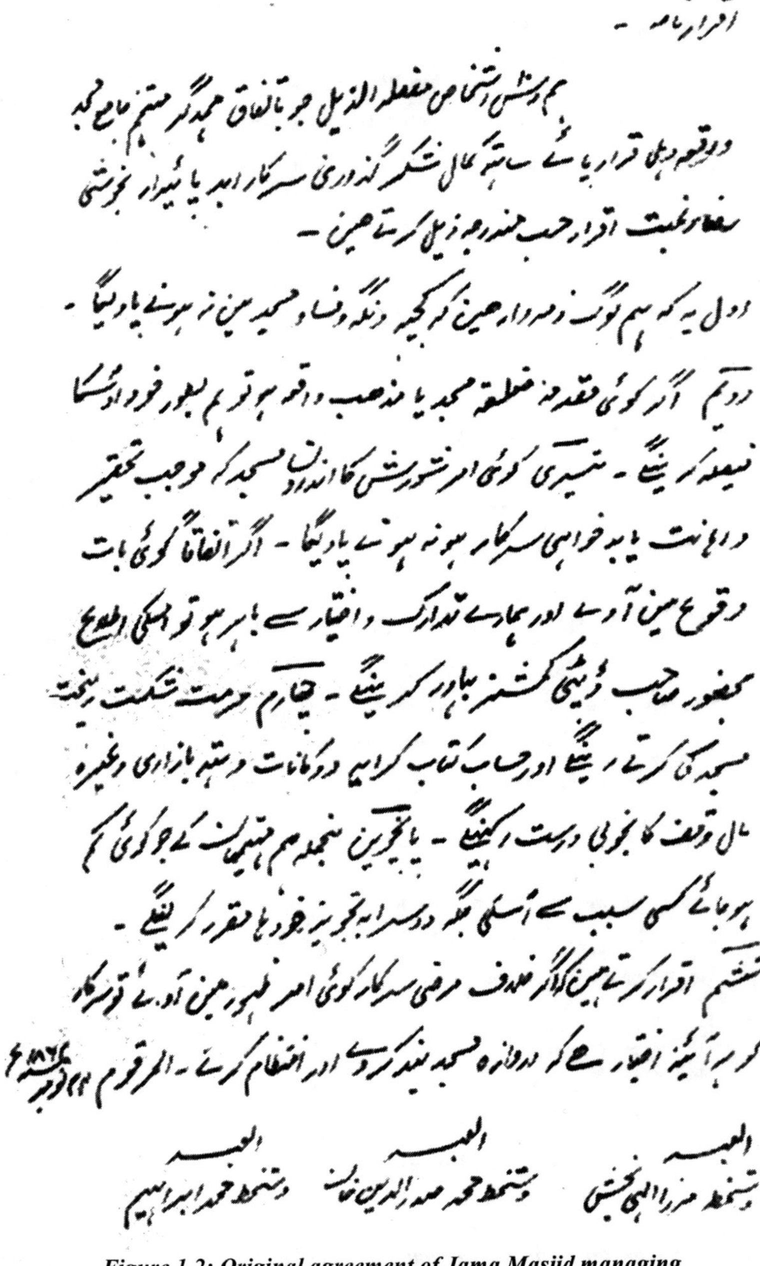
اقرار نامہ ۔

ہم اشخاص مفصلۂ الذیل جو باتفاق ہمدیگر مہتمم جامع مسجد
در قلعہ دہلی قرار پائے ہیں ساتھ کمال شکرگذاری سرکار ابد پائیدار بحرمتی
سعادت نعمت اقرار حسب مندرجہ ذیل کرتے ہیں ۔

اول یہ کہ ہم لوگ ذمہ دار ہیں کہ کچھ دنگہ و فساد مسجد میں نہ ہونے پاویگا ۔
دوئم اگر کوئی مقدمہ متعلقہ مسجد یا مذہب واقع ہو تو ہم بطور خود اوسکا
فیصلہ کرینگے ۔ تیسری کوئی امر شورش کا اندرون مسجد کہ موجب تحقیر
در اہانت یا بدخواہی سرکار ہو نہ ہونے پاویگا ۔ اگر اتفاقاً کوئی بات
وقوع میں آوے اور ہمارے تدارک و اختیار سے باہر ہو تو اسکی اطلاع
حضور صاحب ڈپٹی کمشنر بہادر کو کرینگے ۔ چہارم مرمت شکست ریخت
مسجد کی کرتے رہینگے اور حساب کتاب کرایہ دوکانات واقعہ بازاری وغیرہ
مال وقف کا بخوبی درست رکھینگے ۔ پانچویں منجملہ ہم ہشت کے جو کوئی کم
ہو جاوے کسی سبب سے اوسکی جگہ دوسرا بہ تجویز خود ہا مقرر کرینگے ۔
ششم اقرار کرتے ہیں کہ اگر خلاف مرضی سرکار کوئی امر ظہور میں آوے تو سرکار
کو ہر آئینہ اختیار ہے کہ دروازہ مسجد بند کر دے اور انتظام کرے ۔ المرقوم ۲۴ نومبر ۱۸۶۲ء

العبد دستخط مرزا الٰہی بخش
العبد دستخط محمد صدر الدین خان
العبد دستخط محمد ابراہیم

Figure 1.2: Original agreement of Jama Masjid managing committee in Persian language dated 24th November, 1862. (File No. 11/1860, Deputy Commissioner Vol. I, Delhi State Archives).

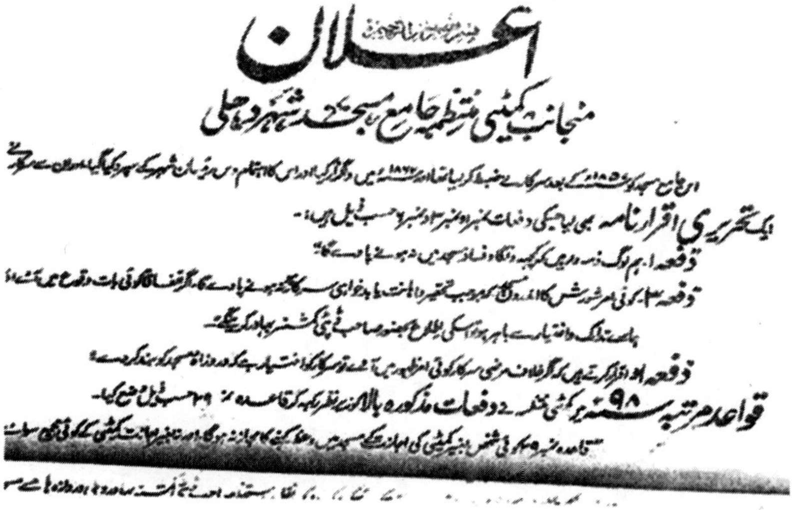

اعلان

منجانب کمیٹی منتظمہ جامع مسجد شہر دہلی

Figure 1.3: Declaration by the Managing Committee regarding the restoration of Jama Masjid. (File No. 11/1860, Deputy Commissioner Vol. I, Delhi State Archives).

Chapter - 19

Fishing in the 'Troubled Waters'

The Revolt of 1857 and Jung Bahadur Rana, the Prime Minister of Nepal

—*Professor Syed Najmul Raza Rizvi*
Dept. of Med. & Modern History
D.D.U. Gorakhpur University

The revolt of 1857 was one of the largest and strongest anti-imperialist or anti-colonial revolts in the whole world during the nineteenth century. The revolt involved millions upon millions of people scattered over a wide region. It originated with the sepoys in the Meerut on 10th May 1857. The sepoys after some deliberations decided to go to Delhi, the capital of Mughal Emperor. They reached Delhi on 11th of May and declared Bahadur Shah "Zafar" as the King. After Delhi, the revolt spread all over north India and other parts of the country. Very soon, it turned into the revolt of the people. The British officers and army placed at different places were unable to handle the situation. By the end of June, a considerable portion of North-West Provinces and Oudh fell into the hands of rebels. Delhi and Awadh, became their main centers and they posed a serious challenge to the British Government. Therefore, the British Government considered its first objective to reoccupy both the centers. Lord Canning, the Governor-General, coming to the decision affirmed that, "paradoxical, as it may appear, I think it of more importance to re-establish our power in the centre, and the capital of Oudh, which has scarcely been in our hands since two years and to recover our older possessions. Every eye in India is upon Oudh as it was upon Delhi. Oudh is not only the rallying place of the sepoys, the place to which they all look, and by doings in which their own hopes and prospects rise or fall but it represents a dynasty, there is a king of Oudh seeking his own lost kingdom. Oudh and our dealings with it, have been in every native's mind for the last two years. The attention of all native chiefs is drawn to see whether or not we can retain hold of what we have taken[1]. The Governor General further adds that, "Then, there is the most formidable of all lurking places of damages and revolt. Hyderabad had, especially Mohammadan deeply sympathizing with Oudh, because fearing however, unreasonably, the same fate. The recovery of Oudh would be of the greatest value to the company, while the penetrating into Rohilkhand, leaving Oudh untouched, would be little thought of"[2] But the British were not in a position to meet out the challenge of the rebels, immediate help was needed for handling the situation. At this critical moment Nepal entered the scene.

The story of Nepal's role has two sides: On the one hand Nepal sent its troops to British against the rebels and on the other, it also gave shelter to rebel leaders. This paper deals with both the sides separately in two parts showing their in how Nepal fished in the troubled waters during the revolt of 1857?

(I)

Nepal was the bad neighbor of British Government and its interest in Indian events were always suspected by the British.[3] News of revolt reached Kathmandu by mid-May. According to Major George Ramsay, the resident at Kathmandu, "The outbreak of rebellion in Hindustan created very little sensation among the people generally or even in the Gorkha Army. When the intelligence of the mutiny at Meerut, of the massacre at Delhi and afterward of the occurrences at Lucknow and Cawnpore reached Jung Bahadur's ears, his course appeared to be taken without the least hesitation. He admitted the seriousness of the crisis, but had no misgivings as to the eventual turn affairs would take".[4] Jung Bahadur Rana knew the British power after his Europe visit in 1850. He was of the opinion that British were certain to win and therefore, Nepal should help the British in the crisis as it would be gainful. Later on, he himself openly expressed his motives behind his offer of military help. In his farewell speech before leaving Kathmandu on December 10th, 1857 he declared, "I have three motives for acting as I am now doing. First, to show that Gorkhas possess fidelity and will shed their blood in defence of those who treat them with honour and repose confidence in them. Second, I know the power of the British government and was I to take part against it, although I might have temporary success, my country would afterwards be ruined and the Gorkha dynasty annihilated. Third, I know that upon the success of British arms and the re-establishment of British power in India, its government will than ever and that I and my brothers and my country will all then benefit from our alliance"[5]. An examination of the above mentioned motives Jung Bahadur Rana, shows that the first motive that Jung Bahadur Rana professed was somewhat doubtful as he was not a feudatory chief, but the Prime Minister of an independent country, who was under no obligation to display fidelity to the British. The second motive was misleading since it implied that Nepal was obliged to make a choice between supporting the British or supporting the rebels. It ignored another possible option-that of remaining neutral. Nepal's support of the British was an act of deliberate policy and not of helplessness or compulsion, Jung Bahadur's third motive was the real motive, as might be inferred from the order in which he listed the beneficiaries: first came "I" then "my brothers" and lastly "my country"[6] Besides this, another reason for offering the military assistance to the British was to seek employment of the troops who had been discharged after the Nepal - Tibet War of 1855-56.[7]

However, the atmosphere in Nepal was not in favour of British Many Bhardars and even some of Jung Bahadur's brothers had sympathies with the rebels. It was not an easy task for Jung Bahadur to take the unanimous decision in favour of the British. Therefore, he convened a meeting of the state council to know their opinion. According to the Buddhiman Singh's *Vamsaval*, "The Maharaja. assembled all the Bhardars and officers and asked them whether or not, Nepal should help the British. Everybody said that Nepal should not help the British"[8] Pudma Jung Bahadur Rana, the son and biographer of Jung Bahadur Rana also wrote in 1909, that, Jung Bahadur held a council composed of all the Sirdars of the State, who were asked to give their opinion on the question of advisability of the Nepalese assisting their British neighbours. Many spoke in favour of the proposal, many murmured dissent, many again advocated a policy of strict neutrality"[9].

Aware of the widespread dissatisfaction in Nepal Darbar, Jung Bahadur held several council meetings to convince the anti-British lobby He argued that the British were certain to defeat the rebels and Nepal could by assisting them regain the territory, which was lost in the 1814-16 war. He also appealed to the religious prejudices of the Nepali-Hindus who had borne a grudge against the Muslim ruler of Awadh ever since his predecessor had "loaned" the British twenty five million rupees during the Anglo-Nepalese war of 1814-16 and had received as payment title to certain districts in Tarai.[10] According to Leo E. Rose, "The Darbar's objections to the use of the Nepali army in India might well have been more vehement if its operations had not been directed against the predominantly Muslim rebel movement in Oudh".[11]

However, it seems that Jung Bahadur could not fully convince the anti-British lobby, but he was firm in his determination to help the fully British. Exercised the power of Maharaja, as the Prime Minister was bound to follow the advice. The Nepal Government offered the services of his troops to British through Major George Ramsay, the Resident at Kathmandu on May 31, 1857. It was said in the letter of Nepal Government, that, "There is no probability that this Government will receive any order from the British Government on such a trifling occasion, yet in consideration of the friendship which subsists between the two states it would not be consistent with the rules of friendship to keep silent on hearing such intelligence. I, therefore, desire to say that we are ready to execute any order that may be given to this Government by the Right Honorable Governor General"[12] In June, 1857, Jung Bahadur offered services of his troops to the Resident. He also desired to personally lead fifty thousand troops to India.

The offer was not taken seriously because it was made in a rather vague and casual manner. Captain Byers, the assistant resident thus commented, "The offer of the Durbar is something like a general invitation to dinner, "Come my dear fellow. Whenever you like, there is always a plate for you"[13] but alarming reports came pouring in from Awadh. Therefore, Ramsay accepted the offer. He replied that, "I have no hesitation in accepting on the part of my Government, the services of three small bodies of Nepalese troops consisting of 1000 men each[14].

Nepal Durbar debated Ramsay's proposal for two days and finally informed him that (1) the Nepal Government's offer was conditional on the reception of a direct request for troops from the Governor-General, (2) Nepal being currently engaged in a border dispute with Tibet, could not send 3000 troops from Kathmandu and (3) Nepal would lend the troops if the British agreed to bear all the expenses involved.[15] But later, on June 5th, the Nepal Durbar modified its policy and consented to send six regiments (3000 men) into the British provinces.

Ramsay made prompt arrangements for dispatching three thousand Nepalese troops to Lucknow, Banaras, and Patna and two hundred to Gorakhpur. The authorities at these places had been making urgent requests to the Resident to send Nepalese troops. Checking the spread of the revolt from Gorakhpur to Champaran and Tirhut in Bihar had now become a pressing necessity.[16] But the Ramsay's proceedings appeared "extraordinary" to the Governor-General Lord Canning. The Resident had no authority for what he did. Therefore, the Resident was censured for his unauthorized proceedings. He was asked to request Jung Bahadur to recall the troops. There were many reasons for rejecting the offer by the British Government. The British Government was suspicious of Nepal's help in the beginning and was apprehensive that the Gorkha troops might be won over by the rebels, Lord Canning feared that if the Nepalese were allowed entry into the disturbed districts they would plunder them. Their sudden descent into the plains might also strengthen the rumour that Nepal had sent her army to assist the rebels. He also knew that Jung Bahadur had a strong opposition in Nepal and most of the Sardars, Bhardars and officers were sympathetic to the rebel in India. Moreover, there were evidences that some of the Gorkha regiment had been infiltrated by the rebels and a Gorkha officer had attempted to assassinate Jung Bahadur in June 1857. Thus Lord Canning had the knowledge of a powerful enemy group opposing Jung Bahadur's pro-British policy. The British Government, moreover, was suspicious of Jung Bahadur as some of the rebels had written him for help against the British. One such letter written by the king of Oudh to Jung Bahadur had been intercepted by the British Resident at Kathmandu. The Governor-General was unwilling to accept the Nepalese offer of help as the rebels believed that the British would be defeated and in the prevailing situation, there was the danger of the

Gorkha troops taking side with the rebels. He was hesitant to take the Nepalese help "until the head of the rebellion should be crushed by the truimph of British arms and the effect of the truimph should manifest" Therefore, Lord Canning rejected the offer in the beginning. The refusal paid heavy price as Danial Wright wrote in 1876 that, "however the measures adopted by the Resident General G. Ramsay were not approved of, by the Governor General and the troops were recalled. Had they gone on, it is probable that the massacre at Cawnpore would never have occurred".[17]

Hardly ten days had elapsed after this refusal when the Governor General, Lord Canning frantically appealed to the Nepal Durbar through the Resident for the help. It was realised that without the Nepalese aid Lucknow could not be held. On 23rd June, new instructions were sent to Ramsay in which he was ordered to obtain from the Government of Nepal, the services of 3000 men and dispatch them at once to Lucknow. The embarrassed Resident made fresh request to Nepal Durbar that "the six regiments Nepalese troops be sent to Lucknow".[18]

Jung Bahadur Rana reassumed the office of Prime Minister of Nepal, second time by the order of king Surendra on June 28th and also obtained the 'supreme power' through the Lal Mohar. The Lal Mohar of June 28th 1857 was concluded with the statement of the king that, "in fact he may do...... whatever he may think proper, but I have desired him at once to put to death all who will not obey him".[19] Therefore, according to Perceval Landon, "On this occasion, Jung Bahadur acted entirely on his own initiative. The great council of State was, as a matter of fact by no means agreed as to the wisdom of this intervention".[20] On June 30th, the first detachment sent out to India and two others followed shortly thereafter.

The Nepalese troops were still on their way when the defense of Lucknow collapsed on 4th July 1857 and in August Gorakhpur was also lost to rebels. The Nepalese troops entered British territory at a point north of Gorakhpur. Instead of marching towards Lucknow they were ordered to occupy Azamgarh and Jaunpur. The Nepalese troops occupied Azamgarh on the 13th of August and Jaunpur on the 15th. But in the third week of September a large body of rebels entered Azamgarh again The Nepalese forces drove them in one day. Azamgarh and Jaunpur were small and comparatively insignificant stations. The area infected was much larger than could properly be dealt with by the British forces supplemented as they had been by a small army from Nepal. The rebels had concentrated at Lucknow and it was feared that the Kingdom of Awadh was, forever, slipping out of the hands of the British.[21] Therefore Lord Canning concluded a new arrangement with the Nepal Government, by which it was settled that Jung Bahadur should personally take the command of a fresh army from Nepal and proceed to the scene of action as promptly as possible. Lord Canning promised to bear all the expenses of their allies, to reward the wounded in action and present medals to all after the termination of war.

On the 10th December, 1857, Jung Bahadur Rana himself left Kathmandu as the head of 8000 or more troops, and reached the frontier on 21st December. There he met General G.K. Macgregor, the British Political Agent, appointed by Governor-General. Continuing his march he reached in the vicinity of Gorakhpur on January 5th, 1858. Gorakhpur was, at that time in the hands of rebels. Mohammad Hasan was the Nazim of Gorakhpur. The Gorkha army defeated him and occupied Gorakhpur.[22] Some parts of Gorakhpur district being still infested by rebels, Jung Bahadur moved his forces rapidly from place to place and this had the desired effect of sweeping the enemy out of the district. Leaving behind two regiments of infantry for the defence of Gorakhpur, Jang Bahadur moved to restore British authority over Lucknow and reached Bari on the left of bank of Ghagra on the 19th of February. After crushing all the resistance, Jung Bahadur reached in the vicinity of Lucknow on March 10th, 1858. On 11th March, Jung Bahadur's troops along with those of Colonel Pahalwan Singh Basnayt were employed in operation against the seize of Lucknow. By March 13th, the whole of Lucknow was freed from the rebels. The Nepalese troops took part in the capture of *Begum, Kothi Alam Bagh, Chhuter Manzil, Moti Mahal and Tara Kothi, Kaiser Bagh and Musa Bagh in Lucknow.*[23] While restoring British rule at Lucknow, the Nepalese joined in the general loot and spoliation of that rich city.[24] In brief, over a period of one hundred days Jung Bahadur's forces engaged with, the rebels in several major actions, and finally assisted British troops in the recapture of Lucknow.

Towards the end of March 1858, the Gorkha troops started to head home taking with them 4000 bullock carts laden with plunder.[25] Two months later, as a reward for services rendered, Lord Canning informed the king of Nepal through Jung Bahadur of the British Government's intention to restore to Nepal the whole of Nepal's former territory below the hills, extending from the River Ghagra (Karnali) on the west to the British territory of Gorakhpur on the east, and bounded on the south by Khairagarh and the district of Bahraich and on the north by the hills.[26] The territory was known, thereafter, as the *Naya Muluk* or new territory, that had been seized in the war of 1814-16, then conferred upon the Nawab of Awadh as repayment of a loan of 25 million rupees, which he had made to the British Government.

The expenditure on Nepal army was also met out by the British Indian Government. According to Ramsay, "A sum of between 4,000,000- 5,000,000 rupees was paid as donation Batta to Maharaja Jung Bahadur's army and to various bodies of Gorkha troops that were engaged in assisting in the suppression of the rebellion in the British provinces, and gratuities in lieu of pensions were given to the families of all officers and men who had been killed in action. It was also decided that the Indian mutiny medals with clasps for Lucknow should be given to all fighting men who by the rules of our own service would be entitled to them".[27] Rishikesh Shaha gives the detailed and exact amount of expenditure which was paid by the British Indian Government. According to him, "The expenditure involved in employing the Nepali troops in India and training them was borne by the British Indian government. It amounted to Rs. 2,30,615. An additional sum of Rs. 4,50,000 was paid as cash gifts to all those men and officers who had taken part in suppressing the mutiny, as gratuities in lieu of pension and compensation to the families of officers and soldiers who had lost their lives in action".[28]

Though, according to Rishikesh Shaha, "Jung's role in suppressing the mutiny was not a significant and vital from the military point of view as it was made out,[29] but the British Indian government recognised his services and made him a G.C.B. In October, the Resident delivered to Maharaja Jung Bahadur at a grand Darbar the Insignia of a Knight Grand Cross of the order of Bath.[30]

Thus, the British did not deny the help rendered to them by Jung Bahadur Rana during the dark days of the rebellion. Nepal played a crucial role in quelling the revolt and earned name, fame, wealth and land in exchange from the British.

(II)

During the revolt of 1857, the rebel leaders also tried to seek help from Nepal. Many rebel leaders wrote to Jung Bahadur urging him not to help the British and to fight for their cause against the British. Kamaluddin Haider, the author of *Qaysarat-Tawarikh* writes that "The Revolutionary leaders made several attempts to remind Jung Bahadur that the policy of supplying mercenaries to a foreign power against his neighbours and co-religionists was not good. Mohammad Husayn (the Nazim of Gorakhpur) was the first of these leaders to make and attempt to persuade the Nepalese Minister to change his policy, but he failed in his efforts"[31] Pudma Jung Bahadur Rana also refers a correspondence between Nawab Ramzan Ali Khan Mirza Birjis Qadr Bahadur and Jung Bahadur Rana the Prime Minister of Nepal. Birjis Qadr wrote a letter to Jung Bahadur which ran as follows:-

> After compliments.
>
> "It is well known that my ancestors gave the English footing on Indian soil. It was we that wrested the province of Benaras from the Maharaja who owned it and put the English in possession of it. In recognition of these favours they signed a treaty, the purport of which was that they would remain faithful to our house, as long as the sun and moon lasted. But after a short time these ungrateful *Feringhees* cancelled that treaty and with the aid of some of our treacherous servants dethroned my father Wajid Ali Shah, seizing his state palaces, Jewels and everything else that belonged to him. They then collected a large force and vast quantity of ammunition at Colonelganj, near the foot of the hills, for the purpose of over running our country. The cause of the late disturbances was that some time ago the English, in order to corrupt the faith of the Hindus and Musalmans, introduced a new kind of cartridge, greased over with the fat of cows and pigs, and ordered the native soldiers on the parade to bite them with their teeth. On refusing to obey

this offensive order, the sepoys were commanded to be blown away by guns, the truth of which must have come to your notice, "We are quite astonished that the Nepalese, pure Hindus as they are, should be induced by the English to come down to India, to assist them in their diabolical work of demolishing holy temples and mosques, and to fight against their own brothers of the plains. I appeal to your honour to come forward, not as the destroyer of the religion, but as defender of the faith of both Hindus and Musalman. In the name of all the Hindus and Mohammadans of India, I sincerely pray that your Highness will not hesitate for a moment to combine your strong arms with our own, in the cause of our ancient faith. We assure you that without your help the English will not be able to stand against us, and thus the Kingdom of Nepal shall extend as far as the banks of your sacred Ganges, and shall be recognized by one and all as the suzerain power of India"[32]

Raja Devi Bakhsh Singh of Gonda, another rebel leader of Awadh also wrote to Jung Bahadur that "he should aid the Begum Hazrat Mahal because the country is losing its (*Dharam*) faith through the oppression of the English and without your Highness's aid it will be impossible for us to preserve its religion"[33] Jung Bahadur's reply to Birjis Qadr reveals his attitude towards the rebels. He replied him in the following words:

After compliments,

"I acknowledge the receipt of your letter dated the 13th of Jetha 1915 (May 1858) stating that English are resolved to destroy the faith of Hindus and Musalmans and calling upon me to side with the natives of India in the defence of their religion. It is more than a hundred years since the English first established their power in India and yet it has never been heard that they attempted to interfere with the faith of the people in a single case. Had I have, the slightest evidence of what you allege against the English, with regard to their attitude towards the religion of their subjects, I would have bestowed serious consideration on the matter".

"Be it known to all that as both Hindus and Musalmans have been guilty of the murder of innocent women and children, and of other excesses which humanity should be ashamed of, the Hindu government of Nepal will never uphold their cause against the authority of the English".

"As you have addressed me a friendly letter, written in friendly terms, I as a friend, advise you to make your surrender, with all possible speed to Mr. Montgomery, the Commissioner of Lucknow, and I assure you, you will be pardoned along with your followers, with the exception of those who have murdered English women and children". "If you do not listen to my counsel and still think of waging war with the British, I assure you that death will be the inevitable result".[34]

The above mentioned correspondence shows that Jung Bahadur Rana stood firm in favour of the British. However, he had to face a difficult situation in Nepal. Many of the rebel leaders and their followers fled to Nepal and sought shelter of the Government of Nepal. The British Government had asked Jung Bahadur not to give asylum to them. The Begum Hazrat Mahal and her son Birjis Qadr, Nana Sahib, Bala Rao Devi Deo of Nasirabad Brigade, Khan Bhadur Khan of Bareilly Mohammad Hasan, Raja Drig Bijay Singh, Beni Madho Singh of Shankerpur and Raja of Gonda etc. had taken shelter in the Tarai region. When the intelligence reached Jung Bahadur that a guerilla band of rebels had penetrated the jungles of *surbi khola*, in the western part of the Nepal Tarai, the Maharaja at once dispatched four companies of soldiers under Colonel Pahalwan Singh with orders to take up his headquarters in the fort of *Changmi* to watch the movements of the enemy, to prevent their climbing up the hills, and if possible to disarm and detain them, pending further instructions. Colonel Pahalwan Singh took up his station at *Changmi* at the end of May 1859. He was surprised to find that their numbers were much more, and it was no more roving band of rebels but a regular force of 2000 armed with matchlocks, guns and swords. Their number was increasing day by day. Pahalwan Singh carefully observed their movements for two months and in the middle of August, he applied for reinforcements as his forces were wholly inadequate to the task of subjugating such formidable numbers. On the 24th of September the Maharaja sent another four regiments under Colonel Ranuzir with orders to await the Maharaja's arrival at Noakote. Meanwhile on 13th of October Col. Pahalwan Singh sent word to rebels that they should surrender their arms to him. But the rebels hesitated. He then summoned Beni Madho of Shankerpur to appear alone before him, assuring him that his life would be safe, if he obeyed. He too hesitated. This taxed his patience too far and he gathered all his men together and demanded the surrender of Beni Madho a second time. The delay from the rebel side fretted his nerves and he marched with his troops towards the rebel camp. He again demanded the immediate surrender of their arms. When Beni Madho came out of his tent to confer with Col. Pahalwan Singh, some of the rebels fired upon the Nepalese. Infuriated at this show of violence, Pahalwan Singh ordered an indiscriminate slaughter, in which Beni Madho and two other rebel chiefs along with their 400 followers were slain. On the 14th November Jung Bahadur Rana arrived at Noakote where he was greatly enraged to hear that "our hundred of the rebels had been shot down by Colonel Pahalwan Singh, who had orders simply to watch their movements and if possible to disarm and detain them without causing any bloodshed" He suspended the Colonel for his unwanted action.[35] However, he pushed on to *Noakote*, where he learned that the rebel horde that had entered Nepalese territory were the personal followr of Nawab Birjis Qadr, who with his mother, the Begum Hazrat Mahal had fled to Nepal to seek refuge in the highlands of India. Both mother and son had an interview with Jung Bahadur at Noakote, the Maharaja received them in a manner befitting the position they had lately lost, and assured them of every care and protection promising not to hand them over to the British. According to Pudma Jung, He bestowed on them a handsome allowance and fixed their residence in a house near his own palace.[36]

Jung Bahadur protected Nana Sahib and his family also. He was unwilling to surrender Nana Sahib whom the British were anxious to capture as he had been responsible for the massacre at Cawnpore. He could not hand over a Brahmin to be executed. It is believed that Nana Sahib and some other rebel leaders received a subsidy of Rs. 400 per month from Nepal Government. Dr. R.C. Majumdar believed that both Nana Saheb and Bala Rao lived and died in Nepal. This could not have been possible without the help of Jung

Bahadur.[37] Pudma Jung also says that, it was also discovered that Nana Rao, Bala Rao and Azimullah had all perished in the western jungles.[38]

Jung Bahadur then proceeded to *surhi khola* to disperse the other rebels. Their number was more than 23,000 of whom 11,000 were under arms. The insurgents quickly laid down their arms before Jung Bahadur.[39] Khan Bahadur Khan of Bareilly and the several thousands of the rebels were examined by Jung Bahadur and those who had taken part in the massacre of the English women and children were sent back to British India under a strong Nepalese guard and rest were liberated and made to settle down as peaceful cultivators in the Nepal Tarai, though they latter found opportunities of going back to their houses.[40]

It is noteworthy that Jung Bahadur helped only those rebel leaders who had brought immense wealth with them from India. Perceval Landon also says that Jung Bahadur bought the jewels of Nana Saheb and of the Begam Hazrat Mahal of Lucknow for a very small sum. According to him, Nana Sahib took with him from Bithur the most valuable jewels in his possession. They included the famous *"Nau Lakha"*, the principal jewel of the Peshwas. It is- for it exists still - a long necklace of pearls, diamonds and emeralds and is perhaps without a rival in the world. The quite unsympathetic Prime Minister, Jung Bahadur Rana, offered 93,000 rupees and Nana Saheb, compelled to take the offer or leave it, accepted the money. But Kashi Bai, the Nana's wife, with shrewdness beyond her years, made a personal appeal to Jung Bahadur and was given in place of the money the revenues of two villages *Dhangra and Raharia*, in return for an annual payment by her of 4,500 rupees. Jung Bahadur accepted her request.

Among other jewels belonging to Nana Sahib that were then transferred to the keeping of the Prime Minister's family in Nepal, was a remarkable single emerald three inches in length, which Nana Sahib had, had mounted as a seal. It is now the chief stone in the official head dress of the Prime Minister. Below it, is a cluster of fine emeralds of great size like a bunch. This also is part of the treasures of Nana Sahib.

The Maharaja of Darbhanga also possesses a finger-ring set with a single diamond of the purest water and of great size. It also belonged to Nana Sahib".[41]

Perceval Landon further writes that "Of other jewels brought by Nana Sahib into Nepal, we have description sent by Siddhiman Singh in the letter to Jung Bahadur. He describes a Necklace of 48 pearls and 24 emeralds. The shape is 3 inches in length and 2 inches in width. The central diamond was of 5/8 of an inch in length and 1/2 inch width. It was surrounded by 34 diomand close set. There was also an armlet 3'h inches by 2 inches consisting of a large Table diamond with 31 diamonds reound it. Another smaller one is one and three quarter by 7/8 inches A certain number of these jewels were offered as bribes to Sidhiman Singh or to Jung Bahadur".[42]

Colonel Ramsay reports that a jeweler came up from Delhi to value the jewels of Nana Sahib and the Begum Hazarat Mahal of Lucknow. Jung Bahadur bought jewels from the Nana's family estimated to be worth between 50,000 to 60,000 rupees for 36,000 rupees; and from the Begum, 40,000 rupees worth of jewels for 15,000 rupees".[43] We also find that the treatment of Jung Bahadur towards the rebel leaders was not satisfactory.[44]

Thus, Jung Bahadur had no sympathy with rebels. He had given the sanctuary only to those rebel leaders who could afford to pay for it. He exploited the situation in his favour and earned costly jewels from rebel leaders.

It is clear that Nepal's Jung Bahadur Rana made the best out of the situation by pleasing the British on the one hand and on the other hand getting money, jewels, etc. for providing shelter to rebels. Nepal and Jung Bahadur both were great gainers. Nepal got back its lost territories and Jung Bahadur accumulated immense wealth.

This story of Nepal's role in 1857 shows how an independent neighboring country exploited the crisis in British India.

Notes and References

1. Letter from Canning to Campbell, 8 Ja. 1958 cf. B.D.Sanwal, *Nepal and the East India Company*, Bombay, 1965, p. 288.
2. Ibid, 30 Dec. 1857, cf. B.D. Sanwal, op. cit., pp. 288-89.
3. For Nepal's relations with East India Company, See, Leo E. Rose, *Nepal Strategy for Survival*, Oxford University Press, 1971. pp. 95-102; Ramakant, *Indo-Nepalese Relations*, New Delhi, 1968, pp. 80-81, 141-45, 204.
4. Events at the court of Nepal III-1852-61, The narrative by Major G Ramsay, Resident at Kathmandu, dated 13 Oct. 1961. Foreign Dept. Political Basta No. 145-164, March 1875 (I), Cf. Bikramjit Hasarat, (ed.) *History of Nepal as told by its own Contemporary Chroniclers,* Hoshiarpur, Punjab, 1970). pp. 133-34.
5. Cf. Adrian Sever, Nepal Under the Ranas, New Delhi, 1993, p. 125, Rishikesh Shaha; *Modern Nepal, A Political History, 1769-1955,* Vol. I, New Delhi, 1990, p. 252.
6. Adrian Sever, op. cit., pp. 125-26.
7. *Ibid.,* p. 126.
8. Buddhiman Singh, *Vamsavali, Nepali Chronological Manuscript* cf. Leo E, Rose, op ct., p. 128.
9. Pudma Jung Bahadur Rana, *Life of Maharaja Sir Jung Bahadur,* Allahabad, 1909, (second reprint, Kathmandu, Nepal), 1980, pp. 198-99.
10. Leo E. Rose, op. cit., p. 129.
11. *Nepal Strategy for Survival,* p. 129.
12. Secret consultation No. 4787A, September 25, 1857, cf Leo, E. Rose, op. cit., p. 129.
13. Byers to Holmes, 4 June 1857, Nepal Residency Papers, Vol. 12, cf Kanchan Mojumdar, *Anglo-Nepalese Relations in the Nineteenth Century,* Calcutta, 1973, p. 71.
14. Secret consultation No. 487 B, Sept 25, 1857, Yaddashat, Ramsay to Krishna Bahadur, June 4, 1857, cf. Leo E. Rose, op. cit., p. 129. f.n. 6
15. Leo E. Rose, op. cit., p. 130.
16. Secret consultation, No. 489: *Nepal Residency Papers,* Vol. 9.
17. Daniel Wright, *History of Nepal,* Cambridge University Press, 1877, Ce ci (Second Edition, Calcutta, 1958) p. 38.
18. Secret consultation, No, 542, Sept. 25, 1857, Yaddasht, *Ramsay to Krishna* Bahadur, June 26, 1857.
19. Secret consultation, No. 473, Sept. 25 1857, Lal Mohar, Surendra to Jung Bahadur, June 28, 1857.
20. Percieval Landon, *Nepal,* New Delhi, 1993 (First Published, 1928) pp. 148-49.

21. Pudma Jung Bhadur Rana, op. cit., pp. 199-200.
22. Shah Sayyid Ahmad Ali, *Kashful. Baghawat* (Gorakipur) Mirzapur, 1860 (in Urdu) p. 27-30, Pudma Jung Bahadur Rana, op. cit, Pp. 200-206.
23. For details, see, Pudma Jung Bahadur Rana, op. cit, pp. 208-14.
24. Nepal Residency papers, Vol. 8, Reports of Brigadier Macgregor, a political officer attached to Jung Bahadur to Ramsay cf. Kanchan Mojumdar, op. cit., p. 73.
25. Adrian Sever, op. cit., p. 126.
26. Foreign secret consultation, 30 July 1858, No. 121, Cf. Rishikesh Shaha, op. cit., PP. 252-53 and f.no. 36 on page 270, Bikramjit Hasarat, op. cit., p.337.
27. Bikramjit Hasrat, op cit, p. 339.
28. *Modern Nepal: A Political History 1769-1955,* Vol. I, p. 253.
29. Ibid, p. 252.
30. Bikramjit Hasrat, op. cit., pp. 339-40, Foreign Political Consultations, 23 Sep. 1859, No. 8, Kanchan Mojumdar, op. cit., p. 79, Pudma Jung Bahadur Rana, op. cit., pp. 226-28, Perceival Landon, op. cit., p. 151.
31. *Qaysar al-Tawarikh* (In Urdu) Part-II, p. 305, Lucknow, November 1879 Syed Moinul Haq, *The Great Revolution of 1857,* Karachi, 1968, p. 305, f.n. 2.
32. *Life of Maharaja Sir Jung Bahadur,* p. 217-18.
33. Abstract translation of the letter dated 19 Sept. 1858.
34. Pudma Jung Bahadur Rana, p. 218.
35. Ibid, p. 222, 224-25.
36. Ibid, p. 223, Perceival Landon, op. cit., p. 150.
37. *The History and Culture of the Indian People,* Vol. IX, Pat-I, Bombay, 1965, 588.
38. *Life of Maharaja Sir Jung Bahadur,* p. 223, For details see also, Kanchan Mojumdar, op. cit., p. 80-99, Perceival Landon, op. cit., pp. 156-170.
39. Perceval Landon, op. cit., p. 150, Pudma Jung Bahadur Rana, op. cit., p. 223.
40. Pudma Jung Bahadur Rana, op. cit., pp. 223-24.
41. Perceval Landon, op. cit., pp. 158-59, Kashi Bai was only thirteen years old at the time of flight. See, p. 157.
42. *Ibid.,* pp. 159-60.
43. *Ibid.,* pp. 162-63.
44. *Ibid.,* p. 158, Perceval Landon refers the statement of Lal Singh, who was sent by E.C. Bayley, Secretary to Colonel H.M.Durand, the Indian Foreign Secretary, and writes, "Jung Bahadur behaves as though Nana Sahib's women- who had been given shelter in Kathmandu-"were his wives.

He goes to their house every three or four days and sends for them" "Jang Bahadur he says, borrowed their jewels on the occasion of his son's marriage; he did not return them but gave them some additional lands instead". See. p. 167, also see the foot notes 2 &3 According to Surendra Nath Sen, "The fugitives moved from place to place between *Chitwan*, Bhutwal, and Nayakot and suffered terrible privations. Some of the sepoys had to sell even their muskets to buy their food-The Nepal Government employed their troops for their capture and expulsion". See, *Eighteen Fifty-Seven,* New Delhi second reprint, 1977, p. 368.

The Memory

Khwaja Hasan Nizami of the *Dargah* of Hazrat Nizamuddin Auliya, and his Remembering of 1857

Chapter - 20

Literature, History and Memory
A Study of the Selected Writings of Khwaja Hasan Nizami on the Great Uprising of 1857

— ***Professor Saiyid Zaheer Husain Jafri***
Department of History,
Delhi University, Delhi

The events of 1857 have been variously studied and interpreted on the basis of the official documentation, as well as the indigenous discourse. There are fewer studies on the basis of literature produced much after the suppression of the event. The city of Delhi was, of course, the Mughal capital and it represented the center of the Mughals past glory. In the imagination of the people it represented the seat of legitimate power and authority. Therefore, it was natural for the sepoys from Meerut cantonment to rush to the city proclaiming the end of the British rule. They begged and cajoled the aged (and powerless) Mughal king Bahadur Shah Zafar to assume the command and the leadership of the rebellion. The British were also aware of this significance of the Mughal capital and put all their might in re-establishing control over the city. They focused on capturing the city from the rebel sepoys and dealing with the 'Mughal Royal Family' and their 'loyalists' before taking any action in other major centers of the uprising. They were finally able to subdue the city on the 14th of September 1857 letting loose a virtual reign of terror on the city and its inhabitants. The retribution was so swift and brutal that Begum Hazrat Mahal commented that seldom there has been a case 'where the entire city was punished for the crimes of a few.' The magnitude of the destruction of the imperial buildings and other civil buildings (in the process of remaking of the city!) had been massive, but hardly detailed in the official records, except of course, some mentions here and there like the personal letters of famous poet Mirza Ghalib and other notable citizens of the city.

The history of the 'sepoy mutiny', as it was officially labeled, was commissioned and John W Kaye, who was a military historian, was assigned the task of writing. He began his project faithfully, describing the course of events purely from a military point of view. But even when he wrote a small section on the destruction of the imperial capital, quite a few eye-brows were raised. It is generally assumed that since he had crossed certain 'limits', the project was later assigned to G.B. Malleson who completed the account. Perhaps, the memory of 1857 was very 'agonizing' to be recalled by the British. Therefore, not a single work was produced which had any description of the actual destruction[1]. For the moment one is not concerned about the possible factors for such attitude of the Colonial administrators.

On the other hand, some British officials firmly believed the theory of 'Muslim conspiracy', which resulted in such a massive catastrophe. This suspicion was further reinforced, when it was found that the *wahabis* were now directly confronting the British, after the collapse of Sikh power in Punjab, and were regularly recruiting the mercenaries and the volunteers and were also receiving the funds from the regions as far as Bengal and Bihar. This was followed by a series of *wahabi* trials between the years A.D. 1863-72.

At the same time it needs to be pointed out that it was not a 'simple military victory' for the English, rather, it was the systematic destruction of a culture, however decadent it might have been; the dislocation of an order, however outdated it might have been. Last but not the least; it was also a total extermination of the erstwhile ruling house and the class dependent on it. One finds a feel of such devastation, in the couplets ascribed to Bahadur Shah Zafar, himself, *'ye riyaya e Hind tabah hui, kaho kya kya in pe jafa hui'[the people of India utterly ruined; what cruelties they have not suffered!]*. Sir Syed Ahmad Khan, an eyewitness and a loyalist could somehow muster the courage to write, *Asbab-e Baghawat-e Hind* in March 1858 itself, in spite of the advice of his well-wishers not to antagonize the colonial masters for writing such an account. However, it is interesting to point out that there is not a single word in this very incisive pamphlet about the subsequent repression unleashed on the city of Delhi. Sir Syed could never think of revising his *Asar us Sanadid* (first published 1847 reprinted in 1854), as it would have necessitated a description of the havoc caused to the physical landscape of the city by the British after 1857.

It was only in A.D 1874, that Khwaja Altaf Husain Haali, lamented the destruction in his famous elegy on Delhi by saying: *mit gaye tere mitane ke nishan bhi ab to; aye falak is se zyada na mitana hargiz'* [*even the traces of what reminded us of the city's destruction are gone; O!Heaven, can there be a greater oblivion than that*]'. Similarly, Maulana Abul Kalam Azad, describing the city of Delhi, used the oriental metaphor, for the city being a 'virtual graveyard of our by-gone civilization', (hamari guzashta tehzib ka qabristan).

Besides these sporadic mentions, no systematic study of the destruction, both physical violence to the city's landscape and the sort of 'ethnic cleansing' of the then ruling race that took place was done. The tone and the tenor of the Urdu novels by scholars like, Deputy Nazir Ahmad (1833-1912) and Rashid ul Khairi (1870-1936) are altogether different in nature. For, they were more focused on the reform of the decadent society; and advised their audience to adopt the 'new culture', which was, represented by the British. Within such an agenda, one could hardly expect any description of the English repression unleashed on the city of Delhi.

It is in this background that a study of the writings of Khwaja Hasan Nizami (1873 - July 31, 1955)[2] on 1857 becomes quite important. He was the *sajjada nashin* of the *dargah* Hazrat Nizamuddin Auliya in Delhi. At the time of the uprising of 1857 his maternal grandfather was the *sajjada nashin* of the *dargah* and was in constant contact with the residents of the *Qila e Mubarak* [Red Fort] and Emperor Bahadur Shah Zafar. These writings are not to be considered simply as imaginative pieces, written in a semi-historical and even romanticized manner. They are reflective of the original writings, files and records from the official sources. Some of these writings are the exact translations of the well-known works like the *Trial of Bahadur Shah Zafar*[3]as well as the Urdu newspapers, published from Delhi during 1857 like *Sadiqul Akhbar* and the memoirs of the *kotwal* Muinuddin Hasan[4], and Jiwan Lal[5], the famous British spy. Similarly, he has made extensive use of the diary of Zaheer Dehalvi[6] especially in describing the massacre of the citizens in various parts of Delhi.[7]

In the Urdu literary circles, he is considered as a person with a literary style of his own, and justly described as *Musawir-e fitrat* for his powerful and moving style of writing. Some of these pieces are considered as representative pieces in Urdu literature. His mastery over the pen was so perfect that later on, an entire generation of writers and critics was inspired to imitate his style. His writings had a very large audience; especially the house-holds of the Muslim middle class in Upper Gangetic Valley' who were much inspired by his writings. It may be argued that some of his writings led to the formation of a sort of 'community consciousness', especially in the light of his debates with the Arya Samaji leader, Swami Shardhanand over the issue of *shuddhi*. Apart from this, his place in the history of Urdu literature as a stylist and prolific writer is seminal. It has been rightly said that

> "a prolific writer who wrote in a simple, colloquial style with an intimacy, mystic perception and light-heartedness that enlivened any subject he touched. He has written an over hundred books and pamphlets, including the moving story of the Great Rebellion of 1857 in twelve parts in the form of a romance..."[8]

His writings on 1857 have been so far largely considered as literary pieces depicting his unique style, which was matchless and had the powerful impact of arousing the sentiments of sympathy and pity for the fallen regime and thus, invoking anti-imperialist sentiments. But a systematic study of these writings has yet to be undertaken either in English or in Urdu.[9]

It is difficult to assign the dates to all his writings but it is certain that he started writing on the subject of the Uprising of 1857 around early 1920's and continued it till the next two decades. All these volumes have gone into numerous prints (too numerous to be counted) and these writings created a sense of sympathy and pity and at the same time invoking anti-British sentiments. His works were all written at the different point, depending on the availability of certain works. As he himself says that the volumes are published without a chronological sequence and he was intending to revise them and to make them more compact. However, in spite of the intended revision, we find that somehow he was trying to do an act of balancing. He also shares the revulsion the people of Delhi had for the sepoys. In fact, he puts the onus on the sepoys of all the misfortune of the royalty, misery of the citizenry and the devastation of the city on the sepoys.[10]

Some of these writings were the land-mark studies like, *Begmat ke Aansu* (first published in 1922),which is mainly based on his personal research and observation of the life of the survivors of the erstwhile ruling house, who were living in the most critical condition on some meager pension or the charity. This became extremely popular text with the audience as by 1946, eighteen editions of this text were already published. The description invokes pity and sympathy for the fallen regime and also invokes a sense of anguish for the British, all the events are described in the first person narrative giving a feel that they are original. Some real characters also appear; in a manner one can connect them to their genealogies. It is this book only, which is the sole authority for mentioning the tradition that after coming out of the Red Fort and before going to Humayun's Tomb, Bahadur Shah Zafar is said to have visited the *Dargah* of Nizamuddin Auliya, and handed over the relics of holy hair of the Prophet from the Royal treasury to the *Pirzadas* for its safe upkeep. These relics are still displayed by the custodians of the *Dargah* annually on the birth anniversary of the Prophet.[11]

Some of these volumes were quite popular among the Urdu speaking audience and therefore have run into dozens of reprints. Not only this but some sections as well as chapters were reproduced in numerous Urdu monthlies published from Delhi, Kanpur and Lucknow. But this is true only for the period 1920s-1940s; after the Partition and Independence of the country, the issues for the Urdu reading audience changed drastically. Facing new problems of settlements and rehabilitations, few could have any interest in the tales of the British repression or the details of the sufferings of the Mughal royal family. Therefore, we don't find any of these twelve volumes printed after 1946, when the thirteenth edition *Dehli ki Jaankani* was reprinted (first published in 1923). These volumes were available only in the libraries and it was difficult to locate the entire set anywhere. Numerous modern Urdu works dismiss these writings, just in few sentences. It was only in AD 2007 that a reprint of the entire set was published from Lahore immediately followed by a photo Indian edition.[12]

It may also be pointed out here that during the period of publication of Khwaja Hasan Nizami's work, the Urdu print culture was firmly established and the Urdu Indian elite were also quite well grounded in this culture. After the 'dislocation' of this culture, post-1947, the memory of 1857 became irrelevant on both sides of the border. There were few takers for such reading material. It is in no way to suggest that there was any decline in the Urdu print culture, rather it proliferated but in different direction.

We notice that after the partition on one hand, a lot of 'pulp literature' was available while on the other hand there was a huge market for the religious and polemical literature, often fueling the sectarian divide. Such works led to the sharpening of the divide within the Sunni community, while the 'pulp' literature ultimately led to the perversion of the taste of the audience.

As it has been pointed out earlier, most of the volumes in the series are the faithful renderings of the well-known works, written in the lucid literary style to make them popular among the audience. The two works, namely, *Dehli ki Jankani* and *Begmat ke Aansu* are the works based on his personal information, interviews of the survivors of the Royal family and the data from the other less known works like the diary of Zaheer Dehalvi, given below the two appendices take a note of these works in some details.

Notes

1. Beside the official accounts, not a single work survives either in Urdu or in English describing the destruction of the city of Delhi or the systematic extermination of the Mughal Royal family or even of the city's elite.

   Of course, there are hints like in the letters of Ghalib and some poems which were in the form of Elegy. Perhaps, it was more than a fear - psychosis, it was the fear of the English that nobody could dare to describe it. Last, but not the least, few people (capable to write on the issue) were left alive in the city to write the story of the atrocities committed during the 'white terror'.

2. Besides numerous works in Urdu, both original as well as secondary literature, a good description of his works, including the journals, he has edited and brought during his long and eventful career, see Carl W. Ernst and Bruce B. Lawrence, *Sufi Martyrs of Love: Chishti Order in South Asia and Beyond*, Palgrave, New York, 2002, pp. 113-117

3. *Proceedings on the Trial of Muhammad Bahadur Shah, Titular King of Delhi, Before a Military Commission, upon a charge of Rebellion, Treason and Murder, held at Delhi, on the 27th Day of January 1858, and following days,* London 1859.

4. For an early attempt to present his report into English, see Metcalfe, C.T. *The Two Narratives of the Mutiny*, Delhi, 1974; See also in Urdu, Khan, Muinuddin Hasan, *Khadang-e-Ghadar: Surguzisht-e-Inqlab 1857* (ed) Ibn Kanwal, Kitabi Duniya, Delhi, 2008.

5. See Metcalfe, op cit

6. Zaheer Dehlavi, *Daastaan-iGhadar/Traz-e Zaheeri,* ed. Afghan Ulla Khan, 2003, Gorakhpur.

7. These pamphlets' and books are: *Begmat ke Ansu* (1), *Angrezon ki Beepta* (published five times under the different titles *Angrezon ke Qisse* was the last publication to be published in 1927) (2), *Muhasra Ghadar Dehli ke Khutut,* (3) *Bahadur Shah ka Muqaddama* (reprint in 1923), (4) *Ghadar ke Farman* (*Griftar Shuda khutut*, published in 1919, 1923, 1948) (5), *Ghadar Dehli ke Akhbar* (*Ghadar ke Akhbar* published three times in 1919, 1923, 1940 and translated by Hasan Aziz) (6), *Ghalib ka Roznamcha*, (7) *Dehli ki Jaankani*,(8) *Dehli ki Akhri Sans* (*Bahadur Shah Zafar ka Roznamcha November 1844- March 1848* (first published in 1925, reprint in 1935) (9), *Ghadar ki Subah-O-Sham*, (reprint 1926) (10), *Dehli ka Yadgar Mushaira* (*Dehli ki Akhri Shama*) (11) *Dehli ki Saza*, (*Ghadar ka Nateeja* first published in 1930) (12), *Dehli ke Resident ki Diary* (*Sar Thamas Metkaf ki daeri*) (13). The original trail of Bahadur Shah Zafar available in English translated into Urdu and incorporated into the three separate parts, titled *Bahadur Shah Ka muqaddama*, *Ghadar ke Farman*, and *Delhi ke Dastawez*, this last account is related to the Delhi Mutiny papers.

   Likewise Persian newspapers and texts are also translated. Nizami discussed this series in his twelve book's publication, see Nizami, Khawaja Hasan *Ghadar Delhi ke afsano ka Barwah hissa, Ghadar ka Nateeja, Ghadar ke zamane ki ek farsi kitab ka tarjuma,* Barqui Press, Delhi, 1930, Apart from it, Nizami also translated the Persian account on Delhi, titled '*Nawab Dargha Quli Khan Bahadur ki Farsi Kitab ka tarjuma*, in 1933, reprinted, 1949; and *Purani Dehli ke Halaat*, Barqui Press, Delhi, 1949.

8. Ali Jawwad Zaidi, *A History of Urdu Literature,* Sahitya Akademi, Delhi, 1993, p. 262.

9. In fact the histories of Urdu Literature and other works in Urdu take very little notice on his voluminous writings on 1857. These writings are simply

dismissed in only few sentences. These are seldom examined for its content but only for the style and diction. See Muhammad Saddiq, *History of Urdu Literature*, Delhi, OUP, 1984; see also Imam Murtaza Naqvi, *Khwaja Hasan Nizami: Hayat aur Adabi Khidmat*, Lucknow 1987.

It is only by way of exception that William Dalrymple, *The Last Mughal: The fall of a Dynasty, Delhi, 1857,* Delhi 2006 has made use of some of his writings in the chapters describing the massacre and the reign of terror unleashed by the British in the city of Delhi.

10. He had quite approvingly quoted the verses composed by Mufti Sadruddin Khan Azurda, putting all the onus for the destruction and the havoc brought on the city of Delhi to the bad deeds of the king and also the arrival of black (sepoys) from Meerut had disastrous consequences, while few verses from poet Dagh are also cited comparing the arrival of *purbias* as the wrath of God on the city!
11. See Appendices.
12. Mohammad Ikram Chaghtai, *1857: Majmua Khwaja Hasan Nizami,* Sang-e Meel Publications, Lahore, 2007, this volume includes a two short pieces by Rashidul Khairi namely, *Ghadar ki mari Shahzadiyan* and *Dilli ki Akhiri Bahar,* pp. 829-880; while its Indian reprint is titled as, *1857: Shamsul Ulema Hazrat Khwaja Hasan Nizami ki barah Qadeem Yadgar Kitabein,* reprnt by Khwaja Hasan Sani Nizami, Delhi, 2008, this reprint has excluded the appendices of Rashidul Khairi and has included a short moving piece by Khwaja Hasan Sani Nizami on Mirza Sohrab Shah Mijji, pp. 829-834.

Appendix - A

Dehli ki Jankani: The Horrors of Delhi during the Uprising[1]

— ***Dr. Shaheen Islamuddin***
Bhagini Nivedita College,
University Delhi

Dehli ki Jaankani, is not a translation of any work but the author has used authentic reports from the surviving data and memory of the people. It is important to examine this text and to see how far the memory of the destruction has survived in almost 60 years after the event and also the manner in which the days of horror were recalled.

Dehli ki Jankani presents the various forms of the British violence during 1857 in detail and explains its different layers on the basis of the written and the oral sources. Regarding the oral sources, writer says that there are more oral sources available and accessible (to him) than literary ones, as he had been much interested, since his childhood days, in meetings, listening and knowing the conditions of those people who had witnessed the rebellion of 1857.[2] Thus, Khwaja Hasan Nizami was the first modern recorder who freely uses oral sources and offers the different meanings that people had given to it. One third part of the account is devoted to highlight the impact of the revolt on the city and the Mughal household. Thus, *Dehli ki Jankani* (Agony of Delhi) can be considered as an impact oriented text. The title was chosen by the author as he tried to explain most of the episodes related to the execution, death, escape, loot, torture and humiliation experienced by the Mughal Emperor, Bahadur Shah Zafar, royal members of imperial household and the inhabitants of the city, on the basis of the popular perceptions. The text is divided into sub headings and every sub heading carries interesting description of the revolt. Writer seems very sympathetic towards the last Mughal Emperor and the rebels. He becomes emotional when he describes the position of Bahadur Shah Zafar, whose legitimate status was obliterated by the British by holding a mock trial.

Khwaja Hasan Nizami was writing when the feeling of anti-British sentiments was in the air and spreading fast. The unity between the Hindus and the Muslims had been displayed in the form of Lucknow pact of 1916, non-corporation and the *Khilafat* movements against the

British's exploitative policies. Mahatma Gandhi as a leader of the common man had taken stand and was ready to make his movement into a mass movement.[2] Whereas, Mohammad Ali and Shaukat Ali, the two '*khilafat*' brothers were actively preaching against the British and inviting Muslim to join the front in Delhi. Revolutionaries' activities were on the rise. Nizami saw this period as the beginning of another revolt which could once again be brutally suppressed by colonial Raj. Therefore, he was in support of maintaining peace and writes that any *ghadar* could be very harmful to both the innocent and the participators. Therefore, he states:

> The main reason of writing this book is to make the nation aware of the affects of the revolt on the capital of Hindustan. It is also to show that what misery and horror caused by the war and disturbances. This book will awaken the present day youth to the possible consequences of their war like intentions. It will also make the youth aware that it is quite dangerous to carry out sedition against the present day British Government as the last time efforts of the Hindustan could not manage to get rid of the British ruler.[3]

He accepts British as an unsurpassable power against whom any action could prove to be more dangerous and hazardous. He tries hard to convince his readers to understand the repercussion of the revolt which was still alive in the minds of the people and prevented them from speaking against the present government.[4] In doing this, he gives sufficient space to the Indian (Delhi) vision of the uprising. In other words, his aim can be examined further by applying the theory of William Cronon.[5] According to William Cronon, people work in multiple ways; on one side, they work with the system but simultaneously raise their demands in the opposition of the very same system, both aspects operate together. The same can be said of Khwaja Hasan Nizami, who was doing the same thing in this context. He offered his support to the colonial government by giving warning to the young generation of Indians not indulging in any revolutionary activities but at the same time describing the various atrocities committed by the British on Indians. He clearly blames the British for the outbreak of the revolt and considered them responsible for the mass massacre, devastation and the loot that took place in Delhi during aftermath of the revolt. He writes that the intense and bloody terror that was unleashed was because of sleeping of Simon Fraser's delay and *Goura* soldiers of Meerut who did not care enough to follow the armed force (rebels) at a time.[6]

Nizami highlights the popular version of the event which is interesting for us to note. He claims that in the surrounding areas of Delhi, the tale of the laziness of Simon Frazer is still popular. He remarks that in Delhi it was commonly accepted that his sleep configured the fire of the mutiny.[7] He further mentions that it was also popular during the revolt that Simon Fraser had drunk more and therefore was not able to read the letter which had come to him on the night of 10th May from Meerut, warning him about the upcoming danger. He also cites the statement from the account of Munshi Zakaullah's *Tarikh-e Hindustan* and then compared and rationalized the matter by saying that this story cannot be considered entirely wrong. British must have been interested in hiding the reality as they did not want to show their mistake and may have wanted the dead person (Simon Fraser) relieved from any charge of fanning the revolt. Otherwise, this incident may not have been much popular among the Indians as there was no necessity to popularize the wrong statements by them.[8]

The texts also reveal that some British personalities were extremely notorious in the popular imagination because of their cruelty, during the aftermath of the revolt, in executing and murdering the Royal members and the city's residents. In that category, Simon Frazer, Metcalfe and William Hudson were counted among the top. Their deeds had turned them into 'careless' and 'cruelest' creatures. Major Hudson was the head of the Intelligent Department during the revolt and arrested the Mughal Emperor, Bahadur Shah Zafar on 22nd September 1857. On the very next day, he apprehended and brutally killed the Mughal princes named Mirza Mughal, Mirza Khizr Sutan, and Mirza Abu Bakr. These actions of Hudson not only gave him a certain place in the colonial official and non- official records but also in the popular imagination. Nizami states that there are two versions of the murder of Bahadur Shah Zafar's sons; one has already been explained by Munshi Zakaullah Sahib, while the other is also very much popular among the local people. Later version was told to Nizami's father by one of the relative of Mirza Ilahi Bukhsh and others: That story is that Hudson not only murdered the princes but also sipped their blood. He considered that it necessary and thought that if he did not do that he will turn mad because they (the princes) were responsible for killing the people (especially women and children) of the British community.[9]

The British anger was presented through a variety of violence perpetuated. One such incident often highlighted was such a famous incident of *Kucha Chelan* where many people were put to death without any reason. *Kucha Chelan* was one of the famous mohallas located in Darya Ganj where several prominent personalities had been living before 1857.[10] In this regard, Nizami provides detailed description of the event.[11] During the searches of the houses by the army, the son of Shamsheer Jung Khan, resident of that area prevented an English officer from entering the female compartment of his house. This innocuous defensive step taken by a man caused so much anger to the whole British army that an order was issued to arrest all the living people (especially males) of the locality and shoot them on the banks of the river Yamuna. Among them, according to the writer, only two people could escape by chance, named Mirza Mustfa Beig and Waziruddeen Beig, the son in- law of Maulana Sahbai. Nizami tells us further that, twenty one members of the family of Maulana Imam Bakhsh Sahbai were murdered in that incident and this give us an estimate of the large numbers of people killed.[12]

Similarly, the description of the loot given by Nizami is very informative. The colonial archival records provide some information on this 'legalized loot' the details related to its sale, ways of searching, use of *havellies* for storing the collected 'prize' in the forms of books, vessels, beds (*charpoyes*), doors, and windows is available in this account. As he explains,

> All these material (looted material) were stored in various *godam*. Haveli of Mansur Ali khan was secured for keeping the aluminum vessels, while books were deposited to the *haveli* of Professor Ram Chandra. Digging took place to such an extent that hidden *asharfiyan* [gold coins] of the old age fallen into the hands of British. It has been said that sixty thousands rupees container was found from the house of Nawab Muhammad Mir Khan whose family members were unaware of this hidden wealth.[13]

Besides this, the period of suppression of 1857 was also a period of 'denouncement' and 'betrayal' where innocent people were hanged and shot dead without any investigation or on the basis of the wrong testimonies. In this context, he narrates a story of a prince Amir-ul Mulk alias Mirza Balaqui who was alive and living at Chandni Mahal. Mirza Balaqui told him the notoriety of one Gami Khan, a spy of the British from whom, the mother of Mirza Bulaqi had saved him by sending him out of the city and going to the suburb. Thus, false witnesses, testimonies and espionage were a matter of the daily occurrences through which one could target the innocent easily.[14] In the same vein, Nizami also highlights the precarious conditions of the women by giving the description of the events of women jumping into the well to save their chastity. He writes the story of two ladies, one younger and the other aged. He starts the story by saying that 'two ladies were brought out from the well of the Farash Khana. One was young but blind and second was old. The statement of the old lady revealed that she had the only son, who was murdered by the British at home. After that *sepoys* were willing to attack on the young girl. As she knew the well of her house, she immediately jumped and following her, the old woman also did the same. They were floating inside the well when someone pulled them out.' Further, he mentioned that situation had worsened to such an extent that the people were killing their daughters and wives to save them falling into the hands of the British sepoys.[15]

The text shows the ways of memorizing the past by people and opens the layers of the local level realities which are usually missing in the colonial sources. As we know the local memories of a past and the event is very different than the dominant narrative. The past is presented by a process of selection and forgetting. The issues pertinent to local level realities can be seen in this text too. The author throws light on the common people's saying and reveals the ways of experiencing and presenting the same event. This popular version of the revolt makes the text even more useful for historians. If we compare this account to other primary sources of 1857, then we are able to consider its exceptionality not only in discussing the depressed condition of that time, but also by quoting 'the eyewitness statements and oral sources from whom the writer has met and listen. 1857 revolt was brutally crushed by the victorious British, who showed their anger with great ferocity. During that period, slaughter was common and the air of suspicion was rife. Although Delhi had faced obliteration before,[16] but this devastation was incomparable. Behind all this, the British wanted to establish their control on India with an element of terror. Therefore, the long silence on the British atrocities and repression was broken by the author. In short, it can be said that his account traces the history of 1857 with diverse outlooks. People remembered the event as a traumatic event in their life and by using their statement, author points out each aspect of the English fury. In other words, he shows their experiences, lamentation, sorrows and painful condition and breaks the silence which had been imposed on them.

Notes

1. Abridged from Shaheen Islamuddin, 'Upheavel in the Social Life of Delhi During and After 1857 with special Reference to *Dihli ki Jaankani* text of Khwaja Hasan Nizami', in *Pluralities of Past: Upper Gangetic Valley through the Millenium*, ed S.Z.H. Jafri and N.R.Farooqui, Proceeding of UP History Congress, 2012, Anamika, pp. 267-77
2. M. Akram Chaghatai, *1857, Majmua-e-Khwaja Hasan Nizami*, Sang-e-Meel publication, Lahore, 2007, pp. 481, In written sources, he relied mostly on English sources and the Shams-ul Ulema Munshi Zaka ullah's *Tarikh-e-Hindustan*.
3. Farooqui, Mahmood, *Besieged: Voices from Delhi 1857,* Penguin Viking, 2010, introduction.
4. Writing in his other book, he remembers that how the people were griped with that terror (terror of 1857) that they constantly intimidating me not to write such a history otherwise (I) would have to face execution. M. Akram Chaghatai, *1857Majmua-e-Khwaja Hasan Nizami*, Sang-e-Meel publication, Lahore, 2007, p. 138.
5. William Cronon, *Changes in the Land: Indians, Colonists and Ecology of New England*, Hill and Wan, New York, 2000.
6. M. Akram Chaghatai ,*1857:Majmua-e Mazamin –e Khwaja Hasan Nizami*, op. cit., p. 493.
7. *Ibid. Dehli ki Jaankani*, p. 492.
8. *Ibid.,* p. 492.
9. *Ibid,* p. 508.
10. The Families of Shah Waliullah, Shah Abdul Aziz, Sir Saiyid Ahmad Khan, Maulana Sahbai and Mir Mohammad Amir urf Mir Punjakash had been staying there before the revolt. Nizami further praises Maulana Sahbai and Mir Punjakash, and describes them as 'moon and sun' of India who were killed in that general massacre. Maulana Sahbai was one of the most popular

and well known Persian language masters and Mir Punja kash was famous for his calligraphic skills in all over India. see for Maulvi Sahbai, Maulvi Abdul Haq, *Marhum Delhi College*, Anjum-e-Traqqui Urdu (Hind), Delhi, 1989, pp. 162-63; Pernau, Margrit., *The Delhi College: Traditional Elites, the Colonial State and Education before 1857,* OUP, 2006.

11. *Ibid;* p. 513-14.
12. Rashid-ul Khairi's account is differed on the detail on those people who had escaped. Rashid-ul- Khairi says that people who could escape from the incident of Kucha Chelan was only Qadir Ali, the nephew of Sahabai, whose was a good swimmer and because of this ability, he could save his life. Story about this event is told by Qadir Ali himself to Rashid. Zahir Dehlavi also discussed this event in his memoir called *Dastan-e Ghadar.*
13. *Dehli ki Jaankani*, p. 523.
14. *Begmat ke Ansu*, pp. 76-82.
15. *Dehli ki Jaankani*, pp. 512-513.
16. Delhi's destruction can be seen in the constant attack of Nadir Shah (1738-39) and Ahmad Shah Durrani. For *Takht-e- Taoos*, see NAI, Foreign Department, Branch (Political), Cons 15/April/1859, Nos-121-124.(there is a detail about *Takht-e-Taoos* or Peacock Throne, which were carried out by the Nadir Shah in his country, after conquering Delhi)

Appendix - B

Some Stories from *Begumat ke Aansoo*[1]

— *Ms. Rana Safvi*
Historian and Journalist
New Delhi

After the fall of Delhi on 14th September 1857, the British gained control over the city of Shahjahanabad. They captured and imprisoned the emperor, killed many of his sons and grandsons and the notables of the walled city. Many of the royal residents of the fort escaped to live their in utter penury and incognito. After a travesty of a trial by the British in 1858, Bahadur Shah Zafar was exiled to Rangoon. We often commemorate the heroes of the 1857 Uprising but rarely give a thought to those who survived to live a life worse than death. The major description of the plight of the innocent Mughal prince and princesses is found in Khwaja Hasan Nizami's *Begumat ke Aansoo* where he documents eyewitness records of the survivors he finds in Delhi. Zahir Dehalvi's *Dastan-e-Ghadar*, Mirza Ahmad Akhtar's *Sawaneh Dehli*, Syed Wazir Hasan Dehlvi's *Dilli ka Aakhiri Deedar* and *Fughan-e-Dehli* or the dirges written by many Urdu poets on the condition of royals left in Delhi are some other accounts. *Begumat ke Aansoo* was first published in 1922. I have translated these stories with the permission of Syed Mohammad Nizami, the heir of Khwaja Hasan Nizami from a collected volume of his writings on 1857 titled*1857 Shams-ul Auliya Hazrat Khwaja Hasan Nizami ki Barah Qadeem yaadgar Kitabein (New edition)*.

(a) From 'Royalty' to 'Beggary'

Had Bahadur Shah not got involved in the *ghadar* [mutiny] he would have lived in great comfort and ease as a *derwesh* [mendicant]. However, he got caught in the trap of the rebel forces and spent the last days of his life in great trouble. My mother had heard from her father Hazrat Khwaja Shah Ghulam Hasan that the day Bahadur Shah left the Qila [Red Fort] of Delhi he came straight to the *dargah* of Mehboob e Ilahi [Hazrat Nizamuddin Auliya]. At that time he was in a state of great despondency and despair. Only a few *khwajasara* [eunuchs] and the porters of his *hawadar* [sedan chair] were with him. His face was lined with worries and he was covered in dust and his white beard was matted with dirt. As soon as my father heard that the Emperor had come to the *dargah* my father presented himself before him. He found the emperor leaning against the head of the *mazaar* [shrine]. As soon as he saw my father he gave a faint smile. My father said that I sat in front of him and started asking him about his welfare. He replied with great simplicity, "I had already told you that these accursed rebel soldiers are headstrong and trusting them was a mistake. They will go down themselves and take me with them. Finally this is what transpired. They have run away. Though I am a mendicant in seclusion (*gosha nasheen faqeer*) I am also a descendant of the Timurid race, which has the instinct and courage to go down fighting. My ancestors went through tougher times and never gave up hope. But my end has already been revealed to me. There is no doubt that I am the last Timurid to sit on the throne of Hind. The lamp of the Mughal dynasty is about to be snuffed out. It's just a guest of a few more hours. Why then should I indulge in unnecessary bloodshed? That's why I left the Qila myself. The country is God's and he can bestow it on whomsoever He pleases. For hundreds of years we have ruled Hindustan through force and fear. Now it is the turn of others to rule. We will be the ruled and they the rulers. This is not a reason to mourn for after all we also removed someone from the throne and destroyed their dynasty to establish ours."

After this the Badshah gave me a box and said he was entrusting it to me, "When Amir Timur had conquered Constantinople he had acquired this from the treasure of Sultan Yaldram Bayazid. It has five hairs from the blessed beard of our beloved Prophet (Pbuh). This has been passed on in our family as special *tabarruk* [blessings]. Now there is no place in this whole wide world for me and I don't know where I can take them. I am giving it into your trust as you are the most worthy person to take care of them. They have provided so much solace to my heart over the years. Today in the most calamitous day of my life I part from it." My nana took the box and put it in the *toshekhana* [treasury] of the *dargah* and they are still present there till today. On every 12 *Rabi-awwal* people are given a *ziarat* [sight] of it. The Badshah told my Nana *Saheb*, "I have not had time to eat the last three meals. If there is some food ready in the house please bring it."

My nana sahib said, "We are also standing on the edge of death and no one has had any time or peace to cook, I will bring whatever I can for you from my house. In fact why don't you grace my humble home with your blessed presence? As long as my children and I are alive no one can touch you. We will die before anyone can harm you."

The Badshah said, "This is your kindness to say it but I will not jeopardize the lives of my Peer's children to defend this old body. I have done the *ziarat* of *mehboob e Ilahi*, I have entrusted my sacred trust to you, now if I can eat a few morsels I will go to Humayun's *maqbara*. Destiny will fulfill what is written in my fate." Nana Saheb came home and asked if there was something available to eat and was told that there was only some *besan ki roti* and *sirke ki chutney* [gram bread and vinegar chutney]. This he brought that on a covered tray and presented it to the Badshah. The Badshah ate it and thanked God for his mercy. After that he left for Humayun's *maqbara* and was arrested there. He was later exiled to Rangoon. In Rangoon the Badshah continued his spiritual pursuits. As long as he lived, he lived like a forbearing and pious *derwesh*. This is a tale from which one should take as a warning.[2]

(b) The Princes are dragged in the *bazaar*[3]

When this Delhi, which is the heart of India and its capital, was flourishing and the flame of the Mughals was flickering and it was on the precipice of destruction, the first change was seen in the lifestyle of its people. First the rulers went and then the subjects both were destroyed. A year before the mutiny, a few princes had gone for *shikar* into the jungle and were killing doves and small birds, which were resting in the branches of the trees from the hot summer sun. A *faqeer* dressed in rags came out and with great respect presented his *salam* to the princes and said, "*Miyan Sahib zado'n* why are you tormenting these innocent birds? What wrong have they done to you? They are also living creatures. They too can feel pain like you but are helpless to express it. Show them mercy for they too are part of this country and deserving of royal clemency."

The eldest prince who was 18 years old was embarrassed and he kept his slingshot away. The younger one Mirza Nasir-ul Mulk got very angry and said contemptuously, "Go away, you! A worthless man like you wants to preach to us? Who are you to tell us what to do? Everyone hunts and we are also not committing a sin." The *faqeer* said with humility, "*Sahib e Alam* don't get angry. We must only hunt in a manner that even if one animal is killed a few others can feed people from it. What can you achieve by killing these tiny birds? Even if you kill 20 of them a single man won't be full." Nasir Mirza was enraged and aiming his slingshot at the *faqeer's* leg let fly a stone at his knee. The *faqeer* fell face forward and cried out, "Oh! You have broken my leg." The princes both mounted their horses and left for the *Qila*. The *faqeer* dragged him to a nearby cemetery and kept repeating, "How can a dynasty flourish, whose heirs are so merciless! Young Prince you have broken my leg, May God break your leg too and force you to drag yourself like me."

The sound of cannons and gunshots had filled Shahjahanabad and there heaps of corpses lying everywhere. Delhi was being deserted. A few Mughal Princes were seen running in a disheveled and bewildered state from the *Lal Qila*. They were riding towards Paharganj. There were being chased by some 25 British soldiers on horseback. They let lose a volley of gunshots on these princes. Very soon the horses and prince were writhing in pain on the ground. When the British soldiers came close they saw that two princes were dead. But one was still breathing. One of the soldiers pulled him up and found that he was unhurt except a few scratches from falling off the horse. He was frightened out of his wits by the turn of events.

The soldiers tied his hands with the reins of his horse and were sent in captivity to the camp with 2 soldiers. The camp was on the ridge where there were Indian soldiers who were supporting the British. When the Senior Officer was told that this is the grandson of the Emperor, Nasir-ul Mulk he was very happy and asked him to be kept in safe captivity. When the rebel sepoys started running away in disarray and the British army entered the city in triumph, Bahadur Shah was arrested from Humayun's tomb and the lamp of the Timurid dynasty was snuffed out, the jungles started flourishing with the disheveled and uncovered hair and faces of the Mughal princesses, and fathers were slaughtered in front of the eyes of their children, mothers saw their sons being writhing in the throes of death in the dust.

Mirza Nasir-ul Mulk was tied in ropes and sitting on the ridge when a Pathan soldier came to him quietly and said, "Run away quickly, I have taken permission from Saheb to release you. Go before they catch you again." The poor Mirza had never walked on foot and was at a loss what to do. However, the survival instinct was strong and thanking the Pathan he set off. He walked aimlessly for a mile; his feet were badly blistered; his throat was parched; tongue swollen. When he was unable to bear it anymore he fell down under the shade of a tree and looked imploringly towards the sky, "O Lord, why has this calamity struck us? What should I do? Where can I go?"

When he looked up he saw a young dove on the tree sitting on her eggs in her nest. Seeing her ease and freedom the prince said enviously, "O Dove, you are thousand times better than me that at least you sit without a care in your nest. There is no place for me in this whole wide world." He spied a habitation at a distance and gritting his teeth he decided to go there. The blisters on his feet were bleeding but somehow he managed to reach it. There he was met with a strange spectacle. Hundred of villagers were surrounding a platform on which a 13-year-old girl was sitting in a state of complete shock. Her ears were bleeding in the places from where her earrings had been pulled out and the villagers were laughing at her. As soon as Mirza and the girl saw each other they started screaming in shock. She was his sister. They both embraced each other and wept copiously.

She had left the *Qila* with her mother, in a bullock cart for Mehrauli to Qutub Saheb's *dargah*. Mirza had no idea that she was caught in this situation. He asked her, "Malika how are you here?" She replied, "Aka ji, the *gujars* looted us and killed the servants. People from another village forcibly took Ammajan [paternal uncle] to their village and these people brought me here. They snatched my ear rings and kept slapping my face." She was crying so copiously by now that she couldn't speak further. The Mirza consoled his sister and started pleading with the villagers to let her go. The *gujars* said with contempt, "Go away you are a fine one to talk like this. If we hit you even once your neck will be separated from your body. We have bought her from those villagers. Now you can buy her from us." Mirza replied, "Chaudhry I am not in other position except to beg for food from you. Please have mercy on us. Till yesterday we were your rulers and you were our subjects. Please don't torture us. We are going through a bad time. If we come back to power we will reward you handsomely." The villagers laughed loudly, "Oho you are the Emperor! Now we will sell you to the *firangi* [foreigners] and this girl will now serve our village: she will sweep it, look after the cattle and clean up after them." They were talking when the British forces came and surrounded the villagers. They captured the *gujar* chief and the young prince and princess. In the *bazar* of Chandni Chowk gallows had been erected. Whoever the British pronounced as guilty was hanged. Every day thousands were hanged. Some were shot and others had their heads struck off by swords. Mirza Nasir-ul Mulk and his sister were presented before the Bade sahib. Bade sahib pronounced them innocent and let them go. These two took employment with a trader. The princess looked after his children and Nasir ul Mulk did the outside work including buying provisions. A few days later the princess died of cholera that was raging in the city. Mirza took up employment in various houses. Finally the British government fixed a pension of Rs 5/ pm for all the Mughal princes and he could now afford to leave employment.

After a few years later a *peer baba* [saint], who looked as if he was from the Timurid-Chengezi lineage used to drag himself around Chitli Qabr and Kamra Bangash area. His legs had been struck by paralysis. He had a bag tied around his neck and he would look at passersby mutely to ask for help. Those who knew who he was would throw in a few coins in his bag. Someone asked who he was and was told that his name is Mirza Nasir ul Mulk and he is the grandson of Bahadur Shah. He had wasted his pension and taken heavy loans against it. Now begging was his only means of living. Khawaja Hasan Mirza had heard this tale from him and some other princes. The *faqeer's* curse had come true.

Notes

1. The appendices are based on a selection of the stories translated by Ms. Rana Safvi (the stories under publication)
2. *1857 Shams-ul Auliya Hazrat Khwaja Hasan Nizami ki Barah Qadeem yaadgar Kitabein*,2008, Khwaja Hasan Nizami, p. 15.
3. In Ahmed Ali's *Twilight in Delhi* there is a description of the Delhi Darbar held in 1911 to celebrate the coronation of King George V a few months earlier. The British Emperor and his wife Queen Mary left the Red Fort, as the *Qila-e-Mubarak*, was called by the British in a state procession. Almost every prince and ruler and notable attended it and presented tribute to King

George V. In the background as this princely convoy is moving a beggar known as Bahadur Shah is dragging himself on useless legs, begging on the streets of Shahjahanabad. I found this story in *Begumat ke Aansoo* and have included it. *1857 Shams-ul Auliya Hazrat Khwaja Hasan Nizami ki Barah Qadeem yaadgar Kitabein,* 2008, Khwaja Hasan Nizami, p. 16.

REVIEW ARTICLE

Recovering the Biography of Bahadur Shah Zafar: An Evaluation of *The Life and Poetry of Bahadur Shah Zafar* by *Aslam Pervez*

— ***Dr. Sana Aziz***
Centre of Advanced Study,
Dept. of History Aligarh Muslim University

Bahadur Shah Zafar, the last Mughal ruler in India, has been the subject of interest for historians, litterateurs and poets alike, both for the versatility of his personality and the complexity of the times he lived and ruled in. A scholar of Persian, a poet of Urdu, an excellent calligrapher and a passionate patron of literature and arts, he ascended the throne in 1837 when he was already at the dusk of his age. His character is treated with diverse approaches from scholars, foiled from love and respect to sympathy and contempt. While historians have critically analyzed his political potence/ impotence, the litterateurs have focused more on the poetry composed by him. His verses become the synecdoche of the times when Urdu poetry reached its zenith with poets like Ghalib (d.1869), Zauq (d. 1854), and Momin (d.1851) adorning his court.

Percival Spear while describing the character of the last Mughal Emperor regards him as the philosopher prince who could have adorned any court and opined that Delhi during his time was a Weimer with Ghalib as its Goethe.[1] Delhi during his time is known to be resonating the past glory of the Mughals that persisted during the zenith of the Mughal Empire from Akbar to Shahjahan's times as far as literature and poetry were concerned. In Urdu historiography/ literature metaphors such as *Delhi ki Akhri Shama* and *Delhi ka Akhri Deedar* etc. began to be associated with his times as it was believed that times like those would never return and was the last phase of the efflorescence of the

Urdu poetry in Delhi. His existence as the Mughal Emperor and his court were important catalysts for blooming of the social and intellectual life of Shahjahanabad before the outbreak of the revolt of 1857.

Despite the fact that the king adored Urdu language and patronized it passionately in his court, we do not find any authentic biography of the King in Urdu till 1986 when the book under review came out. One does find an intellectual apathy towards the last king of the Mughals from the Urdu litterateurs. As far as historians are concerned, the revolt of 1857 has over shadowed the very existence of Bahadur Shah Zafar. The revolt broke out when he was eighty-two years old and became the decisive event that marked the end of his reign. This revolt not only characterized and overshadowed his rule but also invoked varied reactions from historians for his role in the revolt with Syed Mahdi Husain calling him a 'patriot', 'hero' and 'martyr' in the cause of India's liberation' during the course of this revolt.[2] In response to this R.C. Majumdar wrote a rejoinder labeling Bahadur Shah as a 'traitor' for siding with the British in the revolt.[3] According to him 'Bahadur Shah's title of the Emperor of Hindustan was a mere 'hollow and mockery'. Even the recent works like William Dalrymple's *The Last Mughal Emperor* has focused on the revolt of 1857 while discussing the last Mughal Emperor only in the context of the revolt.[4] A number of critics including the travelers and soldiers who witnessed Delhi during the revolt have accused him of joining the rebels and leading the mutiny. Most of these critical accusations are marked by their racial prejudices and xenophobic sensibilities towards the last Mughal ruler. For a poet king that he was, he should be judged by his own words and the evidence of his life rather than believing the harsh accounts written about the king in the backdrop of the war of 1857.

The book, *Life and Poetry of Bahadur Shah Zafar* originally written by Aslam Parvez in Urdu and now translated into English by Ather Farouqui attempts to cover the life of Bahadur Shah Zafar and his experiences- political, social, personal and literary. Though a Ph.D. thesis in the discipline of Urdu, completed in 1964-65 and finally coming out as a book twenty years later in 1986, it does try to make some historical inquiries into his life and times. The book is divided into three parts; the first part tracing the political trajectory of the late

Mughal rulers, from Shah Alam II to Bahadur Shah Zafar. The second part focuses on Bahadur Shah's encounters with the British and his literary engagements while in the third part, the author, very briefly, discusses the verses composed by the Emperor himself. While narrating the brief history of the later Mughals, Pervez stresses more on Shah Alam II as it was during his reign that Delhi finally succumbed to the British indirect rule in 1803 A.D. Moreover, Bahadur Shah spent most of his time with him and also learned the nuances of poetry from him as he had an expertise in *Braj Bhasha*, Punjabi, Persian, Arabic, Sanskrit, and Turkic (P. 20) and also wrote poetry with the *takhallus* 'Aftab'. Though for discussing him, the author has solely relied on the secondary sources such as Percival Spear's *Twilight of the Mughals* and Maulavi Zaka Ullah's *Tarikh-e Urooj-e Sultanat-e Inglishia*. The author tries to weave together in the first part, in as much brevity as possible, the political events of Delhi from 1803 A.D., the accession of Bahadur Shah Zafar, the political developments- internal tussle for succession and the British interference- that led to his accession, and the role of the imperial women in the court politics along with the still popular courtly culture and ethics.

In this backdrop, it becomes important for us to assess author's engagement with the primary sources of this period. The author has attempted to derive information from the *Mutiny Papers* and contemporary Urdu and Persian newspapers preserved in National Archives of India in order to depict the popular perceptions and sentiments emerging about the Emperor and his role in the revolt. But only selected issues of *Delhi Urdu Akhbar*, *Siraj-ul-Akhbar*, *Khulasa-e Akhbar*, *Akhbar-e Delhi*, *Aina-e Sikandari* and *Jam-e Jahan Numa* have been used. For citing references from *Ahsan-ul Akhbar*, the author has completely relied on secondary work such as Hasan Nizami's *Bahadur Shah Zafar ka Muqaddama*. His discussion could have become more comprehensive if Atiq Siddiqui's *1857 ke Akhbarat aur Dastawez* (1966), which extensively uses the Mutiny papers at the National Archives of India, including the contemporary newspapers, magazines, and other relevant material of 1857 and Syed Athar Abbas Rizvi's *Swatantra Delhi,* (1957), covering the period of four months of the revolt at Delhi and additional archival material regarding Bahadur Shah Zafar, preserved in Delhi Department of Archives were also consulted. In the introduction of the translated version of the book (P.13), its translator, Ather Farouqui claims that this book is also based- along with the archival sources- on the literary sources of Urdu and Persian, which have been largely ignored by historians. However, ignoring the most authentic work, *Bahadur Shah Zafar and the War of 1857 in Delhi* (1956) by Agha Syed Mahdi Husain, (who makes the best use of archival as well as Urdu and Persian literary sources) both, the author as well as the translator overlook historians' efforts in doing research using literary sources.

At several occasions throughout the book, Pervez is critical of the ways the emperor led his personal life and managed his finances. For instance, he equates his love for women or him marrying in old age with debauchery (P. 46). He also holds Zafar guilty of being greedy and 'scheming all the time about how to raise loans' (P. 39). This might be factually true considering his sinking political situation, but 'greed' would still be an appropriate gesture to use for his helplessness. His indifference towards Bahadur Shah's fate during and after his trial is also depicted by the way he accuses the Emperor of cowardice for having a 'lust for life at the age of 80' and hence choosing to live the life of a prisoner than dying like a rebel (P. 89). At another instance, (P. 93) the author asserts, and quite repeatedly, that while the emperor was being taken away to Rangoon, the British authorities were compassionate towards him and fully took care of him.

According to him, the British were not as callous as they had been painted by writers and historians. He completely debunks the narrative put forward by various historians that Bahadur Shah Zafar and his family were kept in pathetic conditions during his exile. Contradistinctively, the measure of their callousness can be verified by the way Zafar was deprived of pen and paper in his exile, forcing him to often scribble his verses with charcoal on the walls of his cell. But what can be more callous than the way the three princes- Mirza Mughal, Mirza Khizar Sultan and Mirza Abu Bakr- were shot point blank with their clothes removed right at the entrance of the city at Delhi Gate.

This also attempts to nullify or neutralise the overall 'white terror' unleashed on innocent Indians in retaliation to the atrocities committed on the English people by the rebels. Although it is believed that the English exaggerated the magnitude of the violence committed on them and in return began a reckless pogrom upon the Indian people. Kaye, in his *History of the Sepoy War* records his dilemma:

> An Englishman is almost suffocated when he reads that Mrs Chambers or Miss Jennings was hacked to death by a dusky ruffian; but in Native historians, or, history being wanting, in Native legends and traditions, it may be recorded against our people, that mothers and wives and children, with less familiar names, fell miserable victims to the first swoop of English vengeance; and these stories may have as deep a pathos that rend our own hearts.[5]

An author writing about the fall of the last Mughal Emperor should be contextualizing the fate of the Emperor with the persecution and violence that was unleashed on the Indians in the aftermath of the revolt. Ignoring such instances and making sweeping generalisations would not only be a historical but also a literary blooper.

The book, however, celebrates the poetic genius of Zafar under whose reign the *Qila-e Muálla* became the hub of poetry. It was during these times that the strictures of Delhi school of poetry were taking their form and when Zafar's own literary consciousness was shaping up. The poetic endeavours that flourished in the *Qila-e Muálla* under his patronage, no doubt, gave Delhi school of poetry new heights across the literal continuum of India at that time. His own verses in Urdu come down to us in the form of four *diwans* that he compiled, the first one being published in A.D. 1845. Though the author lists his complete works, one followed by the other, but doesn't write any exposition on their contents or the major themes of his *diwans*. Rather he focuses on the publication details of each of his *diwans* that were published in his lifetime and also after his death.

In sixteenth chapter, titled *Zafar and Zauq,* the author while highlighting the intense bond between Zafar and Zauq, also nullifies the charges that Muhammad Husain Azad in his *Ab-e Hayat* levels against Zafar that his *diwans* were written none other than by Zauq. By citing numerous evidences, he establishes the individuality of Zafar's writing style and differentiates it from Zauq in order to puncture this 'ghost writing' theory of Azad that was much propounded later by

Aloys Sprenger and C.F. Andrews. However, it should be pointed that this argument had already been earlier made by Khalil-ur-Rehman Azmi in his *Nawa-e Zafar* (1958)[6], which the author has also used for this book. The most striking absence with respect to Zafar's poetry in the book is his verses that were composed during his exile in Rangoon. For instance, *Gai Yak –ba Yak* that had become so popular that it was already being sung by 'the minstrels of India', according to a report of the Political Agent of Bhopal, dated 14 June 1862 is missing from the book.[7]The last quatrain of this composition fully explains the pain of the last Mughal Emperor and his existence as a tragic figure during his exile in Rangoon. The lines are worth quoting here:

Main Wo Kushta Hun ki Jiski Laash par ae Dosto,
Ek Zamana Deeda-e Hasrat se Takta Jayga;
Ae Zafar, Qayam Rahegi Jab Talak Iqleem-e Hind,
Akhtar-e Iqbal is Gul ka Chamakta Jayga.

English Translation:

'Friends, I am that slaughtered man, at whose corps,
A whole world will continue to look with grief and envy,
O Zafar, so long as the country of India endures,
the star of the glory of this flower will ever shine.'

The translation of this text came out in 2017, around thirty-two years after the original Urdu version making the translator more accountable. In this case, the translator did a verbatim translation of the Urdu text where there were places where the author could have added a few footnotes to introduce the reader to the new studies that have come up on the theme and explained the terms for non-Urdu knowing audience. Moreover, inclusion of some documents regarding the arrest and trial of Bahadur Shah Zafar, which are readily available in various archives would have been very insightful for the study. The translation - that came out in 2017- throughout, has linguistic and typographical errors. For instance, *tasawwuf* is spelled as *tassawuf* and Aloys Sprenger, the European orientalist officer is constantly written as Springer. Also, a map of Shahjahanabad, especially around the period of 1857, could have better introduced the reader to the political geography of Delhi that Zafar loved immensely. Good quality colored pictures included in between does add to the value of the book. However, after Syed Mahdi Husain's work another book on Bahadur Shah Zafar in English is a welcome addition.

Notes

1. Percival Spear, *Twilight of the Mughal* , Oxford University Press, 1973, pp. 225-226.
2. Syed Mahdi Husain, 'Emperor Bahadur Shah II: His Role in the War in 1857', in *Amrita Bazar Patrika,* 18th November, 1956.
3. R.C. Majumdar, 'Martyr or Traitor', in *Amrita Bazar Patrika,* 28th November, 1956. It was in response to this rejoinder that Syed Mahdi Husain began his elaborate researches about the theme and wrote a full book in 1958 on Bahadur Shah's role in the revolt of 1857 which is titled as 'Bahadur Shah II and The War of 1857 in Delhi with its Unforgettable Scenes'.
4. William Dalrymple, *The Last Mughal: The fall of a Dynasty, Delhi, 1857,* Penguin Books, 2006.
5. Irfan Habib, *Resisting Subjugation: Historical Markers,* Sahmat, New Delhi, 2017, p. 57.
6. Khalil-ur Rehman Azmi, *Nawa-e Zafar,* Anjuman Taraqqi Urdu (Hind), 1958.
7. Irfan Habib, 'Remembering 1857', in *Delhi in 1857: Studies, Images and Documents,* Indian History Congress, Seventieth Session, 2010.

The Images

[The images and the photographs reproduced below are accessed from the mutiny papers to highlight the indigenous and the British official records for the study of the Uprising of 1857. The meticulous details of the measures taken up by the rebel commanders, like ban imposed by Bakht Khan on cow slaughter during the Muslim festival of sacrifice [*Id-ul Azha*], his appeal to Hindu and Muslim sepoys for a joint fight to repulse the British forces; the attempts by the Mughal household to administer the city in an organized manner are visible through these papers. Similarly, the excellent communication network maintained by the British proved to be highly beneficial to them; they could communicate the news of sepoys uprising with in no time to all their cantonments and military headquarters .This timely alert could prevent the similar incidents at other places and townships.

The photographs of the street fights, sorties, blasting of the Magazine and the maps of the battle lines are from dispatches and diaries of the war correspondents and official military records of the British officers. These photos are available in numerous publications and they have been put recently on *Abhilekh Patal* of the National Archives of India and other websites as well; a selection from such records is made here to give an idea of the nature and magnitude of the repression to the physical landscape of the city and also the manner in which the rebel leaders are blown up from the cannons and guns. Some of these photos depict theologians and the members of the religious elite tied up with the guns; ready to be blown, something apparent from their attires and looks. These photos supplement the initial suspicion of the British officers, which regarded 'Muslims as the prime suspects and chief ideologues behind the entire conspiracy'.

Three photographs of Bahadur Shah Zafar depict the various phases of the struggle; as the leader of the rebellion with his well known couplet where he has pinned his hopes on the 'sepoys, the *Ghazis*, whose attachment with their Faith i.e. *Iman* would ensure their armed struggle against the British going up to London, the centre of their ultimate authority'.' The 'swansong' of the King saw the highest personal tragedies for him in his lifetime with ultimate imprisonment and death in exile. His last photograph taken just before his death perhaps depicts the helplessness and the ultimate fate of the third world countries, their leaders and people included under the clutches of colonialism.]

Mohammad Wasim
Ph.D. candidate, Department of History,
University of Delhi, Delhi-110007

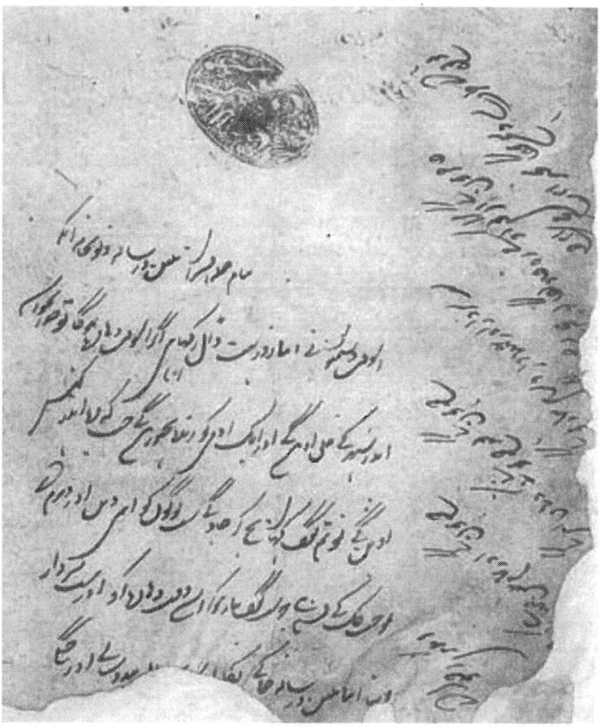

Proclamation by Bakht Khan the Commander-in-Chief of the rebel army in Delhi, fearing that the English may enter the town. He exhorts Hindu and Muslim troops to fight the enemy with zeal. (National Archives of India, Collection No. 57, Serial No. 461, dated 10 September 1857)

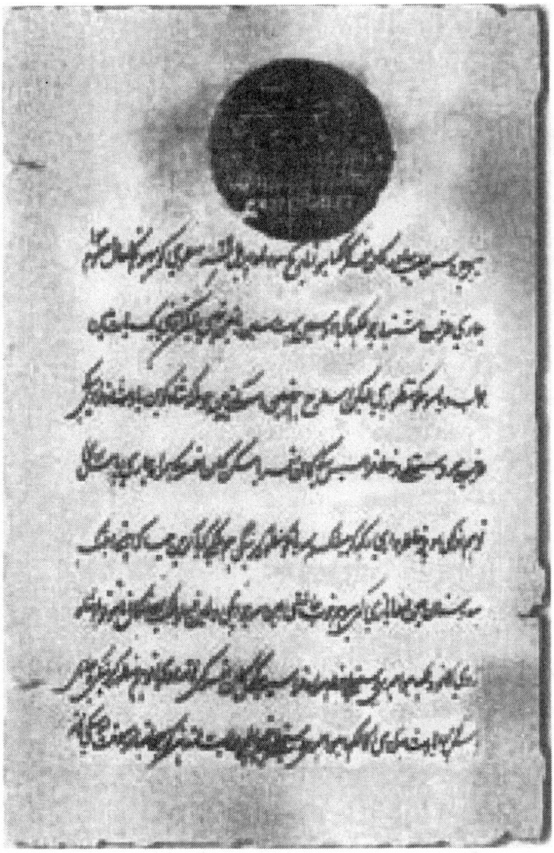

Constitution of the Mutineers The original document in Urdu is available at the National Archives of India. (Reference Collection No. 57, Serial Nos. 539-41, Mutiny Papers).

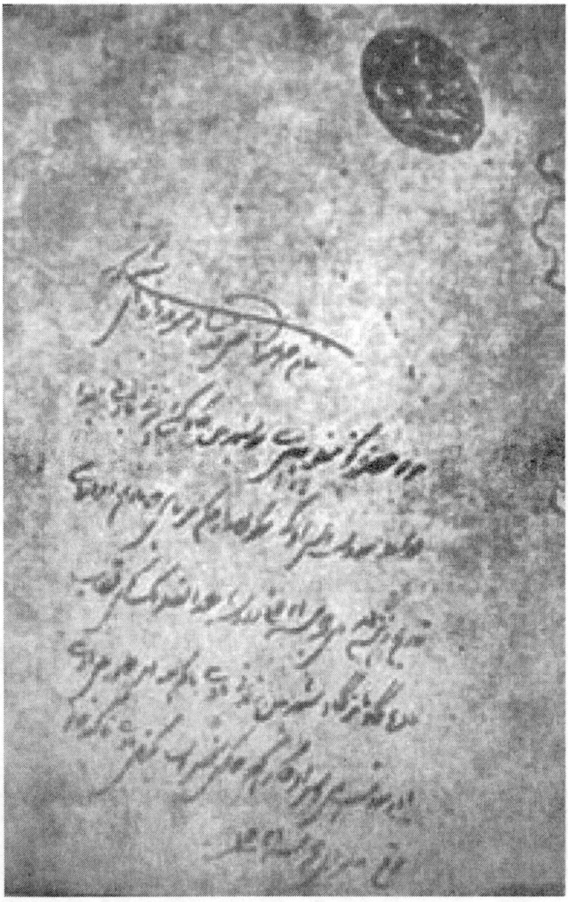

Bakht Khan's* Hukumnamah *dated 30 July 1857, barring cow-slaughter in Delhi.

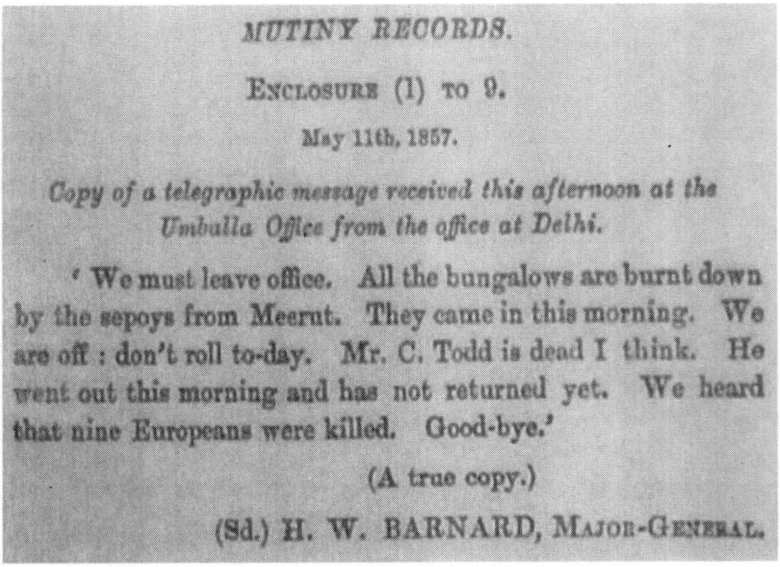

MUTINY RECORDS.

ENCLOSURE (1) TO 9.

May 11th, 1857.

Copy of a telegraphic message received this afternoon at the Umballa Office from the office at Delhi.

'We must leave office. All the bungalows are burnt down by the sepoys from Meerut. They came in this morning. We are off : don't roll to-day. Mr. C. Todd is dead I think. He went out this morning and has not returned yet. We heard that nine Europeans were killed. Good-bye.'

(A true copy.)

(Sd.) H. W. BARNARD, MAJOR-GENERAL.

The telegraph which saved Punjab and the Indian Empire for the British

Mounted rebel sepoys charging through the streets of Delhi, 11 May 1857.

Rebel's attack on the British Magazine, Delhi, 11 May 1857.

Fight for Delhi, August 1857.

Night sortie and an attack on a baggage wagon near Delhi.

Repulse of a sortie from Delhi.

غازیوں میں بو رہے گی جب تلک ایمان کی
تخت لندن تک چلے گی تیغ ہندوستان کی

"Ghāzion mén bū rahegi jab talak imān ki;
Takht-e-London tak chalegi tégh Hindustan ki"

"As long as there remains the scent of faith in the hearts of our heroes, so long shall the sword of Hindustan flash before the throne of London"

Emperor Bahadur Shah Zafar.

Surrender of Bahadur Shah Zafar to the English. After the last stand of the rebels in Delhi, the king took refuge in Humayun's tomb (20 September 1857) . The next day he gave himself up to Captain Hodson.

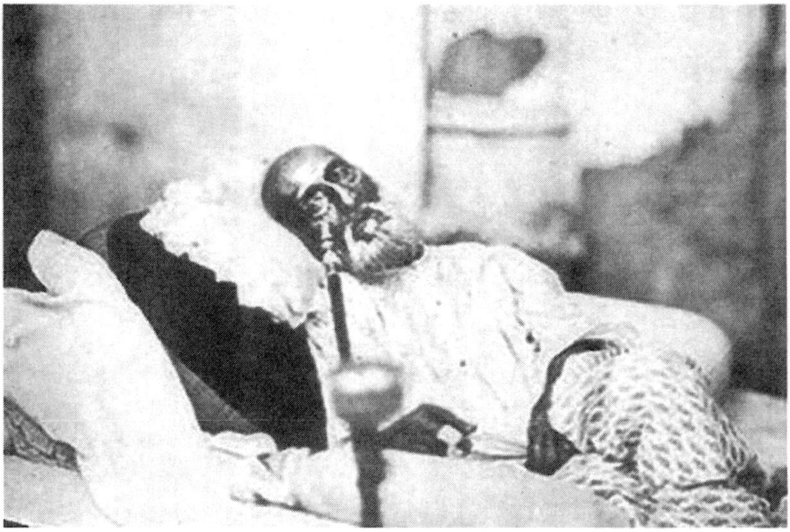

The well known photograph of Bahadur Shah Zafar taken just before his death at Rangoon.

The city of Delhi before the British siege.

The battle at Najafgarh.

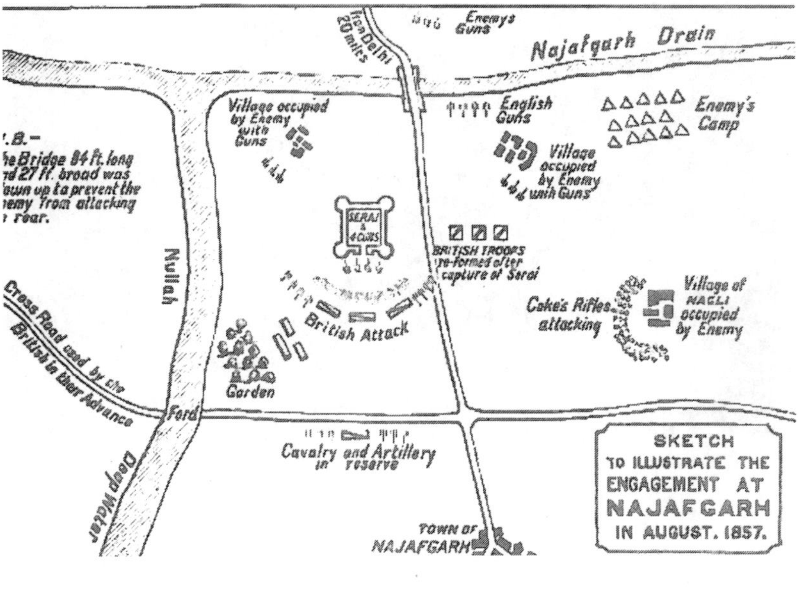

The British artillery fire targeting the city of Delhi.

Blowing up the Kashmiri Gate.

Assault of Delhi and capture of the Kashmiri Gate.

The final charge, 11 September 1857.

Delhi in the shadow of the White terror, January 1858.

The imperialist revenge and the martyrs of 1857.

The Jantar Mantar observatory in Delhi in 1858, damaged in the fighting.

Humayun's tomb in Delhi.

Hindu Rao's house in Delhi was extensively damaged in the fighting in 1858.

THE DOCUMENTS

[The documents, reproduced below, are the one which represents the perspective of the rebels and their anti-imperialists sympathizers. They also provide a glimpse of the way events were remembered and recalled by the contemporaries soon after the rebellion was suppressed. The two 'elegies' on the fate of the city and its cultural past could very well match with the similar elegies on the earlier catastrophes. The sepoys and their leaders tried to control the lawlessness in the city of Delhi after it was captured by them; hence, a *dastur-ul amal*, which has been translated by the scholars as the Constitution was drafted. It is the most important document of the collection in the mutiny papers. Hence, along with its English translation, the original facsimile is being reproduced for its intrinsic value. Similarly, the editorial of *Delhi Urdu Akhbar,* by Maulavi Muhammad Baqar on his perceptions of the nature of colonial tribute and the description of Zaheer Dehalvi about the treatment meted to him and his family at a Jat village, located between Anola and Shahabad [in Rohilkhand region] [both translated from Urdu for the first time by Professor Irfan Habib in the volumes of *People's History of India*] are included here for a better understanding of the aspirations of the intelligentsia and the 'other side' of the communitarian relations existing during the course of uprising.

It is well known that Karl Marx and Friedrich Engels were keeping a close watch on the developments taking place in the Indian subcontinent during the period of rebellion. They offered most realistic analysis to the attempts by the rebels and they were quite aware of the ferocity of the suppression and the reign of terror unleashed by the English forces against them. Their two dispatches are reproduced here, providing details of the elaborate, and out of proportion operations undertaken by the forces of East India Company in Awadh area. Though sympathetic to the rebel's cause, yet they were well aware of the might of English forces; hence, they offer realistic assessment of the inevitable fall of the rebel strongholds.

Queen Victoria's proclamation of November 1858 is often referred as a document representing the changed British policy towards its eastern colonies. However, what is little known is the way in which Begum Hazrat Mahal, the fugitive Queen of Awadh has responded from Nepal Terai to it. The point by point rebuttal to Victoria's promises has been replied in most logical manner. Both the documents make an interesting reading specially to highlight the defiance on the part of the Begum at a time when the East India Company has almost crushed the rebellion.

The memory of the last Mughal Emperor Bahadur Shah has never faded from the imagination of the people of this country. His well known elegy on the fall of the Mughal regime became quite popular in his lifetime so much so that even the road side 'minstrels use to recite this elegy in the principal towns of Central India'. The official correspondence regarding this 'elegy' is reproduced to underline this fact. Similarly, the question of raising a memorial over his mortal remains became an important issue for the Muslims of Burma also. Their powerful appeal for the construction of his tomb became an emotive issue for the Muslim of Indian subcontinent as well. Similarly, his couplets full of pathos and touching the deepest sentiment became quite popular; hence these are reproduced here to catch up those sentimental outpourings. Another elegy on the destruction of the city of Delhi by an eyewitness, namely Khawaja Altaf Husain Hali captures some images of the by gone era; his poem is also full with heart rendering descriptions of the devastations of the city of Delhi during the white terror. It is included here for a better 'understanding of the bitter memory'.]

Yusra Farooqi
Ph.D. Candidate, Department of History,
University of Delhi, Delhi-110007

1

Constitution of the Mutineers in Delhi, 1857

Court of Administration

In the name of God most merciful

Framing of a *constitution in order* to *dispel the confusion in Departments and* to *remove* mismanagement from the Military and Civil Administration which is proper and indispensable *for the working of the Constitution and the Institution of* a *Court'* which is essential-the* following being the important regulations for the same:

(i) A court shall be instituted which shall be named 'Court of Administration', i.e. *'Jalsa-i Intezamia-Fauji Wa Mulki'.*

(ii) Ten members shall be appointed (elected to) on this court, as per details-six military and four civil. Of the military members, two should be selected from the infantry platoons, two from the cavalry and two from the artillery.

(iii) Out of these ten men, one should be appointed president *(Sadr-i-Jalsa)* and another vice president *(Naib Sadr-i-Jalsa)* by a unanimous majority of votes. In every department there should be appointed secretaries according to need. The quorum for the Court meeting should be five whereby work should be done satisfactorily.

(iv) At the time of appointment of these ten men they should take oath that they would do court work with honesty, sincerity, great industry and with deep thought and care; and that they will not neglect even the slightest detail in matters administrative and that they would not covertly or overtly have resort to taking and seizing, or to partiality of any kind and in any manner or at the time of dealing with matters of administration in the Court. On the contrary they will always keep themselves engaged in and apply themselves attentively and diligently to executing the State matters whereby the state should obtain security and the people should enjoy peace and repose; and that they would not divulge any item of the Court work under consideration before its enforcement plainly or by allusion without the permission of the Court and *Sahib Alam*.

(v) Election of the Court members should be in this manner: by the majority of votes two men should be elected from the infantry platoon, two from the cavalry troops and two from the artillery; such men must possess a long record of service and must be clever and well versed, able and intelligent. Should any person be highly clever, intelligent and learned and an adept in the administration of Court work but lacking long service, this latter disqualification in that case will not obstruct the appointment of such a person. And in the same way will be appointed four civil members.

(vi) After ten members have been appointed, if any member gave his vote before the full Court regarding any matter in such a manner as to be against honesty and sincerity or calculated as partial to anyone, then that member will be removed from the Court by the definite majority of votes; and another person will be elected in his place according to regulation (v). All the items of administration to be considered should be first treated in the Court and after the approval of *Sahib Alam* the decision of the Court should be communicated to His Majesty *(Huzur-i Wala)*.

(vii) After the programmes have been drawn by the majority of votes it will be submitted for the approval to *Sahib Alam*

Bahadur and the Court will remain under the control of the *Sahib Alam Bahadur.* And no matter of administration, whether military or civil will be executed without the sanction of the Court and the approval of *Sahib Alam* and without the information of the same being given to His Majesty *(Huzur-i Wala).* In the event of a difference of opinion and after being re-considered by the Court, the same matter-the difference still continuing-will be sent up through the *Sahib Alam* to His Majesty the Shadow of God *(Huzur Zille Subhani),* The order given thereupon by His Majesty *(Huzur)* will be final.

(viii) In the Court none, barring the *Sahib Alam Bahadur* and His Majesty the Shadow of God *(Huzur Zille Subhani)* who will be entitled to be present, no non-member will be present, nor will he join the meeting. When out of the specified number of the Court members, anyone for some valid and acceptable reason be unable to attend the court meeting, then the votes of the remaining members of the Court will be tantamount to the vote of the Court in full strength.

(ix) Should a member of the Court desire to express his opinion regarding any matter, he would first secure the consent of another member; then he may make the proposal of the same as a matter already agreed upon by two members.

(x) When an item is to be considered in the Court according to regulation (ix), then the proposer should first speak in the Court meeting. No one will interrupt his speech until he has finished it. If a member of the Court has any objection to make regarding it, he should explain it and no will interrupt him either, until he has finished speaking. Should a third man make a speech amending or adding or subtracting from the objection, and if the remaining members of the Court observe silence regarding it, then every member of the Court should write out his opinion separately. After consulting regulation (viii), a decision will be arrived at by the majority.

(xi) Those who from every section of the military are elected according to regulation (ii), should be appointed managers and administrators of that section. Under their control should work a committee of four men according to regulation (iv): in that committee secretaries should be appointed according to need. And whichever proposal is formally put up in that committee by the majority of votes that proposal will be presented to the Court by those very officers of that Committee. It should be executed by the Court according to regulation (vii). The same process should be adopted in every military and civil section.

(xii) At any time according to the demand of the occasion right should be vested in the Court to make amendments by majority of votes in this constitution.'[3]

Notes

* The document has been taken from Mahdi Husain, *Bahadur Shah II and The War of 1857 in Delhi with Its Unforgettable Scenes,* Delhi, 1958, pp. 182-7. See also S.AA Rizvi and M.L. Bhargava, ed.,*Freedom Struggle in Uttar Pradesh,* Vol. I, Publication Department, U.P., 1957, pp. 419-21.

1. This court has been called the Court of Mutineers. Spear (p. 206) puts its information in the month of July. But it was surely a part of the Constitution *(Dastoor-ul Amal-i Saltanat)* which according to Zakaullah (T.U.A.S.I., p. 687), Maulvi Fazl Haq had drawn up for the government of Bahadur Shah.

2. Muinu'ddin says that the period between 11 and 25 May was occupied in restoring order and discipline in the city-a task which could never have been performed without a constitution. Cf. Metcalfe, T.N.N., p. 61.

3. (i) Mutiny Papers, Box 57, Nos. 539-41.

   (ii) Translated by the writer from the original Urdu text. *Vide* facsimile of the document facing p.187.

Appendix A

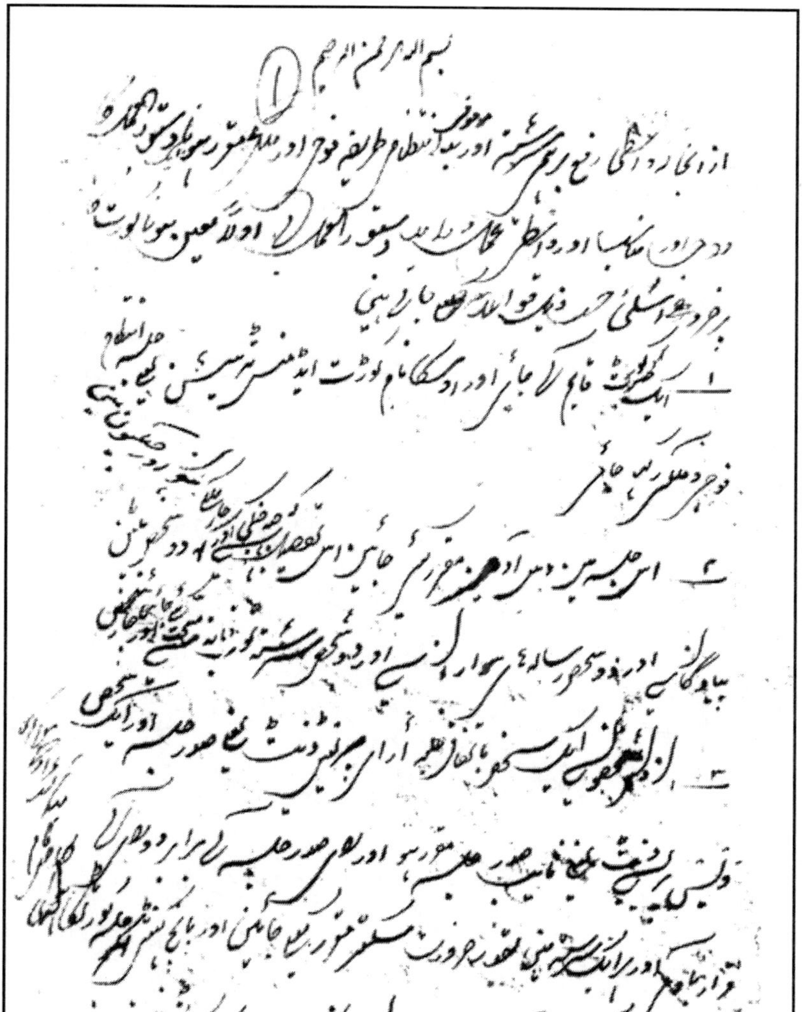
بسم اللہ الرحمن الرحیم

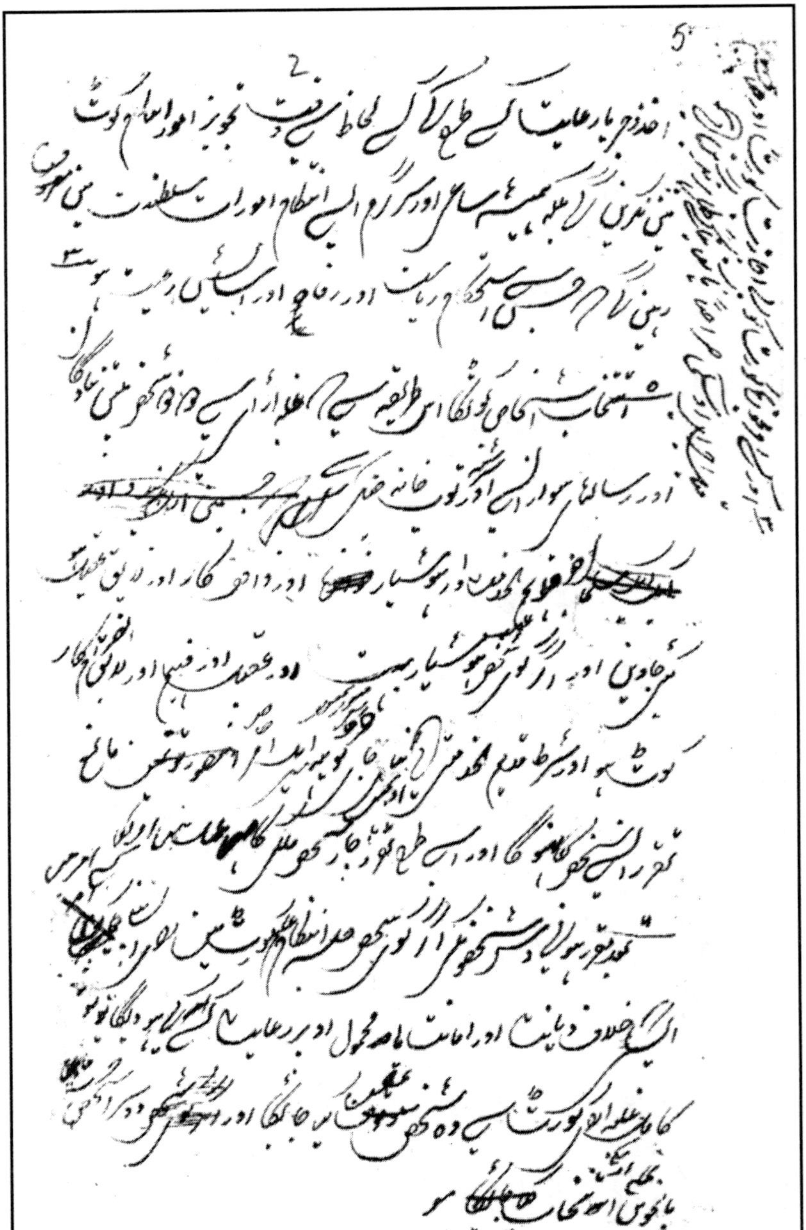

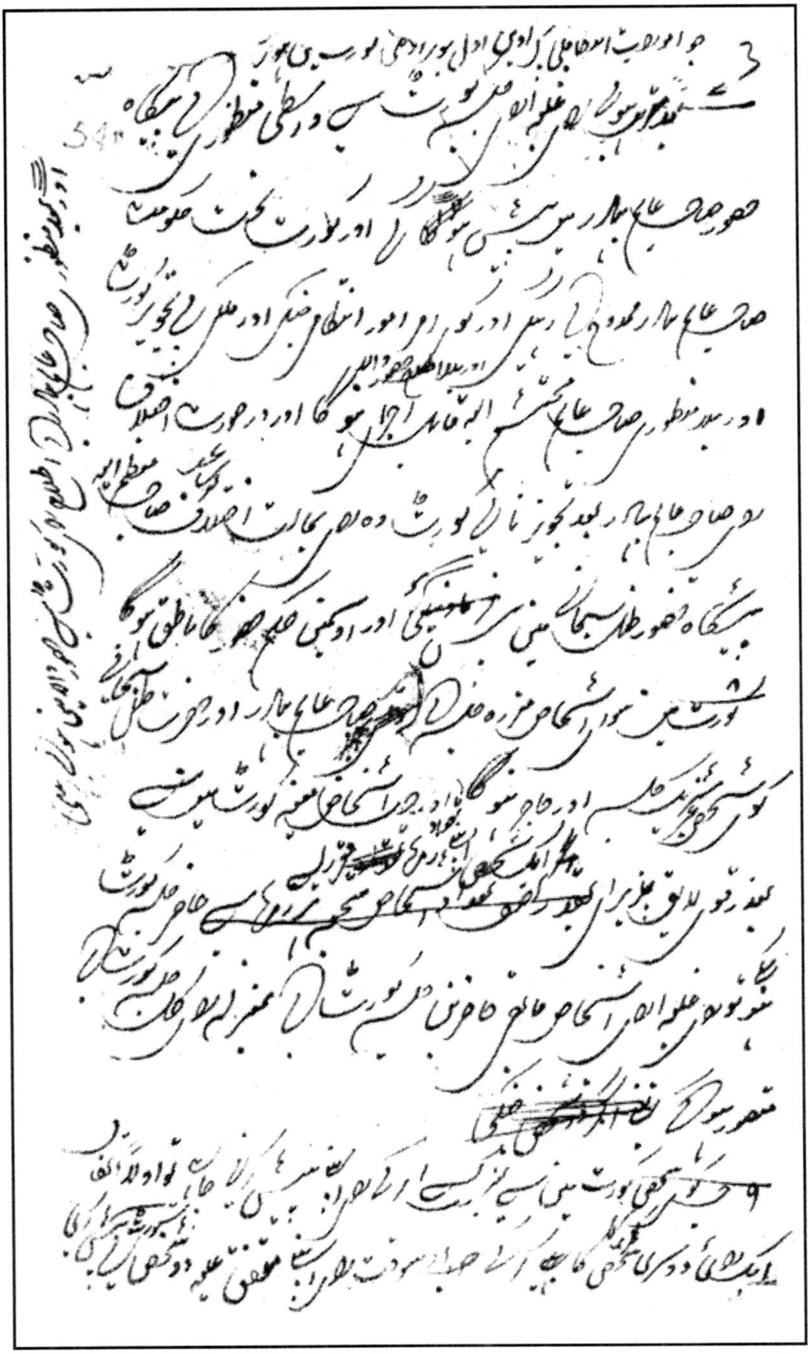

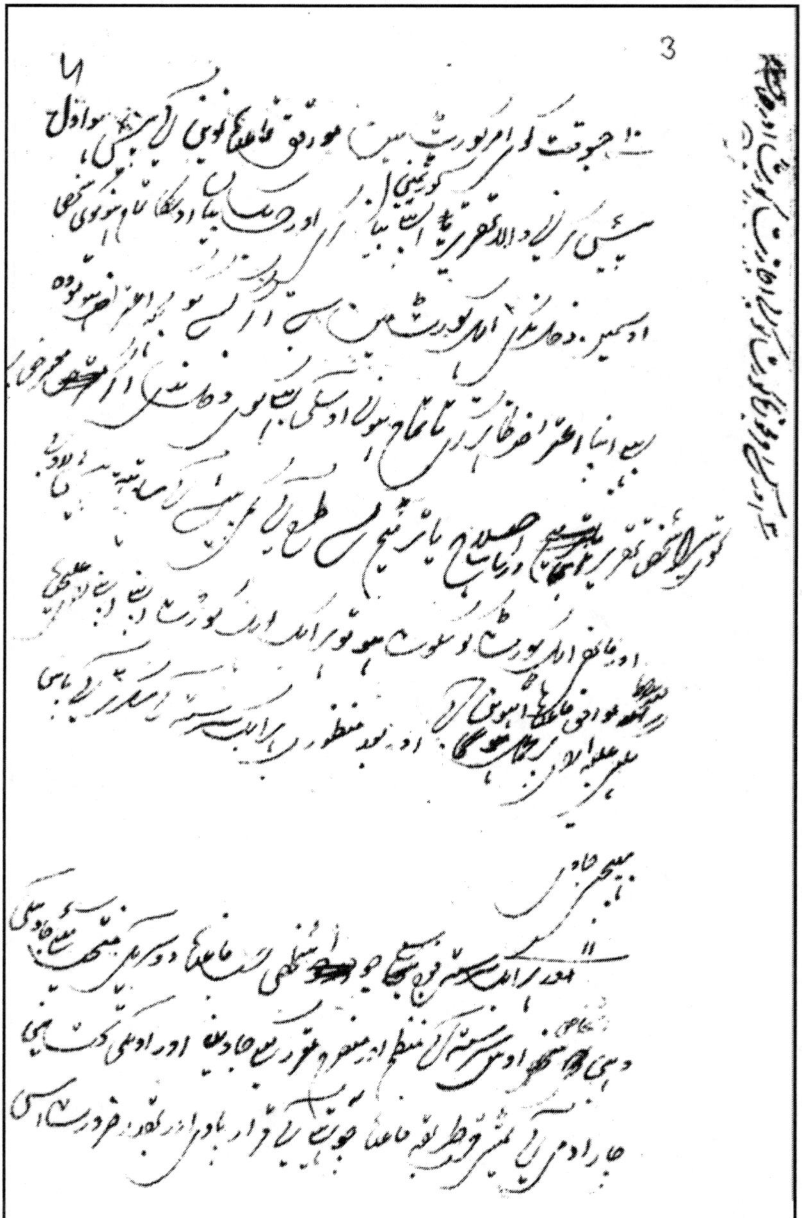

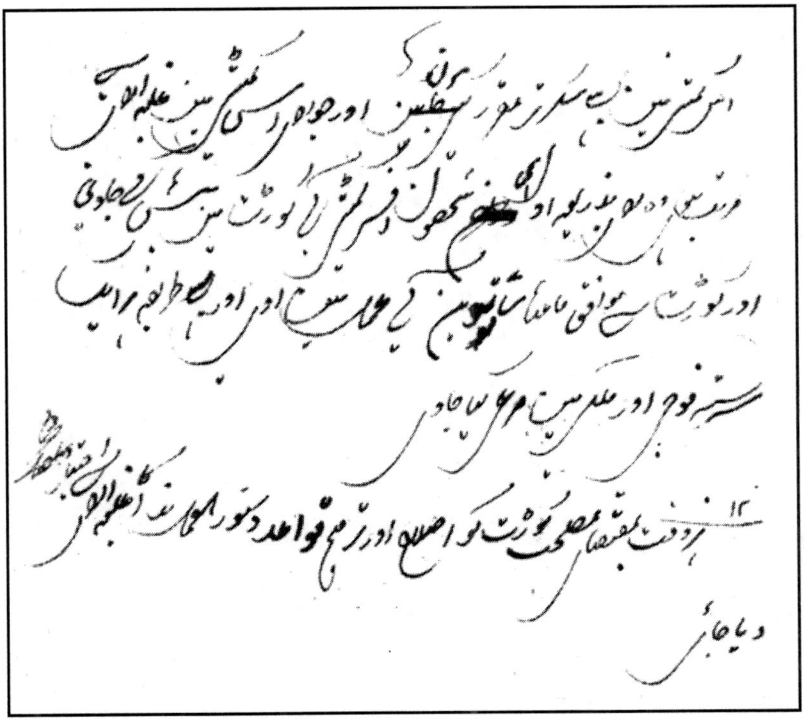

2

Proclamation of Azamgarh Prince Feroz Shah

It is well known to all, that in this age the people of Hindustan, both Hindus and Mohammedans, are being ruined under the tyranny and oppression of the infidel and treacherous English. It is therefore the bounden duty of all the wealthy people of India, especially of those who have any sort of connection with any of the Mohammedan royal families, and are considered the pastors and masters of their people, to stake their lives and property for the well-being of the public. With the view of effecting this general good, several princes belonging to the royal family of Delhi, have dispersed themselves in the different parts of India, Iran, Turan, and Afghanistan, and have been long since taking measures to compass their favourite end; and it is to accomplish this charitable object that one of the aforesaid princess has, at the head of an army of Afghanistan, and c., made his appearance in India; and **I, who am the grandson of Abul Muzuffer Serajuddin Bahadur Shah Ghazee, King of India,** having in the course of circuit come here to extirpate the infidels residing in the eastern part of the country, and to liberate and protect the poor helpless people now groaning under their iron rule, have, by the aid of the Mujahdeens, or religious fighters erected the standard of Mohammed, and persuaded the orthodox Hindus who had been subject to my ancestors, and have been and are still accessories in the destruction of the English, to raise the standard of Mahavir.

Several of the Hindu and Mussalman chiefs, who have long since quitted their homes for the preservation of their religion, and have been trying their best to root out the English in India, have presented themselves to me, and taken part in the reigning Indian crusade, and it is more than probable that I shall very shortly receive succours from the West. Therefore, for the information of the public, the present *ishtahar,* consisting of several sections, is put in circulation, and it is the imperative duty of all to take it into their careful consideration, and abide by it. Parties anxious to participate in the common cause, but having no means to provide for themselves, shall receive their daily subsistence from me; and be it known to all, that the ancient works, both of the Hindus and the Mohammedans, the writings of the miracle-workers, and the calculations of the astrologers, pundits, and rammals, all agree in asserting that the English will no longer have any footing in India or elsewhere. Therefore, it is incumbent on all to give up the hope of the continuation of the British sway, side with me, and deserve the consideration of the Badshahi, or Imperial Government, by their individual exertion in promoting the common good, and thus attain their respective ends; otherwise if this golden opportunity slips away, they will have to repent of their folly, as it is very aptly said by a poet in two fine couplets, the drift whereof is 'Never let a favourable opportunity slip, for in the field of opportunity you are to meet with the ball of fortune; but if you do not avail yourself of the opportunity that offers itself, you will have to bite your finger through grief.'

No person, at the misrepresentation of the well-wishers of the British Government, ought to conclude from the present slight inconveniences usually attendant on revolutions, that similar inconveniences and troubles should continue when the Badshahi Government is established on a firm basis; and parties badly dealt with by any *sepoy* or plunderer, should come up and represent their grievances to me, and receive redress at my hands; and for whatever property they may lose in the reigning disorder, they will be recompensed from the public treasury when the Badshahi Government is well fixed.

I

Regarding Zamindars

It is evident, that the British Government in making zamindary settlements have imposed exorbitant jumas,' and have disgraced and ruined several zamindars, by putting up their estates to public auction for arrears of rent, in so much as, that on the institution of a suit by a common ryot, a maidservant or a slave, the respectable zamindars are summoned into court, arrested, put in gaol and disgraced. In litigations regarding zamindaries, the immense value of stamps, and other unnecessary expenses of the civil courts, which are pregnant with all sorts of crooked dealings, and the practise of allowing a case to hang on for years, are all calculated to impoverish the litigants. Besides this, the coffers of the zamindars are annually taxed with subscription for schools, hospitals, roads, etc. Such extortions will have no manner of existence in the Badshahi Government; but, on the contrary, the jumas will be light, the dignity and honour of the zamindars safe, and every zamindar will have absolute rule in his own zamindary. The zamindary disputes will be summarily decided according to the Shurrah and the Shasters, without any expense; and the zamindars who will assist in the present war with their men and money, shall be excused forever from paying half the revenue. Zamindars aiding only with money, shall be excepted in perpetuity from paying one-fourth of the revenue; and should any zamindar who has been unjustly deprived of his lands during the English Government, personally join the war, he will be restored to his Zamindary, and excused from paying one-fourth of the revenue.

II

Regarding Merchants

It is plain that the infidel and treacherous British Government have monopolised the trade of all the fine and valuable merchandise, such as indigo, cloth, and other articles of shipping, leaving only the trade of trifles to the people, and even in this they are not without their share of the profits, which they secure by means of customs and stamp fees, and c. in money suits, so that the people have merely a trade in name. Besides this, the profits of the traders are taxed, with postages, tolls, and subscriptions for schools, and c. Notwithstanding all these concessions, the merchants are liable to imprisonment and disgrace at the instance or complaint of a worthless man. When the Badshahi Government is established, all these aforesaid fraudulent practices shall be dispensed with, and the trade of every article, without exception, both by land and water, shall be open to the native merchants of India, who will have the benefit of the government- steam -vessels and steam-carriages for the conveyance of their merchandise gratis; and merchants having no capital of their own shall be assisted from the public treasury. It is therefore the duty of every merchant to take part in the war, and aid the Badshahi Government with his men and money, either secretly or openly, as may be consistent with his position or interest, and forswear his allegiance to the British Government.

III

Regarding Public Servants

It is not a secret thing, that under the British Government, natives employed in the civil and military services, have little respect, low pay, and no manner of influence; and all the posts of dignity and emolument in both the departments, are exclusively bestowed on Englishmen, for natives in the military service, after having devoted the greater part of their lives, attain to the post of soobadar (the very height of their hopes) with a salary of 60r. or 70r. per mensem; and those in the civil service obtain the post of Sudder Ala, with a salary of 500r. a month, but no influence, jagheer, or present. But under the Badshahi Government like the posts of colonel,general, and commander-in-chief, which the English enjoy at present, the corresponding posts of Pansadi, Punj-hazari, Haft-hazari, and Sippah-salari, will be given to the natives in the military service; and, like the post of Collector, Magistrate, Judge, Sudder Judge, Secretary and Governor, which the European civil servants now hold, the corresponding posts of Wuzeer, Quazi, Safir, Suba Nizam (Nazim) and Dewan, and c.. with salaries of lacs of rupees, will be given to the natives of the Civil Service, together with Jagheers, Khilluts, Inams, and influence. Natives, whether Hindus or Mohammedans, who fall fighting against the English, are sure to go to heaven; and those killed fighting for the English, will, doubtless, go to hell. Therefore, all the natives in the British service ought to be alive to their religion and interest, and, abjuring their loyalty to the English, side with the Badshahi Government, and obtain salaries of ₹ 200 or 300 per month for the present, and be entitled to high posts in future. If they, for any reason, cannot at present declare openly against the English, they can heartily wish ill to their cause, and remain passive spectators of passing events, without taking any active share therein. But at the same time they should indirectly assist the Badshahi Government, and try their best to drive the English out of the country.

All the *sepoys* and *sawars* who have, for the sake of their religion, joined in the destruction of the English, and are at present, on any consideration, in a state of concealment, either at home or elsewhere, should present themselves to me without the least delay or hesitation.

Foot soldiers will be paid at the rate of three *annas,* and sawars at eight or twelve *annas* per diem for the present, and afterwards they will be paid double of what they get in the British service. Soldiers not in the English service, and taking part in the war against the English, will receive their daily subsistence money according to the rates specified for the present; and in future the foot soldiers will be paid at the rate of ₹ 8-10, and sawars at the rate of twenty or thirty rupees, per month; and on the permanent establishment of the Badshahi Government. will stand entitled to the highest posts in the state, to jagheers and presents:

Particulars	Amount
1. Matchlockmen	2 *annas* a day.
2. Riflemen	2½ *annas* a day.
3. Swordsmen	1½ *annas* a day.
4. Horsemen, with large horses	8 *annas* a day.
5. Horsemen, with small horses	6 *annas* a day.

IV

Regarding Artisans

It is evident that the Europeans, by the introduction of English articles into India, have thrown the weavers, the cotton dressers, the carpenters, the blacksmiths, and the shoemakers, and c., out of employ, and have engrossed their occupations, so that every description of native artisan has been reduced to beggary. But under the Badshahi Government the native artisans will exclusively be employed in the services of the kings, the rajas, and the rich; and this will no doubt ensure their prosperity. Therefore these artisans ought to renounce the English services, and assist the Majahdeens, or religious fighters, engaged in the war, and thus be entitled both to secular and eternal happiness.

V

Regarding Pundits, Fakirs and other Learned Persons

The pundits and fakirs being the guardians of the Hindoo and Mohammedan religions respectively, and the Europeans being the enemies of both the religions, and as at present a war is raging against the English on account of religion, the pundits and fakirs are bound to present themselves to me, and take this share in the holy war, otherwise they will stand condemned according to the tenor of the Shurrah and the Shasters; but if they come, they will, when the Badshahi Government is well established, receive rent-free lands.

Lastly, be it known to all, that whoever, out of the above named classes, shall after the circulation of this ishtahar, still cling to the British Government, all his estates shall be confiscated, and his property plundered, and he himself, with his whole family, shall be imprisoned, and ultimately put to death.'

Notes

1. Majahid-A labourer, endeavourer, striker, a warrior (in the cause of religion), Steingass, *A Persian English Dictionary,* p. 1175. Its translation as religious fanatics is most misleading. However, in the contemporary *English Historical Literature,* the word was invariably translated as religious fanatics.
2. Published by *The Delhi Gazette,* 1857, and reproduced by *The Friend* of *India,* published from Serampur, in its issue of 7 October 1858, under the heading, The Delhi millennium' with the following comments:

   The Delhi Gazette publishes a most valuable contribution to the history of the rebellion. It is the first manifesto in the European sense which has been published in India, the first of grievances, the first step to stir up the people by promises unconnected with religion. It is in the form of a Proclamation issued by the King of Delhi on 25 August, 1857, to the people of Hindoostan. The grievances of each class are specified, and a remedy promised if they will but fight boldly for the old regime. It is scarcely conceivable that such a document can be wholly without foundation, that intriguers plotting for a throne should promise reforms they knew were not desired, the removal of grievances they knew were never felt. And yet if these were indeed the changes for which the people sighed, how fatally Anglo-Indians mistaken their temper and their wants, after attending to the plot which the princess have been framing for years, and the prophesies current among both Hindoos and Mussalmans of the approaching extirpation of the British, the King addresses to the *zamindars*: (as above) The declaration that the land tax is oppressive, and ought to be lowered was only to be expected. Leaders who appeal to the populace, from Jack Cade to Mr. Cobden, have always promised cheap bread and lowered rents. The promise, too, that every *zamindar* should be absolute on his domain was natural from one who knew what we did not know, that the feudal aristocracy was still strong. But if we have prided ourselves on one popular innovation, it has been on the demolition of privilege. That the *ryot* and *zamindar* could stand in the same court was in one belief the one thing which made our rule savoury to the mass. It is quoted here (in the Proclamation) as one of the heaviest oppressions. *(The Friend* of *India,* 7 October 1858, p. 939).

3. Charles Ball, *The History* of *the Indian Mutiny,* Vol. II, pp. 630-2.
4. Foreign Political Consultations, No. 2132, 31 December 1858 (National Archives, New Delhi).

3

A Popular Perception of Colonial Tribute: Editorial in a Rebel Newspaper, Delhi, June 1857

In the time of English rule the high posts of office, to whose number there was no limit, with each carrying a monthly pay of, at least, hundreds of Rupees, were all- given to men of their own race, for, as the proverb runs, 'Let even a blind man distribute sweets, he too would give them only to his own kin.' The amount they spent here is well-known: they would spend with great 'care, thrift and miserliness'. They saved thousands and hundreds of thousands of Rupees and took that wealth to their own country. Thus their money was not spent and spread out of our India *(hamare Hindustan)*, and we gained nothing from their money and wealth. But when [before the coming of British rule] Indians were employed in [government] service, then from the expenditure by a few such men, hundreds stood to gain. Now, God willing, as the administration and governance of several districts would soon have to be conducted [after the English are expelled], you would see that there would be so many areas [to administer] for which there would be difficulty in finding competent men from amongst our countrymen. Only at the present time, as the new change of regime ('*amaldari*) is in the process of taking place, just a few more days of discomfort remain for you.

- From editorial, 'Seize this Opportunity', in the major Delhi weekly newspaper, *Dehli Urdu Akhbar* ('The Delhi Urdu News'), 21 June

1857. By then Delhi had been in rebel hands for over a month. Its editor, Muhammad Baqir, one of Urdu's well-known early journalists, was summarily executed by the English after the city of Delhi fell to them in September, Irfan Habib *Man and Environment: The Ecological History of India* [No. 36 with series, *A people's History of India*], Tulika Delhi, 2010, pp. 141.

4

Maulavi Syed Sarfaraz Ali, *Ameer ul Mujahideen*

Maulavi Sarfaraz Ali is often referred to as an important ideologue and a person who propagated hatred for the English rule among the sepoys at the various cantonment towns. His presence in Shahjahanpur cantonment where numerous sepoys were his *murid* (disciples) is attested by the British spies' report reproduced below. Syed Moinul Haq (*The Great Uprising of 1857*, Pakistan Historical Society, 1968 p. 63-4.) and Mohd Ayyub Qadri (*Jang-e Azadi 1857: Waqiyat wa Shaksiyat*, Pak Academy, Karachi, 1976 pp. 466-68, 451-2.) have reproduced a letter of Maulavi Sarfaraz Ali addressed to one Sardar Khan *Risaldar*, resident of Sagar, Madhya Pradesh, who was, at that time, residing at the *Eidgah* Delhi. They were supposed to reach on the occasion of annual *'Urs* celebration of Khwaja Baqi Billah, the famous Naqshbandi saint, at Sabzi Mandi area of old Delhi.[1] The dates of the *'Urs* synchronized to the month of Feb, 1857. Moinul Haq and Ayyub both have hinted that his presence at this crucial juncture in the city of Delhi and also his meeting with the army officers points to a 'conspiracy'. It is also said that when Bakht Khan has called the theologians of the city to issue a *fatwa* of *jihad* against the British, Maulavi Sarfaraz Ali was one of the signatories.

The local history of Shahjahanpur mentions that after the rebellion was suppressed, he migrated to Nepal, where he was treated well. He died there and lie buried at the same place. He is described in superlatives as a great scholar and a sufi who was addicted to the practice of *sama* as well.

Role of Sarfaraz Ali

This evening the sepoys went off in a body towards Bareilly and (a) *Molvee* by name Surfuraz Ulee (Sarfaraz Ali), a resident of Goruckpur (Gorakhpur), accompanied them; it appears that this man has arrived at the station about 20 days before the mutiny., and doubtless was chiefly instrumental in exciting the sepoys to revolt; Surfuraz Ulee was frequently in the habit of coming to Shahjehanpoor where he has several disciples in the city, among the number Koodrut Ulee[2] (Naeb Foujdaree Surishtahdar)[3] and his brother Neaz Ulee (Niaz Ali) both of whom are with the rebels..............[4]

Sarfaraz Ali and Damman Khan in Nepal Tarai

Surafraz Ally (Sarfaraz Ali), a *Moulvie* who some time before the outbreak left his home at Goruckpoor to preach a religious war, and Dumman Khan, the chief insurgent on the Bansee frontier who has proclaimed himself the Moulvie's "*Murid*" or disciple, are said to be in the Nepaul Terai. It is further reported in the Goruckpoor district that the former has been admitted to interviews with the Nepalese authority in the capacity of Agent to the Begum. The collections were 76,000 Rs. Making a total of Rs. 1,55,805 realized since the reoccupation of the district in spite of the disturbed condition of a portion of it.[5]

Notes

1. Ayyub Qadri op. cit., pp. 466-68; 451-52.
2. Spelt for 'Qudrat Ali'.
3. Spelt for 'Naib Faujdari Sarishtadar'.
4. Extract from letters No.21 from from G.P. Money, Magistrate and Collector of Shahjehanpoor (Shahjahanpur), to R. Alexander, Commissioner of Rohilkund (Rohilkhand), dated 9th September 1858, cf. S.A.A. Rizvi, *Freedom Struggle of Uttar Pradesh*, Vol. V, p. 297.
5. Foreign Department, North-Western Provinces, Narrative (Abstract Proceedings). Narrative of events for Gorakhpur for the week ending 18th July 1858. Secretariat Records Room, Lucknow; cf. S.A.A. Rizvi, *Freedom Struggle of Uttar Pradesh*, Vol. IV, Publications Division, 1957, p. 347.

5

The Revolt in India*

—Karl Marx
London, 17 July 1857

On 8 June, just a month had passed since Delhi fell into the hands of the revolted *sepoys* and the proclamation by them of a Mogul Emperor. Any notion, however, of the mutineers being able to keep the ancient capital of India against the British forces would be preposterous. Delhi is fortified only by a wall and a simple ditch, while the heights surrounding and commanding it are already in the possession of the English, who, even without battering the walls, might enforce its surrender in a very short period by the easy process of cutting off its supply of water. Moreover, a motley crew of mutineering soldiers who have murdered their own officers, torn as under the ties of discipline, and not succeeded in discovering a man upon whom to bestow the supreme command, are certainly the body least likely to organise a serious and protracted resistance. To make confusion more confused, the checkered Delhi ranks are daily swelling from the fresh arrivals of new contingents of mutineers from all parts of the Bengal Presidency, who, as if on a preconcerted plan, are throwing themselves into the doomed city. The two sallies which, on 30 and 31 May, the mutineers risked without the walls, and in both of which they were repulsed with heavy losses seem to have proceeded from despair rather than from any feeling of self-reliance or strength. The only thing to be wondered

---

* Taken from *New-York Daily Tribune,* 4 August 1857.

at is the slowness of the British operations, which to some degree, however, may be accounted for by the horrors of the season and the want of means of transport. Apart from General Anson, the Commander-in-Chief, French letters state that about 4,000 European troops have already fallen victims of the deathly heat, and even the English papers confess that in the engagements before Delhi the men suffered more from the sun than from the shot of the enemy. In consequence of its scanty means of conveyance, the main British force stationed at Umballah consumed about twenty-seven days in its march upon Delhi, so that it moved at the rate of about one and a half hours per day. A further delay was caused by the absence of heavy artillery at Umballah, and the consequent necessity of bringing over a siege-train from the nearest arsenal, which was as far off as Phillour, on the further side of the Sutlej.

With all that, the news of the fall of Delhi may be daily expected; but what next? If the uncontested possession by the rebels during a month, of the traditionary centre of the Indian Empire acted perhaps as the most powerful ferment in completely breaking up the Bengal army, in spreading mutiny and desertion from Kolkata to the Punjaub in the north, and to Rajpootana in the west, and in shaking the British authority from one end of India to the other, no greater mistake could be committed than to suppose that the fall of Delhi, though it may throw consternation among the ranks of the sepoys, should suffice either to quench the rebellion, to stop its progress, or to restore the British rule. Of the whole native Bengal army, mustering about 80,000 men-composed of about 28,000 Rajpoots, 23,000 Brahmins, 13,000 Mahometans, 5,000 Hindoos of inferior castes, and the rest Europeans-30,000 have disappeared in consequence of mutiny, desertion, or dismission from the ranks. As to the rest of that army, several of the regiments have openly declared that they will remain faithful and support the British authority, excepting in the matter in which the native troops are now engaged: they will not aid the authorities against the mutineers of the native regiments, and will, on the contrary, assist their 'bhaies' (brothers). The truth of this has been exemplified in almost every station from Kolkata. The native regiments remained passive for a time; but, as soon as they fancied themselves strong enough, they mutinied. An Indian correspondent of *The London Times* leaves no doubt as to the 'loyalty' of the regiments which have not yet pronounced, and the native inhabitants who have not yet made common cause with the rebels.

'If you read: he says, 'that *all is quiet,* understand it to mean that the native troops have not yet risen in open mutiny; that the discontented part of the inhabitants are not yet in open rebellion; that they are either too weak, or fancy themselves to be so, or that they are waiting for a more fitting time. Where you read of the "manifestation of loyalty" in any of the Bengal native regiments, cavalry or infantry, understand it to mean that one half of the regiments thus favourably mentioned only are really faithful; the other half are but acting a part, the better to find the Europeans off their guard, when the proper time arrives, or, by warding off suspicion, have it the more in their power to aid their mutinous companions. In the Punjaub, open rebellion has only been prevented by disbanding the native troops. In Oude, the English can only be said to keep Lucknow, the residency while everywhere else the native regiments have revolted, escaped with their ammunition, burned all the bungalows to the ground, and joined with the inhabitants who have taken up arms. Now, the real position of the English army is best demonstrated by the fact that it was thought necessary, in the Punjaub as well as the Rajpootana, to establish flying corps. This means that the English cannot depend either on their sepoy troops or on the natives to keep the communication open between their scattered forces. Like the French during the Peninsular War, they command only the spot of ground held by their own troops, and the next neighbourhood domineered by that spot; while for communication between the disjo-ined members of their army they depend on flying corps, the action of which, most precarious in itself, loses naturally in intensity in the same measure that it spreads over a greater extent of space. The actual insufficiency of the British forces is further proved by, the fact that, for removing treasures from disaffected stations, they, were constrained to have them conveyed by *sepoys* themselves, who, without any exception, broke out in rebellion on the march, and absconded with the treasures confided to them. All the troops sent from England will, in the best case, not arrive before November, and as it would be still more dangerous to draw off European troops from the presidencies of Madras and Mumbai-the Tenth regiment of Madras Sepoys, having already shown symptoms of disaffection-any idea of collecting the regular taxes throughout the Bengal Presidency must be abandoned, and the process of decomposition be allowed to go on. Even if we suppose that the Burmese will not improve the occasion, that the Maharajah of Gwalior will continue supporting the English, and the Ruler of Nepaul, commanding the finest Indian army, remain quiet; that disaffected Peshawur will not combine with the restless Hill tribes, and that the Shah of Persia will not be silly enough to evacuate Herat-still, the whole Bengal Presidency must be reconquered, and the whole Anglo-Indian army remade. The cost of this enormous enterprise will altogether fall upon the British people. As to the notion put forward by Lord Granville in the House of Lords, of the East India Company being able to raise, by Indian loans, the necessary means, its soundness may be judged from the effects produced by the disturbed state of the North-Western Provinces on the Mumbai money market. An immediate panic seized the native capitalists, very large sums were withdrawn from the banks, government securities proved almost unsaleable, and hoarding to a great extent commenced, not only in Mumbai but in its environs also.

6

Frederick Engels

The Fall of Lucknow

*(*New York Daily Tribune, *on 30th April 1858 carried a detailed report on the military operations by the East India Company in the erstwhile kingdom of Oudh. Precisely this was the time when large number of rebel leaders along with their retainers were also operating from the various rebel centres still active in Oudh as it was the last hope of the rebels, hence the British also put all their might for the subjugation of the region and crushing of the rebellion. An extract from this report is given below to have an idea about the importance of the military campaign in Oudh region, see Iqbal Husain (ed.),* Karl Marx on India, *Tulika Books New Delhi, 2006, pp. 155-159).*

The arrangements made for Oudh campaign were on a scale hitherto unprecedented in India. In the greatest expedition ever undertaken by the British there, the invention of Afghanistan, the troops employed never exceeded 20,000 at a time, and of these the great majority was natives. In this campaign of Oudh, the numbers of Europeans alone exceeded that of all troops send into Afghanistan. The main army, led by Sir Colin Campbell personally, consisted of three divisions of infantry, one of cavalry, and one of artillery and engineers. The first division of infantry under Outram, held the Alumbagh. It consisted of five European and one native regiment. The second (four European and one native regiment) and the third(five European and one native regiment),the cavalry division under Sir Hope grant (three European and four of five native regiments) and the mass of the artillery (forty-eight field guns, siege-trains and engineers), formed Campbell's active force, with which he advanced on the road from Cawnpore. A brigade concentrated under brigadier Frank at Jaunpore and Azimghur, between the Goomtee and the Ganges, was to advance along the course of the former river to Lucknow. This brigade numbered three European regiment and two batteries, besides native troops, and was to form Campbell's right wing. Including it, Campbell's force in all amounted to——

	Infantry	Cavalry	Artillery and Engineers	Total
Europeans	15,000	2,000	3,000	20,000
Native	5,000	3,000	2,000	10,000

or, in all 30,000 men; to whom must be added the 10,000 Nepaulese Ghoorkas advancing under Jung Bahadoor from Goruckpore on Sultanpore, making the total of the invading army 40,000 men, almost all regular troops. But this is not all. On the south of Cawnpore, Sir H. Roses was advancing with a strong column from Saugor upon Calpee and the Lower Jumna, there to intercept any Fugitives that might escape between the two columns of Frank and Campbell. On the north –west Brigadier Chamberlain crossed toward the end of February. The upper ganges, entering the Rohilcund, situated north-north-west of Oude, And, as was correctly anticipated, the chief point of retreat of the insurgent army. The garrisons of the town surrounding Oude must also be included in the force Directly and indirectly employed against that Kingdom, so that the whole of this force is certainly from 70,000 to 80,000 combatants, of which, according to the official statements, at least 28,000 are British. In this is not included the mass of Sir John lawrence's force, which occupies at Delhi a sort of flank position, and which consists of 5,500 Europeans at Meerut and some 20,000 Or 30,000 natives of the Punjab..........

The force in Oude consisted of the remnants of most of the mutinous Bengal regiments and of native levies from the country itself. Of the former, there cannot have been more than 35,000 or 40,000 at the very outside. The sword, desertion and demoralization must have reduced this force, originally 80,000, appointed, and totally unfit to take the field. The new levies are variously stated at from 100,000 to 150,000 men; but what their numbers may have been is unimportant. Their arms were but in part firearms, of inferior construction; most of them carried for close encounter only— the kind of fighting they were least likely to meet with. The greater part of this force was at Lucknow, engaging Sir J. Outram's troops; but two columns were acting in the direction of Allahabad and Jaunpore.

The operations of Sir C. Campbell in this campaign, as far as we can now judge , were characterized by his usual prudence and vigour. The dispositions for his concentric march on Lucknow were excellent, and the arrangements for an attack appear to have taken advantage of every circumstance. The conduct of the insurgents, on the other hand, was as contemptible if not more so then before. The sight of the redcoats struck them everywhere with panic. Frank's column defeated twenty times its numbers, with scarcely a man lost; and though the telegrams talk of 'stout resistance' and 'hard fighting', as usual, the losses of the British appear, where they are mentioned, so ridiculously small that we fear there was no more heroism needed and no more laurels to be gathered this time at Lucknow than when the British got there before.

7

Queen Victoria's Proclamation of November 1858 and its point by point rebuttal by Begum Hazrat Mahal of Awadh

Proclamation by the Queen (Of England) in Council, To the Princes, Chiefs, and People of India

1. "Victoria, by the grace of God, of the United Kingdom of Great Britain and Ireland, and of the colonies and dependencies thereof in Europe, Asia, Africa, America, and Australasia, Queen, Defender of the Faith.

"Whereas, for diverse weighty reasons, we have resolved, by and with the advice and consent of the Lords spiritual and temporal and Commons in Parliament assembled, to take upon ourselves the government of the territories in India heretofore administered in trust for us by the Honourable East India Company.

"Now, therefore, we do by these presents notify and declare that, by the advice and consent of aforesaid, we have taken upon ourselves the said government; and we hereby call upon all our subjects within the said territories to be faithful and to bear true allegiance to us, our heirs and successors, and to submit themselves

Rejoinder to Queen Victoria's Proclamation by the Begum of Oude (Awadh)

1. "At this time certain weak minded, foolish people have spread a report that the English have forgiven the faults and crimes of the people of Hindostan; this appears very astonishing, for it is the unvarying custom of the English never to forgive a fault, be it great or small: so much so that if a small offence be committed through ignorance or negligence they never forgive it.

The Proclamation of the 1st November 1858, which has come before us, is perfectly clear, and as some foolish people not understanding the real object of the Proclamation, have been carried away, therefore we, the ever-abiding government, parents of the people of Oude, with great consideration, put forth the present Proclamation, in order that the real object of the chief points may be exposed, and our subjects be placed on their guard.

to the authority of those whom we may hereafter from time see fit to appoint to administer the government of our said territories, in our name and on our behalf.

"And we, reposing especial trust and confidence in the loyalty, ability, and judgement of our right trusty and well-beloved cousin and councillor, Charles John, Viscount Canning, do hereby constitute and appoint him, the said, Viscount Canning, to be our first Viceroy and, Governor General in and over our said territories, and to administer the government thereof in our name, and generally to act in our name and on our behalf, subject to such orders and regulations as he shall, from time to time, receive from us through one of our principal secretaries of state.

"And we do hereby confirm in their several offices, civil and military, all persons now employed in the service of the Honourable East India Company, subject to our future pleasure, and to such laws and regulations as may hereafter be enacted.

2. "We hereby announce to the native princes of India, that all treaties and engagements made with them by or under the authority of the Honourable East India Company are by us accepted, and will be scrupulously maintained; and we look for the like Observance on their part.

"We desire no extension of our present territorial possessions; and while we will permit no aggression upon our dominions or our right to be attempted with impunity, we shall sanction no encroachment on those of other. We shall respect the rights,

"It is written in the Proclamation that the country of Hindostan, which was held in trust by the Company, has been resumed by the Queen, and that for the future, the Queen's laws shall be obeyed. This is not to be trusted by our religious subjects, for the laws of the Company, the settlement of the Company, the English servants of the Company, the Governor General and the judicial administration of the Company are all unchanged. What, then, is there now which can benefit the people, or on which they can rely?

2. "In the Proclamation it is written, that all contracts and agreements entered into by the Company will be accepted by the Queen. Let the people carefully observe this artifice. The Company has seized the whole of Hindostan, and, if this arrangement be accepted, what is there new in it? The Company professed to treat the Chief of Bhurtpore as a son, and then took his territory; the Chief of Lahore was carried off to London, and it has not fallen to his lot to return; the Nawab Shumshoodeen Khan, on one side, they hanged, and, on the other side,

dignity, and honour of native princes as our ownl and we desire that they, as well as our own subjects, should enjoy that prosperity and that social advancement which can only be secured by internal peace and good government.

"We hold ourselves bound to the natives of our Indian territories by the same obligations of duty which bind us to all our other subjects; and those obligations, by the blessing of Almighty God, we shall faithfully and conscientiously fulfill.

they *salaamed*[1] to him; the Peishwa they expelled from Poona, Sitara, and imprisoned for life in Bithoor; their breach of faith with Sultan Tippoo is well known; the Rajah of Benares they imprisoned in Agra. Under pretence of administering the country of the Chief of Gwalior, they introduced English customs; they have left no names or traces of the Chiefs of Behar, Orissa, and Bengal; they gave the Rao of Furrackabad a small monthly allowance and took his territory. Shahjehanpore, Bareilly, Azirngurh, Jounpore, Goruckpore, Etawah, Allahabad, Futtehpore, &c.-our ancient possessions they took from us on pretence of distributing pay; and in the 7th article of the treaty, they wrote, on oath, that they would take no more from us. If, then the arrangements made by the Company are to be accepted, what is the difference between the former and the present state of things? These are old affairs; but recently, in defiance of treaties and oaths, and, notwithstanding, that they owed us millions of rupees, without reason, and on the pretence of the misgovernment and discontent of our people, they took our country and property, worth millions of rupees. If our people were discontented with our royal predecessor, Wajid Ali Shah, how comes it they are content with us? And no ruler ever experienced such loyalty, and devotion of life and goods as we have done. What, then, is wanting that they do not restore our country? Further, it is written in the Proclamation, that they want no increase of territory, but yet they cannot refrain from annexation. If the Queen has assumed the government, why does Her Majesty not restore our country to us when our people wish it? It is well-known that no king or queen ever punished a whole army and people for rebellion; all were forgiven; and the wise cannot approve of punishing the whole army and people of Hindostan; for so long as the word "punishment" remains the disturbance will not be suppressed. There is a well known proverb -"A dying man is desperate" *(murta kya na karta)*. It is impossible that a thousand should attack a million, and the thousand escape.

3. "Firmly relying ourselves on the truth of Christianity, and acknowledging with gratitude the solace of religion, we disclaim alike the right and the desire to impose our conviction on any of our subjects. We declare it to be our royal will and pleasure that none be in anywise favored, none molested or disquieted by reason of their religious faith or observances, but that all shall alike enjoy the equal and impartial protection of the law; and we do strictly charge and enjoin all those who may be in authority under us, that they abstain from all in reference with the religious belief or worship of any of our subjects, on pain of our highest displeasure.

"And it is our further will that, so far as may be, our subjects, of whatever race or creed, be freely and impartially admitted to offices in our service the duties of which they may be qualified, by their education, ability, and integrity, duly to discharge.

"We know and respect the feelings of attachment with which the natives of India regard the lands inherited by them from their ancestors, and we

3. "In the Proclamation it is written, that the Christian religion is true, but that no other creed will suffer oppression, and that the laws will be observed towards all. What has the administration of justice to do with the truth or falsehood of a religion? That religion is true which acknowledges one God, and knows no other. Where there are three Gods in a religion, neither Mussulmans nor Hindoos-nay, not even Jews, Sun-worshippers, or Fire-worshippers can believe it true. To eat pigs, and drink wine, to bite greased cartrid ages, and to mix pig's fat with flour and sweetmeats, to destroy Hindoo and Mussulman temples on pretence of making roads, to build churches, to send clergymen into the streets and alleys to preach the Christian religion, to institute English schools and to pay people a monthly stipend for learning the English sciences, while the places of worship of Hindoos and Mussulmans are to this day entirely neglected; with all this, how can the people believe that religion will not be interfered with? The rebellion began with religion, and,

desire to protect them in all rights connected therewith, subject to the equitable demands of the state; and we will (desire) that generally, in framing and administering the law, due regard be paid to the ancient rights, usages, and customs of India.

4. "We deeply lament the evils and misery which have been brought upon India by the acts of ambitious men who have deceived their countrymen by false reports, and led them into open rebellion. Our power having been shown by the suppression of that rebellion in the field, we desire to show our mercy by pardoning the offences of those who have been thus misled, but who desire to return to the path of duty.

"Already in one province, with a view to stop the further effusion of blood and to hasten the pacification of our Indian dominions our Viceroy and Governor General has held out the expectation, of pardon, on certain terms, to the great majority of those who in late unhappy disturbances have been guilty of offences against our government and has declared the punishment which will be inflicted on those whose crimes place them beyond the reach of forgiveness. We approve and confirm the said act of our Viceroy and Governor General, and do further announce and proclaim as follows:-

"Our clemency will be extended to all offenders, save and except those who have been or shall be convicted of having directly taken part in the murder of British subjects. With regard to such, the demands of justice forbid the exercise of mercy.

"To those who have willingly given asylum to murderers, knowing them to

for it, millions of men have been killed. Let not our subjects be deceived; thousands were deprived of their religion in the North-West, and thousands were hanged rather than abandon their religion.

4. "It is written in the Proclamation, that who harboured rebels, or who were leaders of rebels, or who caused men to rebel, shall have their lives, but that punishment shall be awarded after deliberation, and that murderers and abettors of murders shall have no mercy shown them, while all others shall be forgiven. Any foolish person can see, that under this Proclamation, no one, be he guilty or innocent, can escape.

Everything is written, and yet nothing is written; but they have clearly written that they will not let off any one implicated; and in whatever village or estate the army may have halted, the inhabitants of that place cannot escape. We are deeply concerned for the condition of our people on reading this Proclamation, which palpably teems with enmity. We now issue a distinct order, and one that maybe trusted, that all subjects who may have foolishly presented themselves as heads of villages to the English, shall, before the 1st of January next, present themselves in our camp. Without doubt their faults shall be forgiven then, and they shall be treated according to their merits. To believe in this Proclamation, it is only necessary to remember that Hindostanee rulers are altogether kind and merciful. Thousands have seen this, millions have heard it. No one has ever seen in be such, or who may have acted as leaders or instigators in revolt, their lives alone can be guaranteed; but, in apportioning the penalty due to such persons, full consideration will be given to the circumstance under which they have been induced to throw off their allegiance, and large indulgence will be shown to those whose crimes may appear to have originated in a too credulous acceptance of the false reports circulated by designing men.

"To all others in arms against the government, we hereby promise unconditional pardon, amnesty, and oblivion of all offences against ourselves, our crown and dignity, on their return to their homes and peaceful pursuits.

"It is our royal pleasure that these terms of grace and amnesty should be extended to all those who comply with their conditions before the 1st day of January next.

5. "When by the blessing of Providence, internal tranquility shall be restored, it is our earnest desire to stimulate the peaceful industry of India, to promote works of public utility and improvement, and to administer its government for the benefit of all our subjects resident therein. In their prosperity will be our strength, in their contentment our security, and in their gratitude our best reward. And may the God of all power grant to us, and to those in authority under us, strength to carry out these our wishes for the good of our people".

"G.F. Edmonstone

"Secretary to the Government of India with the Governor General"[3]

a dream that the English forgave an offence.

5. "In this Proclamation it is written, that when peace is restored, public works, such as roads and canals, will be made in order to improve the condition of the people. It is worthy of a little reflection, that they have promised no better employment for Hindostanees than making roads and digging canals. If people cannot see clearly what this means, there is no help for them. Let no subject be deceived by the Proclarnation".[2]

The royal declaration was accompanied by the following notification of the Governor General of India:-

"Foreign Department, Allahabad Nov. 1.

"Her Majesty the Queen having declared that it is her gracious pleasure to take upon herself the government of the British territories in India, the Viceroy and Governor General hereby notifies, that from this day all acts of the government of India will be done in the name of the Queen alone.

"From this day, all men of every race and class, who under the administration of the Hon. East India Company, have joined to uphold the honour and power of England, will be the servants of the Queen alone.

"The Governor General summons them, one and all, each in his degrees, and according to his opportunity, and with his whole heart and strength, to aid in fulfilling the gracious will and pleasure of the Queen, as set forth in her Royal Proclamation.

"From the many millions of Her Majesty's native subjects in India, the Governor General will now, and at all times, exact a loyal obedience to the call which, in words full of benevolence and mercy, their sovereign has made upon their allegiance and faithfulness.

"By order of the Right Honourable the Governor General of India."

Notes

1. Saluted.
2. Foreign Political Consultations, 171h Dec. 1858, Nos. 250/54.; National Archives, New Delhi. The Original text of this proclamation is yet to be located. However; it is available only in the official translation.

   It is pertinent to mention that the official view for this Begum's proclamation was that it has yet to reach to a vider audience and had only a limited circulation. Although within a gap of two weeks (between 17 Dec. 31 Dec. 1858) it was too much to access the circulation of this counter proclamation of For. Pol. Coustn. 31 Dec. 1858, Nos. 3021-25, NAI, New Delhi cf. S.A.A. Rizvi & M. L. Bhargava, Freedom Struggle in Uttar Pradesh Vol. II, reprint OUP, 2011.
3. Charles Ball, *'The History of the Indian Mutiny"*, Vol. II, pp. 518-19.

8

The Martyrs of 1857
A Contemporary Elegy

(Gayi yakbayak* jo *hawa palat...)

Gayi yak-ba-yak jo hawa palat nahi dil ko mere qaraar hae
Karoon is sitam' ka mein kya bayan, mera gham se seena figaar' hae

Yeh riaaya-e-hind tabaah hui kaho kya- kya in pe jafa hui
Jise dhekha hakeme-waqt' ne kaha yeh bhi qebile-daar' hae

Yeh kisi ne zulm bhi hai suna ki dee phaansi logo ko begunah
Vale kalmagoiyoo' ki simt se abhi unke dil mein ghubaar' hae

Na tha shahr Dehli, yeh tha chaman, kaho kis tarhe ka tha yaa aman
Jo khitaab tha weh mita diya, faqat ab to ujdaa dayaar hae

Yahi tang haal jo sab ka hae, yeh karishma' qudrate-rab ka hae
Jo bahaar thi so khizaan hui jo khizaan thi ab weh bahaar hae

Shabo-roz phool mein jo tule, kaho khaare-ghum ko weh kya sahe
Mile taauq qaid mein jab unhe, kahaan gul ke badle yeh khaar hae

Sabhi jaa' weh matam-e-sekht' hae kaho kaise gardishe-bakht' hae
Na weh taj hae na weh takht hae, na weh shah hae na dayaar hae
Na wabal tan pe hae dar mira nahin jaan jaane ka dar zara
Kate gham hi nikle jo dum mera, mujhe apni zindagi baar hae

(TRANSLATED FROM URDU)

How suddenly the wind has changed, how restless my heart has become:

How can I describe this tyranny, so grievously wounded is my breast from sorrow?

The people of India are utterly ruined; what cruelties they have not suffered!

Whomever the present rulers see, they say: 'he is good for the gallows'.

Has anyone heard of such oppression, that people are hanged for no fault at all?

And yet the rulers continue to be bitter in their hearts about those who recite the formula of the faith. (Kalima go)

Delhi was not simply a city-a garden it was. What shall I say of the peace that it had!

They have erased all its repute; now it is simply a place laid waste.

This straitened condition that all are in: this comes from how Lord's will works.

The spring turns into autumn, autumn into spring.

Those who were nourished by flowers day and night, how can they bear the thorns of sorrow?

When chains were put on them in prison, they were told: 'This is your garland, in lieu of flowers'.

No one buried them in the garden; no one gave them a funeral shroud.

They never could get to their native land; nor even leave even a trace of their grave behind.

Everywhere there is loud mourning: What can I say, except that such is the turn of Fate?

No more is there that crown, nor that throne, nor that ruler, nor that country.

Those who dealt well with others, see how they have been dealt with;

Sorely oppressed are they from the wheels of fortune, not a thread remains on their body.

This body of mine indeed has become a punishment on my head.

I do not now fear death at all. When I cease to breathe, the sorrow too will at last cease:

For to live for me is to carry an unbearable burden.

What fear have you now Zafar, of the tumult of Last Day.

Whatever God wills, comes manifestly to pass.

We have the favour of our Prophet: he would help our cause.

– Bahadur Shah Zafar

غزل

ابوظفر سراج الدین بہادر شاہ ظفر

گئی یک بہ یک جو ہوا پلٹ کہ نہ دل کو میرے قرار ہے
کروں غم ستم کا میں کیا بیاں میرا غم سے سینہ فگار ہے

یہ جو رعایائے ہند تباہ ہوی کہو اُن پہ کیا یہ جفا ہوی
جسے دیکھا حاکم وقت نے کہا یہ تو قابل دار ہے

یہ ستم کسی نے بھی ہے سنا کہ دی پھانسی لاکھوں کو بے گناہ
وے کلمہ گویوں کی طرف سے ابھی دل پہ اُن کے غبار ہے

نہ تھا شہر دہلی، وہ تھا چمن دلی، سب طرح کا تھا دہاں امن
وہ خطاب اس کا تو مٹ گیا، فقط اب تو اجڑا دیار ہے

یہاں حال تنگ خوشی کا ہے، وہ کرشمہ قدرت رب کا ہے
یہاں بہار میں تو خزاں ہوئی، وہاں خزاں میں ان کو بہار ہے

شب و روز پھول میں جو بلیں کہوں خار غم سے جب کھلیں
انھیں طوق قید میں جب ملے گویا بدلہ گل کے وہ ہار ہے

سبھی جاں وہ ماتم سخت ہے کہوں کیسی گردش بخت ہے
نہ وہ تاج ہے نہ وہ تخت ہے، نہ وہ شاہ ہے، نہ دیار ہے

یہ وبال تن پہ پڑا ہیں ڈر ذرا جان جانے کا
بچے غم سے نکلے جو دم خدا ہمیں زندگی اپنی پہاڑ ہے

9

Political Agent of Bhopal to Governor General informing him that the minsterals reciting the above verses of the elegy by the Ex-King in principal towns of Central India, Aug, 1862

Foreign Political, Fort William
August, 1862, pp. 23

From Major A.R.E. Hutchinson, Political agent Bhopal to Major R.J Mende, agent Governor General for Central India (No. 493, dated, Sehore, 14th July, 1862)

.... I have the honor to transmit a copy of some stanzas with their translations of an Ode said to have been composed by the Ex-King of Delhi, "Zuffur" (victory) being one of his titles.

2. This Ode, I am told is sung or recited by the Minstrels in India, and can be heard in any town of importance throughout the North-Western provinces.

3. From Stanzas 3, 8 and 9, I am of opinion that the composition is of more recent date and that has been attributed to the Ex- King by the faction of which he was the head for reasons apparent.

Translation of the Odes by Zuffer

1. The wind having changed suddenly my mind is disturbed. What should I relate regarding my injuries? My heart is wounded with grief.
2. What calamity has be-fallen the good people of Hindustan? Can you tell me what oppression they endure? Who so ever the rulers of the times behold, they think deserving of hanging.
3. Has anyone ever heard of such obsession as hanging innocent people by hundreds of thousands? They are yet vexed with the Musalmans.
4. Those they have killed have not been interred in the gardens, nor have they had any grave or winding sheet. Who could have given them interments? No trace can be discovered of their grave.
5. People are so afflicted that they do not fear to die. If I were to die, I would be saved from grief. My life, O God, in a heavy burden.
6. When these who used to always live delicately get over their present grief if they be imprisoned with an iron color round their necks, they will concede it as a garland of flowers.
7. How can I describe the state of these who used heretofore to gain the gratitude of others by their gifts? They have, by the revolutions of the heaven, not now a thread left on their backs.
8. Delhi was not a city, but a garden and the place of delight; it is now changed to become a wilderness
9. Happiness in scare here now in place of spring, it is to us the season when trees become bare, and spring to those to whom it showed have been the sear autumn.
10. O Zuffer, you are concerned about the day of Judgment if God declare openly that the prophet is your supporter, you will be blessed.

True Translation (ARE Hutchinson)

10

Some of the Anti-British Verses of Bahadur Shah Zafar

Composed Before the War of 1857

کیا پوچھتے ہو کج روئی چرخ چنبری
ہے اس ستم شعار کا شیوہ ستم گری

What! Do you enquire about the crooked ways of Fate?
It is oppressive in its nature and cruel in its practise.

کرتا ہے خوار تو انھیں جن کو ہے برتری
اُس کے مزاج میں ہے یہ کیا سفلہ پروری

It humiliates particularly those who are more exalted ;
it is the nature of Fate that it supports and patronizes the mean.

کھائے ہے گوشت زاغ، فقط استخواں ھما
کیا منصفی ہے زاغ کہاں اور کہاں ھما

The crow'[1] enjoys meat while the phoenix'[2] has to live on mere bones.

What justice! There is no comparison whatever between the phoenix and the crow.

بالعکس ہے جہاں میں جہاں تک ہے کاروبار
شیوہ کیا الٹا زمانے نے اختیار

All the affairs of this world are topsy-turvy; the world has adopted perverse ways.

ہے موسم بہار خزاں اور خزاں بہار
آئی نظر عجب روش باغ روزگار

Spring is replaced by autumn and autumn by spring;
such strange scenes are staged in the garden of this world.

جو نخل پر ثمر ہیں اٹھا سکتے سر نہیں
سرکش ہیں وہ درخت کہ جن میں ثمر نہیں

Those of the trees which are fruit-bearing cannot raise their heads;
the trees which raise their heads are those which bear no fruit.

باد صبا آڑاتی چمن میں ہے سر پہ خاک
ملتے ہیں دم بدم کف افسوس برگ تاک

Breeze throws dust on its head in the garden;
the vine trees wring their hands in sorrow, every now and then.

غنچے ہیں دل گرفتہ، گلوں کے جگر ہیں چاک
کرتی ہیں بلبلیں یہی فریاد درد ناک

شاداب حیف! خار ہوں، گل پائمال ہوں
گلشن ہوں خار، نخل مغیلاں نہال ہوں

The buds are afflicted with sorrow; the hearts of the roses are lacerated and the nightingales are chirping painfully as if saying in sad melancholy tones-

'Alas! the thorns flourish while the roses are trampled; the garden is transformed into thorns while the tree of prickly thorns is thriving

جائیں فلک کے احاطہ سے ہم کہاں
ہووے گا سر پہ چرخ یہی جائیں گے ہم جہاں

Where can we'[3] go out of the vault of the sky?
There will be this vault of the sky over our head wherever we go.

جو آگیا ہے اس محل تیرہ رنگ میں
قید حیات سے ہے وہ قید فرنگ میں

Whoever has come into this strange place
is a prisoner of the *Firangis* as long as he lives.

یہ گنبد فلک ہے عجب طرح کا قفس
طاقت نہیں ہے نالے کی جس، میں ایک نفس

جنبش ہو ایک پر کی تو پر ٹوٹ جائے دس
رہ جائے دل میں دل کی نہ کس طرح ہوس

کیا طائر اسیر وہ پرواز کر سکے
جس میں نہ اتنا دم ہو کہ پرواز کر سکے

This vault of the sky is such a strange cage that one has not
the power to raise in it cries even for a moment.

If I move an inch I would suffer breakdown in ten points;
the longings of my heart would surely then remain unfulfilled.

How can a caged bird fly?
e has no strength to fly.

کیا کیا جہاں میں ہوچکے شاھان دی کرم
کس کس طرح کا رکھتے تھے ساتھ اپنے وہ حشم

آخر گئے جہاں سے تنہا سوئے عدم
دارا کہاں؟ کہاں ہے سکندر؟ کہاں ہے جم

کوئی نہ یہاں رہا ہے نہ کوئی جہاں رہے
کچھ اے ظفر رہے تو نیکوئی یہاں رہے

Many kings of might and majesty have been in this world.

What powerful armies of different kinds did they possess!

At last they left this world and departed alone.
Where is Darius? Where is Alexander? Where is Jamshed?

O Zafar! barring good deeds which might remain,

nothing will survive in this world'[4]

اس ستمگر نے مجھے جرم وفا پہ مارا
کوئی لینے کا نہیں نام وفا میرے بعد

This tyrant has killed me on account of my faithfulness, considering it a crime.

After me, faithfulness will not be considered worth a mentions.'[5]

کیا ہم نے ظفر جاکے جب تیرا مذکور
تیری طرف سے انھیں بدگمان پایا

O Zafar! whenever we remembered thee to them,
we found them mistrustful of thee'[6]

تمہاری دوستی میں مرگئے لاکھوں نہ رحم آیا
تم ہی ہو دشمن عالم، بھلا مانو برا مانو

Many people have perished in their attempt to cultivate a friendship with you, but you did not relent.

Verily you are an enemy to the whole world; whether you like this epithet *(dushman-i 'alam)* or not.'[7]

کیا جو تم نے میرے ساتھ اپنے دل سے پوچھو
مجھے بس چپ ہی تم رہنے دو کھلواتے زباں کیوں ہو

What you have done to me! This is a story on which you may draw out your own heart.

Let me remain silent. Why do you make me speak plainly'[8]

میں خوب جانتا ہوں نامعتبر ہیں بالکل
تم لاکھ عہدنامے قول و قسم سے لکھو

I know full well that your words are absolutely unreliable.
You may write a lakh pledges under solemn oaths; it matters little.'[9]

اب جو لکھتا ہے وہ کا ہے کو لکھتا تھا کبھی
دیکھ لو اس بت سے پیر کو پہلا کاغذ

Whatever he (the Governor-General) now writes, he never wrote before; you may look into the previous letters of this accursed fellow.'[10]

ملتے ہیں ہم سے یہ دل سے عداوت رکھتے
جانتے ہم تو نہ ایسوں سے محبت رکھتے

They meet us in so friendly manner but cherish enmity within.

Had we known this before, we would never have been friends with them.'[11]

پاسکے رمزو کنایہ کوئی کیا اس کے ظفر
جس کی ایک بات میں سو طرح کا پہلو نکلے

How can one get at their allusions and references, O Zafar!

A single word of theirs is capable of yielding a hundred different rneanings.'[12]

نہ ہم راہ وفا بھولے نہ تم طرز ستم چوکے
جو اپنی بات تھی اس سے نہ ہم چوکے نہ تم چوکے

We never lost remembrance of the way of faithfulness, and you did not neglect your special pursuit of tyranny.

According to the characteristic habit of each, neither diverted from this path; nor you, nor we.'[13]

نہ کر بدعہدیاں پیماں شکن! انصاف کر دل میں
کئے تھے میرے ساتھ کیا کیا قوم وقسم تو نے

O breaker of pledges! do not be repeatedly untrue to your word.

Do justice, looking into your heart; and recall what remarkable assurances you had given me before.'[14]

تمہاری بات کا کیا کوئی اعتبار کرے
کہ قول دے کے کئی بار ظفرؔ سے پھرے

How can Zafar rely on your word for you have turned your back on your word of honour several times'[15]

Notes

1. 'Crow' stands for the Englishmen who were then known as 'men of black heart'. *Vide Sadiqul Akhbar,* 2 July 1857; *Saptahik Hindustan* of *New Delhi* dated 2 December 1957, p. 16 for facsimile.
2.. 'Phoenix' is a fabulous bird whose shadow, it is believed, is auspicious and anyone, on being favoured with it, secures the throne. Here 'Phoenix' stands for Bahadur Shah.
3. This is the royal 'we'. By means of this and the following verse Bahadur Shah expressed his agony.
4. *Diwan-i Awwal,* pp. 382-383. Newal Kishore Press, 5th edn, 1918.
5. *Diwan -i Awwal,* p. 87.
6. *Diwan -i Duwum,* p. 164.
7. *Diwan -i Chaharum,* p. 122.
8. Idem., p. 120.
9. Idem., p. 114.
10. Idem., p. 44.
11. Idem., p. 223.
12. *Diwan -i Suwum,* p. 144.
13. Idem., p. 116.
14. *Diwan-i Awwal,* p. 271.
15. *Diwan-i Duwuml,* p. 89.

11

The Devastation of Delhi

A Lament

—Khwaja Altaf Husain 'Hali'

Dear friend, I beseech you, speak not of the Delhi that is no more,
I cannot bear to listen to the sad story of this city.
O nightingale, I implore you, sing not a song of autumn,
While we laugh and talk, how can we mourn with you?
O minstrel, at such a time, when my heart craves pleasure,
Do not begin a heart-piercing *ghazal.*
O master-painter, do not open before us an album of paintings,
It will only remind us of the *musha'aras* of the past.
O my heart, take care, do not make me weep like a heavy cloud,
The ocean of blood is throbbing in my veins.
O adventurer, your heart will be seared with pain and grief.
Hearken to me, do not go into the ruins of Delhi.
At every step, priceless pearls lie buried beneath the dust,
No place in the world is so rich with hidden treasure.
Even the traces of what reminded us of the city's destruction are gone.
Dear heaven, can there be greater oblivion than that?

Those who are gone have forgotten us. We too have ceased to think of them.
Times have changed as they can never change again.
Can you point to any family which does not bear scars?
Dear heaven, that made us weep, cease, I beseech you,
But do not let strangers mock us.
If they were to know our plight, not only friends
But the whole world would pity us.
O cup-bearer, who passes the last round of wine.
Do not fill it to the brim, and let no thirst be fully quenched.
For now their long spell of good fortune lies asleep.
Do not awake them, O wheel of time, they are deep in slumber.
O mirth and joy, hasten hence, Delhi is no place for you any more,
Yes, once Delhi was the centre for art and science.
But the art of poetry is dead, never to be born again.
Do not grieve for the glories of the past.
Ghalib, Shefta, Nayyar, Azurda and Zauq will never come again.
After Momin, Alavi and Sehbai, who is left to speak of the art of poetry?
The light of their greatness also shone on us who were not great.
Listen to the poetry of Dagh and Majruh, for after them
No nightingale will warble in this rose garden.
Those *musha'aras* of the past are no more.
And it is unseemly that I should grieve others with my own lament.

(English rendering by Dr Yunus Jaffery)

Note: This *marsiya* was recited by Hali at a *musha'ara* in Lahore in 1874. Dagh and Majruh were among the last survivors of the nineteenth-century Delhi poets. Majruh lived till 1902 and Dagh till 1905.

نوحہ دہلی

خواجہ الطاف حسین حالیؔ

تذکرہ دہلی مرحوم کا، اے دوست نہ چھیڑ
نہ سنا جائے گا ہم سے، یہ فسانہ ہرگز

داستان گل کی خزاں میں، نہ سنا اے بلبل
ہنستے ہنستے ہمیں ظالم، نہ رُلانا ہرگز

ڈھونڈتا ہے دلِ شوریدہ، بہانے مطرب
درد انگیز غزل کوئی، نہ گانا ہرگز

صحبتیں اگلی مُصوّر، ہمیں یاد آئیں گی
کوئی دل چسپ مرقع، نہ دکھانا ہرگز

موج زن دل میں ہیں یاں، خون کے دریا اے چشم
دیکھنا ابر سے آنکھیں، نہ چرانا ہرگز

لے کے داغ آئے گا سینے پہ بہت، اے سیّاح
دیکھ اس شہر کے کھنڈروں میں، نہ جانا ہرگز

چپّے چپّے پہ ہیں یاں، گوہر یکتا تہ خاک
دفن ہوگا کہیں اتنا، نہ خزانہ ہرگز

مٹ گئے تیرے مٹانے کے نشاں بھی، اب تو
اے فلک اس سے زیادہ، نہ مٹانا ہر گز

وہ تو بھولے تھے ہمیں، ہم بھی انھیں بھول گئے
ایسا بدلا ہے، نہ بدلے گا زمانا ہرگز

جس کو زخموں سے حوادث کے، اچھوتا سمجھیں
نظر آتا نہیں، ایک ایسا گھرانا ہرگز

ہم کو گر تو نے رُلایا، تو رُلایا اے چرخ
ہم پہ غیروں کو تو ظالم، نہ ہنسانا ہرگز

یار خود روئیں گے، کیا ان پہ جہاں روتا ہے
ان کی ہنستی ہوئی شکلوں پہ، نہ جانا ہرگز

آخری دور میں بھی، تجھ کو قسم ہے ساقی
بھر کے اک جام نہ پیاسوں کو، یہ پلانا ہرگز

بخت سوئے ہیں بہت جگ کے، اے دورِ زماں
نہ ابھی نیند کے ماتوں کو، جگانا ہرگز

یاں سے رخصت ہو سویرے کہیں، اے عیش و نشاط
نہیں اس دور میں یاں، تیرا ٹھکانا ہرگز

کبھی اے علم و ہنر، گھر تھا تمہارا دلّی
ہم کو بھولے ہو تو گھر، بھول نہ جانا ہرگز

شاعری مرچکی، اب زندہ نہ ہوگی ہرگز
یاد کر کر کے اسے، جی نہ کڑھانا ہرگز

غالبؔ و شیفتہؔ و نیّرؔ و آزردہؔ و ذوقؔ
اب دکھائے گا یہ شکلیں، نہ زمانا ہرگز

مومنؔ و علویؔ و صہبائیؔ و ممنونؔ کے بعد
شعر کا نام نہ لے گا، کوئی دانا ہرگز

داغؔ و مجروحؔ کو سن لو، کہ پھر اس گلشن میں
نہ سنے گا کوئی بلبل کا ترانہ ہرگز

رات آخر ہوئی اور بزم ہوئی، زیر و زبر
اب نہ دیکھو گے کبھی، لطف شبانہ ہرگز

بزمِ ماتم تو نہیں، بزم سخن ہے حالیؔ
یاں مناسب نہیں رو رو کے، رُلانا ہرگز

12

A Jat Village's Reception to Muslim Fugitives from British Terror, 1858

—Zahir Dehlavi's Narrative

[From Bareilly, where chiefs like Nana Sahib and Firoz Shah had gathered, a party of five or six fugitives from Delhi decided to move to Rampur since Bareilly was now threatened by English forces.] So we walked 12 *kos* from Aonla (towards Shahabad, 18 *kos* from Aonla) in one day till we were tired out. We could not walk any further, our feet had got swollen, and the soles of our feet were full of blisters. There was a village inhabited by Jats. We sat down beneath a tree on the bank of a pond outside the village. At that time a Muslim carpenter came from within the village to fetch water. Seeing us he said, 'why are you people lying down here? Be on your way. If the villagers see you, they'll kill you. They are deadly enemies of the Muslim Pathans, because under [the rebel leader] Bahadur Khan's administration those [Pathans] who had lorded over these people, had much oppressed them. Now, these people are out to take revenge.' We said,' we are also seeing ways to die, but we are so strongly tied to life that death just does not come our way. We wish to God, someone should kill us, so at last we are relieved of this daily distress.' The carpenter put the water pot on his head and went away to the village. After a little while he returned and said, 'the headman (*muqaddam*-ji) is summoning you.' We said, 'we are penniless people, what have we got to do in the village? Allow us to stay here. After the night, we'll go away in the morning.' But that man went on insisting and took us with him to the *chuapal* (village meeting place). There we saw a strong big young man, with a beard, who lay on a very large *macha* (cot, bedstead), with a large heavy stick put in front of him. That young man, seeing us, said,'O Muslim gentlemen (O *Miyanji*), sit down.' Besides his cot there was a bed set on higher legs. He allowed us to sit on it. We sat down, and the woman told him, 'we are strangers (*pardesi*), inhabitants of Delhi. Having suffered destruction and ruin, we have abandoned our homes. Afraid for our lives from the English, we are wandering about. We now want to go to Rampur. 'That compassionate man expressed much sadness at our pitiable condition. He made us wash our faces and hands. After some time he set before us ghee-soaked pieces of corn-bread, and lentils and milk in a bronze vessel along with sugar, telling us: 'Do please eat your fill'. He also got bread separately for the women (accompanying us). After eating the food we went to sleep in that *chupal*. When in the morning we were ready to depart, that kindly person said, 'your feet are all swollen. How will you travel on foot?' he called his cart-driver and told him to take us to Shahabad on the cart and then return. In addition, he gave us five rupees and handed over to us provisions for the journey from his own store. However much we refused to accept all this from him that high-minded man did not agree, and, putting us on the cart, got us conveyed to Shahabad.

[Note: The passage here translated is taken from Zahiruddin 'Zahir' Dehlavi's memoirs, in Urdu, posthumously printed as *Dastan-i Ghadr,* Lahore, 1915; reprinted, Lahore, 1955, pp. 189-90. Zahir (pronounced 'Zaheer' was a young officer in Bahadur Shah's entourage when the rebels took possession of Delhi.]

Irfan Habib, A People's History of India Vol. 30, The National Movement Origins and Early Phase, to 1918, Tulika, 2017.

13

Facsimile of the printed appeal-Urdu

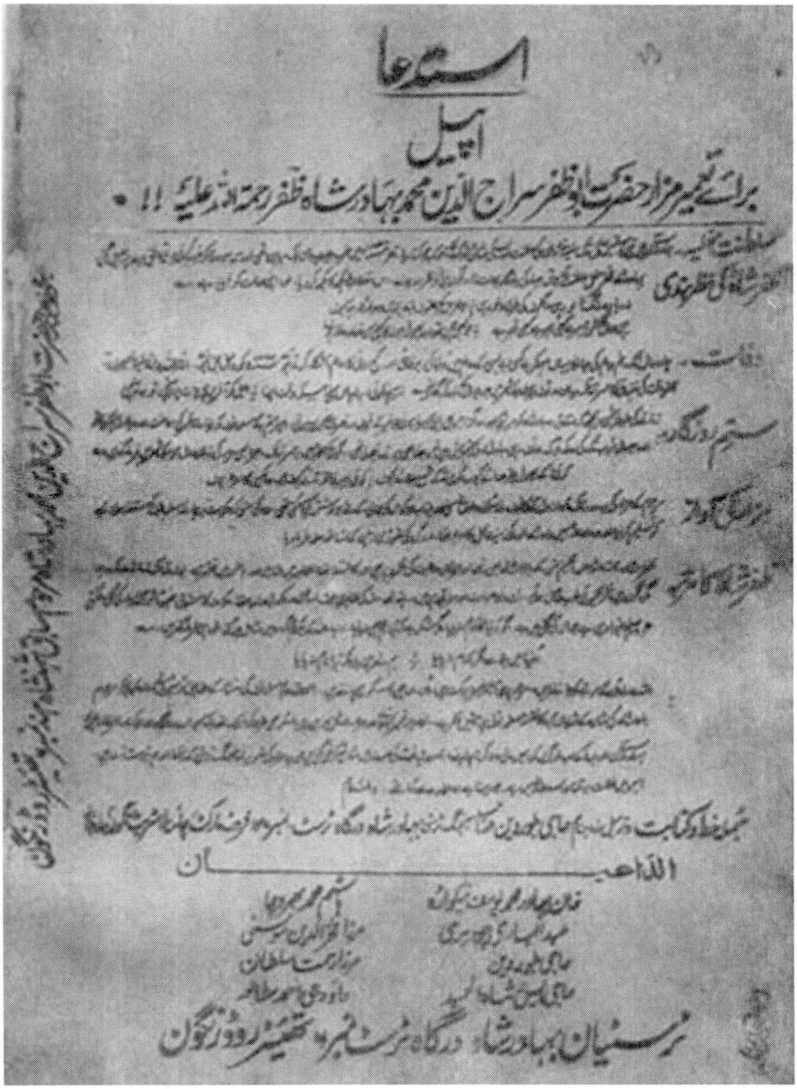

استدعا

اپیل

برائے تعمیر مزار حضرت ابو ظفر سراج الدین محمد بہادر شاہ ظفر رحمۃ اللہ علیہ

الداعیان

ٹرسٹیان بہادر شاہ درگاہ ٹرسٹ نمبر ۶ تھئیٹر روڈ رنگون

14

Appeal made by the Indian devotees of Bahadur Shah Zafar as well as Residents of Rangoon in 1903 to make a Magnificient Mausoleum for the Emperor

AN ENTREATING APPEAL

An entreaty for the construction of the mausoleum of His Majesty Abu Zafar Siraju'ddin Bahadur Shah Zafar; the mercy of Allah on him!

The Mughal Empire: In India the sun of the Mughul Empire shone for 330 years. At last in 1858 a dark cloud sprang from the West (Europe); and drowning that sun spread over the whole of India.

Imprisonment of *Zafar Shah:* Bahadur Shah, the awakener of the memories of the zenith of the Mughul Empire, was brought in a deplorable condition to Rangoon and imprisoned there. Such was the result of the Revolution which transformed him completely. Describing his condition he said:

نہ رہا وہ رنگ نہ بو رہی نہ گلوں کی خوبی و خو رہی
جو خزاں کے ہاتھوں تباہ ہے وہ یادگار بہار ہوں
یہی حال گلشن دہر ہے کبھی مہر ہے کبھی قہر ہے
جو کبھی چمن تھا وہ پھول ہوں جو کبھی سمن تھا وہ خار ہوں

Neither has remained that colour, nor that odour; nor have the flowers their former elegance and beauty.

I am the memento of that spring which has been ruined at the hands of autumn. Such are the ways of Fate; sometimes it is kind and sometimes indignant.

I am the flower of the once-flourishing garden, now reduced to a thorn.

Death : Having suffered from the pangs of sorrow and grief, thus unmasking the faithlessness and crooked ways of the world, the Emperor breathed his last in 1862.

'To God we belong, and to Him is our return'

(Holy Koran, Sura II, verse 156).

Many years before his death, the Emperor had depicted the tragic scene of his death in a verse which forms part of his *diwan* and runs as follows:

نہ پہنچا کوئی اپنے پاس پہنچا جبکہ وقت اپنا
اجل کو آفریں ہے وقت پر پہنچی تو یہ پہنچی

As the hour of death drew nigh, nobody came to us.

Hurrah for Death! it was Death alone who arrived in time.

Tyranny of *the Times:* Look at the mischievous ungratefulness of the Times! After his death such a great Emperor could not obtain even a 2-yard-long piece of land, free from foreign occupation and control. Furthermore the Musalmans were prohibited for many years from visiting his grave and there too were prevented from invoking blessings on his soul by reciting the *Fatiha*... Visualising this tyranny in a forecast of his death the Emperor had composed in Rangoon the following, among many other verses:

کوئی آکے پھول چڑھائے کیوں ؟ کوئی آکے شمع جلائے کیوں؟
کوئی بہر فاتحہ آئے کیوں؟ میں وہ بیکسی کا مزار ہوں

Why should anyone come to my grave with an offering of flowers? Why should anyone visit my grave to recite *Fatiha?* Such an embodiment of misery I shall become, on dying!

Voice from the grave: A voice proceeded from the grave of the afflicted Emperor and was heard by those who were capable of hearing it. They were seized by agony and became restless; and left no stone unturned in there endeavour for the maintenance of that grave. As a result even the then Burmese Government was moved and accepted the prayer made jointly by the Musalmans. They gave away for that purpose, the plot containing the graves of the Emperor and Queen Zinat Mahal together with the surrounding piece of land.

Real Worth of Zafar Shah: Zafar Shah—May God have mercy on him! He was a king of the domain of literature and at the same time a ruler of the dominions of spiritualism. Outwardly he was a king, inwardly he was a *fakir.* In this way he passed his life until his arrival in Rangoon when he gave himself to the pursuit of a single purpose. All the hours—day and night—he spent in prayer and meditation. To all appearances his broken heart had heightened the torment of his soul. When the beloved sweetheart of the kingship was torn from his embrace, he drew to his bosom the Supreme Divinity, thus rising to the eminence of a real saint, as the saying goes: 'The real saint is he who lives in God'.

ع۔ پہنچا ہوا وہی ہے جو اس کی گلی میں ہے

Although Zafar Shah enjoyed no worldly comforts yet, thank God! he was given no bad name. He joined the reputed galaxy of the saints of Allah; and foreseeing this much he himself had said:

'It does not matter if we enjoyed no comforts in this world.

دنیا میں بلا سے اگر آرام نہ پایا
ہم نے یہی پایا کہ برا نام نہ پایا

We have atleast earned this distinction that we have been given no bad name'.

Spiritual men know the real worth of Bahadur Shah. They recognise him also through the Signs of Divine grace and favour that are witnessed at his tomb. In view of all this and in full accord with the longing of the Muslims, the trustees of his *dargah* have resolved that a mausoleum—a fitting memorial to his high position—be raised on the grave of the deceased Emperor. It is also proposed that the land adjoining the said mausoleum be purchased and utilised for building thereupon a mosque and a public resting place. All the people of India and Burma should join hands in financing the proposed construction. Receipt books have been printed bearing a picture of the desired mausoleum along with the signature and seal of the managing trustee.

This matter must not be taken lightly. Whatever you want to give, please give at once.

All correspondence and remittance of money should be addressed to Haji Billouru'ddin Sahib, Managing Trustee, Bahadur Shah Dargah Trust, 178, Fruit Market China Street, Rangoon.

Appealers

Khan Bahadur Muhammad Nekwara, Abdul Bari Chowdhuri, Haji Billouru'ddin, Haji S. Shah al Hamid, Hashim Muhammad Bharocha, Mirza Fakhru'ddin Musa, Mirza Rahmat Sultan, Daudji Ahmad Matali—Trustees of the Bahadur Shah Dargah, Trust No.6, Theatre Road, Rangoon.

Index

H

N

O

P